An Assessment Guide
to Geriatric Neuropsychology

An Assessment Guide to Geriatric Neuropsychology

ନ୍ତ•ଡ଼

Holly Tuokko
University of Victoria
and
Elderly Outreach Service, Ministry of Health,
British Columbia

Thomas Hadjistavropoulos
University of Regina

LEA LAWRENCE ERLBAUM ASSOCIATES, PUBLISHERS
1998 Mahwah, New Jersey   London

Lawrence Erlbaum Associates, Inc., Publishers
10 Industrial Avenue
Mahwah, New Jersey 07430

Cover design by Kathryn Houghtaling Lacey

Library of Congress Cataloging-in-Publication-Data

Tuokko, Holly
    An assessment guide to geriatric neuropsychol-
ogy / Holly Tuokko and Thomas Hadjistavropoulos.
       p. cm.
    Includes bibliographical references and index.
    ISBN 0-8058-1991-6 (cloth : alk. Paper)
    1. Geriatric neuropsychology. 2. Cognition dis-
orders in old age—Diagnosis. 3. Neuropsychological tests. I. Hadjistavropoulos, Thomas. II. Title.
    [DNLM: 1. Cognition—in old age. 2. Geriatric
Assessment. 3. Neuropsychology—in old age. WT
145 T926a 1997]
RC451.4.A5T895 1997
618.97'680475—dc21
DNLM/DLC
for Library of Congress   97-34403
                                    CIP

Printed in the United States of America
10 9 8 7 6 5 4 3 2 1

To Don and Aaron
—H. T.

To Heather and Nicholas
—T. H.

Contents

Preface

More and more studies of the performance of older persons on various neuropsychological measures have been reported in the literature over the past decade in response to the growing demand for clinical practitioners to become involved in the assessment of the elderly. These studies, and others emerging from the area of cognitive aging research, indicate that issues such as educational background are of particular concern when assessing this cohort, and that some cognitive domains are more susceptible than others to the effects of aging. Despite the appearance of more normative information for older persons, we know of no single source in which the findings to date are summarized. This text is designed to fill the gap.

Changes in cognitive functioning occur as a result of aging. Similarly, the prevalence of disorders that adversely affect cognitive functioning increases with age. Neuropsychological measures of cognitive abilities are particularly useful for detecting and monitoring changes in cognitive functioning but only within the context of adequate normative information. This is particularly true when assessing older persons for whom changes in cognitive functioning may or may not be reflective of underlying "pathology."

Neuropsychological assessment of geriatric populations involves not only performance-based measurement of areas of cognitive abilities but heavy reliance on reports of caregivers—both formal and informal—about the functioning of the affected individual. Despite the importance of this information, few standardized and/or validated approaches exist in the field. Those that are available have appeared in scattered reports in the literature. In this text, we bring together relevant information concerning measures designed to obtain information from caregivers. A related issue is the psychological well-being of caregivers and a brief summary is also given of measures useful in the assessment of caregiver well-being.

Another important yet neglected area is that of the ethics involved in conducting geriatric neuropsychological assessment. The issues discussed in this text include informed consent, confidentiality, the right to autonomy and self-determination, and issues pertaining to the provision of feedback to clients. Guidelines for the resolution of ethical dilemmas are also provided.

ACKNOWLEDGMENTS

The preparation of this text reflects the integration of research findings with day-to-day clinical practice issues. Our exposure to these issues within the context of a teaching hospital environment at the Clinic for Alzheimer Disease and Related Disorders at Vancouver Hospital and Health Sciences Centre formed the foundation for our journey into the preparation of this text. We owe our thanks to Dr. Lynn Beattie, Director of the Clinic, for providing a stimulating and fostering environment to staff and students. The support and encouragement provided by Dr. Ian McDowell, Barbara Helliwell, and Betsy Kristjansson, members of the Canadian Study of Health and Aging Coordinating Office, is much appreciated. Data from the Canadian Study of Health and Aging is reported throughout the text. This project was funded by the Seniors Independence Research Program, administered by the National Health and Research Development Program of Health and Welfare Canada. The study was coordinated through the University of Ottawa and the Canadian government's Laboratory Centre for Disease Control. We also thank our dedicated, astute, hard-working assistants—Robert Frerichs, Tamara Goranson, Jocelyn Robinson, and Karen Eso—without whom the task would have been less fun and less rewarding. Finally, we acknowledge our families, who were patient and understanding of our need to make this contribution to the field.

—*Holly Tuokko*
—*Thomas Hadjistavropoulos*

Issues in Psychogeriatric Assessment

The field of clinical neuropsychology is broad-ranging, covering diverse problems and populations. Although the field as a whole has experienced tremendous growth over the past two decades, one of the fastest growing areas within clinical neuropsychology is the assessment of persons over age 65, or *geriatric assessment.*

There are a number of reasons for this development. First, changes in the demographic structure of the North American population have been occurring over the last century such that larger and larger proportions of the population are living past age 65. A variety of factors, most related to improved health status, are contributing to this change. Improvements in public health (e.g., sanitation, sewage treatment, nutritional knowledge), the introduction of antibiotics and immunizations in the middle of this century, and the development of effective interventions for the leading causes of death (e.g., cardiac and cerebrovascular disorders and cancer) are all contributors to this demographic shift. Moreover, in the years following World War II, a record number of births were recorded in North America—the "baby boom." These "baby boomers" are now moving toward age 65 and the consequences of the "graying of the baby boom" has been the source of much economic and political debate (e.g., Barer, Evans, & Hertzman, 1995; Denton & Spencer, 1995), particularly in the context of health and health-related issues.

Age-related changes have been documented in nervous system structure and function as well as other physical systems such as vision, hearing, gastrointestinal functions, and the musculoskeletal system (e.g., Birren, Sloane, & Cohen, 1992; Meneilly & Tuokko, 1994). These normal changes

1

in biological, psychological, cognitive, and behavioral systems seem to occur at differing rates in different persons and result in increased variability on most measures of functioning with increasing age. Moreover, certain disorders or conditions appear correlated with age or occur commonly in older age groups. Comorbidity of physical illness and mental disorders (e.g., anxiety is often seen with cardiovascular, gastrointestinal, or pulmonary disease) is also more common in an aged population than in younger persons (Birren et al., 1992). Thus, distinguishing the anticipated effects of aging from the effects of diseases that are more prevalent with age within the context of comorbid processes is a very important and challenging task.

To fulfill their role, practitioners working with elderly persons require a comprehensive knowledge of processes associated with normal aging (gerontology), as well as a current understanding of the pathological processes associated with aging (geriatrics). Each of these areas has expanded rapidly, most notably since the early 1980s, and is continuing to grow with the realization of, and speculation as to, the impact of the demographic changes within the North American society. This book summarizes the areas of knowledge required to address issues specific to elderly persons. Although many of the principles of neuropsychological assessment presented elsewhere (e.g., Lezak, 1995) may be common to all client populations, the focus here is on the specific issues that may influence the choice of assessment techniques or interpretation of test findings for persons over age 65. Neuropsychological assessments are typically requested when brain dysfunction is suspected or known to exist. The assessment may focus primarily on concerns over diagnostic issues, documentation of change over time, or care planning and management of behavior.

The purpose of this book is to bring together the available normative information for persons over age 65 and to highlight the conceptual and methodological issues pertinent to the use of this information. For example, the variety of factors specific to the individual that may influence test performance or interpretation are raised in the remainder of this chapter. Definitions of what constitutes a normal sample and procedures for determining norms are discussed in chapter 2.

FACTORS ASSOCIATED WITH THE AGING PROCESS

A number of issues specific to the population under investigation must be taken into consideration when selecting and interpreting psychological measures. These include the cognitive, physical, and social processes associated with normal aging.

Cognitive Processes

Cognitive and behavioral changes compatible with normal aging should not be misinterpreted as being indicative of abnormal or pathological change in functioning. Although this may seem obvious, it is extremely important that practitioners appreciate the complexity of this distinction. Diseases commonly manifested by elderly persons may be superimposed on normal age-related changes. Normal age-related changes influence not only the presentation of the disease, but the expectation of response to treatment and the likelihood of potential complications. Cognitive aging research has shed much light on the types of changes in functioning that occur with advancing age.

The introductions to chapters 4, 5, 6, and 7 address age-related expectations for various domains of cognitive functioning (i.e., intelligence, memory, attention, language, visuospatial, perceptual, and motor skills). Briefly, the most striking age-related changes observed in cognitive functioning include:

1. Measures dependent on motor speed (e.g., reaction time, tapping, etc.) are performed less well by older persons. Slowed mental processing appears as the most important component in the characteristic behavioral slowing associated with normal aging (Lezak, 1995). Hence, any task that contains decision points, initiation or redirection of movement may be slowed and will become particularly apparent when timed.

2. Measures of the ability to focus on a simple task and perform it without losing track of the task (e.g., Digit Span Forward) are performed well by most older adults (M. S. Albert, 1988).

3. Semantic knowledge changes significantly with age. Age-related declines have been shown on measures of naming (M. S. Albert, Heller, & Milberg, 1988; Borod, Goodglass, & Kaplan, 1980; Goodglass, 1980; La-Barge, Edwards, & Knesevich, 1986) and verbal fluency (i.e., generation of words within a time period; M. S. Albert et al., 1988; Obler & M. L. Albert, 1981; Spreen & Benton, 1969). These changes appear primarily after age 70 while other linguistic abilities appear to remain relatively intact (M. S. Albert, 1988).

4. Manifestations of changes in memory functioning are dependent on the type of memory task involved. The ability to retain small amounts of information over a brief period of time (once called short-term memory) shows hardly any loss with age (Talland, 1965). Secondary, or long-term, memory declines with age. The degree of loss is related to the type of material to be remembered and the assessment method. Large age-related declines are found in free recall (Botwinick & Storandt, 1974; Craik, 1977;

Gilbert & Levee, 1971; Kausler & Lair, 1966). Decrements are larger for recall than for recognition of material (Erber, 1974; Harwood & Naylor, 1969; Howell, 1972).

5. Visuospatial ability, as assessed by complex visual reproduction and recognition tasks (e.g., Block Design, Figure Integration), declines as individuals age (Doppelt & Wallace, 1955; Wentworth-Rohr, Mackintosh, & Flalkoff, 1974). Similarly, drawing task performance (e.g., three-dimensional cube, clock face) also appear to decline with age (Plude, Milberg, & Cerella, 1986; Tuokko, Hadjistavropoulos, Miller, Horton, & Beattie, 1995). This seems to be true even when the speed components of the tasks are removed (Botwinick, 1977).

6. Abstraction and conceptualization have been assessed in a variety of ways many of which show age-related declines. Of particular interest is proverb interpretation, which shows substantial deterioration with age (M. S. Albert, 1988; Bromley, 1957).

This research emphasizes the need for normative information based on age. Norms can help determine what constitutes a change in functioning above and beyond age-related change. M. S. Albert (1981) noted "age-appropriate norms based on a systematic comparison between elderly normal and pathological populations do not exist for most behavioral tests of brain damage" (pp. 385–386). This situation has changed with the increasing demand for this information.

From the literature on age-related cognitive changes, issues concerning the appropriateness of various measures for use with older persons have been raised. The utility of many standard psychological measures for relating to the performance of everyday behaviors by older persons has been challenged and a need for more "ecologically valid" measures was identified. Moreover, it has been observed that elderly persons may perceive the measures as "meaningless" within the context of their lives and may be unwilling to take part in an assessment. This controversy has resulted in the recent development of measures incorporating real-life situations into the context of the assessment process (e.g., shopping list learning as part of a memory battery), thereby expanding the types of assessment tools available for this population.

Physical Processes

In addition to these age-related cognitive changes, there are a number of *physical factors* that might interact with, influence, or distort the clinical picture. Most notably, changes in sensory processes (i.e., vision and hearing) are common with increasing age and may significantly interfere with a person's performance on measures of cognitive functioning. Most persons over age 60 experience some form of visual compromise (Fozard, 1990). Declines in hearing parallel those of vision and approximately 70% of persons in the 71- to 80-year-old age range suffer some hearing loss (Fozard, 1990). It should be noted, however, that even persons who are legally blind can perform well on many neuropsychological measures containing visual stimuli, because these stimuli are often large and clearly defined. Despite this, the clinician must be cognizant of the possible effects of vision and hearing loss on test performance and ensure that these influences have been controlled (e.g., ensure individuals wear their glasses or hearing aid; use of pockettalker to assist in communicating with hearing impaired) or compensated for by use of measures not dependent on the impaired sensory modality (e.g., use of a verbal measure of memory with a visually impaired person).

Another potential complication to test performance and interpretation when working with this population is the higher prevalence of medical problems than seen in younger individuals. Thus, in addition to normal changes in physiological functioning associated with age, the prevalence of a variety of medical conditions increases with age (e.g., diabetes, heart disease, arthritis). Many of these disorders may be related to observed cognitive impairment in older persons and become important within the context of differential diagnosis. For example, poor metabolic control in diabetics may greatly increase the risk of vascular complications, including retinopathy, nephropathy, and neuropathy (C. M. Ryan, 1988). Observed cognitive deficits may be a function of these micro- and macrovascular changes rather than suggestive of an additional disease process (e.g., Alzheimer's disease). Too often, the role of existing medical disease in disrupting cerebral functioning is overlooked and deficits are attributed to other sources of cognitive impairment. Other disorders, such as arthritis, may limit performance on tasks requiring graphomotor skill or speed of performance, thereby complicating test interpretation.

A related issue is the potential effect of medications on test performance. It is not uncommon for elderly persons to be taking a variety of medications for comorbid disorders. Moreover, older persons have increased sensitivity to medications due to altered abilities to metabolize and excrete medications (e.g., Birren et al., 1992). As drug sensitivity and interactions are often specific to individuals, the potential complicating role of medications must be kept in mind. Thus, it is extremely important to determine the medications a person is taking at the time of the assessment, as well as the dosages. The most effective way to accomplish this is to have the person or a family member bring in all medications for review. It may be necessary to count the tablets to ensure that medications are being taken as prescribed. Inappropriate use of prescription (and nonprescription) medications may contribute to the clinical presentation and needs to be addressed.

Noncompliance with medication regimes may result from an inability to monitor the medications due to memory deficits rather than unwillingness to comply. To ensure optimal functioning, it may be necessary to monitor the individual's performance as medications are introduced or withdrawn.

It is common knowledge that older persons, particularly those with medical problems, may tire easily. Hence, to obtain an estimate of maximal functioning, it may be necessary to limit the length of testing sessions or provide frequent breaks during the testing. This may be done by making it clear to the person that rest breaks are available as needed, or checking with the person at intervals during the assessment as to the need for a break. Increasing agitation or withdrawal from responding may signal that a rest break, or redirection to casual conversation, is warranted. For persons who are very frail, such as those in care facilities, it may be necessary to schedule several sessions to obtain a person's optimal performance. Examination of test results in the context of the order of administration may be of assistance, if there is any concern that the person was fatigued by the assessment process. If there appears to be marked variability between the first and last measures administered, then it may prove beneficial to readminister the latter ones on another occasion to ensure fatigue was not the source of the difficulties. It is also important to view the tendency toward fatigue within the context of the person's activities of daily living. An individual who cannot sustain enough focused attention to complete a 30-minute assessment procedure may have great difficulty performing daily activities when living alone in the community. Similarly, individuals living in a care facility cannot be expected to successfully take part in group recreational activities if they are unable to complete a simple mental status examination without becoming unduly fatigued.

Social Processes

When assessing older persons, the social context of the individual must be kept in mind. Although this is true when conducting neuropsychological assessments at any age, issues specific to older persons center around social change, loss, and the context of the psychological assessment. Retirement may be a major adjustment for some persons and can result in profound feelings of loss and isolation. Change of residence may result in loss of friends and family, social supports, or a sense of belonging. It is common for older persons to have friends and family members who have recently died or are ill. Certainly grieving and bereavement are processes with pervasive effects on a person's functioning. Alternatively, the death of a spouse or caregiver may bring to light the poor cognitive functioning of the remaining partner, which, in the context of the struggle to assume new roles, comes to the attention of others.

Financial limitations and/or sociocultural issues may also complicate the clinical picture and need to be considered in the context of differential diagnosis and planning care. Many persons of this age cohort may lack familiarity with the types of assessment procedures conducted by neuropsychologists, and fear of loss of ability or independence may complicate the assessment process. Careful explanations as to the intent and purpose of the assessment may be required to ensure maximal performance.

PURPOSE OF THE ASSESSMENT

Diagnosis

A neuropsychological assessment may be requested for a variety of reasons. Often, *diagnostic issues* are of primary concern. Identification of dementia is perhaps the most common referral issue in this age group. Dementia may be defined as an overall decline in mental capacity (one or more cognitive domains) that renders the individual unfit to meet the diverse intellectual demands associated with the obligations of everyday life. Within this diagnostic category, there may be a wide variety of individual patterns of cognitive disability. Dementia has been subclassified in a variety of ways: according to most prominent cognitive features (e.g., amnesic, aphasic, visuoperceptive, global), according to anatomical location (e.g., cortical, subcortical, axial; Joynt & Shoulson, 1979), according to reversibility of the underlying etiologic condition (reversible conditions may include Normal Pressure Hydrocephalus, drug toxicity, thyroid dysfunction, neurosyphilis, B12 deficiency, liver failure; irreversible conditions may include Alzheimer's disease, vascular disorders, alcohol-related dementia, Huntington's disease, Parkinson's disease, Amyotrophic Lateral Sclerosis), and severity of functional deficits (i.e., mild, moderate, severe).

In addition to identifying cognitive impairment (i.e., greater than normal age-related decline), it is necessary to differentiate possible dementia from other common disorders affecting older persons. These include depression, acute confusional state, and cognitive changes associated with a variety of remediable medical conditions. Moreover, it is possible that there may be more than one condition present. For example, it has been noted that depression may be present in various neurological conditions (e.g., poststroke, Alzheimer's disease, Parkinson's disease). The identification of coexisting (comorbid) conditions is of importance as treatment for remediable disorders may improve the person's quality of life. When addressing diagnostic issues, the factors described previously must be taken into consideration.

Baseline

Test results may also serve as a *baseline* to monitor change with intervention or the passage of time. In this context, repeated administrations of the measures would be required. In these situations, issues concerning test–retest effects may need to be addressed and it may be prudent to select measures with multiple forms.

Care Planning

The assessment results may also play a role in *care planning* where a careful, detailed delineation of the cognitive strengths and weaknesses of the individual may be translated into management strategies and suggestions for care approaches. As yet, there is little research addressing the link between pattern of cognitive abilities and specific approaches/strategies that are most effective. However, there is no question that understanding a person's capabilities and limitations is essential to a rational care plan. Being able to articulate for individuals and their care providers the nature of the cognitive deficits (e.g., problem retrieving information) is the first step in encouraging creative problem-solving for care providers. For example, a useful premise for assisting care providers in developing problem-solving strategies for persons with dementia (Tuokko & Purves, 1993) is that persons with dementia act on incomplete information. That is, due to cognitive limitations (e.g., new learning problems or inability to self-evaluate), the individual is only processing part of the information in the environment. Once the nature of the deficit is clarified, care providers can actively seek strategies to help the person with dementia accomplish tasks. This might include restructuring the environment, reinterpreting the behavior of the individual, or modifying expectations of the individual with dementia. Other ways of using assessment information in developing care plans have been discussed by S. H. Zarit and J. M. Zarit (1983).

For each of the assessment goals defined earlier, it is necessary to assess a wide range of domains of cognitive functioning, including attention and concentration, motor functioning and praxis, memory, receptive and expressive language skills, reasoning and thinking processes, and visuospatial and verbal reasoning abilities. The assessment may be brief (e.g., screening instrument; see chap. 3) or more lengthy depending on the nature of the issues under investigation. Generally, the information contained in Table 1.1 would be obtained in one form or another so that issues central to differential diagnosis and care planning could be addressed.

The measures selected within each domain depend on the context of the evaluation and the preferences of the neuropsychologist. Measures for use in care planning for a 95-year-old frail woman living in a nursing home may be very different from those selected for use with a 65-year-old, recently

TABLE 1.1
Assessment Information

A. Testing
    Arousal level
    Attention
    Language i) Comprehension
               ii) Expression (naming, repetition, fluency, phrase length, response speed, word finding, paraphasic errors [literal: sounds like; semantic: similar meaning])
    Motor   i) Movements (facial, gait, tremor)
    Memory i) New learning
              ii) Verbal, visual
             iii) Personal information
             iv) Remote memory or information learned in the past
    Visuospatial reasoning
    Verbal reasoning
    Mood
B. Collateral information from family
    History   i) Onset
              ii) Duration
            iii) Course
            iv) Demographic information (education, occupation)
             v) Living situation, hobbies, alcohol consumption
            vi) Medical condition (meds, surgeries, anesthetics, psychiatric/neurological status)
    Present functioning (presence/absence and duration of symptoms)
             i) Personality
             ii) Everyday tasks
            iii) Language skills
            iv) Memory functions
             v) Self-care functions

retired business executive living alone, who may be exhibiting the early signs of dementia. Throughout the assessment process, various hypotheses about the nature of the deficit and underlying disorder may be generated and examined. For example, if a person is unable to follow a simple written instruction, then it may be that vision is impaired, the person never was able to read, or the person can no longer read despite intact vision but can follow the same instruction given orally.

In addition to the material gathered through direct assessment, it is necessary to obtain information from a collateral informant (usually a family member or spouse) to ensure a complete picture is obtained (see chap. 10). Particularly in suspected cases of dementia, individuals may be unaware of changes in their behavior that are readily apparent to others (McGlynn & Kaszniak, 1991). It is rarely the case that persons with dementia seek assessment for themselves. Typically, it is family or friends who make their concerns known to the primary care physician or others on behalf of the affected individual. Material obtained from informants may focus on problems observed in everyday functioning, but would also clarify the nature of the onset, duration, and course of the presenting problems. Moreover, information obtained from informants may include an appraisal of the individuals' living situation and their capability to function within their personal environmental context. All information gathered is examined in relation to the individuals' premorbid level of functioning (see chap. 4), environmental context, and must include as much relevant material as possible.

Assessment over intervals of time is also of particular importance as conditions may evolve gradually (e.g., Alzheimer's disease), may fluctuate (e.g., Lewy Body dementia), or may improve (e.g., treated conditions or stabilization poststroke). Although there are established sets of criteria for many disorders affecting elderly persons (see chap. 9), subtle cognitive deficits may be observed that do not satisfy existing criteria but may be associated with emerging conditions. As yet, these mild deficits in cognitive functioning are poorly understood and only repeated assessment can determine the eventual outcome. In addition, neurodegenerative disorders progress over time, but the rate of progression and the individual features that emerge may differ substantially between persons. Monitoring change over time can be of particular importance in the design of care plans appropriate to the individual's specific strengths and weaknesses at the time of assessment. The elements of the care plan may need to shift and be altered as the characteristics of the affected individual change.

CONCLUSIONS

When assessing older persons, clinicians require a comprehensive knowledge of processes associated with normal aging (gerontology), as well as a current understanding of the pathological processes associated with aging (geriatrics). It is important to evaluate the influences that a variety of factors may have on test performance. These include sensory deficits, physical limitations, and sociocultural issues. Many areas of cognitive functioning must be assessed to determine whether or not cognitive impairment is present, to differentiate between conditions that may give rise to cognitive impairment in elderly persons and to provide meaningful contributions to the care plan for individuals. Monitoring change over time is often necessary as conditions (i.e., underlying disorders) and the needs of the individual may evolve. Supplementing test information with observations of functioning at home or in social contexts and information about the nature of the onset, duration, and course of the behavioral changes obtained from other sources (e.g., family or friends) is crucial for diagnostic and care planning purposes.

Psychometric Issues

Psychometric theory underlies test construction and interpretation but practicing psychologists often have inadequate or obsolete training in measurement theory (Retzlaff & Gibertini, 1994). Unfortunately, clinical neuropsychological assessment is far less precise and sophisticated than some other areas of assessment (e.g., educational or personnel testing). In response to the concern about the appropriateness of measures for clinical use, standards for the development of new measures have been developed (American Psychological Association, 1985). The influence of these standards is apparent in some of the newer measures discussed later in chapters 4 and 5. However, the same attention to psychometric issues has not been afforded to many of the older, more commonly encountered, neuropsychological measures that have been extended to include samples of older persons. Available psychometric information has been included in the descriptions of specific instruments (see chaps. 3–8, 11) when this information was derived from samples of elderly persons. A discussion of the general psychometric properties of specific measures can be found in Spreen and Strauss (1991) or Lezak (1995).

This chapter raises, more generally, issues that need to be considered by the clinician when interpreting individual test results. It is important that clinicians be aware of the limits to inferences that can be made from test performances as the consequences of misinterpretations are often extremely powerful for individual persons. Geriatric neuropsychological assessment often centers on the identification of deficits and/or deterioration in cognitive functioning. It also contributes to the process of determining why this deterioration may be occurring. To identify deficits or deterioration, some ideal must exist against which the individual's performance can be measured. This comparison standard can be normative (derived from performance on the measure by a representative group of persons) or individual (in relation to the individual's own history or present characteristics). This chapter focuses on *normative* issues and provides descriptions of the best available normative samples. It also discusses fundamental characteristics of the measures themselves (e.g., reliability and validity). A basic knowledge of statistical concepts (e.g., mean, standard deviation) is assumed. Readers are referred to basic statistical textbooks such as Ferguson (1981) or those on psychometric theory (e.g., Anastasi, 1988; Nunnally, 1970) for a more thorough discussion of these concepts.

COMPARISON STANDARDS AND NORMS

Clinical assessment typically involves the administration of a variety of measures of cognitive functioning, as well as gathering information through interview with the client and/or a person familiar with the client. The exact measures administered vary depending on the purpose(s) of the assessment (see chap. 1). Direct observation of the person's performance during test administration provides an additional rich source of information about the individual's approach to tasks, tolerance levels, personal style, and coping skills, as well as providing an opportunity for the examiner to note speech and language characteristics and abnormalities in movement that may be clinically significant. Standardized tests are administered to gather objective, readily replicable data that permit reliable interpretation and meaningful comparisons (Lezak, 1995). Both forms of information (i.e., observations and test scores) are essential to the neuropsychological assessment. In isolation, each form of information is subject to misinterpretation. Test scores may be objective but must be considered within the specific context of the individual. Observations lack objective comparability. Notably in geriatric assessment, behaviors associated with normal aging may be readily identified as deficits by someone used to working with a younger population or unfamiliar with the behavioral, cognitive, social, and/or physical correlates of aging.

Psychological test scores are most commonly interpreted in relation to the performance of a *standardization sample*. A standardization sample is a representative group of individuals who are administered the measure in a standardized fashion. Standardization refers to uniformity in administering and scoring the test and is discussed later in the chapter. To accurately determine the individual's performance in relation to the standardization sample, the performance of the standardization sample can be converted to a set of derived scores characterizing the distribution of scores for the sample (standard scores). This allows individual scores to be examined in relation to other persons and to performances on other tests (Anastasi, 1988). Thus, an individual's performance is evaluated in relation to *norms*, or the performance of the standardization sample.

Standard scores come in different forms (e.g., z scores, *T*-scores), but are all based on the mean and standard deviation of the scores in the standardization sample (Lezak, 1995). Comparability of the scores assumes that the underlying distributions of scores have essentially the same form (i.e., typically a normal distribution of scores around the mean or normal curve). The term *normalized standard scores* is used to identify standard scores that have been statistically transformed to fit a normal curve. Scores may also be presented as stanines, percentile equivalents, or merely as means and standard deviations. Wechsler Intelligence Quotients (IQs) are standard scores expressed with a mean of 100 and standard deviation of 15, whereas Wechsler subtest scores have a mean of 10 and standard deviation of 3. Figure 2.1 illustrates relations between these various methods of expressing scores and includes the commonly accepted description terms for classifying ability levels. As noted by Lezak (1995), many measures of cognitive function are affected by age and education (or vocational achievement) and these variables need to be taken into account when generating norms.

Often, the cognitive abilities of interest in neuropsychological assessment are those likely to be normally distributed in the adult population for which standard scores can be generated. However, some behaviors of interest, or domains of cognitive functioning, are not expected to be normally distributed in the population. Some of these have been described by Lezak (1995) as species-wide performance expectations. That is, it is expected that all persons of a certain age (e.g., adults) will manifest these capabilities. The behaviors, then, are rudimentary components of cognitive behavior. If an individual cannot perform this task, impairment is assumed. For example, following simple instructions or copying simple behaviors may reflect this type of task. Other behaviors can be assessed in terms of determining whether or not the individual has attained or maintained the minimum requirements necessary for performing a task (e.g., qualifying for a driver's license). This approach to assessment is a form of criterion-referenced testing (Anastasi, 1988) and is more commonly encountered in the fields of speech language pathology and occupational therapy. Criterion-referenced measures are designed to assess a clearly defined and delimited domain of skills. In addition, performance is evaluated in terms of achievement on the measures, not in relation to other persons (Gronlund, 1973). For example, it may be said that Helen can spell 90% of the words in the unit word list. Although most of the discussion focuses on measures for which the distribution of scores approaches normality, these other forms of measures may be more appropriate for use in certain circumstances.

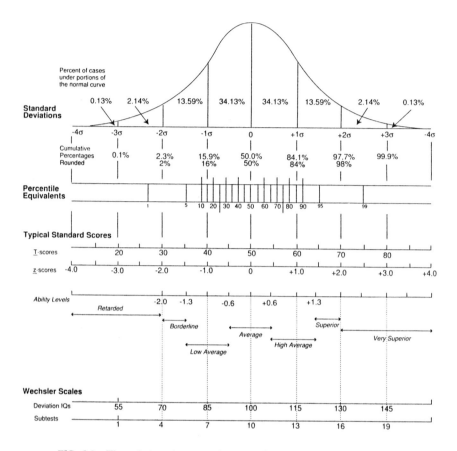

FIG. 2.1. The relations between the normal curve and some commonly used test scores. Data from the Test Service Bulletin No. 48, January 1955 by The Psychological Corporation. Adapted and reproduced with permission. All rights reserved.

Screening measures, or brief measures that sample a broad range of behaviors, are often designed to assess rudimentary behaviors. Although some dispersion of scores is expected, screening measures tend to be skewed to the left such that most persons achieve perfect or almost-perfect scores. Conversion of these scores to standard scores is not appropriate. Often, percentiles may be generated for comparison purposes for a specifically defined group (e.g., by age and/or education; Crum, Anthony, Bassett, & M. F. Folstein, 1993). Cutoff scores are often applied to screening measures, which may be defined to minimize false positive and/or false negative rates of classification. A discussion of cutoff scores is included later in this chapter. Because many screening measures are highly skewed, they tend to lack sensitivity to mild problems or to cognitive deficits in persons with premorbid functioning in the superior range (see chap. 3). Thus, screening measures are similar to the species-wide performance expectations in that identification of a deficit lends support to the hypothesis that the individual is showing cognitive impairment. However, if a deficit is not detected with a screening measure, impairment may still emerge when measures with a normal distribution of scores (thereby allowing for many gradations of performance) are employed.

Individual Comparisons

As is discussed later, the correspondence between the characteristics of the standardization sample and the individual in question is of importance when interpreting the meaning of test results. In addition, comparison to population norms is most useful when the individual's general ability level had been of average caliber (Lezak, 1995). Thus, it is necessary to determine an individual's premorbid level of functioning if interpretations are to be meaningful within the context of the individual. Direct comparisons with test scores (e.g., IQs, school achievement measures) obtained prior to the onset of the cognitive decline are the most desirable, but are rarely available or accessible for this population. Thus, indirect methods—which may involve determining estimates from demographic variables, test performances, or some combination of these (see chap. 4)—are most commonly employed.

By definition, the majority of individuals will fall within the average range with respect to their premorbid level of functioning. However, comparing test performance with an estimate of the original level of cognitive ability, not solely with respect to whether or not the test performance falls within the average range, becomes particularly important when assessing individuals of a superior to very superior or borderline to low average endowment. Although the difficulty in identifying cognitive deterioration in persons of superior intellectual prowess has been emphasized (Naugle, Cullum, & Bigler, 1990), it is of equal importance that persons of low premorbid abilities not be overdiagnosed with dementia. This is of particular importance in light of recent findings from epidemiological studies of Alzheimer's disease, which have shown a very robust association between this age-related disease and low education (D'Arcy, 1994; Mortimer, 1995).

When comparing test performance to estimated premorbid level of functioning, patterns of deficit may emerge. A single discrepant score is expected and unlikely to be of clinical significance. A pattern of scores that conforms to that known to be associated with specific neurological or psychiatric conditions lends support to the diagnosis, if this best accounts for a person's behavioral abnormalities. As noted by Lezak (1995), it is highly desirable to demonstrate statistically significant discrepancies between expected and observed performance levels when identifying patterns of performance. In this context, it must be noted that the patterns of performance described in chapter 9 were derived from reviewing the literature describing performance deficits associated with specific disorders and from personal clinical experience. Also, it must be noted that there will be numerous exceptions to these characteristic patterns of performance associated with different conditions (Lezak, 1995). Nonetheless, pattern analysis is a fundamental component of the assessment, which when used in conjunction with information obtained through observation and interview, may provide important insights into diagnostic and care planning issues.

Standardization Samples

Central to the appropriate use of normative standards to identify areas of deficit or impairment is the correspondence between the characteristics of the standardization sample and the individual in question. For example, it is inappropriate to use norms developed on a sample of 25- to 34-year-old males as a comparison standard for the performance of an 85-year-old woman on a measure of memory. The more similar the individual is to the standardization sample in terms of important demographic characteristics (e.g., age, race, education, and occupational background), the more likely deficits identified will be true and not due to these other factors. Thus, the purpose behind standardization (or administration and interpretation in relation to norms) is to reduce the amount of measurement error (possibility that the test performance is due to things other than a true deficit). The more closely the test administration and the characteristics of the individual are to the standardization procedure and sample, the more likely that the result will be valid. It is important for the standardization sample to be large enough to yield stable values and the sample to be selected as representative of the section of the population for which the test is designed (Anastasi, 1988). As differences exist in the samples used to standardize different measures, the resulting norms will not be directly comparable.

As becomes evident in the following chapters, some large-scale normative projects have been undertaken with elderly persons that have allowed the generation of age-appropriate norms for a variety of measures. Some of these studies include multiple measures whereas others focus on single instruments. Some provide systematic comparisons between elderly normal and pathological populations and others do not. When evaluating the utility of these norms for use in specific situations, it is of utmost importance that the characteristics of the normative sample be carefully considered.

In the descriptions to follow, it will be apparent that the definition of "normal" varies from study to study. There has been considerable debate in the medical and psychological literature as to the definition of normal in the context of aging. Lezak (1995) noted that with advancing age, every organ system, including the brain, undergoes alterations to some degree and age-related changes have been observed in brain size, brain biochemistry, and cerebral blood flow (Duckett, 1991; Wallin & Gottfries, 1990). These brain changes may be reflected in decline from previous levels of functioning as a function of age. However, Rinn (1988) noted that cognitive decline is less pronounced in elderly persons who enjoy unusually good physical health and more severe in those who do not. Pathological medical conditions that occur more frequently with advancing age (e.g., diabetes, high blood pressure) are associated with dementia in their extreme forms and may be associated with lesser cognitive decline in their milder forms. Many older persons have chronic medical conditions, and many more may have a medical disorder, of which they may not even be aware. Rinn (1988) argued that these disorders result in the convergence of multiple small pathological brain changes reflected as normal age-related decline. When comparisons are made to a randomly selected representative sample of the population of older persons, the individual is being compared to a group of people with a high incidence of medical disorders that may compromise mental functioning. Thus, the person may be declared average in relation to persons who are markedly deteriorated or even close to death. Conversely, a comparison group comprised only of older individuals who were highly active and who exhibited extremely good health would not be representative of the normal elderly population. Rinn (1988) recommended to developers of norms that the status of elderly participants be checked about 3 years after data collection and the norms adjusted to eliminate those who were close to death at the time of examination. At this point, Rinn's approach has not been adopted for any of the norms described in this book.

Thus, in selecting appropriate norms for use in a specific context, it is important for the clinician to establish the "best" comparison group: super healthy active volunteers, randomly selected persons screened for major medical illness, or persons deemed "cognitively normal" through screening and/or clinical evaluation. Although the effect of health status may be a more pronounced potential source of error for elderly samples, Lezak (1995) noted that many neuropsychological measures do not have extensive norms and may be standardized on an undefined mixed or nonrandom sample. Comparison of the individual's test performance with several sets of norms may reveal no significant difference in findings. If impairment is identified using some sets of norms but not others, then the clinician must rely on rational judgment. As a number of large-scale projects are referred to throughout the remaining chapters, the normative samples are described here.

R. R. Bornstein (1985). A number of measures were administered to 97 Canadian volunteers age 60 and older. No information about health status was provided.

Framingham Heart Study.   Farmer et al. (1987) presented normative data for various neuropsychological measures collected on 2,123 participants in the Framingham Heart Study. When specific subpopulations were excluded (e.g., those with hearing impairments, the blind, those with documented strokes, those residing in care facilities, and those for whom English was not their first language), 1,195 participants remained. They presented the means and standard deviations for age groups (in 5-year intervals) by education levels (8–11 years, high school, more than high school), and by gender.

Mitrushina and Satz.   Mitrushina and Satz (1989) assessed 156 healthy Caucasian volunteers between age 57 and 85 who completed a self-report medical questionnaire. No persons had a history of neurological or psychiatric disorders and all scored above 24 on the Mini-Mental State Examination (see chap. 3 for a description of this measure). These individuals were well-educated persons functioning independently and living autonomously in the community.

Johns Hopkins Teaching Nursing Home Study of Normal Aging   (e.g., Bolla, Lindgren, Bonaccorsy, & Bleecker, 1990; Bolla-Wilson & Bleecker, 1986). Participants in this study were Caucasian volunteers ranging from age 39 to 89 who were free from neurological and psychiatric disorders and who had never had uncontrolled hypertension, pulmonary edema, liver failure, renal failure, congestive heart disease, uncontrolled thyroid dysfunction, electroconvulsive therapy, sleep disorders, coma, or alcohol/drug abuse.

Ryan, Paolo, and Associates.   These researchers developed norms and examined normative issues primarily for the Wechsler Adult Intelligence Scale–Revised (Paolo & J. J. Ryan, 1993c; J. J. Ryan & Paolo, 1992a, 1992c; J. J. Ryan, Paolo, & Brungardt, 1990). Their sample of 130 persons was chosen to match the 1983 U.S. Census Bureau population figures for persons age 75 and older. Other studies from this group (e.g., Paolo & J. J. Ryan, 1993a; J. J. Ryan, Paolo, & Brungardt, 1992; J. J. Ryan, Paolo, Pehlert, & Coker, 1991) vary in sample sizes. However, in all of these studies, participants lived in the midwestern United States (i.e., Kansas, Missouri, and Iowa), primarily in urban settings (i.e., 90%), and were recruited from senior citizen organizations, retirement communities, newspaper advertisements, and by word of mouth. All participants were screened as healthy and without evidence of current or past psychiatric, neurological, or major systemic illness on the basis of a brief health questionnaire and the Geriatric Depression Scale (Brink et al., 1982). All participants possessed adequate hearing and vision. Minor age-related conditions (e.g., senile diabetes, essential hypertension) were not excluded.

The normative approach used paralleled that of the Wechsler Adult Intelligence Scale–Revised (J. J. Ryan et al., 1990). Raw scores were converted to scaled scores on the basis of the 20- to 34-year-old reference group. The means and standard deviations of the scaled scores on the Verbal, Performance, and Full Scales for the 75 to 79 and 80+ age groups were examined in relation to the WAIS–R standardization sample. The general trend of mild decreases in the sums of scaled scores was maintained with these additional age groups, suggesting they are an appropriate extension to the national sample. To generate IQ scores, Matarazzo's (1972) equation was used to convert each sum of scaled scores to a new score with a mean of 100 and a standard deviation of 15. The distributions were normalized and smoothed (Angoff, 1971) to eliminate minor irregularities.

Tables for age-corrected subtest scores were constructed, converting the means and standard deviations of the raw scores for each subtest to scores with a mean of 10 and standard deviation of 3 using Matarazzo's (1972) formula. The distributions were adjusted to fit a normal curve as closely as possible.

Ivnik and Associates at the Mayo Clinic. These researchers provide age-specific norms for a variety of measures (e.g., Wechsler Memory Scale–Revised: Ivnik et al., 1992b; Auditory Verbal Learning Test: Ivnik et al., 1990; Visual Spatial Learning Test: Malec et al., 1992; Wechsler Adult Intelligence Scale–Revised: Ivnik et al., 1992a). Sample sizes vary across the studies from 394 to 512 participants. These persons ranged from age 56 to 97 and were recruited from a large sample of volunteers for Mayo's Older Americans Normative Studies (MOANS). They lived and functioned independently in the community. They had a variety of medical conditions common to elderly persons but were considered normal by their primary care physicians. Ivnik et al. (1990) noted that care was taken to ensure the representativeness of their data by minimizing selection bias in their sampling, thoroughly documenting health status and specifying a definition of "normal."

Ivnik et al. used overlapping, midpoint age ranges (Pauker, 1988) to provide the maximum amount of normative information in their studies. Raw scores earned on each subtest score were converted to percentile ranks and age-specific scaled scores for midpoint ages occurring at 3-year intervals from 61 through 88 years. The age range around each midpoint was 5 years. For each midpoint range, this approach provides the broadest possible normative base. That is, an 80-year-old person would be compared to the sample with a midpoint age of 79 years for which scores are derived from the performance of all persons 74 to 84 years of age. A 74-year-old person would be compared to the sample with a midpoint age of 73 years for which scores are derived from the performance of all persons 68 to 78 years old. In this way, the size of comparison groups is maximized, thereby ensuring a relatively large *n* in each subcategory cell.

Heaton and Associates. These researchers developed norms for an expanded Halstead Reitan Battery (Heaton, Grant, & Matthews, 1991) based on 486 participants age 20 to 80 with 0 to 20 years of education. The battery included the WAIS, Wisconsin Card Sorting Test, and the Boston Naming Test, as well as a variety of other measures. Participants were derived from several sources (e.g., a number of U.S. states such as California, Washington, Colorado, Texas, Oklahoma, Wisconsin, Illinois, Michigan, New York, Virginia, and the Canadian province of Manitoba) and included both urban and rural areas. All participants were interviewed and denied the presence of psychiatric and neurological disorders. All were rated by their examiners as having put forth sufficient effort to yield valid test results.

A regression approach was employed to develop the norms, using age, gender, and years of formal education as predictor scores (Heaton et al., 1991). This approach requires that raw scores be transformed to scaled scores with a mean of 10 and a standard deviation of 3. A stepwise multiple regression was performed for each test measure using age, education, and sex to predict the scaled scores. Predicted scores, based on age, gender, and education, were generated using this regression formula. For each individual, the predicted score is then subtracted from the obtained scaled score. This difference is then divided by the standard deviation of the residuals for that measure. The resulting value is then multiplied by 10 and added to 50 to yield a *T*-score. Scaled score equivalents of raw scores and *T*-score equivalents of scaled scores for persons up to age 80 by 5-year intervals and levels of education (6–8, 9–11, 12, 13–15, 16–17, 18+ years) by gender are included in their comprehensive norms.

Heaton (1992) also used this approach to develop norms for the WAIS–R. In this project the WAIS–R standardization sample (excluding persons age 16 and 17 years, *N* = 1,680) was used. In the WAIS–R standardization sample, the same stratified sampling basis was used for the older groups as for the younger age groups. The normative data for persons age 55 and over, however, continued to be based on smaller samples than other age groups and persons of advanced age continued to be excluded (i.e., over age 75). Thus, norms were only generated up to age 74.

Heaton, Chelune, Talley, Kay, and Curtiss (1993) examined the Wisconsin Card Sorting Test performance using a sample that included 384 persons age 20 and older. One hundred and fifty of these persons were participants in Heaton et al.'s (1991) normative project. Two additional samples were included for this project. One hundred and twenty-four commercial airline pilots between age 24 and 65 were administered the Wisconsin Card Sorting Task (WCST). All but 5 of these persons were from Colorado. Education levels ranged from 14 to 20 years. The other sample contained 73 of the 80 persons examined by Axelrod and Henry (1992). These were healthy adults recruited for participation in a health promotion project from independent living retirement residences in the Detroit area. Based on self-report, none of these individuals had a history of psychiatric treatment, neurological disease or injury, substance abuse, or significant medical illness requiring treatment (e.g., diabetes, Chronic obstructive pulmonary disease). They ranged from age 50 to 89. Education levels ranged from 6 to 20 years.

The method of continuous norming (Angoff & Robertson, 1987; Zachery & Gorsuch, 1985) was used to derive normative data for a separate census age-matched sample and for the entire sample grouped by age and age by education. This method is recommended to correct for irregularities in the distributions of scores, or the trends in the means and standard deviations across groupings when sample sizes are 200 or less. This approach requires that the line (or curve) of best fit for the data be determined by polynomial regression. The mean, standard deviation, skewness, and kurtosis of the distribution of scores are estimated and percentiles and standard scores are calculated on the basis of this estimate. Norms were generated up to age 90.

The Canadian Study of Health and Aging (CSHA). As a nationwide study of the prevalence of dementia in Canada, the CSHA yielded norms for a variety of measures (e.g., Auditory Verbal Learning Test, individual subtests from the Wechsler Adult Intelligence Scale–Revised, Buschke's Cued Recall paradigm for memory assessment; Tuokko & Woodward, 1996). This demographically corrected normative information was based on the performance of 215 individuals age 65 and older living in the community (i.e., not institutionalized), who completed all of the neuropsychological measures used in the CSHA. All of these individuals scored 78 or above on the Modified Mini-Mental State Examination (3MS; Teng & Chui, 1987) in the screening examination and were diagnosed with no cognitive loss after complete multidisciplinary clinical examinations (see Tuokko, Kristjansson, & Miller, 1995). The performance of 187 persons with dementia, as determined by medical and neuropsychological examination, was examined using the norms to determine the sensitivity and specificity of each measure (Tuokko & Woodward, 1996).

The participants identified with no cognitive loss and dementia in the CSHA differed in important ways from normal volunteers and clinic-based dementia samples more commonly encountered in other neuropsychological studies of dementia. All participants were initially randomly selected from all persons over age 65 living in each region of the country. This being the case, the CSHA sample may be more representative of the general population than other studies. That is, the CSHA sample is less biased in terms of self-selection than most normal samples.

A regression approach to the development of the norms, using age, gender, and years of formal education as predictor scores was used. An approach, essentially identical to that of Heaton et al. (1991) was followed in the development of these norms.

Kaufman Batteries.   Kaufman developed a series of batteries that measure aspects of cognitive functioning and contain norms for persons age 85 and older (A. S. Kaufman & N. L. Kaufman, 1990, 1993, 1994). The standardization sample for each of these measures was described as 2,000 persons from age 11 to 94 selected using a stratified multistage random sampling procedure, to get a cross-sectional representation of the U.S. population as reflected in the 1988 census data. The sample was stratified within each age group by gender, geographic region, socioeconomic status (SES defined by education level), and race or ethnic group. One hundred persons were selected at each 5-year age group between age 65 and 74 (55% and 58% female, respectively) and 100 subjects over age 75 (65% female) were included.

PSYCHOMETRIC ISSUES

Reliability and Validity

The concepts of reliability and validity are fundamental in test construction. There are various forms of reliability and validity that provide information about the measure for interpretation purposes. The reader is directed to other sources (e.g., Anastasi, 1988; Cronbach, 1990; Nunnally, 1970) for a full discussion of these concepts. Only a brief discussion is included here to highlight a few issues of particular importance with respect to geriatric neuropsychological assessment.

Although reliability and validity are important to test interpretation, not all neuropsychological measures easily satisfy the usual requirements for adequate reliability and validity (Kaszniak, 1990). This is not to say that these measures should not be used, but that limitations to the measures must be kept in mind. Moreover, a measure may be valid for one purpose (e.g., identifying persons with dementia) but not another (e.g., predicting rehabilitative success of a person following a stroke). Hence, the adequacy of reliability and validity are relative, and interpreters of test performance are obligated to thoroughly understand these constructs when interpreting test scores. In practical terms, misinterpretation of test data can be highly costly. Overinterpretation of a poor performance on a single, less than adequately reliable or valid measure can potentially place older, highly vulnerable persons at risk of losing their autonomy and self-determination if, on the basis of this performance, it is successfully argued that these individuals are incompetent to make decisions on their own behalf.

In general, *reliability* refers to the consistency with which the underlying behavior is measured. For example, it reflects the degree of similarity in the scores obtained by the same person on the same measure administered at two points in time, or the similarity of scores obtained by two raters scoring the same test protocol. Various forms of reliability have been identified. Methods to examine the consistency within a measure or test (i.e., internal consistency) may be addressed by developing alternate forms, dividing the test items in half and examining the correlations between the halves (i.e., split-half), or by examining the intercorrelations of all items with each other (i.e., Cronbach's alpha).

Another form of reliability evaluates the degree to which two judges (or raters) arrive at the same conclusion regarding an individual's performance (i.e., interjudge reliability or interjudge concordance). This type of reliability is of particular importance when the scoring of a test protocol requires some degree of subjective evaluation on the part of the rater. Most neuropsychological tests boast highly standardized scoring criteria that minimize interjudge differences, but this is not true for all measures. Variations in the administration and scoring guidelines for the original Mini-Mental State Examination (M. L. Folstein, S. E. Folstein, & McHugh, 1975) have given rise to many concerns regarding the replicability of this measure from one practitioner to another (Tombaugh & McIntyre, 1992).

A third form of reliability examines the stability of scores over time (i.e., test–retest). This form is of particular interest in geriatric assessment, because it is often the goal of the assessment to identify true and significant change in performance across time (e.g., deterioration of significant magnitude to suggest an underlying neurodegenerative process). Several coefficients, analogous to the reliability coefficient, have been developed that identify an instrument's ability to detect change within individuals or groups of individuals (Streiner & Norman, 1995). As noted by Retzlaff and Gibertini (1994), differences across time are related to both the reliability of a test and true and natural changes in people's scores across time. Natural changes in test performance over time may be particularly evident with increasing age and it is of great importance that normal changes not be identified as indicative of pathological change.

It is far too common to see practitioners become concerned with a modest (e.g., 3-point) decline on a screening measure such as the Mini-Mental State Examination (MMSE) over a period without consideration for the normal age-related expected change in scores. Formulas for determining significant changes in test performance over time at various levels of significance are available to assist the practitioner in not overinterpreting modest changes in test performance (e.g., Cahan, 1989; Payne & Jones, 1959; Silverstein, 1981). In fact, when assessing the test–retest reliability of a measure in a population with dementia, the time interval is kept short (e.g., a few days) as changes in test scores over longer periods of time could be reflective of cognitive decline as opposed to a limitation of the test.

Validity refers to the degree to which the test measures that for which it was intended. For example, how effective is the measure in identifying a particular diagnostic group, or how well does this test measure depression? Three forms of validity are typically described: *content, construct,* and *predictive validity.* Content validity describes whether or not the content of a particular test is measuring a particular domain. The primary purpose of some measures is to capture or represent a specific universe of content. Classroom examinations, designed to reflect the course content, are examples of this type of measure. Procedures for evaluating content validity are described by Anastasi (1988), who stressed that *content validation* is particularly appropriate for criterion-referenced tests where performance is interpreted in terms of content meaning. Content and face validity are not to be confused. *Face validity* refers to what the test appears superficially to measure, not necessarily what the test actually measures. Face validity plays a role in determining appropriate measures for use with the elderly in that test compliance may be jeopardized if the measure appears irrelevant, silly, inappropriate, or childish. As noted in chapter 4, the face validity of the Wechsler Adult Intelligence Scale for use with older persons was questioned by Kendrick (1982b).

Construct validity refers to the extent to which a test may be said to measure a particular *theoretical construct* or trait. In this case, there is no obvious content corresponding to the behavior of interest (e.g., depression). The construct under investigation is hypothetical and abstract rather than concrete (as with content validity) and must be shown to relate to other measures of the same domain. Construct validation is established when test scores relate to domains in ways that make theoretical sense. For example, a measure of depression should be related to gender because depression is known to be more common in women than men. Construct validation is determined by the gradual accumulation of information from various sources to support this assertion. Some of the procedures providing such supporting evidence include correlations with other tests hypothesized to measure the same construct, factor analysis, and interventions to improve certain abilities (Anastasi, 1988). Thus, a new measure of memory should correlate with existing measures of memory or should have high loadings on the same factor as two or three other well-known memory scales. Retzlaff and Gibertini (1994) noted that construct validity is particularly important within neuropsychology where idiosyncratic test construction techniques are often used.

Criterion-related validity indicates the effectiveness of a test in determining an individual's performance on a criterion measure. Two types of criterion validity are generally discussed: *concurrent* and *predictive*. In both cases, performance on the test is checked against a criterion to determine a statistical relation between them. The difference between concurrent and predictive validity is the timing of the administration of the test and the criterion measure. The most common types of criteria used in geriatric neuropsychology are diagnostic groupings or other biological variables. Because the criterion is available, it is important to determine the function served by the test. For example, does the test provide a simpler, quicker, or less expensive substitute for the criterion data?

Two issues concerning criterion validity that have received relatively little attention in neuropsychological assessment are criterion contamination and operating characteristics of measures. Both of these topics are of importance when determining the criterion validity of a measure. When determining the criterion status of individuals, it is of importance that the test scores do not themselves influence the identified criterion status. That is, if a test score is used to identify groups of cognitively impaired (presumed demented) and cognitively intact persons, one cannot then look for differences between the groups on that test score and infer criterion validity (i.e., the measure is capable of discriminating between the groups). Similarly, when examining the predictive validity of a test score (e.g., whether or not a measure of memory administered at Time 1 can predict diagnosis of dementia at Time 2), the examiner must not be aware of the Time 1 test score when making the diagnosis at Time 2.

Recently, determination of criterion validity in psychology has been approached through examination of the operating characteristics of a measure. Within this framework, the constructs of *sensitivity* and *specificity* are central. Sensitivity and specificity assess how well test scores discriminate between two groups. In a clinical context, the usual goal is to identify those who are disease-positive (e.g., impaired) from those who are disease-negative (e.g., normal), according to some known external criterion (i.e., *gold standard*). The gold standard is the definitive diagnosis of the disease under consideration (e.g., CT-identified lesion, clinically diagnosed Alzheimer's disease, etc.).

The sensitivity of a test at any given cutoff score is the proportion of disease-positive (D+) persons with scores in the test-positive (T+) range. Thus, the sensitivity is the probability of a positive test result given a disease-positive person. The specificity of a test score is the proportion of disease-negative (D−) persons with scores falling in the test-negative range

(T−). Thus, the specificity is the probability of a negative test result given a disease-negative person. In Table 2.1, N is the sample size and A, B, C, and D are the cell frequencies. Thus, A represents the number of disease-positive persons with a test score falling in the test-positive range. Then, the sensitivity and specificity are calculated as follows: sensitivity = A / (A + C) and specificity = D / (B + D).

From Table 2.1, the probability of finding a positive test result in a disease-negative person (false positive; i.e., test identifies a normal person as impaired) can be calculated as 1-specificity. The probability of finding a negative test result in a disease-positive person (false negative; i.e., test identifies the impaired person as normal) can be calculated as 1-sensitivity. A test that discriminates perfectly between the two groups would have both sensitivity and specificity equal to 1.0 at a certain cutoff score (i.e., nonoverlapping distributions of scores) and this would be the optimal cutoff score. However, some overlap in the distribution of psychological scores for impaired and nonimpaired persons often exists. In theory, a good clinical test is both highly sensitive and highly specific at a certain optimal cutoff score. In practice, there may need to be a trade-off between high sensitivity and high specificity (Zweig & Campbell, 1993). The choice, then, of an optimal cutoff score depends on many factors, such as the ultimate cost of false positive and false negative results in the situation under consideration. Usually, high sensitivity is most desirable for screening tools (Essex-Sorlie, 1995), because the point is to make sure no cases of the disease are missed and follow-up testing will then identify the false positive cases (normals). However, in some cases, measures that are both highly sensitive and specific are most desirable. For example, in a disorder such as dementia where no treatment or cure is available, it is important that clinicians can confidently rule out the presence of disease as well as detect it (Essex-Sorlie, 1995).

Needless to say, the approach of identifying a cutoff score to determine who requires further assessment is of practical value and is often a key element of screening tests. Unfortunately, scores on screening tools are often interpreted at face value without consideration of either the need for further evaluation or the context of the assessment. By definition, false

TABLE 2.1
Method for Determining the Sensitivity and Specificity
of a Measure in Relation to Diagnostic Criteria

| Test Results | Gold Standard | | |
	D+	D−	
T+	A	B	A + B
T−	C	D	C + D
	A + C	B + D	N

positive cases and false negative cases are expected to some (predetermined) degree. Moreover, cutoff scores often need to be adjusted by age, education, premorbid intelligence, and race-ethnicity (Adams, Boake, & Crain, 1982). A related issue raised by Meehl and Rosen (1955) is the base rate at which the condition occurs in the sample from which the cutting score was developed. The usefulness of a cutoff score or how much the test score contributes to the diagnostic process is jointly determined by its association with the disease and the base rate of the condition. For example, the use of any valid test will improve predictive or diagnostic accuracy as the base rate approaches 50%. With extreme base rates, the improvement gained by using the test may be negligible (Wedding & Faust, 1989).

CONCLUSIONS

This chapter has addressed some of the psychometric issues of importance to test interpretation. Although many of these issues are common to psychological assessment (e.g., Anastasi, 1988; Cronbach, 1990; Nunnally, 1970) or neuropsychological measurement (e.g., Lezak, 1995; Retzlaff & Gibertini, 1994), in general, particular issues commonly confronted in geriatric neuropsychological assessment were identified. The samples and methods employed in some of the large-scale normative studies for persons over age 65 were described. Because it is often difficult to obtain sufficiently large samples of very old individuals (e.g., over age 90), approaches that provide maximum information from these samples are particularly useful (e.g., regression, overlapping cells). The complexities inherent in assessing samples known to show change in function over relatively short periods of time and for whom many factors are interacting to create the observable behaviors attests to the need for a solid understanding of psychometric theory. Knowledge of more general life-span developmental issues is also important in geriatric neuropsychological assessment.

Chapter 3

Screening Instruments
for Cognitive Impairment

Screening instruments for cognitive impairment have been used extensively by neuropsychologists, neurologists, and other health professionals working with elderly populations. Most of these are brief, easy to administer and score, and are used widely in both clinical and research settings. Their overall diagnostic accuracy can be improved by combining data from several instruments (Eisdorfer & Cohen, 1980).

When using screening instruments, cutoff scores are frequently employed. If performance falls below the minimum level expected, dementia is usually suspected and follow-up testing, as well as additional clinical information, is necessary to establish an appropriate diagnosis. It is not appropriate to derive a diagnosis of dementia solely based on screening instrument performance. No screening instrument is perfectly valid and, consequently, some elders with no clinically significant deterioration will be identified as impaired (false positives) and some individuals with dementia will not be identified (false negatives).

Perhaps the most widely known screening instrument is the *Mini-Mental State Examination* (MMSE; M. L. Folstein et al., 1975). The MMSE is one of the tests recommended by the National Institute of Neurologic and Communicative Disorders and Stroke and the Alzheimer's Disease and Related Disorders Association (NINCDS–ADRDA) to facilitate the diagnosis of Alzheimer's disease (McKhann et al., 1984). M. L. Folstein et al. (1975) included the instrument in its entirety in an appendix. The MMSE is a quick screening tool for the assessment of cognitive impairment in elderly persons. It is divided into two sections, the first of which requires only oral responses and covers orientation, memory, and attention with a maximum score of 21. The second part tests ability to name, follow verbal and written requests, write a sentence spontaneously, and copy interlocking pentagons. The maximum score for the second section is 9, making the highest possible score 30. The items are differentially weighted for the purposes of scoring.

The MMSE takes less than 10 minutes to administer and has satisfactory reliability and validity (Tombaugh & McIntyre, 1992). In terms of internal consistency, community samples yield coefficients ranging from .68 to .77, whereas higher internal consistency is evident when mixed samples of medical patients are being examined (Tombaugh & McIntyre, 1992). Test–retest reliability, with intervals smaller than 2 months, range between .80 and .95 for both cognitively intact and impaired elderly (Tombaugh & McIntyre, 1992), although a study of delirium patients resulted in much lower reliability (Anthony, Le Resche, Niaz, Von Korff, & M. L. Folstein, 1982). Traditionally, scores of 23 or lower are considered to fall within the impaired range (Tombaugh & McIntyre, 1992). A limitation of this instrument is that sensitivity and specificity decrease as the subject's age increases and level of education decreases (La Rue, 1992). For this reason, in this chapter, normative information is broken down by age and educational level (see Table 3.1; Tombaugh, McDowell, Kristjansson, & Hubley, 1996). Tombaugh et al. (1996) presented extensive information on the sensitivity and specificity of the MMSE. In a recent systematic examination of race on the MMSE, it was concluded that there were no significant race effects on total MMSE scores between Whites and Blacks of similar educational background (Murden, McRae, Kaner, & Buchman, 1991). The effects of hearing loss on MMSE performance have also been investigated (Uhlmann, Teri, Rees, Mozlowski, & Larson, 1989). It was concluded that hearing loss was related to significantly reduced cognitive performance in clients with probable Alzheimer's disease regardless of whether the screening measure was administered in written or oral form. They also pointed out that the research participants' visual acuity was at least adequate. Their findings suggested that diminished MMSE performance associated with mild to moderate hearing loss is not necessarily an artifact of the method of administration. In a related investigation, Fillenbaum, George, and Blazer (1988) assessed whether it is preferable to score nonresponses on the MMSE as correct or as errors. Based on a comparison of responders' and nonresponders' abilities to perform activities of daily living, as well as on examination of the relative difficulty level, they concluded that scoring nonresponses as errors is more likely to be correct.

Several variations in MMSE administration exist (see Tombaugh & McIntyre, 1992). Specifically, in the original version, participants are asked to name the hospital and the floor they are on. Alternative questions have been used outside hospital settings. Although the words *apple, penny,* and

TABLE 3.1
MMSE Norms (Percentile Scores) Stratified for Age and Years of
Education for Participants Diagnosed as No Cognitive Impairment

MMSE Score	Age 65–79		Age 80–89	
	0–8 Years Education (n = 58)	9+ Years Education (n = 168)	0–8 Years Education (n = 65)	9+ Years Education (n = 115)
30	98	86	100	93
29	88	62	97	77
28	76	41	89	57
27	62	29	83	37
26	48	21	66	30
25	36	14	58	18
24	26	9	49	11
23	19	6	35	6
22	16	5	23	4
21	10	4	14	3
20	5	4	8	1
19	5	3	5	<1
18	4	1	<5	
17	4	<1		
16	3			
<16	<3			

Note. MMSE = Mini-Mental State Examination. From "Mini-Mental State Examination (MMSE) and the Modified MMSE (3MS): A Psychometric Comparison and Normative Data," by T. N. Tombaugh, I. McDowell, B. Kristjansson, and A. M. Hubley, 1996, *Psychological Assessment, 8*, p. 53. Copyright © 1996 by the American Psychological Association. Reprinted with permission.

table are used to test registration and recall, others have used other words such as *shirt, brown, flag, honesty*. Finally, in the original version, the serial sevens task was always administered, but spelling the word WORLD backward was available as an alternative. However, some administrations include only the WORLD and others only the serial sevens task (see chap. 7 for an additional discussion of the serial sevens task).

There have been several attempts to modify the MMSE in order to improve its sensitivity and specificity (e.g., Bird, Canino, Stipec, & Shrout, 1987; Galasko et al., 1990). The most significant attempt resulted in the *Modified Mini-Mental State Examination* (3MS; Teng & Chui, 1987). The 3MS incorporates four added items, more graded scoring, and some other minor changes. These modifications were designed to sample a broader array of cognitive function, cover a greater difficulty level, and enhance the reliability and validity of the scores. The range of scores was broadened from 0–30 to 0–100. The 3MS was one of the measures administered through the Canadian Study of Health and Aging (see chap. 2 for a description of this study) and normative data are presented in Table 3.2.

TABLE 3.2
3MS Norms (Percentile Scores) Stratified for Age and Years of
Education for Participants Diagnosed as No Cognitive Impairment

| | Age 65–79 | | Age 80–89 | |
| | 0–8 Years Education (n = 58) | 9+ Years Education (n = 168) | 0–8 Years Education (n = 65) | 9+ Years Education (n = 115) |
3MS Score				
100	100	98	100	98
99	100	95	100	97
98	100	86	100	95
97	100	79	100	90
96	95	73	100	88
95	93	67	99	82
94	90	61	99	77
93	86	56	95	70
92	83	52	91	61
91	79	48	90	58
90	78	43	84	54
89	76	38	82	51
88	72	36	81	49
87	69	32	80	42
86	65	29	80	39
85	60	26	80	38
84	57	24	77	37
83	53	22	72	37
82	48	22	71	34
81	47	20	69	31
80	45	20	68	30
79	44	19	66	29
78	43	19	63	28
77	38	16	59	25
76	26	10	51	20
75	17	8	46	17
74	12	7	42	12
73	10	7	38	10
72	9	5	34	7
71	8	5	32	5
70	6	4	25	2
69	5	4	22	<2
68	4	3	19	—
67	3	2	12	—
66	<3	<2	9	—
65	—	—	8	—
64	—	—	3	—
63 or less	—	—	<2	—

Note. 3MS = Modified Mini-Mental State Examination. From "Mini-Mental State Examination (MMSE) and the Modified MMSE (3MS): A Psychometric Comparison and Normative
Data," by T. N. Tombaugh, I. McDowell, B. Kristjansson, and A. M. Hubley, 1996, *Psychological
Assessment, 8,* p. 54. Copyright © 1996 by the American Psychological Association. Reprinted
with permission.

The measure itself appears in an appendix of Teng and Chui. As part of an extensive normative study done within the context of the Canadian Study of Health and Aging, Tombaugh et al. (1996) concluded that the 3MS and the MMSE have comparable degrees of reliability and the two tests are affected in similar ways by age and education. That is, higher education increased specificity and decreased sensitivity, whereas increasing age mainly decreased specificity. An extensive sensitivity/specificity table with cutoff scores was presented by Tombaugh et al. (1996). Information for several age groups of elderly persons was given. The MMSE was found to be superior in identifying cognitively intact persons, whereas the 3MS was better in the identification of persons with Alzheimer's disease. Extensive sensitivity and specificity information for several different educational levels is presented by Tombaugh et al. (1996). This information (see Table 3.2) allows clinicians to select appropriate cutoff scores depending on the client's educational level and risk-benefits analysis (for increasing or decreasing specificity) for each individual client. Additional factor analytic evidence on the validity of the 3MS is also available. Specifically, based on a large sample ($N = 892$) of nursing home residents, Abraham et al. (1993) obtained a five-factor orthogonal solution accounting for close to 59% of the variance and reflecting psychomotor skills, memory, identification and association, orientation, and concentration and calculation. Thus, the instrument appears to map well-recognized dimensions of cognitive performance.

The *CAMCOG* is the cognitive portion of the *Cambridge Examination for Mental Disorders for the Elderly* (CAMDEX; Roth et al., 1986). The developers of the CAMDEX have shown it to be reliable and valid. The CAMDEX consists of three main sections. That is, a structured clinical interview is followed by objective cognitive tests and an interview with a collaborative informant. A simple physical examination, laboratory tests, and radiological investigations are also part of the CAMDEX. The respondent's part of the interview takes approximately 1 hour, whereas the collaborative informant's part takes about 20 minutes (see chap. 10). The cognitive examination part of the CAMDEX (CAMCOG) consists of 14 of the 19 MMSE (M. L. Folstein et al., 1975) items and an additional 43 items designed to provide a wider coverage of cognitive functions than does the MMSE. Maximum score for the CAMCOG is 106. The CAMCOG was designed to assess language, orientation, abstract thinking, calculation, and perception. Roth et al. (1986) presented normative information on a small sample of "normal elderly" ($n = 17$) consisting of both geriatric patients and community residents from warden-controlled sheltered accommodation. The mean MMSE score for that sample was 26.7/30. The mean CAMCOG score was 90/106 with a range of 72–102. It is possible that the means for community dwelling elderly living independently would be higher than those presented by Roth et al. Furthermore, caution should be exercised as performance on this instrument may be affected by age and education (Lindeboom, Ter-Horst, Hooyer, Dinkgreve, & Jonker, 1993). Thus, age- and education-stratified norms would be useful. In fact, the lack of more extensive normative information on this instrument may be the major reason why this instrument is not used widely in clinical settings. The CAMCOG yielded a 92% sensitivity and 96% specificity when using a 79/80 cutoff (Roth et al., 1986). Although a cutoff of 69/70 was found to have 97% sensitivity and 91% specificity when assessing moderate dementia, it is unclear about what would be an appropriate cutoff when the patients are assessed for the presence of mild dementia (Blessed, Black, Butler, & Kay, 1991). A more recent factor analysis of the CAMCOG based on 191 patients with probable Alzheimer's disease yielded factors that differed from the original conceptually based dimensions (Greifenhagen, Kurz, Wiseman, Haupt, & Zimmer, 1994). The empirically derived factors were language/praxis, visuoconstructive abilities, remote memory, and short-term memory. Normative information on the empirically derived factor scores could prove useful. Interrater agreement was studied and was found to be satisfactory. Test–retest reliability data on elderly patients suggests that the measure is stable (Lindeboom et al., 1993).

Kahn, Goldfarb, Pollack, and Peck (1960) presented validity evidence for the *Mental Status Questionnaire* (MSQ), which consists of 10 questions assessing areas such as orientation, memory, calculation, and general personal information. The 10 items were selected from a pool of 31 as being the most discriminating for the determination of mental status. According to Kahn et al., the instrument has satisfactory reliability and internal consistency. Although there have been various versions of the MSQ, most are scored as follows: 0–2 = severely confused, 3–5 = moderately confused, 6–8 = slightly confused, and 9–10 = not confused (Brink, Capri, DeNeeve, Janakes, & Oliveira, 1978). Brink et al. (1978) administered the MSQ to 40 aged community dwelling subjects at a community center. The median was 10 and the range 6 to 10. Brink et al. included the version of the MSQ that they used. They concluded that the MSQ is a valid measure because it can contribute to the differentiation of patients considered by extended care facility staff to be confused from those considered lucid and alert as well as from community participants. On the other hand, they pointed out that the MSQ can result in false negatives. False positives are less likely according to these authors.

Another related instrument is the *Short Portable Mental Status Questionnaire* (SPMSQ; Pfeiffer, 1975), which consists of 10 items tapping mental status (e.g., "What day of the week is it?" and "What is the name of this place?"). The instrument normally takes less than 5 minutes to administer and explores short-term memory, long-term memory, orientation, and ability to conduct serial operations. Pfeiffer (1975) presented validity evidence and the instrument was published in its entirety in an appendix. Additional validity information is also available (Haglund & Schickit, 1976). This instrument has the advantage that norms for persons over age 65 are available (Pfeiffer, 1975). However, Dalton, Pederson, Blon, and Holmes (1987) raised some concerns about the use of this measure. Specifically, they administered the test to a mixed group of neurologic and psychiatric patients with a mean age of 53 and found that the test did not relate significantly to clinical or neuropsychological diagnosis. The latter diagnosis was based on an extensive battery of neuropsychological tests. Dalton and associates gave examples of the types of deficiencies displayed by people with one or no errors on the SPMSQ. Among the examples were difficulties reproducing and recalling immediately geometric designs and impaired short-term memory for both verbal and visuospatial memory. Dalton et al. (1987) attributed their finding to the limited range of skills tapped by this brief instrument and recommended that clinicians use more comprehensive approaches. Fillenbaum (1980) found that the measure is highly correlated with the MSQ. However, when the scores of both instruments were compared to the results of clinical interviews involving 83 patients (29 of whom were diagnosed as having cognitive impairment), a score of two errors in the MSQ and a similar score on the SPMSQ yielded a sensitivity of 55% and a specificity of 96%. The relatively low sensitivity rate is consistent with the conclusions of Dalton et al. (1987). Finally, Winograd (1984) concluded that the SPMSQ is not an adequate predictor of capacity for self-care.

Scherr et al. (1988) administered the SPMSQ to a large sample of community dwelling elderly. Table 3.3 presents the mean performance of the sample. Caution must be exercised when comparing a patient's performance to the data presented in Table 3.3. Specifically, in the study of Scherr et al., one of the SPMSQ items was not administered ("What's the name of this place?") because it was not well received by the initial participants who were responding to the SPMSQ questions at their own homes. It is also worth noting that a substantial portion of the respondents were Italian-American immigrants. Furthermore, Scherr et al. (1988) did not report the standard deviations of the scores because these were not normally distributed. Instead, they provided some information on the frequency of poor performers. Specifically, the proportion of those who did poorly on the test (i.e., three or fewer items correct) was .7% among those age 65 to 69, whereas it was 13.5% among those age 85 to 89. The proportion of those who did well on the test (i.e., eight or nine items correct) was 66.9% among those age 65 to 69 and 29% among those age 85 to 89. Additional normative information on the SPMSQ broken by educational level is presented on Table 3.4. These data were collected by Erkinjuntti,

TABLE 3.3
Short Portable Mental Status Questionnaire Performance
of a Sample of Community Dwelling Elderly Persons

	n	M
Sex		
Male	1,304	7.58
Female	2,034	7.39
Age		
65–69	1,304	7.80
70–74	937	7.70
75–79	589	7.28
80–84	318	6.69
85–89	148	6.05
≥90	42	5.14
Education		
Some grade school	1,657	7.06
Some high school	1,446	7.85
Some college	215	8.12

Note. Only 9 of the 10 items were administered. The item "What is the name of this place?" was not administered. This is only a portion of the table by Scherr et al. (1988), who also presented mean scores "adjusted for age and sex." From "Correlates of Cognitive Function in an Elderly Community Population" by P. A. Scherr, M. S. Albert, H. H. Funkenstein, N. R. Cook, C. H. Hennekens, L. G. Branch, L. R. White, J. O. Taylor, and D. A. Evans, 1988, *American Journal of Epidemiology, 128,* p. 1096. Copyright © 1988 by The Johns Hopkins University School of Hygiene and Public Health. Adapted with permission.

TABLE 3.4
Distribution of Samples by Number of Errors
in SPMSQ and by Educational Level

Number of Errors	Grade School	High School	Post-High School	All
0	63	11	5	79
1	31	1	—	32
2	3	1	—	4
3	1	—	—	1
4	—	—	—	—
5	1	—	—	1
6	—	—	—	0
7	—	—	—	—
8	—	—	—	—
9	—	—	—	1
10	—	—	—	—

Note. N = 119. From "Short Portable Mental Status Questionnaire as a Screening Test for Dementia and Delirium Among the Elderly" by T. Erkinjunttii, R. Sulkava, J. Wikstrom, and L. Autio, 1987, *Journal of the American Geriatrics Society, 35,* p. 414. Copyright © 1987 by the American Geriatrics Society. Reproduced with permission from Williams & Wilkins on behalf of the copyright holder.

Sulkava, Wikstrom, and Autio (1987) and are based on a sample of 119 community residents age 65 or older.

The *Neurobehavioral Cognitive Status Examination* (NCSE) was developed with the aim of distinguishing confusional states from dementia syndromes and differentiating isolated language, memory, and procedural deficits from more "global" dementing processes (Kiernan, Mueller, Langston, & Van Dyke, 1987). According to Kiernan and colleagues, cognitively intact persons require 5 minutes to complete the instrument and persons with impairments require 10 to 20 minutes. First, the instrument assesses three general factors: level of consciousness, attention, and orientation. Then five major ability areas (language, constructions, memory, calculations, and reasoning) are evaluated using independent tasks. The main advantage of the instrument is that, despite its brevity, it offers performance information with respect to several specific abilities. Normative data on volunteers (n = 59) with no medical or psychiatric history that might affect cognition (mean age 77.6 years) are presented in Table 3.5. Although reliability and validity information on this instrument is limited, Schwamm, Van Dyke, Kiernan, Merrin, and Mueller (1987) found that the NCSE had a lower false negative rate (7%) than the MMSE (43%).

The *Mattis Dementia Rating Scale* (MDRS; Coblentz et al., 1973; Mattis, 1976, 1988) was developed to assess mental status in persons for whom impairments are so profound that they would only be able to generate few responses on many other neuropsychological tests. Administration takes less than 15 minutes for normal elderly participants but is significantly

TABLE 3.5

Norms on the Neurobehavioral Cognitive Status
Examination Based on Volunteers With No History
of Medical Conditions That Might Affect Cognition

Scale	M	SD
Orientation	11.7	.7
Attention	7.1	1.2
Comprehension	5.9	.04
Repetition	12.4	.08
Naming	8.2	1.1
Constructions	4.4	1.5
Memory	10.1	2.2
Calculations	3.9	.3
Similarities	5.6	1.3
Judgment	5.0	.08

Note. Based on 59 persons with an average of 77.6 years. From "The Neurobehavioral Cognitive Status Examination: A Brief but Differentiated Approach to Cognitive Assessment," by R. J. Kiernan, J. Mueller, J. W. Langston, and C. Van Dyke, 1987, *Annals of Internal Medicine, 107*, pp. 482–483. Copyright © 1987 by American College of Physicians. Adapted with permission.

longer for elderly persons with dementia. The measure consists of mental status-type items, including measures of conceptualization, memory, attention, initiation, perseveration, and construction. Thus, a briefer mental status test may be more suitable for persons who have difficulties concentrating more than a few minutes. The instrument has satisfactory internal consistency and can differentiate brain-damaged patients from normal elderly persons. One week test–retest reliability estimates range from a high of .97 for the total score to a low of .61 for the attention subscale (Mattis, 1988). However, sensitivity to mild impairment in elderly persons remains to be studied (Coblentz et al., 1973; K. M. Montgomery, 1982; Spreen & Strauss, 1991). The diagnostic value of this measure also requires further study (McDowell & Newell, 1996). Norms, based on a large sample of 4,102 individuals from age 50 to 80 and selected randomly from the official registers of residents in an Austrian city, were published by Schmidt et al. (1994) and appear in Table 3.6. Additional norms on community dwelling elders can be found in the scale's manual (Mattis, 1988).

The second part of the *Blessed Dementia Rating Scale* (BDR; Blessed, Tomlinson, & Roth, 1968) can also be used for screening. The first part is proxy-administered and is discussed in the caregiver chapter of this

TABLE 3.6
Mattis Dementia Rating Scale Scores of Healthy Volunteers

Education Level	Age			
	50–59	60–69	70–80	Total
4–9 years of grade school				
n	119	161	37	317
M	140.7	140.0	139.0	140.2
SD	4.8	3.8	3.7	4.2
10–13 years or high school diploma				
n	245	282	50	577
M	142.1	141.3	140.7	141.6
SD	2.1	3.0	2.4	2.6
College experience or higher degree				
n	33	58	16	107
M	143.1	142.2	141.3	142.3
SD	1.9	1.7	1.7	1.7
Total				
N	397	501	103	1,001
M	141.8	141.0	140.1	141.2
SD	3.2	3.2	3.0	3.2

Note. From "The Mattis Dementia Rating Scale: Normative Data From 1,001 Healthy Volunteers," by R. Schmidt, W. Freid, F. Fazekas, B. Reinhart, P. Grieshefer, M. Koch, B. Eber, M. Schumaker, K. Palmin, and H. Lechner, 1994, *Neurology, 44,* p. 965. Copyright © 1994 by the American Academy of Neurology. Adapted with permission from Lippincott–Raven Publishers.

volume. The second part of the BDR, the *Information–Memory–Concentration Test* (IMCT), assesses cognitive dimensions. The IMCT was included in its entirety in an appendix of Blessed et al. (1968). It is brief and easy to administer. The information part of the test contains orientation-type questions. The memory part requires responses to both personal (e.g., place of birth) and general questions (e.g., the name of the Prime Minister). In addition, the instrument has a 5-minute delayed recall component involving the recall of a name and address that the subject is given. The concentration part consists of three items (counting forward and backward and saying the months of the year backward). Blessed et al. (1968) found test–retest and split-half reliability to be satisfactory. In terms of validity, scores on the test were correlated at the −.59 level with senile plaque counts (Blessed et al., 1968).

Although most screening instruments reviewed this far involve a questionnaire-type approach, *clock drawing* has also been used as a screen for dementia. Although administration procedures vary, subjects are often presented with a predrawn circle and are asked to draw a clock face and place the hands on the clock. Originally, the approach was developed for the evaluation of constructional apraxia that often arises from damage to the parietal lobes (Critchley, 1953; Freedman et al., 1994; Goodglass & Kaplan, 1972). More recently, it has been used as a screening tool for the presence of cognitive impairment in old age. Most scoring procedures for clock drawing are based on rank ordering of severity of errors resulting in a variety of systems for error classification (e.g., Dastoor, Schwartz, & Kurtzman, 1991; Shulman, Sheldetsky, & Silver, 1986; Sunderland et al., 1989; Wolf-Klein, Silverstone, Levy, Brod, & Breuer, 1989). Clinical experience is used to classify clock drawing errors. In one study, Wolf-Klein et al. (1989) identified 10 clock patterns that were related to mental status test performance. Participants were presented with a predrawn circle but were not given a time in which to place the hands. The 10 clock patterns range from 1 (irrelevant figures) to 10 (normal), representing a perfect pattern. In another investigation, Goodglass and Kaplan (1972) asked subjects to draw the face of a clock, place the numbers in the correct location, and set the clock to 10 past 11. They based their scoring on a 3-point system, in which one point each was given for: approximate circular face, symmetry of number placement, and correctness of number. Although such scoring systems may readily identify clearly pathognomic error types, the more subtle differentiation between errors made by normal elders and persons with mild dementia may be overlooked.

Freedman et al. (1994) developed a comprehensive scoring system for predrawn clocks, examiner clocks, and free-drawn clocks. In the first condition, participants are required to place numbers and hands in a predrawn circle. In the examiner clocks condition, the participant is presented with a predrawn circle that contains numbers and is asked to set hands at specified times. Finally, in the free-drawn condition, all aspects of the clock are drawn by the participant. These researchers present normative data on a sample of 348 subjects ranging from age 20 to 90. Their volunteer sample was recruited through advertisements in a major metropolitan area. English was the first language of all participants and none had a history of psychiatric disorder, stroke, transient ischemic attacks, seizures, head injury resulting in loss of consciousness for longer than 1 minute, or subjective memory complaints. Freedman et al. defined a subset of critical items from their comprehensive scoring system. These items were highly likely to occur in their normative sample and were applied to the three clock drawing conditions. An optimal cutoff score for the free-drawn condition yielded sensitivity (for Parkinson's and Alzheimer's cases) and specificity of 78% and 82%, respectively.

Tuokko et al. (1995) developed a scoring system based on objective scoring criteria and allowing for both an overall quantifiable score and a qualitative analysis of specific error types (e.g., misplacements, perseverations). Norms for this test are based on 1,000+ normal elderly persons who participated in the Canadian Study of Health and Aging. These norms are incorporated in the test scoring form. The sensitivity and specificity of this scoring system of Tuokko et al. (1995) has been estimated to be as high as 92% and 86%, respectively (Tuokko, Hadjistavropoulos, Miller, & Beattie, 1992). Other related procedures involve clock setting (i.e., drawing the hands on a clock face to indicate a specific time) and clock reading (e.g., Goodglass & Kaplan, 1972; Tuokko et al., 1995). When clock setting, a procedure similar to the one described by Goodglass and Kaplan (1972) and reading components were added to the Tuokko et al. clock drawing task, sensitivity and specificity increased to 94% and 93%, respectively (Tuokko et al., 1992). The system has good reliability and validity (Tuokko et al., 1995). Analysis has also shown (Tuokko et al., 1995) that the *Clock Test* contributes to the assessment of dementia over and above the 3MS (Teng & Chui, 1987).

Tuokko, Hadjistavropoulos, Rae, and O'Rourke (1996) compared the clinical utility and psychometric properties of a variety of clock drawing scoring approaches. The following systems were compared: Tuokko et al. (1995); Doyon, Bouchard, Morin, Bourgeois, and Cote (1991); Shulman, Pushkar Gold, Cohen, and Zucchero (1993); Watson, Arfken, and Birge (1993); and Wolf-Klein et al. (1989). The following conclusions were drawn: The Tuokko et al. (1995) procedure had higher intra- and interrater reliability than the other procedures. The Watson et al. (1993) procedure yielded lower sensitivity and specificity than the other methods. The Tuokko et al., Shulman et al., and Wolf-Klein et al. approaches detected differences between persons classified as normal, cognitively impaired but

TABLE 3.7
Means and (Standard Errors) for Clock Scores by Age Group
for Normal Subjects

Scoring Procedure	Age				
	65–69	70–74	75–79	80–84	85+
Doyon	18.36	18.85	18.41	18.60	16.63
	(.92)	(.46)	(.43)	(.40)	(.75)
Shulman	2.55	2.53	2.74	2.52	3.41
	(.17)	(.25)	(.12)	(.13)	(.17)
Tuokko CD[a]	3.73	3.17	4.02	3.11	6.64
	(.65)	(.65)	(.53)	(.41)	(.79)
Tuokko CS[b]	9.55	9.77	9.82	9.95	7.34
	(.67)	(.73)	(.35)	(.50)	(.63)
Tuokko CR[c]	12.90	12.63	12.94	13.29	12.31
	(.34)	(.54)	(.30)	(.27)	(.51)
Watson	1.95	2.77	2.55	2.05	3.69
	(.38)	(.48)	(.27)	(.29)	(.38)
Wolf-Klein	8.88	8.27	8.07	8.25	7.00
	(.25)	(.31)	(.20)	(.23)	(.33)

Note. Data are based on sample sizes of 39, 30, 91, 61, and 55 from younger to oldest, respectively. From "A Comparison of the Clinical Utility of Alternative Approaches to the Scoring of Clock Drawing," by H. Tuokko and T. Hadjistavropoulos, 1994. Unpublished manuscript.
[a]Tuokko Clock Drawing.
[b]Tuokko Clock Setting.
[c]Tuokko Clock Reading.

not meeting the *DSM–III–R* criteria for dementia, and subjects who met the *DSM–III–R* criteria for dementia. The Doyon et al. and Watson et al. procedures distinguished only the cognitively intact from the cognitively impaired subjects. That is, the Doyon et al. approach did not discriminate between the subjects with dementia and the subjects who were cognitively impaired but not demented. Table 3.7 presents some normative data on the various clock drawing procedures. These are based on a large sample of normal elderly persons who took part in the Canadian Study of Health and Aging (Rae, 1995).

Where there is flexibility to administer somewhat longer instruments than those that can be considered "screens," one might consider the *Multifocus Assessment Scale* (MAS; Coval, Crockett, Holliday, & Koch, 1985) and *Kingston Standardized Cognitive Assessment Battery* (Rodenburg et al., 1991).

The Kingston Standardized Cognitive Assessment Battery is comprised of 17 sections developed to evaluate concentration, various aspects of memory and language, spatial and psychomotor skill, calculation and evidence of frontal lobe damage as assessed by impairment of abstract thought, and perseveration. It can take 25 to 45 minutes to administer. In terms of psychometric properties, the measure has high interrater reliability and satisfactory criterion validity. More specifically, it was found to discriminate reliably between groups of normal elders, organic patients, and patients with psychiatric disorders (Rodenburg et al., 1991). Rodenburg and colleagues recommended the assessment of individual performance in terms of percentiles because they felt cutoff scores only work well in situations where there is clear separation between the normal and pathological groups, which was not necessarily the case in their samples. Normative statistics on a sample of 97 healthy independent community volunteers recruited from diverse sources (e.g., social clubs) were reported by Rodenburg et al. (1991).

The MAS (Coval et al., 1985) consists of three rating and five performance subscales. The instrument takes about 45 minutes to administer. Ratings are obtained on social behavior skills (adapted from Lawton, 1971), receptive language skills, and accessibility, and sensory abilities. The remaining scales assess mental status, orientation, mood (adapted from Kozma & Stones, 1980), and expressive language skills. Alpha coefficients ranged from .92 to .99 (Coval et al., 1985) and the scale can differentiate among samples of elders on the basis of their ability to live independently in the community (Tuokko, Crockett, Holliday, & Coval, 1987). Normative data on a sample of 70 volunteers with an age range from 50 to 90 years and a mean age of 70.2 years have been reported by Tuokko and Crockett (1991). Recently, the instrument has undergone a revision that remains unpublished (Crockett, Coval, Tuokko, Buree, & Koch, 1991).

COMPETENCE ASSESSMENTS

Clinicians often use screening instruments (and other neuropsychological tests) in order to assess the degree to which patients' cognitive capabilities allow them to make competent decisions for themselves. This can be a difficult determination as individuals who obtain relatively low scores on screening instruments are often capable of making competent everyday life decisions.

Ultimately, clinicians can only make recommendations regarding legal competence as the final decision on such matters rests with the legal system. Nonetheless, a variety of scales designed to assess everyday functioning skills can assist with competence assessments (Grisso, 1994). These include instruments designed to assess Instrumental Activities of Daily Living (see chap. 10), as well as more specialized instruments.

One specialized instrument is the *Cognitive Competency Test* (CCT; see Wang & Ennis, 1996). The instrument adopts a practical approach by simulating daily living situations. It consists of 8 subtests: (a) *personal information*, in which the participant is asked to fill out a printed form similar to application forms used by institutions such as banks. The information is obtained verbally if the participant cannot write; (b) *card arrangement*, in which the participant is asked to arrange sets of cards demonstrating sequences such as making a phone call and baking a pie; (c) *picture interpretation*, in which the participant is asked to use visually presented information to draw conclusions about the interactions of individuals in the picture; (d) *memory*, including immediate and delayed recall; (e) *practical reading skills*, in which 10 pictures are presented and the participant has to read labels and signs in order to respond to questions about the picture; (f) *management of finances*, where actions such as payment of bills are simulated in order to assess individuals' abilities to manage their own accounts; (g) *verbal reasoning and judgment*, which includes questions designed to assess safety judgment and self-preservation strategies; and (h) *route learning and spatial orientation*. The measure was found to discriminate between a sample of 10 subjects who were either living in the community or were hospital patients who were living independently prior to their admission, and 8 subjects who required at least some assistance and supervision. The approach appears promising but more research is necessary to assess the validity and reliability of the test. Other specialized instruments are also available (e.g., the *Hopemont Capacity Assessment Interview*; Edelstein, Nygren, Northrop, Staats, & Pool, 1993). The Hopemont is administered directly to the elderly person and involves areas such as ability to handle financial transactions. Generally, extensive psychometric evaluations of this and other such instruments are needed.

It has been suggested that a multidisciplinary competency panel will find subjects more competent than psychometric test results (Rutman & Silberfeld, 1992), but more information is required to evaluate such decisions against ongoing community functioning. Chapter 12 discusses some related issues pertaining to determination of an elder's ability to consent for neuropsychological assessment.

CONCLUSIONS

It is difficult to make an ideal recommendation about the best procedure to use for screening purposes. As indicated at the beginning of this chapter, combining several of these instruments would likely result in increased diagnostic accuracy. The MMSE is likely the most widely researched instrument. The data presented by Tombaugh et al. (1996) on both the MMSE and the 3MS provide excellent normative information on these instruments taking age and education into account. Such education norms are important because the scores of many screening instruments for elders are correlated with education (McDowell & Newell, 1996). Thus, clinicians may select one of those two instruments depending on whether they wish to maximize sensitivity or specificity. The Clock Test can be used to supplement questionnaire-based procedures both because of the brevity of its administration and its contribution to diagnosis over and above the 3MS and MMSE (Tuokko et al., 1995). Where there is flexibility to administer somewhat longer instruments than those that can be considered "screens," one might consider the Multifocus Assessment Scale (Coval et al., 1985) and the Kingston Standardized Cognitive Assessment Battery (Rodenburg et al., 1991).

It is also imperative to avoid overinterpretation of the findings derived from the use of screening measures. Diagnoses should not be made solely based on these instruments. If a diagnosis is needed, the clinician should follow up with more extensive testing, clinical interview, and consultation with other professionals.

The Wechsler Adult Intelligence Scales

The most widely used and familiar composite measures of adult intellectual functioning are the *Wechsler Adult Intelligence Scales.* Much understanding of the effects of age on intellectual functioning is based on observed age-related performance on these measures. There is a large accumulated literature examining performance on these measures by elderly persons from various perspectives.

There is ample evidence to suggest selective decline on Performance scales by age 60 with little decline evident on Verbal scales until almost age 80. This "classic aging pattern," as described by M. S. Albert and Moss (1988), has emerged repeatedly and consistently, even though cross-sectional and longitudinal studies have yielded difference with respect to the point in time when these declines occur. Cross-sectional studies show more pronounced changes over age 70 than longitudinal studies.

A variety of explanations for the "classic aging pattern" have been generated. Horn and Cattell (1967) put forward the concepts of crystallized and fluid intelligence to describe those overlearned, well-practiced, and familiar skills that hold up with age as opposed to tasks requiring problem solving and reasoning for which no familiar or routine solutions are available. Fluid intelligence was described as being dependent on the integrity of the central nervous system and susceptible to random accumulated insults to the CNS (e.g., from a variety of medical condition and events such as hypertension, diabetes, alcoholism, head injury). The distinction between automatic and effortful processing made by Huff (1990) to account for age-related differences in the context of other tasks (i.e., confrontation naming and verbal fluency) may also apply to tasks defined as

44

representing crystallized (automatic) and fluid (effortful) intelligence. Other researchers, identifying the timed nature of the Performance scales, have proposed increased slowing as the source of age-related deficits. However, subsequently, it has been demonstrated that declines in visuospatial types of tasks are evident even when untimed (Botwinick, 1977; D. B. Howieson, Holm, Kaye, Oken, & J. Howieson, 1993). A third approach has been to propose that particular regions of the brain are more susceptible to aging and have examined cognitive functions ascribed to right hemisphere, subcortical (Van Gorp & Mahler, 1990; Van Gorp, Mitrushina, & Cummings, 1989), or prefrontal competency with equivocal findings (Daignault, Braun, & Whitaker, 1992; Koss, Haxby, & Decarli, 1991; Obler, Woodward, & M. L. Albert, 1984). Finally, M. S. Albert and Moss (1988) noted the difficulty of interpreting changes on the WAIS subtests as reflecting specific areas of cognition (or brain function) as the WAIS subtests are multifactorial and require the integration of several major mental abilities for performance on any particular subscale. Despite this, the WAIS subtests continue to be central to neuropsychological assessment and the effects of age are important in that context.

NORMATIVE DATA

The standardization samples for the WAIS batteries are limited in their inclusion of persons of advanced age. The WAIS standardization sample, selected to be representative of the overall U.S. population (U.S. Bureau of the Census, 1950), ranged in age from 17 to 64 years. However, the WAIS norms were extended to the higher age ranges on the basis of data collected from 475 persons age 60 and older residing in metropolitan Kansas City (Doppelt, 1956; Doppelt & Wallace, 1955). Of note, all the Verbal tests were administered to every participant, but approximately 25% could not be administered all of the Performance measures due to sensory deficits, fatigue, illness, or refusal to complete the scale. The number of older participants used in generating conversion tables for IQs and age-corrected subtest scores was 101 (44 men and 57 women) persons age 60 to 64, 86 (42 men and 44 women) age 65 to 69, 80 (38 men and 42 women) age 70 to 74, and 85 individuals (36 men and 49 women) age 75 and older. Thus, the sample size for the older age groups was smaller than for the younger age groups and the older WAIS samples were not formed on the same stratified sampling basis as the younger age groups. In comparison to other presumably representative groups of older persons (Price, Fein, & Feinberg, 1980), the WAIS scores over age 65 appear slightly elevated, particularly for the Performance scores. Heaton et al. (1991) included the WAIS in their large normative project (see chap. 2). Normative data are expressed in *T*-scores and presented by age group (20–34 . . . 65–69, 70–74, 75–80), gender, and years of education (6–8, 9–11, 12, 13–15, 16–17, 18+).

In the WAIS–R standardization sample, the same stratified sampling basis was used for the older groups as for the younger age groups, but the normative data for persons age 55 and over continued to be based on smaller samples than any other age groups and persons of advanced age continued to be excluded (i.e., over age 75). J. J. Ryan, Paolo, and Brungardt (1990; see chap. 2) extended normative tables for Verbal, Performance, and Full scale IQs and age-corrected subtest scores to persons from 75 to 79 years (*n* = 60) and 80+ years (*n* = 70; see Table 4.1). The VIQ, PIQ, and FSIQ scores are available in Ryan et al. (1990).

In keeping with the procedure used for developing demographic corrections for the WAIS, Heaton (1992) developed age-, education-, and gender-corrected norms for the WAIS–R standardization sample (see chap. 2). Verbal, Performance, and Full scale IQs were examined as well as the nonage-corrected scaled scores on the 11 subtests of the WAIS–R. Because the WAIS–R standardization sample was used, no age groups above age 70 to 74 were included. However, score equivalents were generated up to age 80. Years of education were stratified into six groups (i.e., 0–7, 8, 9–11, 12, 13–15, 16+).

Ivnik et al. (1992a) provided age-specific norms for the WAIS–R (see chap. 2 for a description of the sample and methods). Tables containing raw score, percentile ranks, and age-specific scaled scores for midpoint ages occurring at 3-year intervals from midpoint ages 61 through 88 were generated (see Table 4.2). Ivnik et al. (1992a) referred to the age-corrected scores derived from their tables as MOANS Scaled Scores (MSS). Verbal, Performance, and Full scale sums of MSS (VSumMSS, PSumMSS, and FSSumMSS) were calculated and linear transformations were applied to convert the distributions to the accepted WAIS–R standard setting of IQ means at 100 and standard deviations at 15. In comparing the WAIS–R IQs and MOANS IQs for persons under age 75, strong correlations were obtained for IQs (.97 to .99) and scaled scores (.96 to .98) supporting the contention that despite differences in norming procedures, the same constructs are measured. However, for persons below age 75, the MOANS IQs were consistently lower and more varied than the WAIS–R IQs, which most likely accurately reflects a volunteer's intelligence in comparison to what is considered "normal" in the WAIS–R sample. Given the strong correlations between the WAIS–R IQs and the MOANS IQs, the IQs were recomputed so that the means and standard deviations were set to the known "true" WAIS–R IQ values for persons less than age 75. Ivnik et al. (1992a) referred to these scores as MAYO IQs and present conversion tables for Verbal, Performance, and Full scale IQs. As WAIS–R IQ estimates, the

TABLE 4.1
Age-corrected WAIS-R Subtest Scores for Persons Age 80 and Older

Scaled Score	Verbal						Scaled Score	Performance					Scaled Score
	I	DSp	V	A	C	S		PC	PA	BD	OA	DSy	
19	28–29	24–28	67–70	—	30–32	27–28	19	19–20	17–20	41–51	37–41	69–93	19
18	27	23	66	19	29	25–26	18	18	13–16	38–40	33–36	61–68	18
17	26	22	64–65	18	28	24	17	17	12	35–37	32	52–60	17
16	24–25	19–21	61–63	17	26–27	23	16	16	10–11	33–34	31	49–51	16
15	22–23	17–18	57–60	15–16	25	22	15	15	8–9	30–32	30	47–48	15
14	21	16	51–56	13–14	24	20–21	14	14	6–7	27–29	29	41–46	14
13	19–20	15	48–50	12	22–23	18–19	13	13	5	24–26	25–28	36–40	13
12	17–18	14	45–47	10–11	20–21	16–17	12	11–12	4	20–23	22–24	32–35	12
11	16	13	42–44	9	19	14–15	11	10	—	17–19	20–21	28–31	11
10	14–15	11–12	37–41	8	17–18	11–13	10	8–9	3	13–16	16–19	25–27	10
9	12–13	10	31–36	7	15–16	9–10	9	6–7	2	10–12	14–15	20–24	9
8	10–11	9	25–30	6	13–14	7–8	8	4–5	—	8–9	12–13	15–19	8
7	8–9	8	19–24	5	10–12	5–6	7	3	—	4–7	10–11	13–14	7
6	6–7	7	12–18	3–4	6–9	3–4	6	2	1	2–3	8–9	10–12	6
5	4–5	6	9–11	2	5	1–2	5	1	0	0–1	4–7	7–9	5
4	3	4–5	6–8	1	4	0	4	0	—	—	2–3	4–6	4
3	1–2	2–3	4–5	0	2–3	—	3	—	—	—	0–1	2–3	3
2	0	0–1	2–3	—	1	—	2	—	—	—	—	0–1	2
1	—	—	0–1	—	0	—	1	—	—	—	—	—	1

Note. WAIS-R = Wechsler Adult Intelligence Scale-Revised (D. Wechsler, 1981). I = Information, DSp = Digit Span, V = Vocabulary, A = Arithmetic, C = Comprehension, S = Similarities, PC = Picture Completion, PA = Picture Arrangement, BD = Block Design, OA = Object Assembly, DSy = Digit Symbol. From "Standardization of the Wechsler Adult Intelligence Scale - Revised for Persons 75 Years and Older," by J. J. Ryan, A. M. Paolo, and T. M. Brungardt, 1990, *Psychological Assessment, 2,* p. 410. Copyright ©1990 by the American Psychological Association. Reprinted with permission.

TABLE 4.2

MOANS Scaled Scores, Midpoint Age = 79 (Age Range = 74–84, n = 179)

Scaled Scores	WAIS–R Subtests											Percentile Ranges
	Info.	D.Span.	Vocab.	Arith.	Comp.	Simil.	P.C.	P.A.	B.D.	O.A.	D.Symbol	
2	0–6	0–5	0–16	0–3	0	0	0	0	0–4	0–10	0–7	<1
3	7	6	17–18	4	1–3	1	1	—	5	11	8–16	1
4	8	7	19	—	4	2–3	2	1	6	12	17	2
5	9	8	20–23	5	5–6	4	—	—	7	13–14	18–20	3–5
6	10–11	—	24–28	6–7	7–12	5–8	3–4	2	8–9	15	21–24	6–10
7	12–13	9	29–36	8	13–14	9–10	5–6	3	10–11	16–18	25–27	11–18
8	14–15	10	37–40	9	15	11–12	7–8	—	12–14	19–20	28–30	19–28
9	16–17	11	41–45	10–11	16	13–14	9–10	4–5	15–18	21–22	31–34	29–40
10	18–20	12–13	46–50	12	17–19	15–17	11	6	19–22	23–26	35–39	41–59
11	21	14	51–53	13	20	18–19	12–13	—	23	27–28	40–42	60–71
12	22	15	54–56	14	21	20	—	7–8	24–27	—	43–46	72–81
13	23–24	16	57–58	15	22–23	21	14	9–10	28–29	29–30	47–49	82–89
14	—	17	59–60	—	24	22	15	11–12	30–32	—	50–52	90–94
15	25–26	18–19	61–62	16	25	23	16	13–14	33–35	31–32	53–56	95–97
16	27	—	63	17	—	24	—	15	36	33	57–58	98
17	28	20–21	64	18	26–27	25	17	16–17	37–38	34	59–65	99
18	29	22+	65+	19	28+	26+	18+	18+	39+	35+	66+	>99

Note. MOANS Scaled Scores are corrected for age influences. MOANS = Mayo's Older Americans Normative Studies. WAIS–R = Wechsler Adult Intelligence Scale–Revised (D. Wechsler, 1981). Info. = Information subtest, D.Span = Digit Span subtest, Vocab. = Vocabulary subtest, Arith. = Arithmetic subtest, Simil. = Similarities subtest, P.C. = Picture Completion subtest, P.A. = Picture Arrangement subtest, B.D. = Block Design subtest, O.A. = Object Assembly subtest, D.Symbol = Digit Symbol subtest. From "Mayo's Older Americans Normative Studies: WAIS–R Norms for Ages 56 to 97," by R. J. Ivnik, J. F. Malec, G. E. Smith, E. G. Tangalos, R. C. Petersen, E. Kokmen, and L. T. Kurland, 1992, *Clinical Neuropsychologist, 6*(Suppl.), p. 16. Copyright © 1992 by the Mayo Foundation. By permission of Mayo Foundation.

MAYO IQs are most suitable for general use, whereas the MOANS IQs are reflective of the MOANS project sample functional level. By extrapolation, MAYO IQs also estimate WAIS–R IQ values for persons above age 74, as if valid WAIS–R IQs were available at these older ages. Ivnik et al. (1992a) requested that users specifically designate IQs calculated in this manner so as to avoid confusion between WAIS–R IQ values and MAYO IQs. The utility of scores derived through these proceures is particularly evident for persons over age 74. Unfortunately, similar transformations were not possible with the scaled scores. Ivnik et al. (1992a) cautioned that these scores do not permit intersubtest comparisons of performance levels, and they tend to underestimate true performance (as defined by national as opposed to regional standards) and exaggerate deviations from true performance at the tails of their distributions.

Limitations to the usefulness of the WAIS measures with older persons exist despite the improved normative data. J. J. Ryan et al. (1990) noted from their work that IQs for elderly persons typically do not extend below 52 and it is possible for older persons to obtain age-corrected scaled scores of 4 on some subtests without performing a single item correctly. This limited floor suggests that the WAIS–R will not be of use for providing meaningful evaluations of persons exhibiting more than moderate cognitive impairment.

Other limitations of the WAIS–R battery for use with elderly persons are its length and the fact that memory (and more especially new learning) is not included in the assessment of overall intellectual functioning. Thus, clinicians may find it too time consuming (for the reasons expanded on in chap. 1) to administer the entire WAIS–R as well as supplementary measures of other cognitive domains important for differential diagnosis (e.g., memory).

SHORT FORMS

A number of researchers have developed abbreviated versions of the WAIS–R for use with populations who fatigue easily or cannot maintain motivation for prolonged periods of time. These *short forms* (SFs) have been generally categorized as being made up of selected subtests or selected items (Paolo & J. J. Ryan, 1993c), and are typically used to estimate global functioning.

Selected Subtests

Selected subtest SFs usually consist of two or more subtests and are used to estimate Full scale IQ (FSIQ). Numerous studies have yielded high validity and adequate reliabilities for these SFs, though cautionary notes typically accompany recommendation for using these measures as estimates of FSIQ.

The most common of these are Silverstein's (1982a) two (Vocabulary and Block Design) and four (Vocabulary, Block Design, Arithmetic, and Picture Arrangement) subtest SFs. The Vocabulary and Block Design subtests were selected as the two subtest dyad because this combination has a higher correlation with FSIQ than any other dyad (corrected formula r = .90). The measures in the four subtest SF correspond to those selected for other Wechsler instruments (WISC–R: A. S. Kaufman, 1976; WAIS: Doppelt, 1956), and sample clearly different mental abilities including language, numerical skill, attention-concentration, social planning, and visuospatial problem solving (Sattler, 1982).

Using data from the WAIS–R standardization sample, Silverstein (1982a) generated FSIQ tables for different age groups for both short forms (see Table 4.3). Scaled scores for each subtest are obtained from the WAIS–R manual and summed. These sums of scaled scores were then transformed to a standard score with a mean of 100 and a standard deviation of 15. Although Silverstein noted that standard errors of estimate (SEE, in the customary fashion) cannot be calculated from these data, he commented

TABLE 4.3

Full Scale IQ Equivalents of Sums of Scaled Scores for Two
(Vocabulary and Block Design) and Four (Vocabulary,
Arithmetic, Picture Arrangement, and Block Design)
Subtest Short Forms of the WAIS–R

Sum of Scaled Scores for 2 Subtest Short Form	Age Group 65–69	Age Group 70–74	Age Group 65–69	Age Group 70–74	Sum of Scaled Scores for 4 Subtest Short Form
—	—	—	150	—	62
33	150	—	149	—	61
32	147	—	147	—	60
31	144	149	145	—	59
30	141	146	144	150	58
29	138	143	142	148	57
28	135	140	140	146	56
27	132	136	139	144	55
26	129	133	137	143	54
25	126	130	135	141	53
24	123	127	134	139	52
23	120	124	132	137	51
22	117	120	130	135	50
21	114	117	129	134	49
20	111	114	127	132	48
19	108	111	125	130	47
18	105	108	124	128	46

(Continued)

TABLE 4.3
(Continued)

Sum of Scaled Scores for 2 Subtest Short Form	Age Group 65–69	Age Group 70–74	Age Group 65–69	Age Group 70–74	Sum of Scaled Scores for 4 Subtest Short Form
17	102	104	122	126	45
16	99	101	120	125	44
15	96	98	119	123	43
14	93	95	117	121	42
13	90	92	115	119	41
12	87	88	114	117	40
11	84	85	112	115	39
10	81	82	110	114	38
9	78	79	108	112	37
8	75	76	107	110	36
7	72	73	105	108	35
6	69	69	103	106	34
5	66	66	102	105	33
4	63	63	100	103	32
3	60	60	98	101	31
2	57	57	97	99	30
—	—	—	95	97	29
—	—	—	93	96	28
—	—	—	92	94	27
—	—	—	90	92	26
—	—	—	80	90	25
—	—	—	87	88	24
—	—	—	85	87	23
—	—	—	83	85	22
—	—	—	82	83	21
—	—	—	80	81	20
—	—	—	78	79	19
—	—	—	77	77	18
—	—	—	75	76	17
—	—	—	73	74	16
—	—	—	72	72	15
—	—	—	70	70	14
—	—	—	68	68	13
—	—	—	67	67	12
—	—	—	65	65	11
—	—	—	63	63	10
—	—	—	62	61	9
—	—	—	60	59	8
—	—	—	58	58	7
—	—	—	57	56	6
—	—	—	55	54	5
—	—	—	53	52	4

Note. From "Two- and Four-subtest Short Forms of the Wechsler Adult Intelligence Scale–Revised," by A. B. Silverstein, 1982a, *Journal of Consulting and Clinical Psychology, 50,* pp. 416–418. Copyright © 1982 by the American Psychological Association. Adapted with permission.

that several lines of evidence suggest 6 to 7 IQ points for the two subscale SF and 5 to 6 IQ points for the four subtest SF as reasonable guidelines for accepting variations between the FSIQ and the SF estimated IQ score.

J. J. Ryan, Georgemiller, and McKinney (1984) investigated the four subtest SF of Silverstein in a sample of 55 elderly Veteran's administration hospital inpatients (age 57 to 87). They noted high correlations between the FSIQ and the estimated IQ from the SF ($r = .95$) with no significant difference between the mean IQs [$t(54) < 1$]. When classification of intellectual level was examined between the two measures (i.e., FSIQ and IQ estimated from the SF), differences were noted for approximately one quarter of the patients. The SF corrected categorized 84% of the sample with respect to abnormality of profile as defined by FSIQ less than 79, a Verbal-Performance IQ discrepancy of ≥ 21 points, and/or a scatter range across the 11 age-corrected subtests of ≥ 8 points. They noted that the SF does not provide an accurate estimate of FSIQ but support its clinical utility as a screening device to identify people in need of detailed intellectual assessment, a substitute for the WAIS–R IQ when the participant lacks the stamina for the complete administration, and part of a more lengthy neuropsychological assessment where intellectual factors are not the primary focus.

Cyr and Brooker (1984) examined the "overall psychometric effectiveness" of various subtest combinations. Using data from the WAIS–R manual, the average of the validity and reliability coefficients was calculated for each possible combination of dyads, triads, tetrads, and pentads. Through this procedure, the "best" SF dyad (Vocabulary, Block Design; $r = .93$), triad (Vocabulary, Block Design, Information; $r = .95$), and tetrad (Vocabulary, Block Design, Arithmetic, Similarities; $r = .96$) was obtained. The best pentads were no better than the best tetrads (i.e., $r = .96$), and were more costly in terms of time, so they were not recommended. Table 4.4 can be used to obtain a FSIQ for these SFs by age group (Brooker & Cyr, 1986). To use these tables, the sum of the *age-scaled scores* for the chosen SF is summed and located on the table. The IQ corresponding to this sum of age-scaled scores can then be read under the age group.

Resnick and Entin (1971) suggested three criteria by which to evaluate the usefulness of abbreviated forms of SF measures: The correlation between SF IQ and the FSIQ must be highly significant and account for the majority of the variance shared between the two measures, the difference between the mean SF IQ and the FSIQ must be small and not statistically significant, and a high percentage of persons should be classified correctly into IQ categories by the SF IQ version relative to the FSIQ version. Findings from numerous studies indicate that the SFs already described generally show high correlations with FSIQ but differ with respect to whether or not significant differences between SF IQs and FSIQ are observed. The

TABLE 4.4
Full Scale IQ Equivalents of Sums of Age-Scaled Scores for Two,[a]
Three,[b] and Four[c] Subtest Short Forms for the 65–74 Age Group

Sum of Age-Scaled Scores	Two[a]	Three[b]	Four[c]
76	—	—	154
75	—	—	153
74	—	—	151
73	—	—	150
72	—	—	148
71	—	—	147
70	—	—	145
69	—	—	144
68	—	—	142
67	—	—	141
66	—	—	139
65	—	—	138
64	—	—	136
63	—	—	135
62	—	—	133
61	—	—	132
60	—	—	130
59	—	—	129
58	—	—	127
57	—	151	126
56	—	149	124
55	—	148	123
54	—	146	121
53	—	144	120
52	—	142	118
51	—	140	117
50	—	138	115
49	—	136	114
48	—	134	112
47	—	132	111
46	—	130	109
45	—	129	108
44	—	127	106
43	—	125	105
42	—	123	103
41	—	121	102
40	—	119	100
39	—	117	99
38	150	115	97
37	148	113	96
36	145	111	94
35	142	110	93
34	139	108	91
33	136	106	90
32	134	104	88
31	131	102	87

(Continued)

TABLE 4.4
(Continued)

Sum of Age-Scaled Scores	Two[a]	Three[b]	Four[c]
30	128	100	85
29	125	98	84
28	122	96	82
27	120	94	81
26	117	92	79
25	114	91	78
24	111	89	76
23	108	87	75
22	106	85	73
21	103	83	72
20	100	81	70
19	97	79	69
18	94	77	67
17	92	75	66
16	89	73	64
15	86	72	63
14	83	70	61
13	80	68	60
12	78	66	58
11	75	64	57
10	72	62	55
9	69	60	54
8	66	58	52
7	64	56	51
6	61	54	49
5	58	53	48
4	55	51	46
3	52	49	—
2	50	—	—

Note. From "Tables for Clinicians to Use to Convert WAIS–R Short Forms," by B. H. Brooker and J. J. Cyr, 1986, *Journal of Clinical Psychology, 42,* pp. 483–485. Copyright © 1986 by John Wiley & Sons, Inc. Adapted with permission of John Wiley & Sons, Inc.
[a]Two Subtests = Vocabulary and Block Design.
[b]Three Subtests = Vocabulary, Block Design, and Information.
[c]Four Subtests = Vocabulary, Block Design, Arithmetic, and Similarities.

percentage of samples correctly classified with respect to IQ categories is often less than optimal (Hoffman & Nelson, 1988; Margolis, Taylor, & Greenlief, 1986; J. J. Ryan, 1983; J. J. Ryan et al., 1984; Watkins, Mckay, Parra, & Polk, 1987). Silverstein (1985) examined these three criteria and noted that one would only expect to find correlations that were not highly significant and did not account for a high proportion of the total variance in very small samples or those with a very restricted range of IQs. It was also noted that difference in mean IQ between the SF and FSIQ measures may be determined for even trivial differences with a sufficiently large sample size. Silverstein went on to point out that "sufficiently large" may not be very large at all when a SF is highly correlated with the FSIQ. From the studies examined, differences in IQs ranged from −4 to +3 IQ points, which is about the average standard error of measurement of IQs on the FS in the WAIS–R standardization sample. Finally, Silverstein pointed out that no matter how high the correlation between a SF and the FSIQ (as long as it is not perfect), the percentage of disagreement will prove unacceptably high (e.g., at $r = .95$, disagreements exceed 25%). Although Silverstein acknowledged the importance of examining the "valuable items of information" concerning the relations between the SF IQs and the FSIQs, using them as "criteria" does not appear justified.

Selected Items

Selected items SFs retain all three IQs but involve a reduction in the number of items administered on 9 of the 11 subtests (Adams, Smigielski, & Jenkins, 1984; Paolo & J. J. Ryan, 1993c; Satz & Mogel, 1962). These reduced item SFs maintain the full breadth of intellectual performance and are, thus, meant to replace the full WAIS–R.

The procedure for obtaining the Satz–Mogel SF of the WAIS includes administering: every third item of the Information, Vocabulary, and Picture Completion subtests, and multiplying the obtained score by three; every odd item of the Comprehension, Arithmetic, Similarities, Block Design, Picture Arrangement, and Object Assembly subtests, then multiplying the obtained score by two; and the entire Digit Span and Digit Symbol subtests and using the obtained score in the standard fashion. Results are then converted to scaled scores according to the standard procedure. The Information and Block Design subtests are further weighted by subtracting one point from the obtained scaled scores. The final conversion to IQs is made in the standard fashion. Correlations with VIQ, PIQ, and FSIQ were .99, .97, and .99, respectively. Subtest correlations ranged from .77 (Object Assembly) to .97 (Vocabulary).

Silverstein (1982b, 1990) examined the *validity* and *reliability* of the Satz–Mogel-type of SF using the standardization data reported in the WAIS–R manual. Correlation between the SF and VIQ, PIQ, and FSIQ were reported as .94, .89, and .95, respectively, using a formula for the correlation between the SF and the full scale, which incorporates a statistical correction of the bias introduced by rescoring (A. S. Kaufman, 1977). For VIQ, PIQ, and FSIQ, the reliability coefficients were .93, .88, and .95, respectively, using a formula derived from Gulliksen (1950). Silverstein pointed out that the Satz–Mogel SF is actually less reliable than the best conventional (i.e., reduced subtests) two subtest SF, noting that the use of the reduced items

SFs exacts a steep price in reliability. Paolo and J. J. Ryan (1993c) compared a seven subtest SF (i.e., Information, Digit Span, Arithmetic, Similarities, Picture Completion, Block Design, Digit Symbol) developed by Ward (1990) with the Satz–Mogel SF in a sample of 130 normal persons age 75 and older. They noted that the SFs were highly similar in terms of validity coefficients, average differences in IQ and IQ classification accuracies, and both were able to correctly identify VIQ – PIQ discrepancies 75% of the time.

The preceding studies have examined the SFs in relation to scores on Full Scale as estimates of IQ. SF versions of WAIS–R subtests may also be used as replacements for individual subtests when screening of cognitive impairment within domains. SFs of the Block Design, Comprehension, and Similarities subtests of the WAIS–R were administered as part of the Canadian Study of Health and Aging, a nationwide epidemiological investigation of the prevalence of cognitive impairment and dementia in Canada (Tuokko et al., 1995; Tuokko & Woodward, 1996; see chap. 2 for a description of sample and methods). Table 4.5 contains the raw score to scaled score conversions for the Satz–Mogel SF of the Similarities, Comprehension, and Block Design subtests used in the CSHA. Table 4.6 contains summaries of the predicted scores for the CSHA WAIS–R SFs by age group and education. These summary data are less precise than that of Tuokko and Woodward (1996), which provides exact values for age and education by gender. The standard deviations of the residuals were 2.51, 2.58, and 2.70 for the Similarities, Comprehension, and Block Design subtests, respectively. The T-scores that provided the optimal balance between sensitivity (.70 to .75) and specificity (.68 to .75) when discriminating between persons with dementia and cognitively intact persons were 43, 47, and 45, respectively, for the Similarities, Comprehension, and Block Design subtests.

Two studies have examined the *test–retest stability* of the reduced item SF in samples of elderly persons. This issue is of particular importance when examining elderly persons because evidence of intellectual deterioration is required for a diagnosis of dementia (American Psychiatric Association, 1994). Mitrushina and Satz (1991) administered the reduced item SF of the WAIS–R as part of a larger neuropsychological battery to 122 volunteers from age 57 to 85 (see chap. 2 for sample description and methods). These persons were administered the same comprehensive battery of neuropsychological tests three times at 12-month intervals. Participants were grouped by age: 57–65, 66–70, 71–75, and 76–85. Although the VIQ and FSIQ coefficients were adequate, the PIQ stability coefficients were unacceptable. Of interest, all four age groups uniformly revealed a mild decline on the VIQ over the 3 years. However, the PIQ showed a practice effect of +5 points for the 57- to 65-year-old age group, a lack of improvement or minimal gain for the 65- to 75-year-old groups, and no change or a decline in performance for persons age 75 and older.

TABLE 4.5
Raw to Scaled Score Conversions for CSHA, WAIS–R Subtests

Raw Score	Similarities	Comprehension	Block Design	Raw Score
0	3.20	−.65	2.80	0
1	4.00	.41	3.45	1
2	4.81	1.47	4.10	2
3	5.62	2.52	4.75	3
4	6.42	3.58	5.40	4
5	7.23	4.64	6.05	5
6	8.04	5.69	6.70	6
7	8.84	6.75	7.35	7
8	9.65	7.81	8.00	8
9	10.46	8.86	8.65	9
10	11.26	9.92	9.30	10
11	12.07	10.98	9.95	11
12	12.88	12.03	10.61	12
13	13.69	13.09	11.26	13
14	14.49	14.15	11.91	14
15	—	15.20	12.56	15
16	—	16.26	13.21	16
17	—	—	13.86	17
18	—	—	14.51	18
19	—	—	15.16	19
20	—	—	15.81	20
21	—	—	16.46	21
22	—	—	17.11	22
23	—	—	17.76	23
24	—	—	18.41	24
25	—	—	19.07	25
26	—	—	19.72	26
27	—	—	20.37	27
28	—	—	21.02	28
29	—	—	21.67	29

Note. From "Development and Validation of a Demographic Correction System for Neuropsychological Measures Used in the Canadian Study of Health and Aging," by H. Tuokko and T. S. Woodward, 1996, *Journal of Clinical and Experimental Neuropsychology, 18*, p. 494. Copyright © 1996 by Swets & Zeitlinger Publishers. Used with permission.

Paolo and J. J. Ryan (1993b) examined the test–retest reliability of the Satz–Mogel SF in 61 normal volunteers ranging from age 75 to 87. The entire WAIS–R was administered and then rescored according to the Satz–Mogel procedure. IQ conversions were accomplished using the norms for persons age 75 to 79 and age 80 and older provided by J. J. Ryan et al. (1990). The test–retest coefficients indicated acceptable stability of the VIQ and FSIQ but unacceptably low stability of the PIQ. This did not appear to be related to the differential magnitude of change across the two age groups as was seen in the Mitrushina and Satz (1991) study. Picture

TABLE 4.6
Predicted Score Values for CSHA WAIS–R Subtests*

Subtest	Age			
	65–69	70–74	75–79	80+
Higher Education Group (>12 Years Education)				
Similarities	14.67	14.10	13.62	12.86
Comprehension	14.73	14.35	14.03	13.51
Block Design	14.33	13.63	13.06	17.14
Lower Education Group (<12 Years Education)				
Similarities	8.63	8.06	7.58	6.82
Comprehension	9.23	8.85	8.53	8.02
Block Design	10.69	10.00	9.42	8.50

Note. No sex differences. *Satz–Mogel SF raw scores. SD of residuals for CSHA WAIS–R subtests: Similarities = 2.51; Comprehension = 2.58; Block Design = 2.70. From "Development and Validation of a Demographic Correction System for Neuropsychological Measures Used in the Canadian Study of Health and Aging, by H. Tuokko and T. S. Woodward, 1996, *Journal of Clinical and Experimental Neuropsychology, 18,* pp. 477–616. Copyright © 1996 by Swets & Zeitlinger Publishers. Used with permission.

Arrangement, Block Design, and Object Assembly all fell well below acceptable limits for subtest stability. These findings suggest that the accurate detection of change in IQ scores from test to retest with the Satz–Mogel SF in elderly persons is tenuous and support Silverstein's position that reduced item SFs exact a high price in reliability and other literature questioning the clinical utility of reduced-item methods (A. S. Kaufman, 1990; A. S. Kaufman & N. L. Kaufman, 1990).

SUBTEST SCATTER AND FACTOR STRUCTURE

Three common approaches to the interpretation of performance on the Wechsler scales are comparison between subtest score levels (i.e., intersubtest scatter), examination of the variability within a scale (i.e., intrasubtest scatter), and determination of the Verbal and Performance IQ discrepancy (Lezak, 1995). Examination of these three aspects of performance has led to the identification of score patterns or deviations thought to be characteristic of disorders affecting brain function. Perhaps the most important of these with respect to older populations is the pattern identified by Fuld (1984; Brinkman & Braun, 1984; Tuokko & Crockett, 1987), as occurring frequently (approximately 33% of cases) in persons with Alzheimer's disease and in approximately 50% of persons with drug-induced cholinergic deficiencies. Using the age-corrected scaled scores, the profile is identified as A > B > C < D, where A is determined by summing the scores for Information and Vocabulary then dividing by two, B is determined by summing the scores for Similarities and Digit Span then dividing by two, C is determined by summing the scores for Digit Symbol and Block Design then dividing by two, and D is the score for Object Assembly. The specificity of this profile ranges between 99% (Tuokko & Crockett, 1987 in a sample of 74 normal persons age 59 to 84) and 87.2% (Satz & Van Gorp, 1987) in a sample of 149 persons age 60 to 94. J. J. Ryan et al. (1991) extended this series of investigations to examine profile incidence when 225 normal elderly volunteers over age 75 were grouped according to age, sex, race, years of education, and level of intelligence. Raw subtest scores were converted to scaled scores using the standardization sample reference group provided by D. Wechsler (1981). IQs and age-corrected scaled scores were determined using the norms of elderly persons developed by J. J. Ryan, Paolo, and Brungardt (1990). Overall, 8% of the sample (18 people) manifest the Fuld profile. Differences in profile occurrence by sex, race, and IQ level were not large enough to be of practical significance. Some evidence to suggest an increased frequency of profile occurrence over age 85 was observed, but a steady progression in pattern occurrence across age levels was not apparent. Persons with greater than 13 years of schooling showed a significantly larger proportion of positive profiles than individuals with an educational attainment of 12 years or less. Further examination of age and education effects suggested that persons age 85 and older with 12 or more years of education show the profile relatively frequently (26.3%). These studies emphasize the need to examine frequency of occurrence of various subtest patterns or subtest scatter to determine a normal base rate for comparison to samples with known neuropsychological disorders.

Intersubtest Scatter

McLean, A. S. Kaufman, and Reynolds (1989) determined the base rates of subtest scatter for the WAIS–R and assessed empirically the degree to which WAIS–R subtests are related to age, sex, race, urban versus rural residence, and educational level using the WAIS–R standardization sample ($N = 1,880$). Two indices of subtest scatter were examined: range, or highest subtest scaled score minus lowest subtest scaled score, for the VIQ, PIQ, and FSIQ scales; and the number of scaled scores that deviated significantly ($+/- 3$) from the person's own mean scaled score on the VIQ, PIQ, and FSIQ scales. Base rate tables of normal scatter were developed across the entire standardization sample (age 16 to 74) broken down into five IQ levels (below 80, 80–89, 90–109, 110–119, and 120+). The mean ranges equalled 4.7 for both the VIQ ($SD = 1.9$) and the PIQ ($SD = 2.1$) scales and 6.7 for the Full scale ($SD = 2.1$). This indicates that a profile of normal individuals between age 16 and 74 contains substantial scatter and an average range of scaled scores on the WAIS–R is approximately 7 +/− 2 (McLean et al., 1989). The Verbal scale ranges for males were significantly larger than the corresponding ranges for females and Caucasians had larger ranges than African Americans on the Verbal and Full scales. In general, scaled score ranges were larger on all scales for well-educated persons than those with less education. In particular, persons with at least some college training showed more scatter within all scales than did persons who failed to complete high school.

McLean et al. (1989) generated normative tables of base rate scatter (across all ages 16 to 74) to show the cumulative frequency distributions of the scaled scores ranges and the cumulative distribution of the number of significantly deviating (+/− 3 points) subtests scores. J. J. Ryan and Paolo (1992a) extended this look at normal base rates for WAIS–R intersubtest scatter to persons age 75 and older (see chap. 2 for description of sample) with similar findings. The intersubtest scatter range and number of scaled scores deviating by +/− 3 points from the person's own mean were calculated for the Verbal, Performance, and Full scales. All computations used the regular scaled scores (based on 20 to 34-year-old persons) provided in the WAIS–R manual. The mean ranges for the Verbal, Performance, and Full scales were 4.4 ($SD = 1.7$), 3.4 ($SD = 1.5$), and 6.5 ($SD = 2.1$), respectively. Mean scatter ranges were significantly greater for males and females on all three IQ scales. Caucasian persons exhibited significantly greater scatter than African Americans on the Verbal and Full scales. Persons with 12 or more years of schooling demonstrated significantly more scatter on all three scales than those with less than 12 years of education. In general, the scatter range for the elderly sample was less than that of the persons age 16 to 74 years in McLean et al. (1989).

J. J. Ryan and Paolo (1992a) generated normative tables of base rate scatter (for age 75+ years) to show the cumulative frequency distributions of the scaled scores ranges and the cumulative distribution of the number of significantly deviating (+/− 3 points) subtest scores. It is apparent from these tables that less than 5% of the population had a range of 8, 6, and 11 on the Verbal, Performance, and Full scale, respectively. Less than 1% had a range of 9 on the Verbal scale, 8 on the Performance scale, and 12 on the Full scale.

It is apparent from the tables of J. J. Ryan and Paolo (1992a) that approximately 75% of the sample had fewer than 3 subtests (i.e., 2, 1, or 0) out of 11 that deviate significantly (+/− 3 points) from their own mean scaled score on all WAIS–R subtests. A person must have 2, 1, or 5 discrepant subtest scores on the Verbal, Performance, and Full scales, respectively, to correspond to an amount obtained by 5% of the normal population. J. J. Ryan and Paolo (1992a) provided data that allow the identifi-cation of two levels of abnormality (5% and 1%) at three IQ levels (below 89, 90–109, 110+). As noted by McLean et al. (1989), substantial variability in intersubtest scatter exists in a normal population and it is recommended that practitioners designate a given scatter range as atypical only when it corresponds to that displayed by 5% or fewer of the old-age standardization cases. One difference in findings between the younger standardization sample and Ryan and Paolo's older sample is that elderly persons consis-tently demonstrated less scatter on the Performance scale. This appears to reflect the overall poorer achievement of older persons on these meas-ures ("classic aging pattern" discussed earlier). J. J. Ryan and Paolo (1992a) noted that a major limitation of their study is the use of WAIS–R scaled scores (based on 20- to 34-year-old persons) instead of age-corrected scaled scores. This was done to ensure continuity with past research on WAIS–R intersubtest scatter and must be acknowledged by practitioners using these scatter estimates.

Intrasubtest Scatter

According to Lezak (1995), scatter within a test is apparent when there are marked deviations from the normal pass–fail pattern. On the WAIS–R, items are presented in order of difficulty and it is expected that almost all items preceding the last item passed will be performed correctly. A pattern of failure on easy items and success on harder items has been interpreted as a qualitative sign of intellectual loss (Lezak, 1983).

A number of early studies using the WAIS lent empirical support for this inference (e.g., Hallenbeck, Fink, & Grossman, 1965; Nickols, 1963; Watson, 1965). Mittenberg, Hammeke, and Rao (1989) extended this line of investigation to the WAIS–R and specifically examined whether or not intrasubtest scatter can reliably identify individuals with cerebral impair-ment. Of particular importance, this investigation was conducted within the context of average intelligence as may be encountered clinically when assessing persons with amnesic disorders, dementias, frontal lobe disorders, or persons with high premorbid levels of functioning.

Three measures of intrasubtest scatter were determined for the Vocabu-lary, Comprehension, and Similarities subtests of the WAIS–R: *standard deviation* of item scores, excluding zeros, was used as discontinuation cri-teria; the number of zero-point scores subsequently followed by 1- or 2-point scores yielded *interpolated zeros* (e.g., the scores 2, 1, 0, 0, 1, 2 contain 3 interpolated zeros); and sets of consecutive correct and incorrect responses were tallied to yield *interpolated runs* (e.g., scores of 2, 1, 0, 0, 1, 2 contain five interpolated runs: 2 1; 0 0; 1; 0; 2).

Mittenberg, Thompson, Schwartz, J. J. Ryan, and Levitt (1991) examined these scatter indices in 32 neurologically normal persons ranging from age

75 to 89 and an age-matched group of 32 persons with Alzheimer's disease who met *DSM–III–R* and NINCDS–ADRDA criteria. The indices were highly correlated within the control group. Alzheimer's patients showed more interpolated runs on the Information and Vocabulary subtests, whereas controls showed more interpolated runs and interpolated zeros on the Similarities subtest. However, when discriminant function analysis was used to determine the diagnostic sensitivity of the interpolated runs for Information and Vocabulary, the overall hit rates were poor (59.38% and 60.94 %, respectively). Thus, intrasubtest scatter did not appear to be sufficiently sensitive for diagnostic use on an individual basis.

Verbal/Performance Discrepancies

Examination of the VIQ score in relation to the PIQ score has received much attention in the context of characterizing lateralized (i.e., right and left hemisphere) brain damage (e.g., R. A. Bornstein & Matarazzo, 1982), but other factors (e.g., occupation, magnitude of FSIQ) also appear related to the discrepancy in VIQ versus PIQ of any patient (e.g., Snow, Freedman, & Ford, 1986).

Matarazzo and Herman (1985) stressed the importance of empirical studies specifically designed to provide normative data concerning the base rates with which VIQ and PIQ differences of varying magnitudes actually occur in large samples of persons. The utility of such data relate to the use of the standard error of measurement to determine a VIQ – PIQ discrepancy of "significance" (or *p* value based on size of discrepancy score needed to be different from 0), which reflects *how large* the score needs to be but does not address the frequency of occurrence of the score discrepancy. A series of studies have presented normative base rates of VIQ and PIQ discrepancies (VIQ – PIQ) using the WAIS–R standardization data on persons from age 16 to 74 (Matarazzo, 1986; Matarazzo, R. A. Bornstein, McDermott, & Noonan, 1986; Matarazzo & Herman, 1985). The empirical data generated by Matarazzo and Herman (1984, 1985) suggest that a VIQ — PIQ discrepancy of +/- 15 is worthy of further clinical investigation even though a difference of this magnitude occurred in 15.5% of the standardization data.

J. J. Ryan and Paolo (1992c) extended this look at normal base rates for WAIS–R VIQ – PIQ discrepancies to persons age 75 and older (see chap. 2 for sample description) with similar findings. The VIQ — PIQ discrepancy scores were examined in relation to age, gender, race, years of education, and level of FSIQ. The mean VIQ – PIQ was .13 (*SD* = 10.56) and was very similar to that reported for the younger WAIS–R standardization sample (Matarazzo & Herman, 1985; *M* = –.10; *SD* = 11.12). Positive (52.3%) and negative (46.2%) differences were approximately equal and generally symmetrically distributed.

From these data it is apparent that large discrepancies between the Verbal and Performance IQ scores are common occurrences for elderly persons. For example, more than 16% of the elderly standardization sample showed VIQ – PIQ > 15. Examination of the percentage of individuals with significant VIQ – PIQ discrepancies by gender, age, race, and education did not yield significant differences, and practitioners need not place major emphasis on such factors when interpreting a VIQ – PIQ discrepancy. J. J. Ryan and Paolo (1992c) noted that, as a general rule, VIQ > PIQ is the expected pattern among elderly persons with 12 or more years of education or an FSIQ at or above 110 or both. The VIQ < PIQ pattern is more characteristic of persons with less than 8 years of education or an FSIQ at or below 109 or both. It was also noted that persons at higher levels of psychometric intelligence (FSIQ > 110) are more likely to show significant VIQ – PIQ discrepancies than persons with lower FSIQs.

Paolo and J. J. Ryan (1992b) examined unusual VIQ – PIQ combinations following a formula presented by Silverstein (1987) in their elderly standardization sample of 130 persons age 75 and over. They provided tables that allow the identification of unusual VIQ – PIQ combinations at the .05 and .01 levels of significance. When the VIQ – PIQ discrepancies of a group of 39 neurologically impaired persons at least 75 years of age were examined in relation to this normative data, only two showed discrepancies at the .05 level (5.1%) and none showed discrepancies at the .01 level. However, this finding does not mean that unusual VIQ – PIQ discrepancies lack clinical significance. Further examination of rare score combinations may be more informative.

Factor Analytic Studies

The factor structure of the WAIS–R has been explored using the standardization sample (age 16 through 74) by numerous investigators. The results of these studies typically indicate a global general factor (g), a Verbal Comprehension factor, a Perceptual Organization factor, and, in some instances, a Distractibility or Freedom from Distraction factor (Leckliter, Matarazzo, & Silverstein, 1986; F. F. Ryan & Sattler, 1988).

J. J. Ryan et al. (1990) extended the examination of WAIS–R factor structure to persons age 75 and older (see chap. 2 for sample description) with similar findings. The WAIS–R protocols were analyzed using a principal components analysis with a varimax rotation of two, three, and four factors.

There was clear support for a robust single factor reflecting general intelligence (g) with every subtest showing substantial loadings (.63 or more) on the unrotated first factor, which accounted for 54% of the variance. However, it was noted that the rank order of loading differed from that typically obtained for the younger standardization sample (i.e., Vocabulary, Block Design, Information, Arithmetic for elderly persons versus Vocabulary, Information, Similarities, and Comprehension).

The two-factor rotated solution yielded a structure generally consistent with D. Wechsler's (1981) designation of Verbal and Performance scales. The five loadings at or above .50 on the first factor were for Verbal scales (i.e., Information, Digit Span, Vocabulary, Comprehension, Similarities). The three loadings at or above .50 on Factor 2 were Performance scales (Block Design, Object Assembly, and Digit Symbol). The three-factor solution was generally consistent with factor analytic studies using younger samples. Factor 1 was interpreted as a Verbal Comprehension factor (Information, Vocabulary, Comprehension, Similarities, and Digit Span), Factor 2 was interpreted as a Perceptual Organization factor (Object Assembly, Block Design, and Digit Symbol), and Factor 3 was interpreted as Freedom from Distractibility (Arithmetic). The four-factor solution was considered inferior to the others for explaining the data.

Using A. S. Kaufman's (1975) method for determining specificity of a subtest to a factor, Digit Span, Arithmetic, Picture Completion, and Digit Symbol warranted interpretation (i.e., could be viewed as measuring specific functions), whereas Vocabulary, Similarities, and Block Design were less specific and it was recommended that interpretation be pursued cautiously. The remaining subtests (except Picture Arrangement) appeared sufficiently specific only to be interpreted as measuring *g*.

From this factor analytic study, J. J. Ryan et al. (1990) provided guidance with respect to interpretation of performance on the WAIS–R subtests for elderly persons in three ways. First, they noted that when significant variability on Arithmetic, Picture Completion, and/or Picture Arrangement subtests is encountered, a three-factor model may be most appropriate for interpretation purposes. They suggested that the Verbal Comprehension factor can be estimated by averaging the age-corrected subtest scores (J. J. Ryan et al., 1990) on all the Verbal subtests except Arithmetic. An estimate of the Perceptual Organization factor can be obtained by averaging the age-corrected scores for Block Design, Object Assembly, and Digit Symbol. The Arithmetic score can be interpreted as an estimate of the third, Freedom from Distraction, factor. However, they also noted that the need for considering the three-factor over the two-factor approach emerges relatively infrequently (i.e., 15% of their sample). J. J. Ryan et al. also questioned the standard interpretation of the three-factor model in persons of advanced age. They noted that the two-factor solutions for their sample of elderly persons and the younger standardization sample were essentially equivalent but that Factors 2 and 3 in the three-factor solution differed between the samples. It was suggested that the organization of intellectual functioning on the WAIS–R may show subtle changes with advancing age with greater reliance on verbal skills to perform tasks that may appear to measure other abilities. In this context, they noted that Digit Span does not load on the Freedom from Distraction factor for their elderly sample but clearly loads on the Verbal factor. Finally, it was emphasized that only certain subtests were found to possess high enough levels of specificity to be interpreted as indicators of the underlying factor. However, they encouraged caution when making specific inferences about specific subtests even if they have high or intermediate specificity as common variance exceeded specific variance for almost every subtest.

TEST–RETEST RELIABILITY

As a decline in overall intellectual functioning in later life may be a sign of a dementing process, retest reliability of measures is of particular importance. Berkowitz and R. F. Green (1963), using the Wechsler–Bellevue (Form I), reported test–retest correlations of .93 for VIQ, .86 for PIQ, and .92 for FSIQ in 184 hospitalized male Veteran's Administration Hospital patients with a mean age of 65 years at reassessment (an average of 8.6 years after their initial assessment). Snow, Tierney, Zorzitto, Fisher, and Reid (1989) examined the 1-year test–retest reliability of the WAIS–R in 101 Canadian normal volunteers recruited through a radio station advertisement who ranged in age from 50 to 84 years ($M = 67.1$, $SD = 7.7$) with an average of 15.0 years of education (range = 6–23). Pearson correlations of .86 for VIQ, .85 for PIQ, and .90 for FSIQ were obtained with standard errors of estimate (*SEE*) of 3.25, 4.73, and 3.45, respectively. The reliability of the Verbal-Performance discrepancy was .69 (*SEE* = 2.88). The retest reliabilities of the subtests ranged from .51 (Comprehension) to .91 (Digit Symbol). To examine the amount that test scores varied over the 1-year interval, the proportion of the population showing changes of different magnitudes were tabulated. More persons improved (49%) on reassessment than declined (40.2%). Fewer than 10% of the sample showed changes greater than 10 points in either direction (less than 5% showed decline with 10% showing improvement). Both of these extreme changes were seen for the PIQ values. VIQ and FSIQ were smaller (1% showing decline of more than 10 points; 2% and 5%, respectively, showing improvement of more than 10 points). The reliability of the VIQ – PIQ discrepancy was less adequate and they recommended caution when interpreting change in VIQ – PIQ discrepancies over time.

J. J. Ryan et al. (1992) extended this look at the test–retest reliability of the WAIS–R to a sample of 61 American elderly persons ranging in age from 75 to 87 ($M = 78.93$, $SD = 3.46$) with 12 or less years of education ($M = 9.74$, $SD = 1.91$). All persons were considered free from neurological disease, medical conditions with known CNS complications, and/or significant depressive symptomatology. The 11 WAIS–R subtest scores were converted to scaled scores using the WAIS–R standardization sample. IQs were calculated using the WAIS–R norms as well as those for elderly persons provided by J. J. Ryan et al. (1990). The test–retest correlations for VIQ, PIQ, and FSIQ using the Wechsler norms were .92, .88, and .94, respectively. Using the Ryan et al. norms, the test–retest coefficients were .92, .89, and .93, respectively. The retest reliabilities for the subtests ranged from .49 (Picture Arrangement) to .94 (Vocabulary).

The percentages of persons who maintained the same intelligence classifications at retest for the Ryan and WAIS–R IQs were .74 and .75 for VIQ, respectively; .66 and .77 for PIQ, respectively; and .80 and .75 for FSIQ, respectively. Practice effects typically seen for middle-age adults (i.e., 3, 8, and 6 points, respectively, on the VIQ, PIQ, and FSIQ; Wechsler, 1981) did not occur as reliably or in as robust a fashion in this older population. More persons in Ryan's sample showed improved performance at retest (Ryan norms: 72%, 62%, 72%; WAIS–R norms: 69%, 64%, 71%, respectively, for VIQ, PIQ, and FSIQ) than showed declines (Ryan norms: 26%, 23%, 20%; WAIS–R norms: 28%, 21%, 21%, respectively, for VIQ, PIQ, and FSIQ). Gain or loss in IQ points ranged from −15 to 13, −10 to 19, and −9 to 14 for VIQ, PIQ, and FSIQ, respectively, using Ryan's norms. For Wechsler norms, gain or loss ranged from −11 to 11, −9 to 22, and −9 to 11 on VIQ, PIQ, and FSIQ, respectively. No relations between initial FSIQ and gain or loss at retest were apparent. Similarly, magnitude of gain or loss was unrelated to age or educational level. Ryan et al. recommended that a retest decline of 7 points or more in IQ or 3 or more scaled score points prompt further investigation. However, they noted that declines of this magnitude fall within approximately two standard errors of prediction and may result from measurement error.

PERCEPTIONS OF THE WAIS–R

It has been suggested that the WAIS–R is an inappropriate measure to administer to elderly persons because the subtests are irrelevant to the examinee's everyday behaviors and certain subtests appear childish and may decrease motivation and interest in continuing with the testing (Kendrick, 1982a, 1982b). To assess examinee's perceptions of the test and to ascertain whether or not these perceptions had an impact on test performance, Paolo and J. J. Ryan (1993a) asked 224 healthy volunteers from age 75 to 87 ($M = 80.67$, $SD = 4.99$) who had between 2 and 19 years of education ($M = 10.88$, $SD = 2.92$) a 12-item opinion questionnaire after completing the WAIS–R. More than 92% of the sample felt the WAIS–R was interesting, challenging, motivating, and within their endurance.

Persons rating the overall scale and subtests negatively in at least one area (e.g., fair vs. tricky) were matched on age, education, gender, and race to those who rated the test in a completely positive fashion. Only 24 (10.7%) viewed the overall WAIS–R negatively. Those rating the tests negatively earned lower scores than those who perceived them positively on all WAIS–R variables except the Picture Arrangement subtest. However, no statistically significant difference between groups was apparent. Thus, it appears that rating a test negatively is not significantly related, on the average, to lower WAIS–R scores in normal persons age 75 and older. However, it may be that the design of the opinion questionnaire was inadequate to yield accurate reflections of the examinees' perceptions. Moreover, Kendrick's (1982a) assertions may have been based on observations of the responses of demented or physically ill older persons. Further research is required before the WAIS–R is abandoned as a clinical instrument for use with elderly persons.

ESTIMATES OF PREMORBID INTELLECTUAL FUNCTIONING

A common difficulty encountered by the geriatric neuropsychologist is the determination of premorbid intellectual functioning. This is of particular importance when determining whether or not a person meets certain sets of diagnostic criteria (e.g., *DSM–IV*) that require a "decline" in intellectual functioning be present. The ideal method for determining premorbid functioning is to have test results collected prior to the onset of the neurological disorder. Because this is rarely possible, a number of methods for estimating premorbid IQ have been developed.

Using Subtest Scores

One approach involves estimating premorbid ability from test scores. For example, within the WAIS–R battery, the distinction is made between "Hold" and "Non-Hold" tests. The former are thought to be relatively less sensitive than the latter to the effects of intellectual decline. Specifically, it has been argued that Vocabulary and Picture Arrangement are good indicators of premorbid performance and the highest of the two should be considered as the premorbid index (McFie, 1975; Yates, 1956). However, attempts to estimate premorbid IQ from "Hold" tests have not always led to satisfactory results (e.g., Matarazzo, 1972).

Thorp and Mahrer (1959) suggested the examination of the variance among scores of WAIS subtests as an estimate of premorbid ability. The higher the variance, the greater the premorbid ability is assumed to be.

Thorp and Mahrer also recommended "testing the limits" as a possible means to evaluate premorbid function. For example, after the completion of the formal part of the WAIS–R, extra time may be given to try various subtests again. Examiners could then estimate premorbid ability based on the discrepancy between the better performance on each subtest and the lower performance. The latter performance is assumed to reflect current functioning. Nonetheless, performance on all Wechsler subtests could be affected by neuropsychological dysfunction (Russell, 1972) and methods based on WAIS–R subtests could often underestimate premorbid ability.

Using the Best Performance Method

This method rests on the clinician's assumption that the best estimate of premorbid ability is the highest level of performance regardless of whether this performance is reflected on a test score, historical information, or any aspect of current behavior (Lezak, 1995). The assumption is based on the well-documented phenomenon that performance on many different tasks that require cognitive ability shows an intercorrelation across tasks. The method necessitates that the examiner surveys adequately a wide array of abilities. Lezak (1995) pointed out that, in some cases, the method could produce underestimates or overestimates of ability. For example, the premorbid ability of some individuals with excellent memory may be overestimated because memory is the least reliable indicator of overall cognitive ability. This problem is less likely to occur in samples of dementing elderly, however, as memory declines are usually among the first symptoms of dementia. Generally, the best performance method is most likely to lead to valid estimates when several indices of relatively higher performance can be obtained.

Using Reading Tests

It has been proposed that reading tests would be good indicators of premorbid ability as they assess knowledge obtained before the onset of the neurological disorder (Nelson, 1982; Nelson & O'Connel, 1978). More specifically, the use of words with irregular pronunciation requires knowledge of the pronunciation. "Intelligent guesses" would likely lead to incorrect responses.

Crawford (1989) found the Nelson Adult Reading Test (NART; Nelson, 1982; Nelson & O'Connel, 1978) to be an effective method for estimating premorbid IQ. Unlike other neuropsychological tests, performance on the NART does not appear to be substantially related to age (Crawford, 1989). Although satisfactory reliability and validity evidence for the approach exists (e.g., Crawford, 1989; Nelson & McKenna, 1975), Stebbins and his colleagues have shown that NART estimates of premorbid IQ may be affected by dementia severity and the presence of language disturbances (Stebbins, Gilley, R. S. Wilson, Bernard, & Fox, 1990; Stebbins, R. S. Wilson, Gilley, Bernard, & Fox, 1990). They also argued that the test, although not insensitive to dementia, can still provide an estimate of the lower limit of premorbid IQ. It is also worth noting that the NART appears to be less sensitive to dementia than the WAIS Vocabulary subtest (Sharpe & O'Carroll, 1991). O'Carroll (1992) noted that the ability to correctly pronounce irregular words "holds" better than other "current" ability measures, at least in the earlier stages of dementia where diagnostic problems tend to occur.

Although the NART can be affected by severity of dementia, Crawford (1989) pointed out that it would be unrealistic to expect any neuropsychological test to be completely insensitive to dementia severity. He suggested that where cognitive dysfunction is severe enough to markedly impair performance on the NART, the comparison of obtained IQ scores to premorbid estimates would be unnecessary as intellectual deterioration would be evident.

Crawford (1990) developed a regression equation that allows for the prediction of NART scores from demographic variables. He suggested that, by comparing the predicted with the obtained NART score, clinicians might be able to estimate the likelihood that the NART is an underestimate of premorbid ability.

J. J. Ryan and Paolo (1992b) estimated WAIS–R IQ scores from the NART in a sample of 126 normal elderly persons over age 75. All IQs were calculated using the norms for persons over age 75 developed by J. J. Ryan, Paolo, and Brungardt (1990). The following equations were derived from separate linear regression analyses (SEE = Standard Error of Estimate):

Estimated VIQ = 132.3893 + (NART errors) (−1.164) (SEE = 7.70)
Estimated PIQ = 123.0684 + (NART errors) (−0.823) (SEE = 12.08)
Estimated FSIQ = 131.3845 + (NART errors) (−1.124) (SEE = 8.83)

These equations were applied to a sample of 20 neurologically impaired older persons (75+ years of age) revealing a significant difference between obtained and estimated IQ scores ($p < .001$ for all three IQ scores), as would be expected. An additional study (Zacharewicz, Pliskin, Neumann, Berent, & Buchtel, 1994) comparing various premorbid IQ estimations in dementia patients ($n = 49$; age range 50 to 91, mean age = 72, $SD = 8.7$) noted this particular method appeared to provide the most clinical utility as an estimate of premorbid IQ in dementia samples.

J. J. Ryan and Paolo (1992b) noted that regression to the mean may result in poorer estimated IQs for persons falling at the extremes of the distribution of scores (i.e., high or low IQs) and encourage the use of other available information (e.g., clinical observation, education, and occupational histories) as supplements to the NART estimates.

As the NART was developed in the United Kingdom, Blair and Spreen (1989) adapted the test for use with U.S. and Canadian populations. Their North American Adult Reading Test (NAART) and the equations that estimate premorbid IQ based on the test appear in the Compendium of Neuropsychological Tests (Spreen & Strauss, 1991). However, the work of Blair and Spreen (1989) was not based on samples of elderly persons. Thus, the utility of the NAART with older adults merits further investigation. However, if the NART research findings generalize to the NAART, the NAART would appear to be a very promising tool for the estimation of premorbid function in elderly persons.

Using Demographic Variables

Formulas that estimate WAIS premorbid IQ based on demographic information are also available. Originally developed by R. S. Wilson, Rosenbaum, and Brown (1979), Verbal, Performance, and Full scale IQ scores were estimated. The moderate success of the WAIS formulas (Crawford, 1989) led to similar efforts for the WAIS–R. Specifically, the Barona Index was originally based on formulas derived from analysis of the 1,880 persons of the WAIS–R standardization sample. The formulas are presented in Table 4.7. On the positive side, such formulas are practical, easy to use, and their use is explained well by their developers (e.g., Barona, Reynolds, & Chastain, 1984). Eppinger, Craig, Adams, and Parsons (1987) found that the

TABLE 4.7
The Barona Index

VIQ = 54.23 + .49(age) + 1.92(sex) + 4.24(race) + 5.25(education) + 1.89(occupation) + 1.24(residence)

PIQ = 61.58 + .31(age) + 1.09(sex) + 4.95(race) + 3.75(education) + 1.54(occupation) + .82(region)

FSIQ = 54.96 + .47(age) + 1.76(sex) + 4.71(race) + 5.02(education) + 1.89(occupation) + .59(region)

Note. Age: 16–17 years = 1; 18–19 = 2; 20–24 = 3; 25–34 = 4; 35–44 = 5; 45–54 = 6; 55–64 = 7; 65–69 = 8; 70–74 = 9. Sex: male = 2; female = 1. Race: Black = 1; other ethnicity = 2; white = 3. Education: 0–7 years = 1; 8 = 2; 9–11 = 3; 12 = 4; 13–15 = 5; 16+ = 6. Region: Southern = 1; North Central = 2; Western = 3; Northeast = 4. Residence: urban = 2; rural = 1. Occupations: professional and technical = 6; managers, officials, proprietors, clerical, and sales workers = 5; craftspersons and skilled workers = 4; not in the labor force = 3; operatives, service workers, farmers and farm managers (semiskilled) = 2; farm laborers, farm forepersons, and unskilled workers = 1. From "A Demographically Based Index of Premorbid Intelligence for the WAIS–R," by A. Barona, C. R. Reynolds, and R. Chastain, 1984, *Journal of Consulting and Clinical Psychology, 52,* pp. 885–887. Copyright © 1984 by the American Psychological Association. Used with permission.

Barona Index can help in the discrimination of neurologically impaired and neurologically normal patients. Nonetheless, formulas based on demographics lead to inaccurate conclusions in over one quarter of the cases (Lezak, 1983). In addition, they tend to overestimate very low IQ and underestimate IQ scores over 120 (e.g., Barona et al., 1984; Sweet, Mober, & Tovian, 1990).

Paolo and J. J. Ryan (1992a) applied the formulas of Barona et al. (1984) and Barona and Chastain (1986) to a sample of normal males age 75 and older (see chap. 2 for sample description). A neurologically impaired sample consisting of 20 males, age 75 and older ($M = 78.65$, $SD = 5.62$) with MMSE scores less than 21 and/or at least three areas of impairment on the Neurobehavioral Cognitive Status Examination (Kiernan et al., 1987) was also examined. The WAIS–R IQ scores were calculated using the norms for persons over age 75 developed by J. J. Ryan et al. (1990).

The correlations between the actual WAIS–R IQs and the estimated IQs for the normal sample were moderate and similar for each estimated procedure (1984: FSIQ = .73, VIQ = .72, PIQ = .61; 1986: FSIQ = .72, VIQ = .71, PIQ = .57). These findings are similar to those reported for the younger samples (Barona & Chastain, 1986; Eppinger et al., 1987). For the normal sample, VIQ was underestimated by both the 1984 and 1986 equations. FSIQ was also underestimated by the 1984 equation. All underestimates fell within one standard error of estimate of the 1984 and 1986 prediction procedures. All three predicted IQ scores for both (1984 and 1986) methods were significantly higher than the actual IQ scores obtained by the neurologically impaired older sample. The accuracy of the predicted IQs (i.e., percent of obtained IQ falling within one standard error of estimate of the formula-estimated IQ) was similar to that reported for normal younger samples (Eppinger et al., 1987). Specifically, FSIQ prediction accuracy was 77.3% by the 1984 procedure and 72.0 % by the 1986 procedure. VIQ prediction accuracy was 73.3% by the 1984 procedure and 64.0% by the 1986 procedure. PIQ prediction was poor (< 70%) for both methods (1984 = 65.3%; 1986 = 64.0%). Thus, it appeared that the 1984 procedure was slightly better in estimating WAIS–R IQs than the 1986 procedure. Both the 1984 and 1986 methods overestimated the obtained WAIS–R scores for the neurologically impaired sample with the 1984 procedure, once again, providing slightly better estimates.

The same cautions as noted for use of these formulas in younger samples apply to their application with older persons. The equations work best when predicting FSIQ. Estimation of PIQ was poor and should be done with extreme caution. For this sample of normal elderly persons, underestimates of the IQs tended to occur that may lead to underestimates in the accurate identification of cognitive decline, particularly for persons in the above-average levels of intelligence. Thus, these procedures should not be used in isolation but in conjunction with historical information and/or other prediction methods.

An important relevant issue relates to the question of how well clinicians' IQ estimates relate to the actuarial formulas. Kareken and Williams (1994) examined the way in which clinicians' beliefs about the relation between demographic characteristics and premorbid IQ relate to the relations that have been identified actuarially in the research literature. The two investigators concluded that the clinicians believed the relations between IQ and demographic predictors to be stronger than has been established by research. Furthermore, although the clinicians' estimates of the IQ of hypothetical individuals were close to those of an actuarial formula using the same information, their confidence was considerably higher. In other words, the clinicians' confidence intervals were considerably smaller than the standard error of estimate of the formula. They argued that clinicians diagnose impairment on the basis of an obtained score that falls outside a range of error that surrounds an estimated value. Thus, clinicians' smaller confidence intervals could lead them to overdiagnose cognitive decline. Research is needed, however, to compare directly the actual accuracy of formulas and clinicians' estimates when predicting IQs.

Combining Reading Tests and Demographics

Preliminary work suggests there may be some value to statistically combining demographic variables and reading test scores (e.g., NART) in single equations (Crawford, 1989). Such estimates appear to have higher construct validity than estimates based on the NART alone (Crawford, 1990; Crawford, Cochrane, Besson, Parker, & Stewart, 1990). The work of Crawford and colleagues on NART/demographic prediction is based on the WAIS administered to samples from the United Kingdom.

The WAIS–R IQ has been estimated from a combination of NART and demographic variables in an Australian study. Willshire, Kinsella, and Prior (1991) revised the NART for use with a non-British population, arrived at by modifying the pronunciation guide (i.e., Australian English), and determined a revised equation including demographic variables for persons ($n = 49$) age 55 to 69. This equation was then cross-validated on a sample of 28 persons from age 55 to 69. Using a backward multiple regression analysis of IQ on NART error score, sex, education, age, and occupation, the following equation was produced:

IQ = 123.7 − (.8 × ERRORSCORE) + (3.8 × EDUCATION) − (7.4 × SEX).

From this equation, 56% of the variance in the WAIS–R IQ was predicted on the basis of the NART, education and sex, whereas only 38% of the variance in the WAIS–R IQ was predicted by the NART alone. When this equation was used to compute IQ scores for the cross-validation sample (n = 28) and the resulting scores were correlated with their actual IQ scores, a correlation of .81 was obtained. Willshire et al. (1991) noted that this equation may be applicable to persons over age 69 but should only be done with caution.

Grober and Sliwinski (1991) developed a regression-based method for estimating premorbid intelligence by examining the relations between errors on the American version of the Nelson Adult Reading Test (AMNART), WAIS–R VIQ, education, and gender. The model using AMNART and education best predicted current VIQ in a group (n = 215) of nondemented elderly persons. Double cross-validation showed high accuracy and stability of estimating VIQ. The resulting equation was: VIQ = 118.2 – .89 (AMNART errors) + .64 (years of education). The model was used to estimate premorbid IQ in a group (n = 25) of mildly demented elderly persons. Estimated VIQ exceeded actual VIQ by at least 10 points. Only 10% of the nondemented sample showed discrepancies of that magnitude.

Recently, another method of estimating premorbid WAIS–R IQ has been proposed (Paolo, J. J. Ryan, & Troster, in press; Vanderploeg & Schinka, 1995). This method combines demographic information with individual WAIS–R subtest scores to generate regression equations with IQ predicted by one subtest scaled score in combination with demographic characteristics (11 different equations for each of the three summary scores = 33 equations). Using the 1880 participants in the WAIS–R standardization sample, Vanderploeg and Schinka (1995) found R^2 values ranging from .36 to .78, with little shrinkage on cross-validation. The samples were combined to generate more stable estimates and the correlations between the actual and estimated IQs for FSIQ, VIQ, and PIQ ranged from .70 to .82, .66 to .87, and .57 to .81, respectively. These figures exceed those of Barona et al. (1984) for demographically based regression equations.

Paolo et al. (in press) extended this methodology to their sample of persons age 75 and older (see chap. 2 for sample description). The obtained WAIS–R VIQ, PIQ, and FSIQs were calculated using the norms developed by J. J. Ryan et al. (1990). Premorbid IQs were estimated using the coding scheme and methodology presented by Vanderploeg and Schinka (1995; see Table 4.8). Race, gender, and SES from Table 4.8, and age-corrected subtest scores were used as independent variables in the equations. The correlations between obtained and actual IQ scores ranged from .51 to .88 and equal or exceed those reported for the younger sample (Vanderploeg & Schinka, 1995). Data from an additional sample of 95 healthy persons over age 75 were collected for cross-validation (mean age = 79.95, SD = 4.57). Although some shrinkage occurred on cross-validation (average magnitude = 17%), only one significant difference emerged when the obtained and estimated IQ scores were compared. Additional cross-

TABLE 4.8
Predictor Variable Codes for the
WAIS–R Premorbid Predictor Equations

Sex	Male = 1; Female = 2
Race	White = 1; Other ethnicity = 0
Age	16–17 years = 1; 18–19 = 2; 20–24 = 3; 25–34 = 4; 35–44 = 5; 45–54 = 6; 55–64 = 7; 65–69 = 8; 70–74 = 9
Education	0–7 years = 1; 8 = 2; 9–11 = 3; 12 = 4; 13–15 = 5; 16+ = 6
Occupation	Unemployed = 1; Farm Laborers, Farm Foremen, & Laborers (unskilled) = 2; Operatives, Service Workers, Farmers, & Farm Managers (semiskilled) = 3; Craftsmen & Foremen (skilled workers) = 4; Managers, Officials, Propietors, Clerical, & Sales Workers = 5; Professional & Technical = 6
SES	Sum of Education Code and Occupation Code (If unemployed, SES = 2 × Education)

Note. Reprinted from *Archives of Clinical Neuropsychology, 10,* R. D. Vanderploeg and J. A. Schinka, "Predicting WAIS–R IQ Premorbid Ability: Combining Subtest Performance and Demographic Variable Predictors," p. 230. Copyright©1995, by the National Academy of Neuropsychology, with kind permission from Elsevier Science Ltd, The Boulevard, Langford Lane, Kidlington, 0X5 1GB, UK.

validation was accomplished using information from 60 neurologically impaired persons.

Despite the promise of some of the procedures for estimating premorbid IQ, caution should be exercised when applying them to the individual case. The various methods discussed leave substantial portions of the variance in estimated IQ unaccounted for and individual case estimates may often be in error. Reading test results may frequently lead to better estimates of IQ than the formulas based on demographics but demographics-based formulas have the advantage of being unaffected by current performance (Crawford, 1989). Thus, demographic estimates may be more useful with patients who have significant language impairments (e.g., elderly persons with focal strokes affecting the speech areas of the brain). The "best performance method" could be used in conjunction with actuarial approaches. However, more research comparing the various methods and their combinations is needed.

CONCLUSIONS

Much information has accumulated about the WAIS–R to support the clinician in providing appropriate interpretation for older adults. However, floor effects are apparent on the WAIS–R that limit its usefulness for monitoring the progression of disorders. Of particular importance to diagnostic decision making is the discussion of estimates of premorbid level of functioning. A variety of procedures are available to assist clinicians in this complicated task.

Chapter 5

Measures of Intellectual Functioning and Neuropsychological Batteries

Measures of intelligence typically assess a number of semi-independent kinds of abilities to determine a person's general ability level (Nunnally, 1970). How many constructs or factors underlie intelligence is reflected in the theories of intelligence. Binet and Simon (1908), for example, adopted a "global" conception of intelligence and designed their measures to assess the "end products" of intellectual functioning. This approach implicitly assumes that intelligence is general or that all test items are reflections of only one factor (*g*). Other schools of thought, including much of what is reflected in neuropsychology, propose a large number of separate, highly specific capacities, such as attention, memory, reasoning, and perceptual processes. Studies of the relations between measures of cognitive processes that include both measures of specific abilities and those thought to reflect a more general single factor of intelligence suggest that neither extreme point of view is correct. Most tests of abilities correlate positively, supporting the general factor theories. However, factor analytic studies suggest there are definite clusterings of tests that seem to measure a common construct differing from (or do not correlate as strongly with) other tests.

It is beyond the scope of this book to go into the various theories of intellectual functioning in detail. The WAIS–R performance of older persons is discussed in chapter 4. This chapter focuses on other measures of intelligence and neuropsychological batteries that have been specifically designed to assess the broad range of cognitive functions that may be affected in different ways by brain damage depending on the extent and location of the damage. Only those measures for which information on older persons is available are addressed.

MEASURES OF INTELLIGENCE

The Raven's Progressive Matrices were intended to be "culture free" in that verbal instructions are kept to a minimum. Responses do not require verbalization or skilled manipulation ability and are not timed. Although three forms of this measure are available (i.e., Advanced, Colored, and Standard), only the latter two have been used with elderly persons.

The *Standard Progressive Matrices* (SPM; J. C. Raven, Court, & J. Raven, 1976) consists of a series of visual pattern matching and analogy problems. Each item contains a pattern problem at the top of the page with a part (or piece) missing. Below are alternative solutions (6 for sets A and B, 8 for sets C through E) to complete the pattern problem. The 60 items on this measure are divided into five sets (A–E), with each set involving different principles of matrix transformation and increasing in difficulty from Item 1 though Item 12 within each set. Percentile norms provided in the manual (J. C. Raven et al., 1976) range in ages from 6½ to 70. Although the scale is intended to assess the entire range of intellectual development, the very old are not expected to solve more than the problems in Sets A and B of the scale and the easier problems on Sets C and D (Spreen & Strauss, 1991).

Studies by Burke (1985) and O'Leary, Rusch, and Guastello (1991) observed negative correlations between SPM score and age. Relations of the SPM with education and WAIS–R FSIQ differed between the studies. However, it must be noted that few persons (i.e., 20) in these studies were over age 65. Peck (1970), using Orme's (1966) norms, provided a method for converting SPM scores to estimated IQ scores. Raw scores were plotted against percentiles to yield a curve, which then allowed interpolation of intermediate raw scores and extrapolation of more extreme scores. Once an exact percentile was obtained, this was converted to standard scores using the normal curve tables. The standard scores corresponding to IQs ($M = 100$, $SD = 15$) were then determined. At age 65, raw scores of 13, 17, 25, 35, and 43 are equivalent to the 5th, 17th, 50th, 85th, and 95th percentiles, respectively. The corresponding IQ scores were 75, 86, 100, 115 and 125, respectively. Peck (1970) noted that for the age groups from 35 to 65 years, data at the 10th percentile and below are based on Orme's interpolated data. Thus, in Peck's tables for persons age 65, the information for percentiles less than 10 is an interpolation of an interpolation and should be viewed with caution.

The *Colored Progressive Matrices* (CPM; J. C. Raven, 1965) is the shortest, simplest version of the Progressive Matrices and was originally developed for use with children, older persons, anthropological studies, and clinical work. The visual problems are printed in color and can be administered in a booklet form or as boards with movable pieces (Spreen & Strauss,

1991). The CPM requires approximately 25 minutes to complete and consists of 36 items divided into three 12-item sets (A, Ab, B).

As already noted for the SPM, Orme (1966) generated "hypothetically true norms" for persons age 65 to 90 for the CPM (see Table 5.1). These norms differ marginally from percentile norms provided in the CPM manual (J. C. Raven, Court, & J. Raven, 1990) for persons age 65 to 85. Specifically, Orme's (1966) norms require a higher raw score than J. C. Raven et al. (1990) to obtain an equivalent percentile score. For example, the raw scores 18, 17, 16, 14, and 12 are equivalent to the 25% according to J. C. Raven et al. (1990) for persons age 65, 70, 75, 80, and 85, respectively, in contrast to Orme's (1966) raw scores of 21, 19, 18, 17 and 15.

The normative database from which Table 5.1 was derived consisted of 271 persons age 60 to 89. This sample was not a representative cross-section of British people but was drawn from the Rutherglen Centre, a clinic visited by approximately one third of all people over age 65 living in the neighborhood. According to Orme (1966), this sample did not contain people suffering from dementia or other mental disorders. The most common errors made by normal elderly persons (mean age 70 years) on the Board Form of the CPM were repetition of a pattern (e.g., the same pattern as the figure immediately above the space to be filled; 76% of all errors when corrected for frequency of presentation) with an average of 21 items correct (J. C. Raven et al., 1990). The distribution of error types was similar to that seen for persons age 10½ years who obtained a total correct of 27.

Measso et al. (1993) administered the CPM to 894 persons age 20 to 79 who were randomly drawn from the Local Residents Registers of six Italian cities. Of these, 107 were females over age 60 and 90 were males over age 60. The sample was stratified by age and gender and allocation to strata were proportional to the weight of each stratum in the general

TABLE 5.1
Colored Progressive Matrices Amended
Norms Age 65–85, Extrapolated 90–100

Percentile Points	Age							
	65	70	75	80	85	90	95	100
95	33	31	30	29	28	27	27	26
90	30	29	28	27	27	26	24	23
75	27	26	26	25	24	22	21	19
50	25	23	22	21	19	18	17	15
25	21	19	18	17	15	14	13	11
10	17	16	14	13	12	11	9	8
5	15	13	12	11	9	8	—	—

Note. From "Hypothetically True Norms for the Progressive Matrices Tests," by J. E. Orme, 1966, Human Development, 9, p. 228. Reproduced with permission of S. Karger AG, Basel.

population. Persons were screened on the basis of their medical records in collaboration with their family physicians to exclude any current or previous condition that could interfere with their cognitive abilities. Using a regression approach, a model was used to correct for the relations between CPM scores and gender, age, and education (in years of schooling). From this model, correction values were computed for specific subgroups of subjects (see Table 5.2). These scores are added to the raw scores to produce Adjusted CPM values.

Adjusted CPM values provided by Measso et al. (1993) and falling at two different confidence levels include the proportion of the population scoring above a given adjusted value, and the degree of confidence with which this statement can be made. An adjusted score lower than 18.6 would be obtained by only 5% of the population and this assertion has a probability between 95% and 99% of being true. With greater than 99% confidence, it can be said that fewer than 5% of the population obtain adjusted scores of 18.3 or less.

Moreover, Measso et al. (1993) noted that the CPM item grouping proposed by Vallardita (1985) was more sensitive to age than the traditional grouping. Vallardita (1985) grouped items according to whether or not the detection of the correct response involved the principles of: sameness (dependent on perceptual abilities), symmetry (implying internal verbalization for the analysis of stimulus features), or analogy (dependent on conceptual thinking). It was proposed that this newer grouping may allow clinicians to more precisely control for the effects of age when examining for cognitive pathology in older adults.

As is apparent from the studies already reviewed, there is comparatively little information on Raven Matrices performance in the older population. Test–retest reliability data are acceptable in younger samples (above .8)

TABLE 5.2
Adjustment Values for Raven's Colored Progressive Matrices Total
Score by Sex and Educational Level

		Years of Education				
Age	Sex	0–3	4–5	6–8	9–13	>14
60–69	F	7.51	4.78	3.23	.60	−2.08
	M	5.87	3.46	1.88	−.51	−3.56
70–79	F	10.08	5.76	4.73	1.5	−.26
	M	7.07	4.45	2.36	.30	−1.5

Note. From "Raven's Colored Progressive Matrices: A Normative Study of a Random Sample of Healthy Adults," by G. Measso, G. Zappala, F. Cavarzeran, T. H. Crook, L. Romani, F. J. Pirozzolo, F. Grigoletto, L. A. Amaducci, D. Massari, and B. D. Lebowitz, 1993, *Acta Neurologica Scandinavica, 88*, p. 73. Copyright © 1993 by Munksgaard. Adapted with permission.

but have not been addressed for older persons. Although the Raven Matrices measures correlate with WAIS measures, the correlations are not particularly high and conversions of RPM scores to IQ scores have been discouraged (Spreen & Strauss, 1991) as they are not interchangeable types of measures. In all studies of the SPM, the numbers of persons included over age 65 have been small and resulting normative information is of limited value. This may not be of great concern as the CPM appears to be a better measure for use with elderly persons. Orme's (1966) data are limited in that percentile equivalents are not given for each raw score and age but state the raw score only at certain percentile and age values. Thus, interpolation of intermediate score and extrapolation of more extreme scores is required and lacks precision. Further examination of Vallardita's (1985) grouping of items may yield useful information when studying older persons.

The *Shipley Institute of Living Scale* (SILS: Shipley, 1940; Shipley & Burlingame, 1941; revised manual: Zachary, 1986) is an easily administered paper-and-pencil test containing two subtests: a 40-item multiple choice vocabulary test, and a 20-item subtest requiring concept formation and solution finding of verbal and arithmetic abstract problems. The original normative sample was 1,046 students from 4th grade through college. In the revised manual (Zachary, 1986), T-score conversion tables were included for the following three raw scores: Vocabulary score, Abstract score × 2, and Conceptual Quotient (CQ) as reflected in the Abstract score divided by the Vocabulary score, age corrected to age 64.

Morgan and Hatsukami (1986) administered the SILS to 61 healthy, high functioning 60- to 85-year-old volunteers. Only 5% of this sample performed within the "normal" CQ range. Thirty-eight percent of this sample attained scores of four or less on the Abstract subtest. Of those persons with a minimum of a high school education, only 33% attained four or fewer items correct on this subtest. Thus, given the restricted range of scores obtained by elderly persons, serious questions were raised about the potential relations between the Abstract and CQ measures. Morgan and Hatsukami (1986) noted that the presence of a "floor effect" for the Abstract subtest makes the SILS unlikely to be a useful measure for identifying organic impairment with this population.

The *Kaufman Adolescent and Adult Intelligence Test* (KAIT; A. S. Kaufman & N. L. Kaufman, 1993) is composed of separate Crystallized and Fluid scales (Horn, 1968; Horn & Cattell, 1967). As noted in discussing the WAIS, crystallized intelligence refers to acquired concepts and depends on schooling and acculturation for success. Fluid intelligence refers to the ability to solve new problems. The KAIT is organized into six Core Battery subtests and can be administered in about 1 hour. The Expanded Battery consists of 10 subtests (see Table 5.3) and requires approximately 1½ hours to administer.

TABLE 5.3
Subtests of the Kaufman Adolescent and Adult Intelligence
Test (KAIT; A. S. Kaufman & N. L. Kaufman, 1993)

Subtest #	Name	Description
1	Definitions	(Crystallized). A word, with missing letters is shown and a clue about its meaning is given.
2	Rebus Learning	(Fluid). Words are associated with particular drawings (rebus). Phrases and sentences composed of rebuses are then read.
3	Logical Steps	(Fluid). Logical premises are explained (visually and aurally). A response to a question making use of the logical premise is then required.
4	Auditory	(Crystallized). A short news story is presented. Responses to literal and inferential questions about the news story are then required.
5	Mystery Codes	(Fluid). A set of pictorial stimuli are associated with identifying codes. The code for a novel pictorial stimulus must then be determined.
6	Double Meanings	(Crystallized). Two sets of word clues are presented. A word that relates closely to both sets of clues is required.
7	Rebus Delayed Recall	Phrases and sentences composed of rebuses learned earlier (45 minutes) are read.
8	Auditory Delayed Recall	Responses to literal and inferential questions about news stories heard earlier (25 minutes) are required.
9	Memory for Block Designs	(Fluid-alternative). A printed abstract design is exposed briefly. A copy of the design from memory using six yellow and black wooden blocks and a tray is required.
10	Famous Faces	(Crystallized-alternative). Photographs of people of current historical fame are presented with a verbal cue about them. Each of these people are to be named.

Like the Wechsler scales, the KAIT IQs have a mean of 100 and a standard deviation of 15 for each of the three intelligence scales: Crystallized, Fluid, and Composite Intelligence. The IQs are derived from age-based norms for persons age 11 through 85+. Subtest raw scores are converted to standard scores (mean of 10, standard deviations of 3) by age group. The three Core Crystallized subtests are summed, as are the three Core Fluid subtests. Alternatives for Core subtests are available and substitutions for a Core subtest may be made. The sums of the Crystallized and Fluid scales are added together to determine the Composite Intelligence scale. The three scale score sums are then converted to IQs in tables that contain the 90% and 95% confidence intervals, percentile rankings, and mean scaled scores. A difference between Crystallized and Fluid IQ scores is computed with a discrepancy of 8 (and 11) being significant at the .05 (and .01) levels, respectively, for persons age 35 and older.

A Profile Analysis page is available that presents the size of the difference required for significance at the .05 level when comparing each subtest scaled score to the mean scaled score earned by the person on all subtests in that particular scale (e.g., Crystallized or Fluid). Guidelines are provided for capturing strengths and weaknesses in the subtest scaled score profiles.

As with the Wechsler scales, interscale scatter is expected for the KAIT. Differences between the Crystallized and Fluid scales of 24 and 22 points, respectively, were observed in only 5% of persons age 55 to 69 and 70+ in their standardization sample. Data concerning the magnitude of difference between highest and lowest subtest scale scores within the three intelligence scales are also presented in the manual but are not broken down by age group. Only 5% of the standardization sample ($N = 2,000$) showed discrepancies of 7, 8, and 10 points between the highest and lowest subtest scale scores on the Crystallized, Fluid, and Composite scales for the Core Battery.

In the Expanded battery, comparisons can be made between the immediate and delayed recall scores. A 10-item supplementary subtest, Mental Status, gives a general estimate of alertness and orientation to the testing situation and the environment. Raw scores are converted to descriptive categories by age grouping. Scores of 6, 5, and 3–4 define the upper bounds of the "lower extreme" category for persons age 65–69, 70–74, and 75+, respectively. It is suggested in the manual that this measure may prove valuable for the clinical assessment of abnormal individuals (e.g., those with Alzheimer's disease).

High internal consistency is demonstrated for the Crystallized, Fluid, and Composite IQs and the six core subtests for persons over age 65 (A. S. Kaufman & N. L. Kaufman, 1993). Stability coefficients from 54 persons age 55 and older, administered the KAIT twice (mean retest interval = 31 days), were high for Crystallized, Fluid, and Composite Intelligence and for the Core Battery subtests. Modest average gains (i.e., approximately four IQ points) were observed. The Mental Status performance of this same sample of 54 persons showed very high agreement with respect to category classification for each person.

Examination of age changes on the subtests and IQ scales revealed that after age 54, the mean scores on the four Crystallized subtests declined steadily but not dramatically. Conversely, a precipitous decline is apparent for Fluid mean scores after age 54. Of all the subtests, the means on the two delayed recall measures show the most marked declines after age 54. These cross-sectional data follow the patterns of age-related changes predicted by Horn and Cattell (Horn, 1968; Horn & Cattell, 1967) and lends support to the construct validity of these measures. Factor analytic studies revealed that two-factor solutions appeared the most meaningful. For all age groups, the Crystallized subtests formed one factor and the Fluid subtests formed the other.

The KAIT performance of a small clinical sample of persons with Alzheimer's disease ($n = 10$) was compared with matched control subjects. It is noteworthy that 2 of these 10 were only able to complete the Mental Status subtest and the average scaled score performances for the remaining 8 suggest that performances may have been at or near the floor of subtests. Little information about the severity of impairment represented in this sample is given, but it appears that the KAIT may be of little use to track the course of cognitive decline in Alzheimer's disease, particularly in very old persons.

The *Kaufman Short Neuropsychological Assessment Procedure* (K–SNAP; A. S. Kaufman & N. L. Kaufman, 1994) was designed as a brief (25-minute) measure of mental functioning at three levels of cognitive complexity: least complex or attention/orientation, medium complexity or simple memory and perceptual skills, and most complex or reasoning and planning abilities. Although this measure is intended for full range of ages from 11 to 85 years, Kaufman and Kaufman indicated that this measure is especially useful with cognitively impaired populations such as persons suspected of having a dementia.

The K–SNAP is composed of four subtests ranging in level of complexity from low (Mental Status) to medium (Number Recall and Gestalt Closure subtests) through high (Four-Letter Words subtest). The two subtests of medium complexity are combined to yield a Recall/Closure Composite score by summing the scaled scores. The subtests of medium and high complexity are combined to yield a K–SNAP Composite score by summing of the Recall/Closure Composite scaled score with the Four-Letter Words scaled score. An impairment index (scores ranging from 0 through 8) is calculated to provide an estimate of the person's level of cognitive impairment. The K–SNAP was designed to be interpreted in the context of various neuropsychological theories (e.g., Luria's blocks, sequential vs. simultaneous processing, automatic vs. representational organization).

The K–SNAP yields the same descriptive categories for the Mental Status subtest as the KAIT. Scaled scores with a mean of 10 and standard deviation of 3, percentile ranks and descriptive categories are presented for the other three subtests and the Recall/Closure Composite score. Standard scores with a mean of 100 and standard deviation of 15, percentile ranks and descriptive categories are presented for the K–SNAP Composite score. An Impairment Index score of 3 or above suggests the presence of neurological impairment and more comprehensive evaluation is recommended. K–SNAP normative subtest scores were based on 14 age groups for persons age 11 through 85+. K–SNAP norm tables present confidence intervals at the 90% and 95% confidence level.

The K–SNAP Composite score for persons over age 65 shows high internal consistency. Split-half reliability coefficients and test–retest reliability coefficients are available in the manual (A. S. Kaufman & N. L. Kaufman, 1994). An average gain of six IQ points was observed for the K–SNAP Composite score. The Mental Status data from KAIT standardization also pertain to its use as part of the K–SNAP.

Examination of age changes on the subtests revealed that the mean scores on all subtests showed declines after age 50 with some declines beginning in early adulthood. This is consistent with previous literature in that all three subtests reflect abilities vulnerable to the aging process. The K–SNAP was factor analyzed with the KAIT, WAIS–R and K–FAST. No K–SNAP subtests loaded on the first Verbal/Crystallized factor. One subtest was associated with the Perceptual Organization factor, one subtest was associated with the Fluid factor, and one subtest was associated with the memory/sequencing dimension that included WAIS–R Digit Span. Correlations of the K–SNAP with the KAIT were higher than K–SNAP correlations with the WAIS–R.

The K–SNAP performance of a heterogeneous clinical sample of neurologically impaired persons ($n = 49$), including those with Alzheimer's disease ($n = 10$), was compared with matched control subjects. It is noteworthy that the clinical group ($n = 49$) scored significantly lower than the control group on the K–SNAP Composite score but the other differences fell short of significance.

The Impairment Index was examined to determine its usefulness in discriminating between samples with known cognitive/neurological impairment and those without such impairment. When Alzheimer's patients were combined with mentally handicapped persons and compared to their matched controls, an Impairment Index of 3 or more points occurred over 90% of the time in relation to 11.9% of the controls. When this group was combined with other neurologically impaired persons ($n = 91$), less than 60% earned scores of 3 or more in relation to 8.8% of the controls. Certainly, more of the persons obtaining high Impairment Index scores (i.e., 4 through 8), were neurologically impaired than were normal controls.

The *Kaufman Brief Intelligence Test* (K–BIT; A. S. Kaufman & N. L. Kaufman, 1990) was designed as a brief (15–30 minutes), individually administered measure of verbal and nonverbal intelligence composed of two subtests: Vocabulary and Matrices. This measure is not viewed as a substitute for a comprehensive measure of intelligence. The K–BIT was designed for use when a brief measure will suffice and trained professionals may be unavailable (e.g., large-scale screening, estimate of IQ is of lesser importance in the assessment, time constraints, research purposes). Because the measure is easy to administer, Kaufman and Kaufman suggested that technicians or paraprofessionals may be trained by qualified personnel to administer this measure.

Vocabulary is viewed as a measure of Crystallized thinking and contains two parts: Part A, Expressive Vocabulary, consists of 45 items and requires the person to provide the name of pictured objects; Part B, Definitions, consists of 37 items and requires the person to provide the word that best fits: a phrase description (e.g., a dark color) and a partial spelling of the target word (e.g., BR_W_). The Definitions subtest is an alternate form of the identical task on the KAIT Crystallized Learning Scale but the actual items on the two tests do not overlap. The Matrices subtest is a 48-item measure of nonverbal skills and the ability to solve new problems. It is viewed as a measure of fluid thinking. The measure is composed of several types of visual stimuli (e.g., meaningful and abstract) and all items require an understanding of the relations among the stimuli. All items are multiple choice and require the person to point to the correct response or say the letter associated with it. The majority of the items involve abstract stimuli and require the solution of 2×2 or 3×3 matrices or to complete a dot pattern. Each item demands nonverbal reasoning and flexibility in applying a problem-solving strategy.

As with the other Kaufman batteries, age-based standard scores having a mean of 100 and a standard deviation of 15 are provided for each subtest and the overall score or K–BIT IQ Composite. Age-based standard scores were developed by dividing the sample into 17 separate age groups (i.e., 4, 5, 6, . . . 13–14, 15–16, 17–19, 20–24, 25–34, 35–44, 45–59, 60–90). Later a linear interpolation was applied to expand the linearly equated raw scores to tables for 53 age groups (including 65–69, 70–74, and 75–90). The two subtest standard scores were summed to develop the composite standard scores and smoothed within the 17 original age groupings. Split-half reliability coefficients and test–retest reliability coefficients, with a mean test–retest interval of 15 days, are described in the manual (A. S. Kaufman & N. L. Kaufman, 1990) for 50 persons age 55 to 89. Although 20 validity studies are reported in the manual, none contain persons over age 50.

The *Quick Test* yields Mental Age and IQ scores but is actually a measure that examines vocabulary in situational contexts. A card containing four pictures is shown to individuals and they are instructed to point to the picture that best fits the word read by the examiner. There are three forms of this measure, each containing 50 words. The original normative sample (R. B. Ammons & C. H. Ammons, 1962) contained persons age 2 to 43. Adult norms are applicable only up to age 45.

Sinnett, Holen, and Davie (1988) administered the QT to 100 volunteers, 20 (10 males and 10 females) from each of five age categories (60–64,

65–69, 70–74, 75–79, and 80+ years). Within each gender, five persons of relatively higher socioeconomic backgrounds and five with relatively lower socioeconomic backgrounds were chosen. Ten percent (one man and one woman in each age category) were members of identifiable ethnic/racial minorities. The QT IQs were derived from the sum of scores for Forms 1, 2, and 3, given in that order. The overall IQ values (i.e., all age categories) had a mean of 109.71 and a *SD* of 15.7. The means for the age categories did not differ significantly from one another except for the oldest group (age 80 to 96), which was significantly below all other age categories. Sinnett et al. suggested a correction of approximately 10 points might be adopted as a guideline to equate the scores of the oldest age group with the other age categories.

Levine (1971) administered the QT to 50 volunteers (25 males and 25 females) age 60 to 100 from old age homes, senior citizen clubs, residents of a retirement village, or referred to the examiner in relation to the WAIS. A mean level of education of 10.6 years was attained for this sample. All three forms of the QT were administered to all subjects (as was the WAIS). The QT was significantly correlated with all WAIS IQs (e.g., QT with FSIQ, $r = .88$) but more highly with the VIQ ($r = .89$) than the PIQ ($r = .78$). Levine concluded that the QT taps essentially the same construct as the WAIS IQ and may be a useful, brief instrument for assessing the intellectual level of older persons.

NEUROPSYCHOLOGICAL TEST BATTERIES

The *Halstead–Reitan Neuropsychological Test Battery* (HRB; Halstead, 1947; Reitan & Davidson, 1974; Reitan & Wolfson, 1993) began as seven measures chosen to discriminate between brain-damaged persons and normal subjects: Category Test, Tactual Performance Test, Rhythm Test, Speech Sounds Perception Test, Finger Oscillation Test (i.e., Finger Tapping), Critical Flicker Fusion Test, and the Time Sense Test. The latter two measures have been dropped from more recent modifications of the battery because they have not been shown to identify those with brain damage with sufficient accuracy. In addition to the individual test scores, an Impairment Index is calculated by applying cutting scores to determine the number of measures falling within the impaired range. The present battery yields seven scores and abnormal functioning is identified if 60% or more of the measures fall within the impaired range. Other measures often included in this battery are the Trail-Making Test and the Aphasia Screening Test.

Reitan and Wolfson (1986) reviewed ample evidence that the measures within the Halstead–Reitan Battery are sensitive to age even under age 65. Over age 65, these decrements are even more marked. Meyerink (1982) examined 25 persons with no past or present evidence of cerebral disease or damage in each of five age decades beginning at age 20. Comparisons between the age groups revealed that complex tasks and those most heavily dependent on abstract reasoning were observed to decline most significantly with age. Based on these findings, Reitan and Wolfson (1986) recommended the inclusion of the Category Test, Tactual Performance Test–Localization Component, and Part B of the Trail Making Test as measures of general integrity of the cerebral hemispheres when assessing for age effects.

The original norms for the HRB (Halstead, 1947) were not well founded (Lezak, 1995) and consisted of only 28 persons (age 14 to 50). This has raised serious concerns about the appropriateness of the cutting scores for older populations as most of the measures decline with age (e.g., Bak & Greene, 1980). More recently, norms for the HRB have been developed (Heaton et al., 1991) based on 486 participants age 20 to 80 using a regression approach (see chap. 2 for description of sample and methods).

It has been noted (Feurst, 1993) that transforming raw scores into demographically corrected scores using the Heaton et al. (1991) manual can be laborious and a computer program has been developed to automate this procedure. However, Feurst (1993) noted some problems with the computer program, as well, which may deter all but the most avid HRB enthusiasts. It is to be expected that these problems will be corrected in future versions of the software.

Despite improvements to procedures for using the norms of Heaton et al. (1991) for older age groups, Lezak (1995) noted that the HRB may not be chosen for use with elderly persons for other reasons. Most notably, older persons may be unwilling or unable to tolerate the length of the testing session required to administer the HRB. Moreover, the difficulty level is such that older persons may withdraw from testing or be unable to perform sufficiently well on measures to warrant the cost in terms of time and effort. Certainly older persons suspected of neurological disorders would be fatigued by the HRB easily with little useful information concerning strengths and weaknesses yielded for diagnostic or rehabilitative purposes.

Faibish, Auerbach, and Thornby (1986) addressed these issues and proposed a form of the HRB modified for older adults. The measures chosen for alteration included: the Category Test, the Tactual Performance Test, the Seashore Rhythm Test, the Speech Sounds Test, and the Trail Making Test. The Category Test for Younger Children was selected and modified for use with elderly persons. The Tactual Performance Test was changed radically with the presentation of two 5-form boards for each hand (i.e., four trials). Faibish et al. (1986) reported that over 95% of the trials were completed in less than 5 minutes with a moderate age effect being seen ($r = .53$). Modifications to the Speech Sounds Test focused on reduced length and response intervals were increased on the Seashore Rhythm

Test. The Trail Making Test for Older Children was adopted in favor of the standard adult form. Whether or not these changes are sufficient to create a battery of suitable length that is sensitive to forms of deterioration of concern in an aging population (e.g., dementia) is yet to be determined.

The *Luria Nebraska Neuropsychological Battery* (LNNB) is made up of examination techniques described by Luria, the preeminent Russian neuropsychologist, and organized by Christensen. These techniques were converted into test items in this battery, which as noted by Speirs (1981) is not to say that "the test is an operationalization of Luria's method" (p. 339). Golden, Moses, Graber, and Berg (1981) selected items from Christensen's manual, which discriminated between normal subjects and an unspecified group of neurologically impaired persons. The 269 items were organized into 11 clinical scales: C1 = motor; C2 = rhythm; C3 = tactile; C4 = visual; C5 = receptive language; C6 = expressive speech; C7 = writing; C8 = reading; C9 = arithmetic; C10 = memory; C11 = intellectual processes; and C12 = intermediate memory.

Form II of this measure largely parallels Form I but contains an extra subtest, Intermediate Memory (10 items), which assessed delayed recall of some of the previously administered short-term memory items. Performance on each item is evaluated on a scale from 0 (normal) to 2 (severely impaired). The 11 clinical scales are derived from the sums of the items within each scale. Five summary scales (Pathognomic, Right Hemisphere, Left Hemisphere, Profile Evaluation, and Impairment scales) are also derived by summing particular items. For example, the Right Hemisphere scale is composed of the sums of all tactile and motor function items for the left side of the body. Other scales, derived from summing particular items, have been generated since the publication of this measure (see Lezak, 1995), including a 66-item list of qualitative aspects of test performance to allow for the examination of the nature of a failure.

Initial normative data were limited (i.e., 26 female and 24 male hospitalized medical patients). The *critical level* is defined by calculating the person's age × .214 for every age between 25 and 70 years. The number of years of education (0 through 20) is multiplied by 1.47, which is then subtracted from the critical level. These corrections assume simple linear relations between age, education, and performance on every skill or function that does not correspond to studies on cognitive changes with aging. Other limitations of this measure include the heterogeneity within scales (e.g., verbal, visual, visuospatial, auditory all within one scale) and the limited breadth within each domain of each scale (e.g., some aspects of memory not addressed) (Lezak, 1995).

Spitzform (1982) first examined the performance of persons age 65 to 83 on the LNNB ($n = 14$). MacInnes, Gillen, Golden, and Graber (1983) extended this look at the performance of normal elderly persons to 78 volunteers with a mean age of 72.2 years. The mean performance of this group fell within the average range for 14 clinical scales, localization scales, and factor scales. When this group was divided into young–old (60–74) and old–old (75+) groups, the mean performances of both groups fell within the average range and the only statistically significant differences between groups on the clinical scales were in favor of the old–old group (Expressive Speech and Writing). When males ($n = 26$, mean age = 73.4) and females ($n = 52$, mean age = 71.6) were examined, the males performed significantly better than the females on the Visual scale and the females performed significantly better than the males on the Expressive Speech and Pathognomic scales. When a group of 100 neurologically impaired older persons was compared with this normal sample using the objective rules reported by Golden et al. (1981), 72 of the 78 normal persons were correctly classified and 86 of the 100 neurologically impaired persons were correctly classified. Golden et al. noted that the lack of age-related cognitive decline on the LNNB may be the result of sampling (i.e., 75+ were selected to be as healthy as 60- to 74-year-old group); simpler items on the LNNB (other neuropsychological batteries contain more complex tasks that are affected by normal aging); or more crystallized items on the LNNB (age-related effects are most pronounced for fluid tasks). They concluded that the LNNB may be a useful measure of neuropsychological functioning with elderly persons.

A normative study for Form II of the LNNB was conducted by Wong, Schefft, and Moses (1990) with 100 normal individuals age 17 through 70 ($M = 38.5$, $SD = 14.7$). They presented the means and standard deviations for each scale and noted that the average mean predicted performance level score or baseline (critical level) = .171 (age) − 1.16 (education) + 59.7. They noted that more research is needed before the norms could be used in clinical situations on a regular basis. The effects of age, sex, race, education, and health status on test performance were not examined.

Moses, Schefft, Wong, and Berg (1992) extended these norms to include a total of 392 persons age 12 to 80. They recommended the use of uniform T-scores over standard T-scores as this method makes percentile equivalents of the scaled score the same for the clinical scales and maintains the sensitivity of the test to outliers. The uniform T-score value for 316 persons in the normative sample was then predicted using a multiple regression procedure with age and education entered as the independent variables. The prediction equation that estimates the baseline was: 57.482 − (1.629 × educational level) + (0.078 × age).

The application of this formula was validated in a sample of 55 control subjects (age 18 to 71) and 55 neurologically impaired subjects (age 18 to 73). The formula (baseline value plus 10 T-score points = critical level) correctly classified 85.5 % (47/55) of the normal participants when four or fewer scales were elevated above the critical level (including C12, Intermediate Memory and excluding C7 and C9, Writing and Arithmetic, respectively, from the sum). Using this criteria, 87.3% of the neurologically impaired subjects were correctly classified. Moses et al. noted the differences in mean values between this sample and that reported earlier (Wong et al., 1990) indicate that the earlier norms were too stringent to account for the range of normality likely to be encountered in clinical practice. They also recommended the use of this uniform T-score approach rather than the previously used normative prediction method recommended by Golden and colleagues for the LNNB II.

A short form containing approximately half (141) of the original items (269) has been proposed for use with elderly persons (McCue, Shelly, & Goldstein, 1985). This short form was designed to specifically address referral issues of dementia, differential diagnosis of type of dementia and distinguishing between dementia and depressive pseudodementia. Thus, the Memory, Intellectual Processes, and Pathognomic Scales of the LNNB were administered in their entirety and the Rhythm Scale was deleted. The remaining scales were shortened and modified.

When a heterogeneous sample of persons age 55 and older ($n = 247$) was examined, correlations between the T-scores generated from the abbreviated scales and those derived from the full battery ranged from .8 to .9. McCue, Goldstein, and Shelly (1989) administered this short form of the LNNB to 79 elderly persons, 34 diagnosed with probable Alzheimer's disease and 45 meeting DSM–III criteria for depression. Discriminant function analysis yielded a correct classification rate of 86.1%. Examination of specific scales (e.g., Memory scale, Overall Mean T-score, and Pathognomic scale) yielded slightly poorer classification (i.e., 79.7%, 81%, 79.8%, respectively). Of note, the mean profile for the depressed group was completely normal when critical level age and education adjustments were applied.

The LNNB has been roundly criticized for various flaws, including poor norms and diagnostic insensitivity (Lezak, 1995). The advantages of this measure for use with older adults is the simple, generally nonthreatening nature of the items and its brevity.

CONCLUSIONS

This chapter highlighted efforts to extend knowledge about measures of global functioning to persons age 65 and older. As seen with the WAIS–R, floor effects (e.g., HRB) may limit the use of some measures with older persons. New measures of intelligence have emerged (i.e., Kaufman's measures) based on different theoretical constructs than the WAIS–R. Whether or not these batteries will be of particular use in the assessment of older persons is yet to be determined.

Chapter 6

Memory Assessment

Assessment of memory is the central issue in most referrals of elderly persons for neuropsychological evaluation. Many comprehensive sources are available that detail proposed theories, classifications, and subdivisions of memory functioning (e.g., Squire, 1987). Reeves and Wedding (1994) noted that memory processes involve registration, encoding, storage, consolidation, and retrieval, at least. Moreover, memory tasks may be classified within a temporal framework as involving immediate, recent, and remote memory. Because the structure of memory assessment tools may reflect these concepts, some of the more common constructs are discussed briefly.

It is generally assumed that information must be *registered,* or *encoded,* if it is to be remembered. Specific encoding operations are performed on what is perceived and information is processed further into short- and long-term storage. Short-term memory is a limited capacity store with extremely rapid decay (i.e., seconds to a minute). *Working memory,* a type of short-term memory, is most related to active processing, and is discussed with measures of attention and concentration in chapter 7. Information that has been encoded into short-term storage must then be maintained or elaborated if it is to be *consolidated* into long-term storage (held for minutes, hours, or longer). Only information that has been adequately encoded and stored is available to then be *retrieved* from storage. Retrieval may be facilitated by semantic prompting, cued recall, and recognition procedures. This facilitation of memories implies that some of the to-be-remembered material must have been adequately encoded and stored for it to be revealed under these conditions. Differences in the duration of maintenance of the information in long-term memory (e.g., 3 to 5 minutes,

15 minutes, or longer), *speed of memory decay* or *retention over time* may also be of significance for characterizing memory functioning. Abundant evidence to support a relation between anatomical substrates and various components of memory processing has been described and detailed elsewhere (e.g., Lynch, McGaugh, & Weinberger, 1984) but as yet is not fully understood.

The majority of memory assessment instruments for which normative information has been collected were not derived from any particular theoretical model. However, some of the newer clinical instruments include constructs that extend beyond the simple presentation of material for retrieval at a later time. In addition, measures of subjective appraisals (e.g., Crook & Larrabee, 1992) of memory functioning have been developed because complaints of memory change may or may not be related to memory performance on objective measures.

It is important to be able to distinguish between normal memory changes and declines in memory functioning resulting from a variety of medical conditions, including Alzheimer's disease. Such conditions may affect memory functioning of older persons and impact on their abilities to meet the complex demands of everyday life (see chap. 10).

MEMORY BATTERIES

The first battery of measures designed specifically to assess memory was the *Wechsler Memory Scale* (WMS; D. Wechsler, 1945; see Table 6.1). The seven subscales are combined into a Memory Quotient with mean of 100 and *SD* of 15, making the scores comparable to Wechsler's IQ measures. The original normative sample did not include people over age 60 (D. Wechsler, 1945). Klonoff and Kennedy (1966) collected normative data on 115 Canadian male veterans between age 80 and 92 living in the community. The same year, Hulicka (1966) examined age differences on the WMS and included persons age 60 to 89 who were hospitalized veterans, residents of homes for the aged, or members of Golden Age Clubs. Cauthen (1977) was the first to collect norms for a 60-minute delayed recall for the Logical Memory subscale in older persons. Since then, norms have been collected from a number of sources addressing a variety of procedural concerns. Differences between the norms in terms of sample composition and scoring systems illuminate the need for care in applying these norms in clinical settings (see Table 6.2).

Age effects have been identified for most subscales of the WMS across studies. Hulicka (1966) noted age differences between scores for Logical Memory (LM), Digit Span (DS), and Associate Learning (AL). Performance on the easy pairs of the AL subtest shows far less change over age

TABLE 6.1
Content of the WMS and WMS–R

Subscale	WMS	WMS–R
Personal and Current Information	Age, date of birth, current and recent public officials	Extended with additional questions
Orientation	Time and place	Extended with additional questions
Mental Control	Automatisms and simple conceptual tracking	Speed credits eliminated from WMS scoring system
Logical Memory (LM)	Immediate recall of verbal ideas from two paragraphs	Stories are more nearly equivalent in difficulty. Scoring system improved. Delayed recall trial added.
Digit Span (DS)	Repetition of forward and backward digit series	Easier items added to both forward and backward series. Scoring procedures changed.
Visual Reproduction (VR)	Immediate visual memory drawing	Item content modified and subtest lengthened. Scoring rules improved. Delayed recall trial added.
Associate Learning (AL)	Verbal retention of easy and hard word pairs	Renamed to Verbal Paired Associates. Two easy paired associates deleted. Scoring system simplified. Material learned to a constant criterion. Delayed recall trial added.
Visual Paired Associates (Visual PA)		New subtest corresponding to Verbal Paired Associates (Verbal PA). Contains delayed recall trial.
Figural Memory		New subtest measuring recognition of abstract visual patterns
Visual Memory Span (VMS)		New visual-spatial subtest corresponding to the verbal Digit span subtest

Note. WMS = Wechsler Memory Scale (D. Wechsler, 1945) and WMS–R = Wechsler Memory Scale–Revised (D. Wechsler, 1987). Wechsler Memory Scale–Revised. Copyright © 1945, 1974, 1987 by The Psychological Corporation. Adapted with permission. All rights reserved. "Wechsler Memory Scale" and "WMS" are trademarks of The Psychological Corporation.

than recall of hard pairs (desRosiers & Ivison, 1986). Persons age 60 to 69 received an average score on the easy pairs (15.05 +/− 2.62 of a total of 18 points), more than four times greater than their average performance on the hard items (3.32 +/− 2.62 of a total of 12). Age effects were evident for Visual Reproduction (VR) and Delayed Recall for both LM paragraphs in Cauthen's (1977) sample. Haaland, Linn, Hunt, and Goodwin (1983)

TABLE 6.2
WMS Normative Studies

Author	N	Age	Sample
Trahan et al. (1988)[a]	255	18–91 years; 50–69 ($n = 51$), 70–91 ($n = 26$)	Healthy, nonhospitalized, neurologically normal with no evidence of major psychiatric illness or mental deficiency.
Abikoff et al. (1987)[b]	339	18–83 years	Age and education norms for gist, verbatim, immediate, delayed, and 24-hour recall; interrater reliability.
Haaland et al. (1983)	175	65–69 ($n = 49$), 70–74 ($n = 74$), 75–79 ($n = 40$), 80+ ($n = 13$)	Volunteers in a longitudinal study on immunology and aging; no prescription medication; living independently; self-report and medical examination to assess health status including history, physical, and appropriate laboratory tests.
Ivnik et al. (1991)	99	65–97 years	Normal volunteers participating in an Alzheimer's disease patient registry; white.
Mitrushina & Satz (1989)	156	57–85 years	Very intelligent (high average to superior IQ), optimally functioning residents of a retirement community in Southern California.
Klonoff & Kennedy (1966)	115	80–93 years	Canadian male veterans residing in an urban community (Vancouver, BC). Most subjects had good global health ratings (from internist) and were moderately or very active; majority had unskilled/semiskilled occupational backgrounds.
Cauthen (1977)	64	60+ years	Canadian volunteers, living in institutional settings.

Note. WMS = Wechsler Memory Scale (D. Wechsler, 1945).
[a]Using only the Visual Reproduction subtest of the WMS.
[b]Using only the Logical Memory subtest of the WMS.

reported that education and income differences did not account for the effects of age on Russell's variant of the LM and VR subtests (i.e., immediate and 30-minute delay). Abikoff et al. (1987) noted effects of age on the LM subscale for immediate, 20- to 30-minute delay and 24-hour delayed gist and verbatim recall—except for immediate recall Form II. Ivnik et al. (1991) found a limited correlation of age with the WMS measures accounting for only 10.7% of the variance in the total WMS raw score. Hence, age stratification was not warranted for their sample. Tables 6.3 and 6.4 summarize some of the available normative data for persons over age 60 on the various subtests of the WMS.

TABLE 6.3
Logical Memory and Visual Reproduction Scores (SD) for Persons
Age 65 and Older From Haaland et al. (1983)

	Age Group			
Variable	65–69 (n = 49)	70–74 (n = 74)	75–79 (n = 40)	80+ (n = 13)
Logical Memory				
Immediate	7.4	6.7	5.9	6.1
	(2.5)	(2.6)	(2.5)	(1.7)
Delayed	4.8	4.2	3.6	4.0
	(2.4)	(2.4)	(2.5)	(1.4)
Percentage Retained[a]	63.1	60.2	56.3	65.7
	(21.3)	(23.0)	(23.9)	(13.2)
Visual Reproduction				
Immediate	6.0	5.1	4.9	3.3
	(2.1)	(2.0)	(2.0)	(2.3)
Delayed	5.4	4.3	4.2	2.8
	(2.5)	(2.3)	(1.9)	(1.9)
Percentage Retained[a]	89.3	83.4	86.8	92.6
	(27.6)	(37.2)	(31.5)	(42.8)

Note. Immediate and delayed scores for Logical Memory are based on the average of the details recalled from two stories, whereas similar scores for Visual Reproduction are based on the total number of details recalled, as proposed by D. Wechsler (1945). From "A Normative Study of Russell's Variant of the Wechsler Memory Scale in a Healthy Elderly Population," by K. Y. Haaland, R. T. Linn, W. C. Hunt, and J. S. Goodwin, 1983, *Journal of Consulting and Clinical Psychology, 51,* p. 879. Copyright © 1983 by the American Psychological Association. Adapted with permission.

[a]Percentage retained = Total number of details recalled on delay / Total number of details recalled immediately (× 100).

Both Cauthen (1977) and Ivnik et al. (1991) noted stronger correlations between IQ and WMS performance than age. They suggested that IQ rather than age deserves consideration in adjustment for nonmemory factors when using the WMS with older persons. Ivnik et al. (1991) also found correlations with education, which they suspected arose from the correlation of both WMS and education with IQ and present normative data by education and IQ (see Table 6.5).

The LM subtest has also received additional attention as a result of problems in interpretation and interstudy comparisons arising from imprecise scoring instructions. The norms generated by Cauthen (1977), Haaland et al. (1983), and Hulicka (1966) are based on Wechsler's imprecise scoring instructions. Abikoff et al. (1987) applied operationalized scoring systems for verbatim and gist recall for immediate, intermediate (25 minutes), and long-term (24-hour) recall intervals. Both age and edu-

TABLE 6.4
Summary of Hulicka (1966) Data for Persons
Age 60 and Older on the Wechsler Memory Scale

		WMS Subscales					
Age	n	Information	Mental Control	Logical Memory	Digit Span	Visual Reproduction	Associate Learning
60–69	70						
M		5.47	6.24	7.34	9.91	6.03	11.94
SD		1.16	2.29	2.90	1.58	3.72	4.53
70–79	46						
M		5.24	5.63	7.35	9.91	4.95	10.98
SD		1.03	2.46	3.83	2.51	3.42	4.78
80–89	25						
M		5.60	6.92	6.80	10.00	4.00	9.98
SD		0.24	2.02	3.19	2.35	2.38	3.28

Note. From "Age Differences in Wechsler Memory Scale Scores." *Journal of Genetic Psychology, 109,* 135–145, 1966. Adapted with permission of the Helen Dwight Reid Educational Foundation. Published by Heldref Publications, 1319 Eighteenth St., N. W., Washington, D.C. 20036-1802. Copyright © 1966.

cation effects were found and Abikoff et al. (1987) provided prediction equations, taking age and education into account (see Table 6.6). The prediction equations can also be used to generate z scores, thereby enabling comparison of individuals at different ages and educational levels. This standard score is obtained by subtracting the predicted score from the actual score and dividing by the *SD* (given in Table 6.6).

Ivnik et al. (1991) expressed delayed free recall on the LM and VR subtests as "percent retention" scores based on the amount of information originally learned and found no relation with age, education, or IQ. Therefore, norms by age were not considered necessary. Haaland et al. (1983) reported a similar finding. This feature of memory performance may prove to be useful clinically, if this lack of relationship to age, education, and IQ can be replicated.

D'Elia, Satz, and Schretlen (1989) critically reviewed the existing studies that provide norms for the WMS. They noted differences between studies in the amount of detail provided concerning the sample and procedural variables such as scoring methods. In addition to these limitations, they commented that there are no reliable delayed recall data for the AL subtest for any age group. Moreover, there are no data available regarding recognition testing on delay for any of the original or modified WMS subtests. They go on to indicate that without assessment of delayed recognition for material not recalled, it is not possible to ascertain whether the manifest deficit is one of encoding or retrieval.

TABLE 6.5
Means and Standard Deviations on
WMS by WAIS–R Full Scale IQ Group

	IQ			
WMS Scales	<90 (n = 27)	90–100 (n = 22)	101–110 (n = 34)	>110 (n = 15)
Information	4.5	5.2	5.5	5.7
	(1.3)	(.7)	(.6)	(.7)
Orientation	4.7	4.8	4.9	6.0
	(.5)	(.4)	(.3)	(.0)
Mental Control	4.9	6.0	6.8	7.9
	(2.2)	(1.5)	(1.6)	(1.4)
Logical Memory	5.6	7.9	9.1	10.5
	(2.3)	(2.6)	(2.7)	(2.9)
Digit Span	9.0	10.2	11.0	10.9
	(1.5)	(1.5)	(1.8)	(2.0)
Visual Reproduction	3.4	6.1	7.1	9.3
	(2.1)	(2.6)	(3.0)	(2.6)
Associate Learning	10.8	13.1	13.3	14.4
	(2.8)	(3.2)	(3.4)	(3.4)
Raw Total	42.9	53.4	57.6	63.6
	(7.5)	(5.8)	(6.6)	(6.4)
Delayed Logical Memory	3.8	6.3	7.0	8.1
	(2.5)	(2.6)	(2.8)	(3.1)
Delayed Visual Reproduction	2.8	5.0	6.1	8.1
	(2.3)	(3.2)	(3.3)	(3.5)

Note. WMS = Wechsler Memory Scale (D. Wechsler, 1945) and WAIS–R = Wechsler Adult Intelligence Scale–Revised (D. Wechsler, 1981). From "Wechsler Memory Scale: IQ-dependent Norms for Persons Ages 65 to 97 Years," by R. J. Ivnik, G. E. Smith, E. G. Tangalos, R. C. Petersen, E. Kokmen, and L. T. Kurland, 1991, *Psychological Assessment, 3,* p. 160. Copyright © 1991 by the American Psychological Association. Reprinted with permission.

To address some of the shortcomings of the WMS, an extensive revision was undertaken in 1987 with modifications to the original WMS subscales (as indicated in Table 6.1). In addition to improving scoring procedures for some subtests, delayed recall components were added for LM, Verbal Paired Associates (VerbalPA), and VR. Two of the three new subtests (Visual Memory Span: VMS; and Visual Paired Associates: VisualPA) were designed as visual counterparts to the DS and VerbalPA subtests.

The subscales from the *Wechsler Memory Scale–Revised* (WMS–R; D. Wechsler, 1987) are combined into four Index scores: Attention/Concentration, Verbal Memory, Visual Memory, Delayed Recall. A General Memory index score is obtained using a sum of the weighted raw scores for the Verbal Memory and Visual Memory components. Each of the five index scores has a mean of 100 and a standard deviation of 15. In addition, the manual

TABLE 6.6
Equations to Predict WMS Subtest Scores From Age and Education

Recall Measure	Equation	SD
Gist		
Immediate	$6.72 + .20$ (age) $+ .93$ (education) $- .003$ (age^2)	6.01
Delayed	$3.40 + .26$ (age) $+ .90$ (education) $- .003$ (age^2)	6.56
24-hour	$3.00 + .19$ (age) $+ .98$ (education) $- .003$ (age^2)	6.41
Verbatim		
Immediate, Form I	$4.39 - .03$ (age) $+ .62$ (education)	4.83
Immediate, Form II	$5.20 - .01$ (age) $+ .57$ (education)	4.32
Delayed, Form I	$2.37 - .05$ (age) $+ .55$ (education)	4.27
Delayed, Form II	$2.92 - .02$ (age) $+ .56$ (education)	4.09
24-hour, Form I	$1.31 - .05$ (age) $+ .58$ (education)	3.77
24-hour, Form II	$2.37 - .05$ (age) $+ .65$ (education)	3.91

Note. WMS = Wechsler Memory Scale (D. Wechsler, 1945). From "Logical Memory Subtest of the Wechsler Memory Scale: Age and Education Norms and Alternate-form Reliability of Two Scoring Systems," by H. Abikoff, J. Alvir, G. Hong, R. Sukoff, J. Orazio, S. Solomon, and S. Saravay, 1987, *Journal of Clinical and Experimental Neuropsychology, 9,* p. 446. Copyright © 1987 by Swets & Zeitlinger Publishers. Used with permission.

contains tables of the following data: cumulative frequencies for the number of Information and Orientation questions answered correctly by each age group (i.e., 55–64, 65–69, 70–74), the percent passing each Information and Orientation question by age, percentile equivalents of raw scores of DS and VMS (Forward and Backward) by age, percentile equivalents of raw scores for LM I by age group, percentile equivalents of raw scores for LM II by age group, percentile equivalents of raw scores for VR I by age group, and percentile equivalents of raw scores for VR II by age group.

The normative sample did not include people over age 74. Moreover, data are only available for some of the individual (i.e., not combination) subscale scores. Test users, then, have limited flexibility in selecting specific subtests from the WMS–R for use. In many circumstances, it is not necessary or possible to administer the entire battery, although specific subtests would be of interest to clinicians.

Additional normative information from the WMS–R has been collected on older age groups. Cullum, Butters, Troster, and Salmon (1990) examined forgetting rates for verbal and nonverbal material for 47 persons age 50 to 70 and 32 persons age 75 to 95. Despite equivalent scores on measures of global cognitive status and attention/concentration, the older group demonstrated significantly more rapid forgetting rates on the VR, VerbalPA, and VisualPA subtests. The severity and pattern of losses appeared useful in differentiating "abnormal" forgetting from that exhibited by normal elderly persons. Lichtenberg and Christensen (1992) extended the normative data on the LM subtests of the WMS–R by examining 66 cognitively intact geriatric medical patients (age 70 to 99) from an urban hospital. All participants scored 129 or greater on the Dementia Rating Scale (DRS; see chap. 3) and showed no evidence of medical conditions of sufficient severity to affect their cognitive functioning on medical history review. Analyses indicated that LM scores for Forms I and II were uncorrelated with education, race, sex, or age (Form I, $M = 17.8$, $SD = 5.8$; Form II, $M = 13.7$, $SD = 6.6$).

Ivnik et al. (1992b) provided age-specific norms for the WMS–R on a sample of 441 cognitively normal persons age 56 to 94 (see chap. 2 for a description of this sample and methods). Some differences in administration and scoring of the MAYO adaptation of the WMS–R exist. The only difference in administration procedure from the WMS–R is that only three learning trials were allowed during both the VisualPA and VerbalPA I subtests. This administration difference, then, precludes computation of the standard WMS–R Delayed Recall index for this sample and these norms. However, delayed recall (30 minutes) data for this administration of the subtest were obtained and combined with the LM and VR Delayed Recall scores to define the MAYO Delayed Recall Index.

The MAYO system contains several major computational differences from the WMS–R but the overall results are similar, though not identical, using the two systems. First, all subtest raw scores are converted to age-corrected and normalized scaled scores (MOANS Scaled Scores). These age-corrected scaled scores have a mean of 10 and a standard deviation of 3 thereby allowing intersubtest comparisons. Second, the MOANS Scaled Score for each subtest is weighted using different weights from the traditional WMS–R. Third, the weighted MOANS Scaled Scores are grouped and summed into the same subtest groupings as the traditional WMS–R. Fourth, the subtotal for the Visual subtests (Figural Memory + VR I + VisualPA I) is divided by 3 before specifying the weighted MOANS Scaled Score sum to be converted to the MAYO Visual Memory Index. Fifth, one new index, the MAYO Percent Retention Index, is computed. This measure evaluates delayed recall as a function of the amount of data originally learned as distinct from the absolute amount of data remembered (already captured by MAYO Delayed Recall Index). To obtain this score, the LM II and VR II scores are expressed as a percentage of the LM I (LMII/LMI × 100) and VR I (VRII/VRI × 100) scores. These values are then converted to age-corrected and normalized MOANS Scaled Scores and weighted. Finally, the six weighted MOANS Scaled Score sums are converted to their respective indices. Ivnik et al. (1992b) provided tables to convert raw scores to MOANS scaled scores and the weighted MOANS Scaled Score Sums to MAYO Indices.

As indicated by Spreen and Strauss (1991), the WMS–R takes longer to administer than the WMS. There is no parallel form and the new "nonverbal" tests are not pure measures of visual learning/memory. The continued absence of recognition tasks limits the capabilities of the scale as noted for the WMS and, although delayed recall tasks have been added, the WMS–R content does not reflect developments in memory theory since the publication of the WMS (D. Wechsler, 1945). As published, the WMS–R lacks norms for persons over age 74 and the lack of normative data for individual subscales (e.g., Verbal PA) limit the user's ability to select specific components of interest from this measure. However, the availability of the MOANS normative data for persons over age 60 overcomes some of these limitations and has made the WMS–R the choice of many clinical practitioners working with older persons. Being able to generate normalized scaled scores for the individual subtests increases the flexibility of the measure and the inclusion of the Percent Retention score makes the WMS–R more contemporary in relation to developments in memory theory. However, the differences in administration and scoring between the traditional WMS–R and the Mayo version must not be overlooked if the obtained scores are to be meaningful. Care must be taken to ensure that *only three learning trials* are administered during the VisualPA and VerbalPA I subtests if the MOANS Scaled Scores are to be calculated for these measures.

The *Guild Memory Test* was introduced in 1968 (Gilbert, Levee, & Catalano, 1968) to assess immediate and delayed recall of paragraphs, immediate and delayed recall of paired associates, digit span (forward and reversed), and recall of geometric designs. The measure was originally standardized on 834 persons between age 20 and 69. Crook, Gilbert, and Ferris (1980) extended the normative data collection to include 228 persons age 60 to 80 residing in the community. Persons with psychiatric disorders and/or medical problems that may have interfered with the assessment were excluded, as were individuals who scored less than a WAIS Vocabulary scaled score of seven. Cutoff scores (i.e., next possible subtest score one standard deviation below the mean score attained) were determined for each subtest. They noted that "we do not suggest that the Guild criterion is suitable for any application other than clinical research" (p. 1318).

More recently, batteries of measures have been developed that address constructs arising from memory theory such as encoding strategies, learning rates, consistency of recall, degree of vulnerability to interference, retention of information over time, error types, and improvement with cued recall and recognition testing. The *Memory Assessment Scales* (MAS; Williams, 1991b) represent a battery of tasks derived from the memory assessment literature in clinical psychology, cognitive psychology, and neuropsychology. Although no one memory battery could reasonably assess all of the tasks identified in the literature, the MAS includes measures of verbal and nonverbal attention, concentration, and short-term memory; verbal and nonverbal learning and immediate memory; memory for verbal and nonverbal material following delay; recognition, intrusions during verbal learning recall, and retrieval strategies. The 12 subtest scores, based on seven memory tasks, are summarized in Table 6.7.

In addition to 12 subtest scores, three Summary Scale scores and a Global Memory Score are calculated: the Short-term Memory score (based on the Verbal Span and Visual Span subtests); the Verbal Memory Summary Scale (based on the List Recall and Immediate Prose Recall); and the Visual Memory Summary Scale score (based on the Visual Reproduction and Immediate Visual Recognition scores). The Global Memory Scale score is based on the Verbal and Visual Memory Summary Scale scores. Verbal Process scores, which probe strategies underlying performance on the list learning subtest, can also be examined. For example, frequent *Intrusions* indicates problems discriminating relevant from irrelevant responses. The content of intrusion (e.g., within semantic category, irrelevant) may provide clues as to type of learning strategy being used. *Clustering* indicates whether or not semantic categories are being used to aid recall, with a high score indicating use of efficient strategy to assist recall. If *Cued Recall* is intact in the context of poor free recall, a retrieval problem is evident. However, if Cued Recall is also poor, an encoding deficit may be implicated. When *List Recognition* is intact in the context of poor free recall, retrieval problems are evident. If both free recall and List Recognition are poor, then a deficit in encoding may be apparent.

The normative sample (Williams, 1991b) consisted of 843 adults age 18 to 90. In the age groups 60–69 years and 70+ years, there were 190 and 156 subjects in the normative sample, respectively. Three sets of normative tables are provided in the manual; 467 subjects reflecting the distribution of the U.S. population, 843 subjects grouped by age decade up to 70+ years, and 843 subjects grouped by age and three levels of education (less than or equal to 11 years, 12 years, and greater than or equal to 13 years).

Raw scores are converted to scaled scores ($M = 10$, $SD = 3$) for each subtest. Scaled scores are summed to derive the four summary Standard scores ($M = 100$, $SD = 15$ for Short-term Memory, Verbal Memory, Visual Memory, and Global Memory). The method of continuous norming (see chap. 2 for a description of this method) was used to derive the separate normative data for age decade and age by education classifications for all subtests, Summary Scales, and Global Memory Scale. Verbal Process scores were too highly skewed to warrant this process. Thus, normative data for the Verbal Process scores were determined by calculating raw score ranges above and below the mean minus one standard deviation.

This battery is new and little research has, as yet, been generated. In its favor, the norms for older persons are substantial and it allows for a variety of memory processes to be examined. Lezak (1995) noted that some information seems to be lost by not scoring the story recall or the

TABLE 6.7

Memory Assessment Scales (Williams, 1991) Subtests

Subtest	Description	Score
List Learning	Auditory verbal learning task of 12 common words; 3 of each from 4 semantic categories (countries, colors, birds, cities); 6 recall trials or until recalls all 12	Total = List acquisition score; additional scores = intrusions, successive clustering
Prose Memory	Auditory verbal prose recall task—recall a short story; then asked 9 questions about details of story	Immediate Prose Recall score = number of correct responses to questions; serves as interference task for next List Recall
List Recall	Recall list learning; recall within cued semantic categories; recognition from printed list of 24	List Recall score = number words recalled. Additional scores = intrusions, successive clustering, list recognition
Verbal Span	Short-term auditory memory; repeat increasing longer series of numbers; forward and backward like Digit Span	Verbal Span score is combination of F and B
Visual Span	Points to series of stars in specified sequence	Visual Span = longest sequence
Visual Recognition	Recognition memory for geometric (nonverbal) designs. 5 = same/different; 5 = recognition from an array	Immediate Visual Recognition score = score of all 109 trials
Visual Reproduction	Two trials, reproduce nonverbal geometric design, distractor between presentation and reproduction. Scored for presence or absence of details	Visual Reproduction score = scores for the two drawings
Names–Faces	Associate verbal and nonverbal material; learn the names of people in photographs, after learning trials must recognize name from brief list of alternatives	Immediate Names–Faces = sum of two trials
Delayed List Recall	Recall words from List Learning, then cued semantic recall	Delayed List Recall = number of words recalled, additional scores = intrusions, successive clustering
Delayed Prose Recall	Asked to recall story, then asked nine questions	Number correct to nine questions = score
Delayed Visual Recognition	20 printed geometric designs, 10 from Visual Recognition	Number recognized = score
Delayed Names–Faces Recall	Asked to identify names from photos	Number correctly identified

101

delayed design recall. Moreover, it was suggested that the designs seem to be fairly verbalizable despite being referenced as nonverbal tasks in the MAS manual. Finally, Lezak (1995) questioned the conceptual pooling of subtest scores to generate summary scores.

VERBAL MEMORY MEASURES

In addition to the aforementioned memory batteries, there are a number of other traditional memory measures for which normative data have been collected for older samples. List learning tasks are perhaps the most commonly used measure of memory functioning in older populations. During informal mental status screening, the examinee is often given a list of three or four words to repeat, with instructions to remember these words for later recall. Repetition is required to ensure that the words have been registered appropriately. Once the words have been adequately registered, individuals engage in other tasks for approximately 5 minutes after which they are asked to recall the words. Although thorough normative data do not exist for this measure, errors are not uncommon in large studies of normal elderly persons and such simple tasks most likely lack sensitivity and specificity.

Other list learning tasks are also available for use with older persons across a range of difficulty levels. The *Hopkins Verbal Learning Test* (HVLT) was designed as a very brief test of verbal memory. Six equivalent forms have been developed and preliminary standardization and validation data were presented by Brandt (1991). Each of the six forms of the HVLT consists of a 12-item word list composed of four words from each of three semantic categories. The examinee is instructed to listen carefully to the words and try to memorize them. The instructor reads the words at a rate of one word every 2 seconds. The examinee's free recall of the list is recorded. This procedure is repeated for a total of three trials. After the third recall trial, the examinee is read a list of 24 words and asked to indicate, after each word, whether or not that word was contained in the recall list. Half of the 12 distracter words were from the same semantic categories as the targets words (related distracters) and the remainder were from other categories (unrelated distracters).

Equivalency of the six forms and the sensitivity of the HVLT to conditions that may affect memory (i.e., Alzheimer's disease, global amnesia) have been demonstrated by Brandt (1991). The availability of alternate forms makes this measure attractive. However, relatively little information is as yet available addressing possible age differences on this measure and it may be that, with only 12 items, it lacks sensitivity to mild memory impairments, particularly in younger people. On the other hand, its brevity makes it an attractive task for use with frail individuals or in settings where limited assessment time is available.

The *Auditory Verbal Learning Test* (AVLT; Rey, 1964) was originally designed in French for children but has been translated into English and used with samples of all ages. A 15-word list is read at a rate of one word per second immediately after which free recall of the words in any order is requested. This procedure is followed for five learning trials. A second list of 15 words is then read and recall of that list is requested (List B). Following recall of this second list, recall of the original list is requested *without re-presentation* of the first list (List 7). A 30-item recognition list may then be administered or a 30-minute delayed recall of the first list may be requested.

In 1983, Query and Megran observed age-related declines in AVLT scores for recall, recognition, and learning. Subjects were 677 male inpatients ranging in age from 19 to 81 years. One hundred and six of these subjects were age 60 or older. They provided means and standard deviations for ages 60–64 ($n = 57$), 65–69 ($n = 26$), and 70+ ($n = 23$). In contrast, Bolla-Wilson and Bleecker (1986) found age was only related to performance on the first two trials in a sample of 114 healthy volunteers between age 40 and 80. Higher verbal intelligence was associated with better performance on the AVLT and women consistently performed better than men (see Table 6.8). G. Geffen, Moar, O'Hanlon, Clark, and L. B. Geffen (1990) examined the AVLT performance of 153 adults grouped into age categories with approximately equal number of males and females per group and matched for intelligence, education, and occupation. Forty-four persons age 60 and over were included, and classified into two age groups (60–69 and 70+ years of age). Overall performance declined with age and females performed better than males. A number of verbal learning indices were derived from the AVLT scores, including recall for each trial, the total recall summed over the five learning trials, total number of repeated words over five trials, the number of extra-list intrusions over the five learning trials, List B recall, List 7 recall, and a 20-minute delayed recall. Following the 20-minute delayed recall trial, the subject was asked to identify the words from the original list from a printed list of 50 words containing the 15 target items, the 15 words from List B and an additional 20 phonemically or semantically similar distracter words. G. Geffen et al. (1990) presented means and standard deviations for age by gender groupings.

Data on the AVLT were collected as part of the Canadian Study of Health and Aging (see chap. 2 for a description of this sample and methods). The True Positive and True Negative scores from the Recognition component were not examined in the same fashion as the rest of the data due to nonnormality of regression residuals. Instead, the frequency distribution for each of these measures was examined with scores of 12 or less

TABLE 6.8
Performance Means and Standard Deviations on the AVLT by Sex
and WAIS–R Vocabulary Subtest Raw Scores

Trial	Men on Vocabulary		Women on Vocabulary	
	<50 *(n = 16)*	*>50* *(n = 39)*	*<50* *(n = 16)*	*>50* *(n = 43)*
1	5.6	6.6	5.9	7.1
	(1.6)	(1.5)	(1.4)	(1.4)
2	7.7	9.5	9.3	9.9
	(1.9)	(2.2)	(1.9)	(1.8)
3	9.6	10.6	11.2	11.4
	(2.0)	(2.7)	(1.6)	(2.3)
4	9.7	11.4	12.0	12.4
	(2.7)	(2.5)	(1.8)	(2.1)
5	10.6	12.6	12.4	13.2
	(2.2)	(2.2)	(2.0)	(2.1)
Recognition	13.6	14.3	14.5	14.3
	(1.8)	(1.1)	(1.0)	(1.0)

Note. AVLT = Auditory Verbal Learning Test and WAIS–R = Wechsler Adult Intelligence Scale–Revised (D. Wechsler, 1981). Vocabulary groups derived from the raw scores on the WAIS–R Vocabulary subtest. From "Influence of Verbal Intelligence, Sex, Age, and Education on the Rey Auditory Verbal Learning Test," by K. Bolla-Wilson and M. L. Bleecker, 1986, *Developmental Neuropsychology, 2*, p. 207. Copyright © 1986 by Lawrence Erlbaum Associates, Inc. Reprinted with permission.

(True Positives) and 13 or less (True Negatives) falling one standard deviation below the mean. Tuokko and Woodward (1996) provided exact predicted score values for age and education by gender and *T*-scores for which provided the optimal balance between sensitivity and specificity for each derived score.

Three sets of normative data for the AVLT have been generated from the Mayo Clinic group. Ivnik et al. (1990) presented age-specific norms based on a sample of 394 persons age 55 years and over (see chap. 2 for a description of this sample and methods). Although Ivnik et al. (1990) presented descriptive statistics on a trial-by-trial basis, they introduced four summary scores for the AVLT (see Table 6.9) and included normative information for each one. Since the Total Learning (TL) score does not capture information about learning occurring after Trial 1, a Learning Over Trials (LOT) score was calculated as an estimate of actual improvement over trials using information from all five learning trials. The two measures of percent retention reflect short-term retention (data recalled at Trial 7) and the other reflecting long-term retention (i.e., 30-minute delayed free recall).

R. C. Petersen, G. Smith, Kokmen, Ivnik, and Tangalos (1992) examined 161 community dwelling, cognitively normal individuals age 62 to 100

TABLE 6.9
Description of Ivnik et al.'s (1990) AVLT Summary Scores

Summary Score Title	Content
Total Learning (TL)	Sum of words recalled across Trials 1 through 5.
Learning Over Trials (LOT)	TL − (5 × Trial 1 recall); that is, TL corrected for immediate word span or number of words recalled on Trial 1.
Short-term Percent Retention (STPR)	100 × (List A Trial 6 Recall/Trial 5 Recall); number of words recalled on List A Trial 6 expressed as a proportion of the number of words recalled on Trial 5.
Long-term Percent Retention (LTPR)	100 × (30-minute Delayed Recall Score/Trial 5 Recall); number of words recalled on 30-minute Delayed Recall expressed as a proportion of the number of words recalled on Trial 5.

recruited as part of the Mayo Clinic Alzheimer's Disease Patient Registry. Total Learning (TL), or acquisition, scores were found to decline with age but were not related to education. Delayed recall, expressed as a change from the fifth learning trial to the 30-minute delayed recall trial (or forgetting) remained stable over age and education level. Means and standard deviations for delayed recall from combined groups were presented.

Ivnik et al. (1992c) updated their AVLT norms to be consistent with the methodology applied to the WAIS–R (see chap. 4) and the WMS–R. That is, AVLT scores (see Table 6.10) were converted to age-corrected and

TABLE 6.10
Ivnik et al.'s (1992) AVLT Summary Scores

Summary Index	Content
MAYO Auditory-Verbal Learning Efficiency Index (MAVLEI)	MOANS Trial 1 Scaled Score + MOANS LOT Scaled Score
MAYO Auditory-Verbal Delayed Recall Index (MAVDRI)	MOANS List A Trial 6 Scaled Score + MOANS 30-minute Delayed Recall Scaled Score
MAYO Auditory-Verbal Percent Retention Index (MAVPRI)	MOANS STPR (see Table 6.9) Scaled Score + MOANS LTPR (see Table 6.9) Scaled Score
	List B
	Recognition

normalized MOANS Scaled Scores ($M = 10$, $SD = 3$), thus making them directly comparable to the MOANS WAIS–R and WMS–R data. The Scaled Scores were then grouped and summed to yield three MAYO Auditory-Verbal Indices: a learning efficiency index, a delayed recall index, and a percent retention index. Tables converting the Scaled Score sums to MAYO Index scores are also presented. The inclusion of summary scores and the elimination of the Total Learning (TL) score are departures from Ivnik et al.'s previous AVLT work, but were done to enable the direct comparison of AVLT scores with WAIS–R and WMS–R scores. They argued (Ivnik et al., 1992c) that TL and LOT are redundant and, within the updated system, Trial 1 and LOT are not redundant and together provide the basis for the Learning Efficiency Index that is conceptually similar to the now abandoned TL.

Perhaps the greatest drawbacks of the AVLT for use with elderly persons are its length and its reliance on auditory input. Hearing problems are common in the elderly and may affect performance on the AVLT. Although most cognitively intact elderly persons are able to complete the AVLT, tolerance of its length and repetitive nature decreases as fatigue and cognitive impairment increase. Thus, the AVLT may be best used with high functioning persons or those for whom the presence of memory impairment continues to be suspect (i.e., very mild deficits). This is not to say that the AVLT cannot be used with persons across the course of a dementia but that compliance problems may increase with disease severity thereby limiting its utility as a monitoring tool.

The basic format of the *California Verbal Learning Test* (CVLT; Delis, Kramer, Kaplan, & Ober, 1987) was modeled after the AVLT (i.e., list learning). The CVLT builds on the knowledge derived from cognitive psychology's understanding of memory functions and incorporates these principles into a test with a scoring system capable of quantifying both the spared and impaired component processes of memory functioning. The CVLT quantifies numerous cognitive components of verbal memory within a single test and provides normative information on how a task is solved, including different strategies, processes, and errors.

In the CVLT, a "shopping" list (Monday list) consisting of 16 words, four words from each of four semantic categories, is presented and followed immediately by a free recall trial. This is repeated for a total of five free recall trials. A second "shopping" list (Tuesday list) is then presented followed immediately by a free recall trial. A "short-delay free recall" of the Monday list is then requested. Next, the participant is provided with a cue for each of the four semantic categories in succession and asked to report all of the items from the Monday list in that category. Nonverbal testing (e.g., block construction or finger tapping) is then administered for 20 minutes, after which a "long-delay" free recall of the Monday list is requested and followed by a "long delay" cued recall of this list. Finally, a list of 44 words is read to participants and they are asked to report whether or not the item was on the Monday list.

The level of the participant's performance on a number of CVLT parameters can then be generated using standard score tables (e.g., short and long delay free recall, clustering, primacy and recency effects, consistency of item recall, perseverations, intrusions, response bias). Delis et al. (1987) described how differences in performance between the various trials may shed light on the underlying type of memory problem manifest. For example, a large negative difference in standard scores between Trial 1 of List A and List B may reflect an unusually high degree of proactive interference.

The normative sample for the CVLT consists of 273 neurologically intact individuals (104 males, 169 females; mean age = 58.93, SD = 15.35; mean educational level = 13.83, SD = 2.70). Because this reference group is a combination of several independently collected samples, smoothed age curves were fitted to raw data using multiple regression. The curve provides an estimate of the mean score at each age for sex, because age and sex accounted for a substantial portion of the variance on all recall measures and for smaller (but statistically significant) proportions on 11 of the 14 other variables. A similar curve-fitting technique was used to estimate the standard deviation at each age and sex. The Standard Score shows the number of standard deviations any raw score deviates from the expected mean for that age and sex. Additional data available in the manual include information on internal consistency, test–retest reliability, validity, factor structure, criterion-related validity, and score patterns of selected neurological groups including Alzheimer's disease and Parkinson's disease.

Normative information is available to age 80 by gender. The scoring systems allow for at least 19 different aspects of memory functioning to be examined. The shopping list nature of the task lends some ecological validity to this measure and may be viewed as assessing something more relevant to daily functioning than other learning lists. However, like the AVLT, the CVLT may be too long for some patient populations, particularly the very old and those with cognitive impairment. According the Lezak (1995), Kaplan developed a 9-item version (3 words from 3 categories) that may be more suitable for these populations, although no norms are as yet available.

Another variant of the list learning task differs in procedure from the aforementioned measures in that selective reminding takes place after the initial recall trial. The earliest and most frequently cited version of this type of measure is the *Selective Reminding Test* (SRT; Buschke, 1973) using a 12-word recall list. Following each trial, only those words not recalled by the subject are presented again by the examiner. Typically, this procedure is repeated until a criterion is met (e.g., 2 consecutive trials completely recalled under the Free Recall condition) or until 12 learning trials have taken place. However, a variety of administration procedures has been employed. In addition, a variety of scores has been derived from the SRT. Other variants (Pictorial cues) have also been developed that use a selective reminding procedure.

Banks, Dickson, and Plasay (1987) administered the SRT to 60 volunteers from seniors' centers, retirement clubs, and churches in Mississippi age 65 to 75. The mean age was 69.2 years ($SD = 3.3$) and the mean number of years of education for this sample was 15.15 (range 6–18.8, $SD = 3.45$). A 12-word list devised by Levin, Benton, and Grossman (1982) was read at a rate of one word every 2 seconds. A maximum of 12 learning trials or 2 consecutive trials completely recalled under free recall was employed. The following salient dependent measures were selected for use in this study: Sum Recall (number of words recalled across all trials), Long-Term Storage (number of words recalled on at least two consecutive trials), Consistent Long-Term Retrieval (number of words recalled on all subsequent trials without reminding), Short-Term Recall (number of words never recalled on two or more consecutive trials), Long-Term Retrieval (number of words not in Consistent Long-Term Retrieval). No age effects were apparent across the age categories 65–69 ($n = 32$), 70–75 ($n = 28$). Females ($n = 37$) performed better than males ($n = 23$) on all summary measures already noted except Long-Term Storage and a significant decrease in recall was apparent from the last recall trial to a 15-minute delay recall trial. Means and standard deviations by gender were presented.

Ruff, Light, and Quayhagen's (1989) normative study of the SRT contained 33 individuals from age 55 to 70. All subjects were screened with an interview questionnaire and selection criteria included no history of neuropathology, no hospitalization for psychopathology, no significant history of drug or alcohol abuse, and English as the primary language. The examiner read a list of 12 discrete words that were individually repeated by the subject to assure initial comprehension of each word. Recall of the list was requested and reminders were subsequently given only for the words not recalled on the free recall trial. This procedure was continued until all 12 words were recalled on two successive trials or when 12 recall trials had been exhausted. Following a 1-hour delay, recall of the list was again requested. No prior warning that a 1-hour delay recall would be requested was given. No significant age or education effects were found within this sample, although a gender effect, with women's performances superior to those of men, was noted.

Larrabee, Trahan, Curtiss, and Levin (1988) provided norms for 7 age groups from age 18 to 91, which include all 11 of the scores defined in Spreen and Strauss (1991). Participants were 271 healthy, nonhospitalized, nonpaid volunteers with no reported history of neurological or psychiatric disorders. The Verbal SRT, Form 1, was administered following the procedures of Buschke (1973) (i.e., words read at 2-second intervals, selective reminding after first recall trial). Learning criterion was recall of all 12 words on 3 consecutive trials or completion of 12 trials. After the final recall trial, a cued recall trial was administered in which cards containing the first two or three letters of the stimulus word were presented and the examinee was asked to identify which word on the stimulus list began with these letters. This was followed by a multiple-choice recognition task. The examinee was asked to discriminate the list word from three foil words (a phonemic foil, a semantic foil, and an unrelated foil) that were printed on 5-by-8 index cards. Thirty minutes later, free recall, without cueing or reminding was assessed. Both age and sex appeared as salient subject variables with education being relatively unimportant. Gender corrections were applied to the data. The normative data for persons age 60 and older are presented in Table 6.11. Note that mean values do not always necessarily sum to the exact totals (e.g., LTR and STR). These small discrepancies appear related to the gender corrections for the different scores (Spreen & Strauss, 1991).

Masur et al. (1989) administered one of four different 12-word versions of the selective reminding task to 134 participants from a longitudinal dementia risk factor study. All persons screened as cognitively normal for 2 consecutive years. The average age of the sample was 80 years with over two thirds being female and less than one third with less than 9 years of education. The words were presented visually (on index card) and were simultaneously read to the persons at 5-second intervals. The person was asked to repeat each word. After the presentation of all 12 words, the person was asked to recall as many words as possible in any order. After 60 seconds, the examiner verbally reminded the individual of words that were not recalled under the free recall condition at 2-second intervals. This procedure was repeated for 6 trials. Immediately after the last trial, the individual was asked to perform 60-second trials of spontaneously generating words within the categories of fruits, animals, flowers, vegetables, and names. Following completion of the 5 category retrieval tasks, subjects were asked to recall as many words from the original list as possible. For words that were not retrieved, during this Delayed Recall (DR) trial, the person was asked to recognize each word from an array of four alternative choices presented verbally and consisting of the word, a semantically related distracter, a phonemically related distracter, and an unrelated distracter. A maximum correct score for Delayed Recall + Delayed Recognition was 12. No significant effects of sex, age, education, or test form were found. Table 6.12 contains the collapsed means and standard deviations for this sample.

TABLE 6.11
Normative Data on the SRT for Persons Age 60 and Older

	Age		
VSRT Measure	60–69 (n = 50)	70–79 (n = 59)	80–91 (n = 27)
LTR	101.52	89.95	77.22
	(24.68)	(29.23)	(26.26)
STR	13.52	17.47	20.74
	(9.52)	(10.41)	(9.62)
LTS	107.00	95.54	87.48
	(21.79)	(24.86)	(25.26)
CLTR	88.92	69.68	54.96
	(35.85)	(35.96)	(29.04)
RLTR	14.66	20.71	22.19
	(11.83)	(14.37)	(10.70)
Reminders	28.12	36.95	43.96
	(15.16)	(15.17)	(15.77)
Intrusions	3.90	4.22	3.30
	(7.29)	(5.76)	(5.09)
Cued Recall	9.58[a]	8.95[b]	8.16[c]
	(1.93)	(2.12)	(2.22)
Multiple Choice	11.96	11.85	11.93
	(.20)	(.58)	(.27)
Delayed Recall	9.58	9.05	8.37
	(2.46)	(2.62)	(2.45)

Note. Correction values for raw scores of males (calculate before entering normative tables). Total = +5; LTR = +9; STR = −4; LTS = +7; CLRT = +13; RLTR = −5; Reminders = −5; Intrusions = 0; Cued Recall = 0; Multiple Choice = 0; Delayed Recall = +1. Caution: Do not correct LTS or CLTR if raw score is 0. From "Normative Data for the Verbal Selective Reminding Test," by G. J. Larrabee, D. E. Trahan, G. Curtiss, and H. S. Levin, 1988, Neuropsychology, 2, p. 179. Copyright © 1988 has been transferred to the American Psychological Association. Adapted with permission.
[a]n = 31.
[b]n = 38.
[c]n = 19.

Deptula et al. (1990) administered five forms of a 16-word SRT to normal young adults and 45 normal elderly persons (age 60 to 79). Of note, these groups had relatively high levels of education (elderly mean = 14.2, SD = 2.9) and age-adjusted performance on the Vocabulary subtest of the WAIS–R (elderly mean = 14.1, SD = 2.4). Words were read at a rate of 3 seconds per word. Seven recall trials of the same list were administered. Each subject received three of the five forms at approximately 1-week intervals (as baseline measures in a drug trial). Scores were corrected for practice effects and the equivalency of the five forms was examined. The five forms showed adequate reliability for the Total Recall measure. Forms 1 and 4

TABLE 6.12
Performance on Components of the SRT for Masur et al.'s (1989)
Normal Elderly Sample ($N = 134$)

Measure	M	SD
Sum Recall	45.53	7.94
LTR	34.97	11.51
STR	10.56	4.77
Storage Estimate	9.05	5.01
CLTS	39.63	11.84
CR	24.09	9.43
CLTR	21.34	11.82
Intrusions	0.82	1.16
SDR	6.79	2.68
SDR + DMCR	11.70	0.54

Note. From "Distinguishing Normal and Demented Elderly With the Selective Reminding Test," by D. M. Masur, P. A. Fuld, A. D. Blau, L. J. Thal, H. S. Levin, and M. K. Aronson, 1989, *Journal of Clinical and Experimental Neuropsychology, 11,* p. 621. Copyright © 1989 by Swets & Zeitlinger Publishers. Used with permission.

showed the lowest correlation. Strongest correlations were between Forms 1, 2, and 3. The subcomponents were less consistently reliable than the total score. LTR and CLTR tended to be the most reliable measures. Forms 1 and 4 were again the weakest.

Trahan and Larrabee (1993) examined rate of forgetting using various indices derived from the Verbal SRT in 287 adults age 18 to 91. One hundred and fifty-nine of these individuals were age 50 or older. A forgetting score was defined as an Acquisition Score minus the number of words freely recalled during the 30-minute delayed recall task. Three acquisition scores were used and examined by age: the number of words recalled on the final learning trial, the number of words in long-term storage in the final learning trial, and the number of words in consistent long-term retrieval on the final learning trial. Significant decrements were observed across age groups (18–29, 30–49, 50–69, 70+). Older persons exhibited a higher rate of forgetting than younger persons using the second forgetting index, although the amount forgotten was very modest. When the third forgetting index was used, older persons actually exhibited no forgetting, obtaining higher scores on the delayed task than during acquisition. Percentile ranks for each forgetting score are presented for persons age 50 and over. Trahan and Larrabee (1993) suggested that the second forgetting index (i.e., Trial 12 LTS) appears to be the most useful because it provides the best fit with most traditional models of long-term memory.

The strength and weakness of the SRT lies in the variety of administration and scoring procedures that have been used with this recall paradigm. None of the set of norms presented here are derived from the same administration and scoring procedures. Some studies use 6 learning trials, others 7, and still others 12. Some studies use 12 words, others 16. Some delayed recall intervals are 60 minutes, others 5 minutes. Not all papers clearly identify their departures in administration and scoring procedures. It has been noted that SRT scores are often redundant, perhaps measuring similar components of memory (Larrabee et al., 1988). Moreover, Spreen and Strauss (1991) noted that the operational definitions for some of the subscales may not, in fact, be tapping the hypothesized underlying constructs adequately.

The selective reminding paradigm has been used in a variety of other formats. Schmidt, Tombaugh, and Faulkner (1992) developed measures of memory for verbal passages, list, and word-pair learning using a selective reminding paradigm for each. The *Passage* measure consisted of an athematic paragraph containing 31 bits of verbal information. After presentations of the passage, a free recall condition was employed, followed by a cued recall condition (i.e., specific questions asked about the content of the passage). Two learning trials were administered. After a 20-minute delay, free recall of the passage was requested. This was followed by cued recall and a recognition task (4-item multiple-choice format) for items missed under both free and cued recall conditions. The *Word List* measure contained 15 unrelated words presented five times. Following each free recall trial, semantic cues were provided for items missed under free recall. The delayed recall trial included free recall, cued recall, and recognition (i.e., 4-item multiple-choice) components. The *Word Pairs* measure contained 3 easy and 11 hard (8 concrete and 3 abstract) word pairs. Four learning trials were administered. Prior to the first recall trial, the entire list was presented, but only pairs that were missed were presented on the subsequent trial. Following each presentation, the first word of the pair was presented and the person was required to recall the second word. Again, a delayed recall trial was administered consisting of free recall, and recognition (4-item multiple-choice format) components.

Age effects were apparent for all three measures. Older persons benefited more from cueing and recognition than younger subjects. Retention scores also yielded significant age effects that may have been due to the lower initial learning levels of older subjects. When retention scores were examined in terms of percent savings (retention trial score/last learning trial score × 100), age effects typically continued to be evident (except for passage free recall). Tables summarizing the normative data for subjects age 60 and older for these three verbal memory tasks were presented. These measures are components from a more extensive battery of memory tests, the Learning and Memory Battery (LAMB; Tombaugh & Schmidt, 1992).

The *Cued Recall paradigm for memory assessment,* another measure based on a selective reminding procedure, was introduced by Buschke (1984) specifically for use with elderly populations. In his original study, Buschke displayed line drawings of 12 common objects in random order to 10 persons over age 60 and asked them to locate and name each picture in response to a stimulus cue (e.g., Which one is a piece of clothing?). Following this search condition, the pictures were removed and the person was asked to count backward from 100 for 60 seconds as a distraction task. After 60 seconds had passed, the person was asked to recall as many of the pictured items as possible in any order. When the subject was no longer able to provide additional responses (> 20 seconds), the semantic stimulus cues were given for all items missed on free recall. If any items were not recalled under free or cued recall conditions, then the pictures were once again displayed and the person was asked to search for and name only those items (i.e., missed under both free and cued recall). The pictures were once again removed from view. The same recall procedures were followed for six learning trials. In developing this measure for use with the elderly, the search procedure was employed to ensure or enhance encoding, because encoding has been implicated as contributing to memory deficits of older persons. Three different channels were employed to assist in encoding (i.e., visual pictures, category cues and naming). Thus, unlike many other memory measures, this procedure was designed to facilitate and control initial encoding of the to-be-remembered items so that deficits in retrieval and acquisition could be more clearly examined. A retrieval score was generated by summing the items across trials under the free recall condition. An acquisition score was derived by summing items across trials for both free and cued recall conditions. This basic procedure was later modified by Tuokko et al. (Tuokko & Crockett, 1989; Tuokko, Vernon-Wilkinson, Weir, & Beattie, 1991) to standardize the layout of the stimulus figures, reduce the number of learning trials to three, and include a delayed learning trial (5-minute delay later modified to 15-minute delay). Four summary scores were identified by Tuokko et al.: FR on Trial 1, Retrieval (sum of free recall over three trials), Acquisition (sum of FR + CR over three learning trials), and Retention (sum of FR + CR for delayed recall trial).

Data on Tuokko et al.'s (1989, 1991) modification of the Cued Recall paradigm were collected as part of the Canadian Study of Health and Aging (see chap. 2 for a description of this sample and method). The Acquisition and Retention scores were not examined in the same fashion as the rest of the data due to nonnormality of regression residuals. Instead, the frequency distribution for each of these measures was examined with a Retention score of 0–11 falling below the 16th percentile. For persons age 65 to 84, an Acquisition score of 0–35 fell more than one standard deviation below the mean, whereas for persons 85+, scores of 0–34 fell in this range. Tuokko and Woodward (1996) provided exact predicted score values for age and education by gender. The *T*-score for Retrieval that provided the optimal balance between sensitivity (.83) and specificity (.94) was 34.

Grober, Buschke, Crystal, Bang, and Dresner (1988) modified the basic cued recall paradigm to include 16 items, presenting 4 items at a time. After each set of four items was searched, identified, and named, immediate verbal cued recall of just those four items was tested by presenting each cue. Once all four items were recalled correctly in response to the cues, the next set of four items was presented for the search procedure. After all 16 items were searched and recalled through immediate cued recall, three recall trials, each preceded by 20 seconds of interference (counting backward) were conducted. Each recall trial consisted of two parts: 2 minutes for free recall and cued recall of those items not recalled under the free recall condition. If an item was not retrieved within 10 seconds of category cue presentations, a reminder of the item was given. Immediately following the last recall trial, the word and an equal number of related and unrelated foils were presented to assess recognition memory. One word at a time was presented and the participant was asked to decide whether or not the word was in the memory list. This procedure has been effective in correctly classifying 71/73 dementia cases and 47/47 cognitively intact individuals (Grober & Buschke, 1987; Grober et al., 1988).

R. C. Petersen et al. (1992) collected data for 161 persons age 60 and older with this basic procedure. Six recall trials were employed and a delayed recall trial was administered after 30 minutes. No recognition task was employed. Correlations with age were noted for a variety of scores derived from this measure. Mean and standard deviations for a variety of scores by age were presented.

Another learning/retention measure developed specifically for use with older persons is the *Aronson Shopping List* (ASL; Aronson, 1985). Tsang, Aronson, and Hayslip (1991) noted that most existing measures of memory have little face validity with respect to personal relevance for an elderly individual and motivational/emotional factors may confound their performance on these measures. The ASL was designed specifically to help differentiate learning/memory dysfunction or impairment from states of benign forgetfulness among older individuals. ASL training requires the person to learn a shopping list of 10 noun–adjective pairs with nouns used as the stimulus for recall. Pairs were chosen to balance gender interests and to form unusual combinations (e.g., wide magazine). The list is presented at a rate of 3 seconds between pairs and 1 second between noun–adjectives. All pairs are presented in a predetermined order in the first through third trials. Thereafter, pairs are eliminated once they are recalled accurately. Immediate feedback is given after each recall attempt. One point is given for each error in the first three trials and two points are given for each error thereafter. The test is terminated after an errorless trial or after 7 training trials. Delayed recall, or ASL retention, is assessed after approximately 30 minutes of additional testing, which does not include verbal memory tasks. Delayed recall responses are given 10 points for each correct adjective, 5 points for each synonym, and 2 points for any adjective that is recalled but mispaired. Unrelated responses or guesses are given 0 points.

Tsang et al. (1991) provided normative information for a group of 81 persons between the age of 61 and 87 recruited through newspaper ads and visits to organizations such as American Association of Retired Persons. They were paid a small hourly wage for participation. Eighty-three percent had more than a high school education and 93% reported their health status as "good" to "excellent."

Participants under age 75 differed from those over age 75, when other demographic variables were controlled, on ASL training error score and number of adjectives recalled after delay. Females made fewer errors than males. Training error and retention scores, adjusted statistically to control for the effects of other demographic variables, were presented. Tsang et al. (1991) suggested that training error scores greater than 10 be used to identify impairment for females under age 75 who graduated from high school. Two additional points could be allowed for those whose education was below eighth grade and one point for those who completed more than grade eight but did not complete high school. They also suggested that two points be added to scores for males, and one point for each 5 years of age beyond 75.

Tsang et al. (1991) asserted that the presence of a problem performing either of these tasks is suggestive of processes other than normal aging but, as yet, it is unclear whether or not the measure will be sensitive to mild memory impairments.

The *Recognition Memory Test* (RMT) is actually two tests, parallel in form but providing verbal (words) and relatively nonverbalizable (faces) stimuli for assessing material specific memory deficits. Each test contains 50 stimulus items and 50 distracters. Diesfeldt and Vink (1989) extended the normative data on the RMT for faces to include 89 subjects between age 69 and 93. The standard recognition for faces was used (i.e., all faces are male and for the recognition trial each item is paired with a photo of man of similar age and degree of hairiness with randomized positions). As in the original version, the stimuli were presented at 3-second intervals. The subject was to judge the pleasantness of the stimulus. Recognition memory was assessed immediately after presentation by asking the subject which item of a pair (item and distracter) had been seen earlier.

In Warrington's (1984) original version, raw scores are converted to percentile scores for three age groups (18–39, 40–54, 55–70, or to standardized scaled scores with a range of 3 to 18), thereby limiting their use with older individuals. Diesfeldt and Vink (1989) found that the RMT for faces was acceptable for use with normal elderly persons in that it was not overly time consuming and that the distribution of scores revealed no ceiling effects. Distribution of scores on the RMT for faces shows a decline across age groups. Diesfeldt and Vink (1989) noted that the RMT for faces is not independent of intellectual ability and this needs to be considered when interpreting performance on this measure.

VISUAL LEARNING MEASURES

A number of visual learning measures have normative data for elderly persons. The most frequently used visual recall test, the *Benton Visual Retention Test* (BVRT), has three forms and various administration procedures. The most common of these is a 10-second exposure of each stimulus card followed by immediate recall by drawing (Administration A). Normative data are provided in the test manual for age 8 to 64 (Benton, 1974) with a progressive decline in recall after age 40. Robertson-Tehabo and Arenberg (1989) provided means and standard deviations for persons age 60 to 69 ($n = 28$), 70 to 79 ($n = 47$), and 80 to 89 ($n = 15$) from the Baltimore Longitudinal Study of Aging. A marked decline in performance, particularly after age 70, was noted. Youngjohn, Larrabee, and Crook (1993) presented data for persons age 18 to 70+ at three education levels. The BVRT Administration A (10-second exposure, immediate recall) was administered to 1,128 volunteers who reported no evidence or history of physical, psychiatric, or neurological conditions that could affect memory on a health history questionnaire and who scored within the nondepressed range on the Affective Rating Scale (Yesavage, 1986). Table 6.13 summarizes these data for persons over age 60. Youngjohn et al. (1993) generated the following predicted score equations for specific individuals: Predicted BVRT # correct (+/- 1.57) = 7.87 − .045 (age) + .098 (years of education); Predicted BVRT # errors (+/- 2.88) = 1.73 + .088 (age) − .126 (years of education).

Administration M (10-second exposure, multiple-choice format) has been used with elderly persons to overcome limitations imposed by the drawing response. A number of physical conditions (e.g., arthritis, tremor) may prohibit use of drawing tasks in older persons. Norms in the manual only extend to age 55. K. M. Montgomery (1982) used the multiple-choice version of the BVRT with a 5-second exposure to assess healthy elderly subjects age 65 to 89. Data are summarized in Table 6.14. The BVRT multiple-choice format was administered as part of the Canadian Study of Health and Aging (see chap. 2 for a description of this sample and method).

TABLE 6.13
Normative Data on the BVRT for Persons
Age 60 and Older By Education

| Education | n | BVRT Performance | |
		Mean Correct	Mean Errors
		Age 60–69	
12–14 years	129	6.18	5.55
		(1.67)	(2.74)
15–17 years	159	6.70	4.99
		(1.47)	(2.78)
18+ years	134	6.80	4.93
		(1.55)	(2.87)
		Age 70+	
12–14 years	53	5.62	7.28
		(1.73)	(3.55)
15–17 years	54	6.06	6.74
		(1.84)	(4.34)
18+ years	49	6.22	6.33
		(1.57)	(3.63)

Note. From "New Adult Age- and Education-Correction Norms for the Benton Visual Retention Test," by J. R. Youngjohn, G. J. Larrabee, and T. H. Crook, 1993, *Clinical Neuropsychologist, 7,* p. 158. Copyright © 1993 by Swets & Zeitlinger Publishers. Used with permission.

TABLE 6.14
Performance of Elderly Persons on the BVRT Multiple Choice
With 5-second Exposure

Score	Percentile
6	2.4
7	4.7
8	12.9
9	24.7
10	42.4
11	55.3
12	82.4
13	95.3
14	100.0

Note. From *A Normative Study of Neuropsychological Test Performance of a Normal Elderly Sample* (p. 79) by K. M. Montgomery, 1982, University of Victoria. Unpublished master's thesis. Adapted with permission.

Raw score to scaled score conversions and exact prediction scaled score for the Correct BVRT–MC scores are provided by age, gender, and education (Tuokko & Woodward, 1996).

Another measure of visual memory that requires minimal motor demands is the *Visual Spatial Learning Test* (VSLT; Malec, Ivnik, & Hinkeldey, 1991). The VSLT requires a person to learn to recognize seven designs that are difficult to verbally encode and to recall the correct placement of these designs on a 6 × 4 matrix. After seeing the design placed on the 6 × 4 grid, persons are given an empty grid and 15 designs from which to select and place the 7 targets as they were when seen on the grid. Five learning trials are administered and a 30-minute delayed recall trial. Scores determined for each trial include: the number of correct designs chosen (D), the number of correct positions chosen (P), the number of correct designs placed in the correct position (PD), and the number of incorrect designs (i.e., intrusion errors) (E). Scores were summed over the five learning trials to yield summary scores identified as DSUM, PSUM, and PDSUM. ESUM is the sum of intrusion errors across all trials (i.e., 5 learning + delayed recall trial). Malec et al. noted that because PSUM and PDSUM were highly correlated, only PDSUM was examined. A normative sample of 455 persons age 56 to 97 from the Mayo Older Americans Normative Studies (see chap. 2 for a description of this sample and method) was administered this task (Malec et al., 1991). Conversion of raw ESUM, DSUM, and PDSUM scores to Scaled Scores with a mean of 10 and *SD* of 3 is presented. ESUM did not correlate with age and was standardized on the entire sample. The D and PD scores for the delayed recall trials were handled differently because of the high correlation between these scores and their respective Trial 5 scores. For each possible score on Trial 5, a delayed score was given an impairment score (IS) of −2 (falling below 15th percentile), −1 (falling between 16th and 35th percentile), or 0 (scoring above 35th percentile). This procedure was developed for the entire sample because it was argued that removing the redundancy with Trial 5 would also remove most of the variance associated with age. This procedure was adopted instead of expressing delayed recall scores as a percentage of original learning as percentage scores are often correlated with both the numerator and denominator and thereby only partially reduce the redundancy with Trial 5.

This measure is quite new so little information is yet available. G. E. Smith et al. (1992), in factor analyzing a battery of measures including the VSLT, questioned the validity of the construct of nonverbal memory as distinct from verbal memory, especially in an older normal adult population. However, this does not mitigate the importance of the development of this nonmotor dependent measure of visual memory. Further research and clinical practice will determine the relative usefulness of this measure in relation to others currently available.

Visual memory abilities have also been assessed using the *Rey Osterrieth Complex Figure* (ROCF) and the *Taylor Complex Figure* (TCF) across age ranges. Typically, persons are asked to copy the figure and are not told that they will be asked to reproduce the figure from memory at a later time. Delayed recall is typically required and some investigators also use an immediate recall condition. If an immediate recall condition is used, this serves as a facilitator for future recall trials (i.e., Delayed Recall), consequently it is imperative to use appropriate norms (i.e., same procedure) for these tasks. Spreen and Strauss (1991) provided data for persons over age 60 on the copy with delayed recall version of the ROCF using the scoring criteria provided in their book. In addition to providing data for the 3-minute recall for persons age 45 to 83, Boone, Lesser, Hill-Gutierrez, Berman, and D'Elia (1993) computed a percent retention score. A sample of English-speaking volunteers were screened for history of psychotic or major affective disorder, current or past history of alcohol or other substance abuse, and documented neurological illness and significant medical illness that could affect the central nervous system. In addition, persons who were found to have abnormal neurological examination, metabolic abnormalities detected with blood tests, or abnormal findings on magnetic resonance testing were eliminated from the sample. The final sample consisted of 91 individuals (34 males, 57 females) with a mean educational level of 14.5 ($SD = 2.5$).

Berry, Allen, and Schmitt (1991) administered both the ROCF and the TCF to 107 persons age 50 to 79. Interrater, alternate forms, test–retest, and internal consistency reliabilities were all adequate to good for the recall trials of the ROCF. The ROCF was significantly correlated with age and education but not gender. No normative data were presented but the observed correlations with age and education suggest that these factors be considered when developing adequate norms. A subsequent study by Berry and Carpenter (1992) found no differences when the length of the delay interval was varied (15, 30, 45, or 60 minutes) between age and gender equivalent groups of persons age 60 and older.

Tombaugh, Schmidt, and Faulkner (1992) adopted a different administration procedure for the TCF to control for the duration of stimulus exposure and provide information on rate of learning and level of retention. New scoring methods were also developed. Participants were told that they would be shown a design they would have to draw from memory, they would be given four tries at this, and they would be required to recall the design later. On each of the four trials, the TCF was exposed for 30 seconds. The figure was removed and the subject was allowed 2 minutes to reproduce the figure from memory. Approximately 15 minutes after the last acquisition trial, during which other measures were administered, delayed recall was requested. Following this, the subject was given 4 minutes to copy the TCF with the stimulus figure present. The average amount of time to administer the test, excluding the delay interval, was approximately 13 minutes. An itemized scoring system (Tombaugh, 1989) yielded a maximum of 69 points. Age effects were apparent (see Table 6.15). Data were also expressed as a percent of the copy score. This may be useful for determining whether or not a person with a mild constructional impairment also has a memory deficit over and above the constructional one.

As noted by Lezak (1995), the revised procedure for Tombaugh's version to the TCF allows for the generation of a learning curve, thereby adding important information not obtained on other complex figure tasks. Tombaugh et al. (1992) asserted that, if comparison between visual and verbal memory measures is important to neuropsychologists, then this new procedure more closely parallels the verbal learning measures typically administered and thereby should yield more comparable data than the traditional ROCF or the TCF. Moreover, the inclusion of normative data assisting in

TABLE 6.15
Summary of Data for Persons Age 60 and Older on the TCF

	Age	
Measure	60–69	70–79
Trial 1		
M	28.5	20.7
SD	9.9	10.8
Trial 2		
M	44.3	31.0
SD	13.2	13.3
Trial 3		
M	51.5	39.1
SD	12.0	14.5
Trial 4		
M	55.0	43.6
SD	11.6	14.1
Total Recall		
M	179.3	134.9
SD	43.7	49.6
Delayed Recall		
M	54.6	43.7
SD	11.0	14.8
Copy		
M	65.3	63.0
SD	3.5	4.4

Note. TCF = Taylor Complex Figure. From "A New Procedure for Administering the Taylor Complex Figure: Normative Data Over a 60-year Age Span," by T. N. Tombaugh, J. P. Schmidt, and P. Faulkner, 1992, *Clinical Neuropsychologist, 6,* p. 69. Copyright © 1992 by Swets & Zeitlinger Publishers. Used with permission.

the differentiation of copy versus memory deficits may prove very useful to clinicians. The detailed scoring system may prove to be a limiting factor for those with little scoring time available.

SELF-REPORT MEASURES

Another type of memory measure that may be of use in the assessment of older adults is the report of self-perceived memory functioning. Complaints of changes in memory functioning may accompany the normal aging process and may be of use when compared to objective measures of memory functioning in the diagnostic assessment process (see chap. 10). Gilewski and Zelinski (1986) critically reviewed 10 questionnaires developed to assess memory complaints in older adults. Of these, the psychometric properties of 6 had been investigated. Although they generally recommended the *Memory Functioning Questionnaire* (MFQ; Gilewski, Zelinski, Schaie, & Thompson, 1983) and the *Metamemory in Adulthood instrument* (MIA; Dixon & Hultsch, 1984), both of these measures were primarily designed as research instruments and are probably of excessive length (64 and 120 items, respectively) for most clinical situations.

A shorter measure has been developed that although less conceptually sophisticated than the MFQ and the MIA, may be more practical in most assessment situations. Crook and Larrabee (1992) reported normative data for a measure containing 21 items reflecting a person's ability to remember specific types of information and 24 items reflecting how often specific memory problems occur (*MAC-S*). Both types of items were recorded on a 5-point Likert scale with choices ranging from "very poor" to "very good" on the Ability Scale, and from "very often" to "very rarely" on the Frequency scale. Volunteers age 18 to 92 were recruited to take part in the normative study. All persons identified through interview as having neurological disorders that could produce cognitive changes, major psychiatric disturbance, or a history of substance abuse were excluded from the sample. The MAC–S was administered to 1,106 persons.

The data were grouped into five Ability factors (Remote Personal Memory, Numerical Recall, Everyday Task-Oriented Memory, Word Recall/Semantic Memory, Spatial and Topographic Memory) and five Frequency factors (Word and Fact Recall or Semantic Memory, Attention and Concentration, Everyday-Task Oriented Memory, General Forgetfulness, and Facial Recognition) (Crook & Larrabee, 1992). Total scores for the Ability (max = 21×5) and Frequency scales (max = 24×5) were also calculated, as was the sum for four items rating global memory functioning (e.g., In general, compared to the average individual, how would you describe your memory?; How would you describe your memory, on the whole, as compared to the best it has ever been?). Normative data for persons age 60 to 69 ($n = 346$) and 70+ years ($n = 157$) were presented. A parallel version for family ratings of patient memory functioning (*MAC–F*; Feher, Mahurin, Inbody, Crook, & Pirozzolo, 1991) has also been used to examine differences between patient and family perceptions of memory functioning in persons with Alzheimer's disease.

This measure is quite new and so little information is, as yet, available. There is reason to suspect that dissociations between objective and subjective measures of memory functioning may be of use in a diagnostic context. For example, persons suffering from depression may complain of memory problems but yet perform within the average range on objective measures. Conversely, some persons with Alzheimer's disease seem unaware of their markedly poor performances on measures of memory functioning. Whether or not self-report measures of memory functioning will yield enough meaningful information to warrant their inclusion in clinical practice is yet to be determined.

CONCLUSIONS

It is apparent that the assessment of memory has broadened substantially from the original formulation of the WMS. Many measures, reflecting a variety of theoretical perspectives, are available to the clinician. The issues of age-related changes in memory performance and sensitivity to age-related memory disorders have been incorporated into the construction of many of these newer measures. Selecting the most effective and efficient measure(s) for use in a particular context remains the challenge for the clinician.

Chapter 7

Attention and Executive Functioning

Attention refers to the ability to focus on a simple task and perform it without losing track of the task. If attention is impaired, the individual will also have difficulty performing many other tasks. Although the concept of attention has been the focus of much debate by cognitive psychologists (see Parasuraman & Davies, 1984, and Hasher & Zacks, 1979, for reviews), normative data are available for relatively few commonly employed measures of attention. It must be noted that these measures tend to assess sustained attention rather than other forms of attention (e.g., selective or divided) and, hence, are not comprehensive measures of attention or attentional capacity. These measures have also been considered as methods for assessing working memory (Lezak, 1995) or immediate memory (Trahan, Goethe, & Larrabee, 1989).

Executive functions refer to those capacities that enable a person to engage in independent, purposive, and self-serving behavior (Lezak, 1995). *Executive disorders* can affect cognitive functioning directly by compromising the development of strategies to approach, plan, and carry out activities, or through defective monitoring of the performance (Lezak, 1995). From a psychosocial viewpoint, persons with executive disorders may lack initiative or be unable to plan or carry out the activity sequences that make up goal-directed behaviors. Persons with these disorders often perform well in structured assessment sessions because most measures of cognition only require responses to focused questions and the person is directed (or follows the "plan" provided) by the examiner.

Executive functions are often ascribed to the frontal lobes but are also sensitive to damage in other areas of the brain, most notably subcortical areas (Lezak, 1995). The tasks included here are similar in that they require planning and abstraction of underlying principles for successful completion. However, not all persons with executive disorders will have difficulty performing these tasks. As noted by Lezak (1995), executive disorders may be manifest in many ways. For example, individuals may be able to perform tasks when asked but may be unable to perform these tasks *unless* asked (e.g., getting dressed). It is also important to keep in mind that poor performance on these tasks is not synonymous with frontal lobe damage. Deficits in planning may arise for a number of reasons (e.g., other areas of impaired cognition). Persons with dense memory impairment will have difficulty with complex "planning" tasks like Wisconsin Card Sorting (discussed later) because they may not remember the instructions to the task or the category they were using to search by. Similarly, the person with poor memory may forget to eat and thereby appear unable to perform a self-serving behavior.

Observation or report of behavior is often the way in which deficits in executive function come to light. Marked discrepancies between the observed test performances and the report of everyday functions may suggest underlying disorders of executive functions.

MEASURES OF ATTENTION

Reverse spelling is one example of the ability to reverse a sequential order that is difficult for persons with aphasia (language impairment) or other organic mental disorders (Bender, 1975). Reverse spelling has been incorporated into some screening measures for cognitive impairment (e.g., the Mini-Mental State Examination and the Modified Mini-Mental State Examination, see chap. 3) and examined, in its own right, in relation to age.

The prevalence and degree of disability in performing reverse spelling of 5-, 4-, 3-, and 2-letter words was examined in three groups of persons over age 60 by Bender (1979). Group 1 consisted of 156 persons between age 60 and 88. Thirty-two of these persons were age 75 and older. Group 2 consisted of 100 persons between age 65 and 90. The 5-letter reverse spelling was, by far, the most difficult of the tasks and the incidence in errors increased with age. Similarly, Jenkyn et al. (1985) reported that the incidence of failure on reverse spelling of WORLD increased from 6% at age 50 to 54 years to 21% over age 80 in a sample of 2,029 persons age 50 to 93. These individuals were volunteers from a population of current and retired employees of E. I. Du Pont de Nemours and Company, Inc., in Wilmington, Delaware. None of these persons had a known history of any central nervous system disease, psychiatric disorder, or medical illness with which neurologic and/or psychiatric dysfunction is frequently associated.

Bender (1979) noted that a deficit in reverse spelling may be due to lack of familiarity with language, defective education, and unrecognized congenital dyslexia; impairment of memory; acquired defect in language or aphasia; disability in learning a new order of reverse sequences; perseverative process; specific disability to reverse a series of meaningful or non-meaningful symbols; or a locatable lesion for defect in reversibility. He suggested that the higher incidence of reverse spelling errors for older persons might relate to rigidity in performance or mild new learning deficits seen as a function of normal aging.

Serial sevens, a popular measure of the ability to attend and concentrate on a task, requires the individual to count backward from 100 by 7s (i.e., subtract 7 from 100 and continue subtracting 7 from the remainder). Deficits have been observed in performance on this task by psychiatric and neurological patients (Hayman, 1942; Luria, 1966), although no comparisons with the incidence and types of errors seen in normal adults were made.

As an alternative for reverse spelling, serial seven performance is present on the Mini-Mental State Examination (see chap. 3) but was removed from the Modified Mini-Mental State Examination. At least part of the reason for its removal relates to the lack of comparability between serial sevens and reverse spelling (Ganguli et al., 1990). Moreover, as age increases, performance decreases—as does its potential utility for differentiating between age-related decline and pathological changes in functioning, such as dementia. For example, A. Smith (1967) examined serial seven performance in 132 adults, including 9 persons between age 56 and 63. Of the total sample, 42.5% (i.e., 56/132) performed the task without error. Only 1 of 9 persons over age 55 performed without error.

Another study examined the serial seven performance of 506 users of care services in the Capital Regional District (CRD) of British Columbia. Persons were screened for cognitive impairment using the Adult Lifestyles and Function Interview (ALFI) version of the MMSE (Roccaforte, Burke, Bayer, & Wengel, 1992) in which only the nonwritten components are administered. Using data collected on separate samples of clinically defined normal and demented participants in the Canadian Study of Health and Aging, a cutoff score that yielded sensitivity and specificity of .70 and .75, respectively, was determined for the ALFI items, without including the serial sevens, and applied to the CRD sample. The distribution of errors by age group is shown in Table 7.1 and the distributions of errors for the normal and "cognitively impaired" groups are shown in Table 7.2. The use of serial sevens as a screening instrument for dementia should be approached with caution as errors are not uncommon in normal elderly persons for this task.

A task that reportedly shows little change with age is the repetition of digit series of increasing length. The *Digit Span* subtests of the Wechsler

TABLE 7.1

Frequency of Errors on the First Five Responses on Serial Sevens
for Cognitively Intact Individuals (*N* = 425) by Age Group

	Age				
Number of Errors	65–69 (n = 28)	70–74 (n = 50)	75–79 (n = 81)	80–85 (n = 111)	85+ (n = 155)
0	57.1	64.0	45.7	44.1	42.6
1	10.7	18.0	25.9	19.8	14.8
2	0.0	6.0	9.9	8.2	15.5
3	3.5	2.0	2.5	5.4	7.7
4	7.3	2.0	7.5	10.8	12.9
5	0.0	0.0	0.0	0.0	0.7
Refused the task	10.7	8.0	7.5	11.7	5.8

Note. From T. Goranson, H. Tuokko, L. Rosenblood, and R. Frerichs (October 1997). *Serial Sevens: Myths and Realities.* Poster session presented at the meeting of the Canadian Association on Gerontology, Calgary, Alberta, Canada. Used with permission.

Adult Intelligence Scale Revised (WAIS–R, see chap. 4) and the Wechsler Memory Scale–Revised (WMS–R, see chap. 6) assess digits repetition in forward and reverse order. Generally, little effect of age is seen on repetition of digits (forward) (Craik, 1990; Jarvik, 1988). Although the digits backward task is somewhat more sensitive to the effects of aging, it is less sensitive than other measures of memory (Granick & Friedman, 1967).

Klonoff and Kennedy (1966) reported the performance of a group of 115 community dwelling Canadian male veterans randomly selected from a larger group (*n* = 172) reported in Klonoff and Kennedy (1965; see chap. 6) on the Digit Span subtest of the Wechsler Memory Scale. This group ranged in age from 80 to 92 with a mean of 83.61 years (*SD* = 2.48). A mean performance of 10.20 (*SD* = 1.97) was obtained on the Digit Span subtest.

TABLE 7.2

Percent of Normal (*N* = 425) and Impaired (*N* = 81)
Cases Refusing the Task or Making 0 Through 5
Errors on the First Five Responses to Serial Sevens

Errors	Normal	Impaired
0	47.1	16.0
1	18.4	12.3
2	11.1	8.6
3	5.2	6.3
4	9.6	17.3
5	0.2	0.0
Refused the task	8.4	39.5

Mitrushina and Satz (1989) investigated the performance of 129 persons over age 65 on the number of digits repeated in forward order from the WAIS–R. Although there was no correlation between performance on this task and age, they reported the means and standard deviation by age group: age 66–70 ($M = 7.9$, $SD = 2.7$); age 71–75 ($M = 7.6$, $SD = 2.9$); and age 76–85 ($M = 6.9$, $SD = 3.9$).

The WMS–R provides norms separately for the forward and reverse sequences to age 74. Approximately 50% of their sample age 65 to 69 ($n = 55$) was able to repeat 7 digits forward (52%) and 6 digits backward (60%). Less than 5% repeated 4 digits forward and 2 digits backward. Approximately 50% of their sample age 70 to 74 ($n = 50$) was able to repeat 7 digits forward (46%) and 5 digits backward (48%). Less than 5% repeated 3 digits forward and 2 digits backward.

Farmer et al. (1987) presented normative data for the Digit Forward and Digits Backward components of the WAIS collected as part of the Framingham Heart Study (see chap. 2 for description of this sample). They included data (mean number of digits recalled) by age group (in 5-year intervals), education levels (8–11 years, high school, more than high school) and gender (see Table 7.3). Scores were very similar for males and females. These data reflect poorer performance than that reported by Mitrushina and Satz (1989) and that seen on the WMS–R subtests at the same ages.

Given the lack of age effects in the traditional digit recall tasks already discussed and their insensitivity to various neurological disorders, Trahan et al. (1989) administered a memory span measure containing more than 8 items (i.e., *verbal supraspan*) to 301 persons from age 18 to 91. All of these persons were screened through clinical interview and persons with neurologic or psychiatric disorders were excluded from the sample.

Free recall of a list of 12 unrelated words taken from the Verbal Selective Reminding Test (VSRT; Levin et al., 1982; see chap. 6) was identified as a measure of verbal supraspan. Significant age differences were found with older persons performing below the levels of younger persons. Table 7.4 shows the cumulative percentile ranks for persons over age 65.

The *Paced Auditory Serial Addition Task* (PASAT) is considered a measure of information-processing speed, efficiency, and concentration skills. Extended normative data have been collected on the Galveston version of this measure (Roman, Edwall, Buchanan, & Patton, 1991). In this version, the individual is requested to listen to a series of single-digit numbers, presented at a fixed speed, and add the last digit presented to the digit immediately preceding it. Four separate series of numbers are presented, each separated by a brief pause, with each series presented at a faster pace. The 41 older adults (age 60–75) performed more poorly than the younger age groups (i.e., 18–27, 33–50). The study included the mean number correct, percent correct for each trial, and the total for all trials.

TABLE 7.3
Means and Standard Deviations by Age Group and
Education Level for Women on WAIS Digits
Forward and Backward (Farmer et al., 1987)

Age Group	Digits Forward			Digits Backward		
	8–11 Years Education	*12 Years Education*	*13+ Years Education*	*8–11 Years Education*	*12 Years Education*	*13+ Years Education*
65–69						
M	5.4	6.1	6.1	3.8	4.6	4.5
SD	1.3	1.0	1.3	1.2	1.1	1.2
n	37	51	67	38	52	70
70–74						
M	5.5	5.9	6.4	3.9	4.1	4.8
SD	1.3	.9	1.2	1.1	1.0	1.2
n	35	36	50	36	36	50
75–79						
M	5.4	6.1	6.1	4.0	4.4	4.4
SD	1.0	1.4	1.1	1.2	1.3	1.4
n	28	36	20	29	36	22
80–84						
M	5.5	6.1	5.7	3.8	4.6	4.4
SD	1.3	1.2	1.1	1.2	1.1	1.0
n	16	15	19	16	15	19
85–89						
M	5.1	5.0	5.8	3.3	4.3	3.8
SD	.7	1.0	1.0	.8	1.5	.5
n	7	3	4	7	3	3

Note. Reproduced with permission of authors and publisher from Farmer, M. E., White, L. R., Kittner, S. J., Kaplan, E., Moes, E., McNamara, P., Wolz, M. M., Wolf, P. A., & Feinleib, M. Neuropsychological test performance in Framingham: A descriptive study. *Psychological Reports, 60*, 1987, pp. 1023–1040. Copyright © Psychological Reports, 1987.

Brittain, La Marche, Reeder, Roth, and Boll (1991) also developed norms for the Galveston version of the PASAT and included a group of persons ($n = 122$) over age 54. Normative data for the PASAT by IQ (Shipley Institute of Living Scale) are presented. Detailed instructions for the administration of the PASAT are included as an appendix.

MEASURES OF EXECUTIVE FUNCTIONING

The *Stroop Test* (Jensen & Rohwer, 1966; Stroop, 1935) contrasts performance on a basic task, like color naming, with performance of the task in the presence of conflicting or incongruent stimuli. The Stroop Test comes in different variations but most involve color words (e.g., red, blue, green)

TABLE 7.4
Cumulative Percentile Ranks for Persons Over Age 65 on Recall of
the 12 Unrelated Words From the Verbal Selective Reminding Test

| | *Cumulative Percentile Ranks by Age Group* | |
Score	*66–77 years* *(n = 83)*	*78+ years* *(n = 40)*
9	100.0	
8	97.6	
7	92.8	100.0
6	88.0	92.5
5	60.2	77.5
4	39.8	52.5
3	18.1	30.0
2	7.2	5.0
1	2.4	—
M	4.94	4.43
SD	1.67	1.36

Note. From "An Examination of Verbal Supraspan in Normal Adults and Patients With Head Trauma or Unilateral Cerebrovascular Accident," by D. E. Trahan, K. E. Goethe, and G. J. Larrabee, 1989, *Neuropsychology, 3,* p. 85. Copyright © 1989 has been transferred to the American Psychological Association. Adapted with permission.

printed in congruent or incongruent colors (see Lezak, 1995, for a full discussion of Stroop Color–Word formats). The task is either to read the words or name the colors. Poor performance on this task has been interpreted as reflecting impaired selective attention, a failure of response inhibition, or concentration effectiveness (Lezak, 1995). Moreover, it is often viewed as a general measure of cognitive flexibility (see Spreen & Strauss, 1991). Graf, Uttl, and Tuokko (1995) presented a picture–word version of the Stroop task containing congruent and incongruent picture–word pairs to determine whether or not two versions of the Stroop task (Color–Word and Picture–Word) in fact reflect the same general, as opposed to test-specific, index of cognitive flexibility in a group of older adults. In addition, they developed normative tables for their measures.

Regardless of the variant of the Stroop Test under investigation, slowing with advancing age has been demonstrated. Spreen and Strauss (1991) reported that slowing of color naming and an increase in the Stroop interference effect (difference between congruent and incongruent conditions) appear as the major changes with increasing age. They reported the mean and standard deviation for 67 persons over age 60 using the Modified Stroop Test (Spreen & Strauss, 1991), which uses a 24-item/card format with a preliminary colored dot naming trial.

Graf et al. (1995) presented norms (see Tables 7.5 and 7.6) for their color–word and picture–word versions of the Stroop task arranged by mid-

TABLE 7.5
Means and Standard Deviations (in parentheses) for the Color–Word Stroop Test Performance
(in msec per item) of Various Midpoint Overlapping Age Groups

	Age Group Midpoint and Range						
Score	68 65–71 (n = 50)	71 68–74 (n = 53)	74 71–77 (n = 58)	77 74–80 (n = 44)	80 77–83 (n = 32)	83 80–86 (n = 19)	86 83–95 (n = 11)
Word	421	430	433	439	466	488	490
	(81)	(76)	(68)	(68)	(70)	(76)	(88)
Congruent	416	433	437	436	463	468	468
	(73)	(71)	(70)	(63)	(63)	(69)	(77)
Color	592	633	659	655	730	803	854
	(109)	(129)	(132)	(127)	(156)	(186)	(250)
Incongruent	1087	1157	1211	1266	1379	1502	1564
	(238)	(304)	(322)	(365)	(332)	(387)	(547)
Color–Word	170	202	224	215	254	315	364
	(96)	(120)	(119)	(108)	(145)	(153)	(204)
Incongruent-Color	495	526	554	610	646	699	710
	(230)	(262)	(256)	(292)	(267)	(305)	(366)
Color/Word	1.42	1.49	1.53	1.50	1.58	1.65	1.74
	(.24)	(.30)	(.30)	(.26)	(.33)	(.32)	(.36)
Incongruent/Color	1.85	1.84	1.85	1.95	1.92	1.89	1.83
	(.40)	(.40)	(.37)	(.41)	(.40)	(.39)	(.37)

Note. From "Color- and Picture-word Stroop Tests: Performance Changes in Old Age," by P. Graf, B. Uttl, and H. Tuokko, 1995, *Journal of Clinical and Experimental Neuropsychology, 17,* p. 399. Copyright © 1995 by Swets & Zeitlinger Publishers. Used with permission.

TABLE 7.6

Means and Standard Deviations (in parentheses) for the Picture–Word Stroop Test Performance (in msces per item) for Various Midpoint Overlapping Age Groups

	Age Group Midpoint and Range						
Score	68 65–71 (n = 50)	71 68–74 (n = 53)	74 71–77 (n = 58)	77 74–80 (n = 44)	80 77–83 (n = 32)	83 80–86 (n = 19)	86 83–95 (n = 11)
Picture	784 (209)	812 (213)	881 (236)	906 (248)	993 (273)	982 (247)	1000 (270)
Congruent	484 (111)	484 (99)	491 (101)	504 (107)	526 (114)	563 (121)	591 (132)
Incongruent	1008 (197)	1052 (208)	1135 (241)	1146 (268)	1224 (279)	1282 (290)	1280 (334)
Picture-Congruent	302 (189)	330 (201)	391 (217)	395 (201)	457 (225)	418 (190)	409 (211)
Incongruent-Picture	232 (256)	240 (219)	259 (281)	246 (312)	240 (318)	300 (263)	280 (225)
Picture/Congruent	1.66 (.43)	1.72 (.46)	1.82 (.47)	1.79 (.41)	1.87 (.45)	1.76 (.32)	1.70 (.34)
Incongruent/Picture	1.34 (.30)	1.34 (.26)	1.34 (.30)	1.32 (.33)	1.29 (.32)	1.34 (.31)	1.30 (.36)

Note. From "Color- and Picture-word Stroop Tests: Performance Changes in Old Age," by P. Graf, B. Uttl, and H. Tuokko, 1995, Journal of Clinical and Experimental Neuropsychology, 17, p. 400. Copyright © 1995 by Swets & Zeitlinger Publishers. Used with permission.

131

point overlapping age groups (see chap. 2 for a description of this method). These tasks were administered to 129 community dwelling adults between age 65 and 95 who participated in the Vancouver Center component of the Canadian Study of Health and Aging (CSHA) and were screened as cognitively intact (see chap. 2 for information about the overall sample). In the color–word task, four cards were used, each containing 27 items that were arranged in 3 columns and 9 rows. The first card (Word) contained color words (e.g., red, blue) printed in black ink. The second card (Color) presented 27 colored (i.e., red, blue or green) series of Xs in the length of the word corresponding to the color of the ink (e.g., *XXXX* printed in blue, *XXX* printed in red). The third card (Congruent) showed the color words printed in their corresponding colors and the fourth card (incongruent) showed the color words (i.e., red, green, blue) printed in incongruent ink colors (e.g., the word "red" printed in green ink).

For the picture–word task, three cards containing four columns and five rows were developed. In each cell was a line drawing of a common object. The first card (Picture) contained only pictures. The second card (Congruent) contained pictures with the name corresponding to the object printed over it. The third card (incongruent) contained the same pictures as the Picture and Congruent cards and names as on the Congruent card but the objects and names were deliberately mismatched (e.g., the word BALLOON printed over a picture of an umbrella).

As noted by Graf et al. (1995), the Color–Word and Picture–Word tasks appeared to measure different constructs in their elderly sample. The Color–Word interference score, but not the Picture–Word scores, appeared related to other presumed measures of cognitive flexibility (e.g., Digit Symbol and Similarities subtests of the WAIS–R). They also noted that analyses of the raw scores and derived scores yielded different age effects. They cautioned against the use of a commonly used index of Stroop Test performance (MacLeod, 1991), the interference difference score (i.e., Incongruent-Color) that was insensitive to age-related slowing. They favored the use of a ratio index of interference (i.e., Incongruent/Color) to capture age-related changes.

Lezak (1995) noted that the Stroop task is unpleasant for participants and recommended a maximum time of 5 minutes for the interference trial. Of particular importance to performing this task is visual competence. Because color-blindness is age related in men and visual difficulties in general increase with age, it is imperative that these factors be evaluated (e.g., as in the Spreen & Strauss, 1991, version) when determining the appropriateness of this measure for a specific elderly individual.

The *Trail Making Test* (TMT) contains two sections: Trails A and Trails B. Trails A is a simple join-the-dots task where the participant must draw a line connecting circles containing numbers, placed about a page, in sequence. Trails B requires the individual to draw a line connecting circles containing both numbers and letters by alternating between the two sequences (i.e., 1, A, 2, B, and so forth). Visual scanning and tracking play important roles in performing these tasks. Performance on this task may relate to the person's ability to follow a sequence mentally, deal with more than one stimulus at a time (Eson, Yen, & Bourke, 1978), or to be flexible in shifting the course of an ongoing activity (Pontius & Yudowitz, 1980). Spreen and Strauss (1991) provided detailed administration procedures. Performance times increase significantly with age and are affected by education in younger samples.

Seconds to completion and number of errors have been examined for a variety of samples of older adults (see Table 7.7). Stanton, Jenkins, Savageau, Zyzanski, and Aucoin (1984) administered the TMT to 102 persons age 60 to 69 in a prospective study of recovery after elective coronary bypass-graft or valve-replacement procedures. R. R. Bornstein (1985) ad-

TABLE 7.7
Means and Standard Deviations
(in parentheses) for the Trail Making Test

Description	Trails A	Trails B
Time in seconds for 60- to 69-year-old medical surgical patients ($n = 102$)	49.3 (23.4)	116.7 (53.7)
Time in seconds for 60- to 69-year-old Canadian volunteers ($n = 97$)	36.7 (10.3)	92.7 (32.5)
Time in seconds for 60- to 69-year-old Canadian employees of a Mental Health Centre ($n = 30$)	35.22 (12.36)	95.02 (34.62)
Time in seconds for 66- to 70-year-old healthy, active seniors ($n = 45$)	43.20 (14.98)	105.20 (43.43)
Time in seconds for 71- to 75-year-old healthy, active seniors ($n = 57$)	50.08 (12.88)	97.79 (30.40)
Time in seconds for 76- to 85-year-old healthy, active seniors ($n = 26$)	59.73 (15.95)	153.09 (62.60)

Note. Data in row 1 reproduced with permission of authors and publisher from Stanton, B. A., Jenkins, C. D., Savageau, J. A., Zyzanski, S. J., & Aucoin, R. Age and educational differences on the Trail Making Test and Wechsler Memory Scales. *Perceptual and Motor Skills, 58*, 1984, pp. 311–318. Copyright © Perceptual and Motor Skills 1984. Data in row 2 come from "Normative data on selective neuropsychological measures from a nonclinical sample," by R. A. Bornstein, 1985, *Journal of Clinical Psychology, 41*, p. 654. Copyright © 1985 by John Wiley & Sons, Inc. Adapted with permission of John Wiley & Sons, Inc. Data in row 3 reproduced with permission of author and publisher from Kennedy, K. J. Age effects on Trail Making Test performance. *Perceptual and Motor Skills, 52*, 1981, pp. 671–675. Copyright © Perceptual and Motor Skills 1981. Data in rows 4 through 6 come from "Neuropsychological processes associated with normal aging," by W. G. Van Gorp, P. Satz, and M. Mitrushina, 1990, *Developmental Neuropsychology, 6*, p. 284. Copyright © 1990 by Lawrence Erlbaum Associates, Inc. Adapted with permission.

TABLE 7.8
Trail Making Test: Percentile Ranking for Time in Seconds

Percentile	60–69 years (n = 90)		70–79 years (n = 90)	
	Trails A	Trails B	Trails A	Trails B
90	29	64	38	79
75	35	89	54	132
50	48	119	80	196
25	67	172	105	292
10	104	282	168	450

Note. From "The Influence of Age on Trail Making Test Performance," by A. D. M. Davies, 1968, *Journal of Clinical Psychology, 24*, p. 97. Copyright © 1968 by John Wiley & Sons, Inc. Adapted by permission of John Wiley & Sons, Inc.

ministered the TMT to 97 Canadian volunteers age 60 and older. Kennedy (1981) administered the TMT to 150 persons age 20 through 69 randomly selected from the 614 healthy active employees of a Canadian Mental Health Center. Thirty individuals (15 male and 15 female) were selected in each age interval (e.g., 60–69). Van Gorp, Mitrushina, and Satz (1990) administered the TMT to 128 healthy, active, well-educated ($M = 14.14$, $SD = 2.86$) volunteers recruited from an independent living retirement community. No persons with a past history of neurologic or psychiatric disorder or chronic substance abuse were included. Davies (1968) reported percentile ranks for 180 persons age 60 and older from the British Medical Research Council's volunteer panel (see Table 7.8).

Age and education corrections were determined by Alekoumbides, Charter, Adkins, and Seacat (1987) through a linear regression approach. Thirty people age 60 and over were included in their sample of 123 neurologically intact individuals. The following regression formulae generate scores corrected for age and education:

Trails A Corrected Score (CS) = Trails A time to completion in seconds − (.456 × age) − (−2.357 × education) + (−5.58); Trails B CS = Trails B time to completion in seconds − (1.468 × age) − (−7.771 × education) + (−20.058).

For ease of interpretation, standardized scores (SS; $M = 100$; $SD = 15$) were developed using the corrected scores (above):

1. For Trails A CS less than or equal to 56, SS = 15 [(Trails A CS − 44.977) / (−12.920)] + 100.
2. For Trails A CS greater than 56, SS = 15 [(Trails A CS − 20.198) / (−43.103)] + 100.

3. For Trails B CS less than or equal to 155, SS = 15 [(time to completion in seconds − 110.145) / (−42.735)] + 100.

4. For Trails B CS greater than 155, SS = 15 [(time to completion in seconds + 32.696) / (−178.571)] + 100.

It becomes evident that the mean time in seconds to completion varies by sample. Stanton et al.'s (1984) medical surgical patients appear slower than other age-related normative groups. Davies' (1968) British volunteers are somewhat slower than comparative North American samples. Van Gorp et al.'s (1990) sample over age 75 is slower on both Trails A and B than all younger samples.

The *Wisconsin Card Sorting Test* (WCST), a measure of the abilities to generate and test hypotheses and to appropriately shift set (Heaton, 1981), is widely used, particularly as a measure of executive functioning. The respondent is given a pack of cards (typically 128 cards) containing one to four symbols (i.e., triangle, cross, star, and circle) printed in red, green, yellow, or blue. The task is to place each card under one of four stimulus cards (i.e., one red triangle, two green stars, three yellow crosses, four blue circles) according to a principle (color, number, or shape) conveyed to the respondent by the examiner indicating whether or not the placement is correct. The examiner changes the principle after a run of 10 correct responses. A number of scores can be obtained from this measure, including total number of errors, number of categories achieved, and perseverative errors (see Lezak, 1995, for discussion of scoring principles). It is to be noted that various versions of this measure exist (e.g., Haaland, Vranes, Goodwin, & Garry, 1987; Heaton et al., 1993; Nelson, 1976).

Age decrements are to be expected on a complex task of this nature because memory and cognitive flexibility have been identified as areas disrupted with aging (Horn, 1968). Haaland, et al. (1987), using a 64-card version of the task, examined the performance of 75 well-educated, medically healthy persons over age 65 (i.e., 64–69, $n = 10$; 70–74, $n = 22$; 75–79, $n = 25$; 80–87, $n = 18$). The oldest group differed significantly from the youngest group on the number of categories attained ($M = 2.4$, $SD = .9$ for youngest; $M = 1.5$, $SD = 1.3$ for oldest) and the total number of errors ($M = 19.1$, $SD = 11.4$ for youngest; $M = 26.1$, $SD = 14.3$ for oldest). Spreen and Strauss (1991) also showed a significant decline in performance, though only after age 80 for categories achieved (i.e., age 60–69, $n = 28$, $M = 5.5$, $SD = 1.1$; age 70–79, $n = 19$, $M = 5.0$, $SD = 1.3$; age 80+, $n = 13$, $M = 4.23$, $SD = 1.5$), and perseverative errors (i.e., age 60–69, $n = 28$, $M = 12.25$, $SD = 10.91$; age 70–79, $n = 19$, $M = 15.9$, $SD = 9.8$; age 80+, $n = 13$, $M = 25.77$, $SD = 12.23$).

Axelrod and Henry (1992) examined WCST performance of 20 healthy persons grouped in each age decade (see chap. 2 for a description of this sample). The progressive age-related decline observed was unrelated to intellectual competence, educational experience, or the general health status of the participant. Axelrod, Jiron, and Henry (1993) used this same sample to examine an abbreviated (i.e., 64-card) WCST. The age-related declines apparent on the full version continued to be evident (see Table 7.9).

Heaton et al. (1993) used the method of continuous norming (Angoff & Robertson, 1987) (see chap. 2 for a description of this method) to provide normative data for a total sample of 899 persons from six distinct samples. These samples included 50 normal persons age 58 to 84 with education levels ranging from 8 to 20 years and 73 healthy adults age 51 to 89 with education levels ranging from 6 to 20 years. Contained in these samples are 99 persons age 65 and over. Normative data are presented by 5-year age span (e.g., 65–69 years through 85–89) and years of educational attainment ($\leq$ 8; 9–11, 12,

TABLE 7.9
Means and Standard Deviations for Scores Derived From
the Wisconsin Card Sorting Test and the Abbreviated
Wisconsin Card Sorting Test (in parentheses)

Variable	*Age Groups (128 cards)*		
	60–69	*70–79*	*80–89*
Correct Responses			
M	69.2	73.8	66.6
SD	43.5	7.0	13.6
Total Errors			
M	40.5 (21.3)	46.0 (22.8)	48.9 (25.7)
SD	26.1 (11.6)	14.2 (6.0)	25.4 (10.8)
Perseverative Errors			
M	22.4 (12.0)	25.5 (12.7)	33.0 (16.2)
SD	14.7 (7.6)	9.5 (4.3)	22.2 (10.1)
Perseverative Responses			
M	25.4 (13.5)	29.6 (14.8)	39.8 (20.4)
SD	17.4 (8.5)	11.5 (5.4)	29.2 (13.2)
Nonperseverative Errors			
M	18.2 (9.4)	21.4 (10.7)	15.9 (9.0)
SD	13.3 (6.3)	7.9 (5.0)	8.4 (4.3)
Categories Achieved			
M	3.8 (2.6)	4.2 (2.6)	3.6 (2.2)
SD	2.1 (1.7)	1.3 (1.1)	2.4 (1.6)

Note. Data that are not in parentheses come from "Age-related Performance on the Wisconsin Card Sorting, Similarities, and Controlled Oral Word Association Tests," by B. N. Axelrod and R. R. Henry, 1992, *Clinical Neuropsychologist, 6,* p. 21. Copyright © 1992 by Swets & Zeitlinger Publishers. Used with permission. Data in parentheses come from "Performance of Adults Ages 20 to 90 on the Abbreviated Wisconsin Card Sorting Test," by B. N. Axelrod, C. C. Jiron, and R. R. Henry, 1993, *Clinical Neuropsychologist, 7,* p. 207. Copyright © 1993 by Swets & Zeitlinger Publishers. Used with permission.

13–15, 16–17, 18+) with raw score conversions to standard scores, T-scores, and percentiles for Total number of errors, Percent Errors, Perseverative Responses, Percent Perseverative Responses, Perseverative Errors, Percent Perseverative Errors, Nonperseverative Errors, Percent Nonperseverative Errors, and Percent Conceptual Level Responses. For Perseverative Errors and Nonperseverative errors, Heaton et al.'s (1993) raw score findings are similar to (and the means do not exceed) those of Axelrod and Henry (1992) presented in Table 7.9.

Nelson's (1976) version of the WCST has been found sensitive to the effects of early dementia of the Alzheimer's type (Bondi, Monsch, Butters, Salmon, & Paulsen, 1993). Bondi et al. (1993) attributed their findings to early impairment of cognitive flexibility with deficits in problem-solving skills or conceptualization arising later. An alternative interpretation may relate to the severity of new learning disturbance exhibited across the course of DAT as memory plays a significant, and often underestimated, role in the performance of the WCST. Bondi et al. (1993) recommended Nelson's (1976) shorter version of the WCST for use with persons with dementia for time saving and ease of administration.

The WCST is one of the most popular putative measures of frontal lobe pathology in persons of all ages. Mountain and Snow (1993) discussed this issue in some detail concluding that "no specific test score has been validated as being uniquely sensitive to the presence of frontal-lobe dysfunction, either in the differentiation of patients with frontal lobe damage from normals, or patients with frontal-lobe damage from patients with nonfrontal-lobe damage" (p. 117). This is particularly true for persons over age 65 who have received little attention from this perspective.

The *Category Test* is a measure of abstract concept formation consisting of 208 visually presented items organized into seven sets. A particular principle underlies the organization of each of the first six sets. For example, the first set shows Roman numerals I through IV for which the respondent is to press the response key containing the corresponding Arabic numeral. For each set, the respondent must deduce the principle and apply it throughout the set. The seventh set is made up of items occurring previously in Sets 1 through 6. All responses can be conveyed using a keypad with the numbers 1 through 4. The score is the total number of errors across sets.

Information about the performance, specifically for older adults, on the Category Test was provided by Mack and Carlson (1978) who screened volunteers age 60 to 80 for signs or symptoms of disease with neurological significance as well as neurological impairment. The 41 individuals selected were well-educated (i.e., $M = 14.05$, $SD = 3.39$) and of above-average intelligence (i.e., $M = 119.90$, $SD = 15.14$). Perfect or near-perfect scores were obtained on Sets 1 and 2. The number of errors on Sets 3 through

5 fell between 25 and 19, respectively. Fewer errors were made on Sets 6 and 7 (means = 15.32 and 7.93, respectively).

J. Ernst (1987) reported on the performance of 110 persons age 65 to 75 on a booklet version of the Category Test (DeFilippis, McCampbell, & Rogers, 1979). The means and standard deviations were reported separately for men ($n = 51$) and women ($n = 59$). As was evident from Mack and Carlson's (1978) study, better performance was evident on Sets 5 and 6 than on Sets 3 and 4 for both men and women. The fewest number of errors were apparent for Set 7.

Heaton, Grant, and Matthews (1986) noted age, education, and age-by-education interaction effects for the Category Test. Their sample included 100 persons age 60 and older derived from the neuropsychological laboratories of University of Colorado, University of California at San Diego, and University of Wisconsin Medical School. None of these persons had a history of neurological illness, significant head trauma, or substance abuse, and all were considered cognitively intact. They reported a mean performance of 66.4 errors for this group (standard deviation not given). Alekoumbides et al. (1987) administered the Category Test to 123 persons selected from the population of a large general hospital, none of whom were suffering from cerebral lesions or had a history of cerebral contusion or alcohol abuse. Thirty of these individuals were age 60 or older. Using a regression approach (see chap. 2), they derived the following formula to correct for age and education for the Category Test:

Corrected Score (CS) = Raw Score − (.672 × age) − (−2.421 × education) + 3.808

The CS can then be standardized with a mean of 100 and $SD = 15$ to allow for ease of interpretation by applying the following formula:

Standardized Score = 15 (CS − 62.607) / (−23.362 + 100)

Also using a regression approach, Heaton et al. (1991; see chap. 2 for a full description of this sample) presented norms to age 80 by gender and education level (i.e., 6–8, 9–11, 12, 13–15, 16–17, 18+). To illustrate the marked age effect on this task, a raw score of 60 errors would be equivalent to a scaled score of 7. If individuals in question had obtained 12 years of education and were age 40, they would receive a T-score of 38 (Mildly Impaired range). If they were age 80, the T-score would be 53 (Average range). If they were age 80 and poorly educated (i.e., 6–8 years), the individuals could make as many as 117 errors and still fall within the average range.

One of the major limitations of using the Category Test with older adults is its length. A number of attempts to shorten the Category Test have been made (e.g., 100-item Short Category Test, Booklet Format: Wetzel & Boll, 1987) but include relatively few older persons in their normative samples.

The *Similarities* subtest of the Wechsler Adult Intelligence Scale–Revised (Wechsler, 1981) assesses verbal concept formation (Lezak, 1995). Pairs of words are presented and the respondent must identify similarities between the words (e.g., carrot–turnip are both vegetables). Age-related decline has been observed in elderly samples. Ivnik et al. (1992a), with data obtained from the Mayo Older Americans Normative Study (see chap. 2), generated age-adjusted scores for the individual subtests of the WAIS–R as well as for summary scores (i.e., VIQ, PIQ, and FSIQ) using overlapping, midpoint age ranges. Table 7.10 contains raw score conversions to age-specific scaled scores and percentile ranks for the Similarities subtest of the WAIS–R from Ivnik et al. (1992a).

Axelrod and Henry (1992) examined performance on the Similarities Scaled Scores in their sample of 60 persons age 60 and older (see chap. 2 for a description of this sample). They noted an age-related decline on this task for the 70- and 80-year-old groups. They also noted that the Age-Scaled score equivalents, presented in Table 21 of the WAIS–R manual (1981), appeared adequate to control for these differences by age.

Farmer et al. (1987) administered the Similarities subtest of the WAIS–R to the 2,123 participants in the Framingham Heart Study (see chap. 2). When examining raw scores, a stronger effect for education than age was noted. In all education groups, scores either remained stable or declined with age.

The *Behavioral Dyscontrol Scale*, a measure of the conscious control of motor functioning, is reportedly based on Luria's theory of frontal lobe functioning (Grigsby, Kaye, & Robbins, 1992). The respondent must perform eight items for which a total of 16 points can be obtained. Five items assess the capacity for inhibition and control of various aspects of simple movement. Two items involve learning simple motor tasks and one item measures working memory and the ability to shift attention flexibly while maintaining concentration on a simple cognitive task. The examiner's rating of the person's insight into personal performance is the final (ninth) item. Each item, except the final rating, is scored on a 3-point scale: 2 = adequate, 1 = moderately deficient, 0 = very impaired. A 4-point scale is used to rate insight and assesses the individual's awareness of the existence, nature, severity, and significance of errors in personal performance.

The normative sample for this measure consisted of 141 persons ranging in age from 63 to 102 ($M = 78.7$, $SD = 7.9$), who obtained scores of 25 or greater on the MMSE (see chap. 3 for a description of this measure). These individuals had a mean educational level of 11.4 years ($SD = 3.6$). The following cutoff scores were suggested by Grigsby, Kaye, and Robbins

TABLE 7.10
Raw Score Conversions to Percentile Ranks and Age-specific Scaled Scores for the Similarities Subtest of the WAIS–R

Percentile Range	Scaled Scores	Midpoint Age								
		64 Range 59–69 (n = 170)	67 Range 62–72 (n = 183)	70 Range 65–75 (n = 187)	73 Range 68–78 (n = 203)	76 Range 71–81 (n = 187)	79 Range 74–84 (n = 179)	82 Range 77–87 (n = 149)	85 Range 80–90 (n = 113)	88 Range 83+ (n = 81)
<1	2	0	0	0–1	0–1	0	0	—	—	—
1	3	1–2	1–2	2	2	1	1	0	0	0
2	4	3–6	3–6	3–6	3–6	2–3	2–3	1	1	—
3–5	5	7–9	7–8	7–8	7	4–7	4	1	1	1–3
6–10	6	10–12	9–12	9–10	8–10	8–10	5–8	2–6	2–5	4–6
11–18	7	13–14	13–14	11–13	11–13	11	9–10	7–9	6–8	7–9
19–28	8	15–16	15	14–15	14	12–13	11–12	10–11	9–10	10–11
29–40	9	17	16–17	16–17	15–16	14–15	13–14	12–13	11–12	12–13
41–59	10	18–19	18–19	18	17–18	16–18	15–17	14–16	13–16	14–15
60–71	11	20	20	19–20	19–20	19–20	18–19	17–18	17–18	16–18
72–81	12	21	21	21	21	21	20	19	19	19
82–89	13	22	22	22	22	22	21	20–21	20	20–21
90–94	14	23	23	23	23	23	22	22	21	—
95–97	15	—	—	—	—	24	23	—	22	22
98	16	24	24	24	24	—	24	23	—	—
99	17	25–26	25	25	25	25	25	24–25	23	23
>99	18	27+	26+	26+	26+	26+	26+	26+	24+	24+

Note. From "Mayo's Older American Normative Studies: WAIS–R Norms for Ages 56 to 97," by R. J. Ivnik, J. F. Malec, G. E. Smith, E. G. Tangalos, R. C. Petersen, E. Kokmen, and L. T. Kurland, 1992, *Clinical Neuropsychologist, 6* (Suppl.). pp. 11–19. Copyright © 1992 by the Mayo Foundation. Adapted by permission of Mayo Foundation.

(1992): 0–6 = severely impaired, 7–10 = moderately severe impairment, 11–15 = mild impairment, 16–19 = normal performance. Given the somewhat subjective nature of the scoring for tasks included on this measure, formal training is imperative for reliable administration, scoring, and interpretation of the scale.

Royall, Mahurin, and Gray (1992) developed a clinically based bedside screening examination for executive cognitive function deficits, the *Executive Interview* (EXIT). This 25-item (maximum score = 50) measure assesses frontal release, motor and cognitive perseveration, verbal intrusions, disinhibition, loss of spontaneity, imitation behavior, environmental dependency, and utilization behavior and can be administered in 10 to 20 minutes. Higher scores indicate greater executive dyscontrol.

Forty persons, randomly selected across four levels of care (i.e., independent living to Alzheimer's Special Care Unit), were selected from a 537-bed retirement community in Texas and administered the EXIT, the MMSE (see chap. 3 for a description of this measure), traditional tests of "frontal" executive function, and a behavior problem checklist (Royall et al., 1992). Interrater reliability was good (r = .90) and the EXIT correlated well with other measures of executive functioning. The EXIT was superior to the MMSE in discriminating between care levels and correlated with the disruptive behavior checklist (r = .79). Impairment on the EXIT has been observed in a variety of disorders associated with frontal lobe dysfunction including Alzheimer's disease, frontal lobe dementia (FLD), major depression, dementia with no cortical features (largely vascular in origin), and schizophrenia (Royall et al., 1993). Thus, the information provided by the EXIT is most useful from the perspective of care planning. Appreciation of the extent of executive dysfunction can lead to specific behavioral and environmental interventions regardless of the etiology.

The *Behavioral Assessment of the Dysexecutive Syndrome* (BADS) was designed to assess individuals' abilities to initiate, monitor, and evaluate their own behavior (B. A. Wilson, Alderman, Burgess, Emslie, & Evans, 1996). The need for such a battery developed from observations that persons with obvious impairments of executive functioning can perform satisfactorily on measures thought to be sensitive to frontal lobe lesions (Shallice & Burgess, 1991). Special effort was taken to design subtests to be similar to real-life activities. Table 7.11 describes the subtests included in this measure. The normative sample included approximately 55 persons age 65 and older with an approximately equal number of persons falling below average, average, and above average on the National Reading Test IQ equivalent score. The BADS profile score (sum of profile scores for each subtest, range = 0–24) is presented by age group (i.e., ≤ 40, 41–65, 65–87) as the overall performance was significantly poorer for the oldest age group. Interrater and test–retest reliabilities were examined with some surprising

TABLE 7.11
Subtest Description for the Behavioral Assessment
of the Dysexecutive Syndrome (B. A. Wilson et al., 1996)

Subtest	Content
Rule Shift Cards Test	Twenty-one nonpicture playing cards are used. In Part 1, a specific response is requested if the card is a specific color, in Part 2, a specific response is requested if a card is the same color as the preceding card. Time taken and number of errors are recorded.
Action Program Test	This novel problem-solving task requires physical manipulation of a variety of materials. The task requires five steps to completion. Prompts may be given after 2 minutes of unsuccessful problem solving.
Key Search Test	The stimulus material consists of a piece of paper with a 100 mm square drawn on it and a small black dot 50 mm below it. The task is to draw a line starting on the black dot to show where they would walk to search the field (i.e., square) to find a set of lost keys.
Temporal Judgment Test	Four questions, concerning how long a specific event takes, are asked.
Zoo Map Test	Two trials of this task are administered and require demonstration of a plan to visit specific locations on a zoo map. Specific rules must be adhered to when planning the routes.
Modified Six Elements Test	Instructions are given to perform three tasks (i.e., dictation, arithmetic, and picture naming), each of which is divided into two parts: A and B. Each of the six subtests must be attempted within a 10-minute interval but two parts of the same task cannot be performed consecutively. The number of subtests completed, whether or not the rule was broken, and maximum amount of time spent on any one subtest are noted.
Dysexecutive Questionnaire	This 20-item questionnaire was constructed to sample a range of problems commonly associated with the Dysexecutive syndrome. Two versions are available: one to be completed by the respondent and another to be completed by a relative or care provider.

low values. Despite these outstanding psychometric concerns, the constructs assessed by this measure appear particularly relevant to the assessment of elderly persons.

CONCLUSIONS

The domains of cognitive functioning discussed in this chapter may be viewed as representative of the spectrum of task complexity. Attention functions are basic and fundamental to the performance of all tasks. That is, impairment of attention will also affect the person's performance on a wide variety of other tasks (e.g., memory, reasoning). Executive functions are often referred to as the most complex of human behaviors being primarily concerned with planning and organization of purposeful behavior. Impairment in many other areas of cognitive functioning may affect a person's performance on executive tasks (e.g., memory impairment). Thus, attention is fundamental to the performance of all other cognitive tasks and executive functions can be disrupted by impairment of most, if not all, lower order skills.

There are a number of other measures of both attention and executive functioning that have been developed for research and/or clinical purposes that have not been applied with elderly persons or they have been addressed in other chapters (e.g., Word Fluency and Figural Fluency in chap. 8). The reader is directed to Lezak (1995) for descriptions of some of these measures. Despite much clinical interest in frontal lobe dementia (see chap. 10) and the report that persons with this condition have difficulty with "frontal lobe tests" (The Lund and Manchester Groups, 1994), only a few studies with small sample sizes have characterized the neuropsychological test profile of these persons (Boone, Miller, & Lesser, 1993). At best, it is generally noted that test performances are good and in distinct contrast to observations of everyday behaviors. Once again, it is important to emphasize that poor performance on measures of executive functioning is not necessarily synonymous with frontal lobe damage.

Chapter 8

Language, Visuospatial, Perceptual, and Motor Functioning

LANGUAGE AND COMMUNICATION

It is often noted that language functions are unlikely to deteriorate with age. Moreover, Schaie (1980) noted that the practical significance of the observed changes in language functions appear quite modest. And, according to Obler and M. L. Albert (1981), certain language capabilities potentially may continue to develop throughout the lifespan.

M. S. Albert (1988) noted that linguistic ability encompasses at least four domains (i.e., phonology, lexical, syntactic, and semantic). These domains differ with respect to the emergence of changes with normal aging. Knowledge of the sounds of words and the rules for their combination (i.e., phonology) is well preserved with age (Bayles & Kaszniak, 1987). Similarly, lexical decision making (i.e., the accuracy with which words are discriminated from nonwords) shows little change with age. The ability to meaningfully combine words (i.e., syntactic knowledge) also does not deteriorate with age unless the syntactic structure under investigation imposes high memory demands (e.g., Kemper, Kynette, Rash, O'Brien, & Sprott, 1989). Memory has also been implicated (Bayles & Kaszniak, 1987) as the source of observed deficits in the comprehension of complex material (e.g., Ulatowska, Hayaski, Cannito, & Fleming, 1986). Semantic knowledge (or the organization of language by meaning) appears the most vulnerable to the effects of increasing age after age 70. Specifically, performance on naming tasks and tasks requiring verbal fluency have been shown to decline with advancing age.

Other aspects of language, including length of oral and written statements and clause structure, have also been shown to decline with advancing age (Kemper et al., 1989). Kemper et al. pointed out the possible effects of limitations in working memory on the linguistic competence of their elderly adults and suggested that the restricted syntactic complexity observed in the responses of older adults is the product of loss of memory capacity.

Here lies the crux of the major interpretation issue when deficits are observed on neuropsychological measures of language. The most commonly employed are naming (e.g., Boston Naming Test) and fluency (e.g., Controlled Oral Word Association, or FAS test) tasks. These tasks, as noted earlier from the psycholinguistic point of view, are also those most heavily influenced by memory functions. Suffice it to say that memory and language are intertwined and a person with verbal memory disturbance is likely to experience some difficulty performing "language" tasks such as naming, word generation, and comprehension of complex material. However, other aspects of language (e.g., syntax) may be intact.

Aphasia, a disturbance of symbol formation that may extend beyond spoken communication to include reading and writing abilities as well, may occur as part of the clinical presentation of many different brain disorders. It is the analysis of discrete patterns of language breakdown occurring with circumscribed brain lesions that has been most influential in determining the neuroanatomical source of the various aphasic syndromes (see Benson, 1993; Lezak, 1995). Circumscribed disturbances of language have been noted as an early key feature of Progressive Aphasia (see chap. 10), whereas the language disturbance seen in neurodegenerative processes is often less clearly defined and more likely to occur in the context of global cognitive impairment.

Aphasia batteries have been designed to specifically characterize discrete verbal functions. These batteries focus on the linguistic processing of verbal symbols and are typically concerned with disordered language functions, per se, in each communication modality (listening, speaking, reading, writing, and gesturing). If communication skills are the focus of the assessment (e.g., rehabilitation planning following stroke), an aphasia battery may prove very useful, detailed information.

Other aspects of verbal production (i.e., speech disorders) may affect verbal communication but are distinct from language functions. These deficits in articulation may be the focus of a speech-language evaluation where particular characteristics of the speech are examined in detail. At a more superficial level, observation of deficits such as delayed responding, effortful speech, use of stereotyped phrases, paraphasic errors (i.e., substitutions of words), or the production of nonwords (idioglossia) during assessment may be especially meaningful. Disorders of phonation, articulation, resonance, and prosody fall within the group of speech disorders denoted as the dysarthrias (Darley, Aronson, & Brown, 1975). The most common disorders that manifest motor-speech disorders and are associated with aging include Amyotrophic Lateral Sclerosis, Parkinsonism, and cerebrovascular disorders (Rosenbek & LaPointe, 1981). Motor-speech disorders are invariably not part of the clinical presentation of Alzheimer's disease.

In this chapter, two batteries for which normative information is available are included. In addition, the two most commonly used measures of language are reviewed, the Boston Naming Test and Controlled Oral Word Association Test, a verbal fluency measure.

Aphasia Batteries

The *Arizona Battery for Communication Disorders of Dementia* (ABCD) test manual (Bayles & Tomoeda, 1991) was designed to assess the functional linguistic communication skills of individuals diagnosed with mild or moderate Alzheimer's disease. Fourteen subtests are included to provide information concerning mental status, episodic memory, linguistic expression, linguistic comprehension, and visuospatial construction (see Table 8.1). The samples presented in the manual are 50 normal control subjects (mean age = 71.15, SD = 21.49) and 50 persons with Alzheimer's disease (mean age = 74.95, SD = 14.31). No age range for the normal controls is given, but they were all English-speaking Caucasians with no history of alcohol or drug abuse, or neurologic or psychiatric disease. This instrument has been shown to discriminate between normal persons and persons with Alzheimer's disease (Bayles, Boone, Tomoeda, Slauson, & Kaszniak, 1989).

The *Montreal–Toulouse–86β Aphasia Battery* (MT–86β; Beland & Lecours, 1990; Beland, Lecours, Giroux, & Bois, 1993) was designed to assess language disorders in a French-speaking population. The normative sample contained 72 persons age 50 to 69 and 53 persons age 70 to 87. Beland and Lecours (1990) reported means and standard deviations and qualitative error analysis for 7 of the 23 subtests of the battery (i.e., repetition, reading aloud, writing to dictation, copy, naming, verbal fluency, and word and sentence picture matching). Beland et al. (1993) reported quantitative data and qualitative analyses on the error types by age group for the remaining 16 subtests (see Table 8.2). Cutoff scores, determined as the highest score achieved by at least 95% of each normative group, are also indicated by Beland et al. (1993; see Table 8.2).

The findings that effects of age, education, or both were apparent for a number of these seemingly simple tasks is important to note when using aphasia batteries that do not present norms for older samples. That is, some language tasks are affected by age, and these age-related changes must be kept in mind when assessing for aphasic disturbances.

TABLE 8.1
Contents of the Arizona Battery for
Communication Disorders of Dementia

Area	Subtest	Subtest Description
Mental Status	Mental Status	Orientation to time, place and person, and general knowledge.
Episodic Memory	Story Retelling Immediate	Immediate recall of a story.
	Story Retelling Delayed	Recall of the story after 30 minutes.
	Word Learning	Learn a set of nouns, known by most literate adults, within the context of the test.
Linguistic Expression	Object Description	Describe a common object in detail, thereby generating a series of descriptors about the stimulus object.
	Generative Naming	Generate names of items in a semantic category.
	Confrontation Naming	Name objects.
	Concept Definition	Define the stimulus words from the naming task.
Linguistic Comprehension	Following Commands	Follow variable level commands suitable for even nonambulatory, hemiparetic individuals.
	Comparative Questions	Respond to simple reasoning and auditory comprehension questions about the relations between two entities.
	Repetition	Repeat six and nine syllable phrases that express conceptually impossible relations.
	Reading Comprehension	Read words and sentences.
Visuospatial Construction	Generative Drawing	Generate drawings.
	Figure Copying	Copy a figure.

Other Language Measures

Perhaps the most common complaint of older persons is the inability to recall a person's name quickly. A selective deficit for this type of word-finding ability in 20 persons in their eighties was observed by Goodglass (1980) using pictures of 24 famous faces. A less dramatic, though still significant, effect was seen for naming objects on the *Boston Naming Test* (BNT; Kaplan, Goodglass, & Weintraub, 1978).

The BNT contains a series of 85 line-drawn pictures graded in difficulty. The total score is typically the number of words recalled without assistance. Providing a functional category description (i.e., semantic cue) and/or

TABLE 8.2
Subtests From the MT–86β With Cutoff Scores for Persons
Between Age 70 and 99 ($n = 32$) Who Had
Obtained 10 or More Years of Education

Subtests Where Normal Persons Obtain Close to Perfect Scores	Subtests Where Differences Are Found Across Age or Education Groups
Interview	Written picture naming; cutoff score = 9/12.
Automatized sequences	Reading a text aloud.
Signature	Reading comprehension of the text read aloud (above).
Verbal body-part identification	Written word and written sentence picture matching; cutoff score = 10/13.
Written body-part identification	Oral picture description; cutoff score = 7/18.
Number repetition	Written picture description; cutoff score = 7/18.
Oral reading of items from number repetition (above)	Written questionnaire; cutoff score = 5/7.
	Object manipulation; cutoff score = 5/8.
	Buccofacial praxis under verbal request and imitation; cutoff scores = 3/6 and 3/6, respectively.

Note. From "The MT–86β Aphasia Battery: A Subset of Normative Data in Relation to Age and Level of School Education (Part II)," by R. Beland, A. R. Lecours, F. Giroux, and M. Bois, 1993, *Aphasiology, 7*, pp. 359–382. Copyright © 1993 by Taylor & Francis. Adapted with permission.

the first sound of missed words (i.e., phonemic cue) allows for further examination of the types of problems the respondent may be having. For example, in Goodglass's (1980) sample of 20 elderly persons, provision of the first sound of missed words resulted in approximately 60% success rate, indicating that no profound dissociation between word and concept was present. Misperceptions accounted for approximately one fifth of the errors made by the elderly persons.

Many investigators have examined performance on the BNT by elderly persons since that time. Moreover, various shortened versions have been developed. Normative data including older persons for the original 85-item version of the BNT (i.e., BNT–85) were described by Borod et al. (1980) and extended by LaBarge et al. (1986) and M. S. Albert et al. (1988) (see Table 8.3). Borod et al.'s (1980) sample contained 31 persons age 60 to 69 and 25 persons age 70 to 85. All were volunteers recruited from the community who were free of neurological disorders, alcoholism, and learning disabilities. Cutoff scores of 47 and 31, based on determination of 2 standard deviations below the mean, were suggested for the younger and older groups, respectively. LaBarge et al. (1986) recruited 58 persons between age 60 and 86 who showed no abnormalities on physical examina-

TABLE 8.3
Means and Standard Deviations (in parentheses) for Performances
on the 85- and 60-Item Versions of the Boston Naming Test

Version	Source	n	Age	BNT performance
85-item	Borod et al. (1980)	31	60–69	70.3 (11.7)
		25	70+	63.2 (16.2)
	LaBarge et al. (1986)	38	70–85	66.8 (9.5)
60-item	Van Gorp et al. (1986)	12	59–64	56.75 (3.05)
		20	65–69	55.60 (4.29)
		24	70–74	54.46 (5.17)
		13	75–79	51.69 (6.20)
		9	80+	51.56 (7.00)
	Van Gorp et al. (1990)	28	57–65	55.5 (4.53)
		45	66–70	55.47 (3.94)
		57	71–75	53.88 (5.73)
		26	76–85	51.00 (6.36)
	Howieson et al. (1993)	17	65–74	54.4 (4.6)
		34	84–100	50.8 (5.2)
	Ross et al. (1995)	40	70–74	43.1 (11.7)
		40	75–79	40.1 (10.9)
		43	80+	35.8 (11.3)
	Neils et al. (1995)	54	65–74	51.83 (6.77)
		61	75–84	47.54 (8.89)
		52	85–97	43.75 (11.72)
			Education	
		48	6–9	41.58 (11.36)
		63	10–12	49.95 (8.29)
		56	12+	50.55 (7.40)

Note. Data from row 1 come from "Normative Data on the Boston Diagnostic Aphasia Examination, Parietal Lobe Battery, and the Boston Naming Test," by J. C. Borod, H. Goodglass, and E. Kaplan, 1980, *Journal of Clinical Neuropsychology, 2*, p. 214. Copyright © 1980 by Swets & Zeitlinger Publishers. Used with permission. Data from row 2 come from "Performance of Normal Elderly on the Boston Naming Test," by E. LaBarge, D. Edwards, and J. W. Knesevich, 1986, *Brain and Language, 27*, pp. 380–384. Copyright © 1986 by Academic Press, Inc. Adapted with permission. Data from row 3 come from "Normative Data on the Boston Naming Test for a Group of Normal Older Adults," by W. G. Van Gorp, P. Satz, M. E. Kiersch, and R. Henry, 1986, *Journal of Clinical and Experimental Neuropsychology, 8*, p. 704. Copyright © 1986 by Swets & Zeitlinger Publishers. Used with permission. Data from row 4 come from "Neuropsychological Processes Associated With Normal Aging," by W. G. Van Gorp, P. Satz, and M. Mitrushina, 1990, *Developmental Neuropsychology, 6*, p. 284. Copyright © 1990 by Lawrence Erlbaum Associates, Inc. Adapted with permission. Data from row 5 come from "Neurologic Function in the Optimally Healthy Oldest Old," by D. B. Howieson, L. A. Holm, J. A. Kaye, B. S. Oken, and J. Howieson, 1993, *Neurology, 43*, p. 1884. Copyright © 1993 by the American Academy of Neurology. Adapted with permission from Lippincott-Raven Publishers. Data from row 6 come from "Normative Data on the Boston Naming Test for Elderly Adults in a Demographically Diverse Medical Sample," by T. P. Ross, P. A. Lichtenberg, and B. K. Christensen, 1995, *Clinical Neuropsychologist, 9*, p. 324. Copyright © 1995 by Swets and Zeitlinger. Used with permission. Data from row 7 come from "Effects of Age, Education, and Living Environment on Boston Naming Test Performance," by J. Neils, J. M. Baris, C. Carter, A. L. Dell'aira, S. J. Nordloh, E. Weiler, and B. Weisiger, 1995, *Journal of Speech and Hearing Research, 38*, p. 1146. Copyright © 1995 by the American Speech-Language-Hearing Association. Adapted with permission.

tions or routine blood work and who did not have a history of neurologic or psychiatric disorders. M. S. Albert et al. (1988) assessed 44 community dwelling males age 60 and older who had been screened to exclude those with alcoholism, psychiatric illness, learning disabilities, severe head trauma, epilepsy, hypertension, chronic lung disease, kidney disease, coronary artery disease, and cancer. This sample showed overall better performances for both age groups than the samples of Borod and LaBarge. In addition to overall performance, M. S. Albert et al. (1988) examined naming error types and observed that semantic errors (i.e., circumlocutions, semantically related associates, nominalizations) and perceptual errors increase with age, whereas other error types do not.

Heaton et al. (1991) included the BNT–85 as part of their expanded Halstead–Reitan Battery (see chap. 2 for a description of this sample). The BNT–85 was administered to 107 persons (mean age = 64.3, SD = 10.4) from their larger sample. The total number of items correct was used in their normative system (see chap. 2 for a description of their approach). Age appears to exert minimal effects in terms of T-score values (e.g., a raw score of 70 is equivalent to a scaled score of 8; for men with a grade 12 education, T-scores of 42, 47, and 49 are obtained by persons age 60, 70, and 80, respectively).

The BNT was revised to a 60-item version (BNT–60) to improve the psychometric properties of the instrument (Kaplan, Goodglass, & Weintraub, 1983). Although other shortened versions of the BNT have been proposed (e.g., Huff, Collins, Corkin, & Rosen, 1986; Mack, Freed, Williams, & Henderson, 1992), little data are available for older persons on these measures. The remainder of this discussion of the BNT focuses, then, on the BNT–60 (see Table 8.3).

Van Gorp, Satz, Kiersch, and Henry (1986) examined the BNT–60 performance of 78 adults ranging from age 59 to 95 who were healthy, independently functioning, and living autonomously in California. None had a history of neurologic or psychiatric disease or alcoholism. Cutoff scores of 51 (59–65 years), 47.12 (65–69 years), 44.12 (70–74 years), 39.29 (75–79 years), and 37.56 (80+ years) were provided based on scores 2 standard deviations below the mean. Mitrushina and Satz (1989) assessed 156 healthy persons between age 57 and 85 (see chap. 2 for a description of this sample). Van Gorp et al. (1990) reported information for a similar, if not the same, group of normal elderly persons as Mitrushina and Satz (1989) with slight differences in means and standard deviations. D. B. Howieson, Holm, Kaye, Oken, and J. Howieson's (1993) sample consisted of 51 persons age 65 and older, all of whom were healthy, community dwelling, functionally independent persons. Special emphasis was made in this study to exclude persons with age-related diseases that may affect the brain. All three of these samples for which normative data were collected on the

BNT–60 can be considered "super healthy" and only minimal differences between these samples are apparent.

Neils et al. (1995) extended this examination of the BNT–60 to include education and living environment (institutional and independent living) in addition to age as important demographic factors for consideration. Educational background accounted for the largest portion of the variance in the BNT–60, followed by age and living situation. They cautioned that poor performance on the BNT–60 may be typical of otherwise normal persons with limited education and emphasized the need for more comparative information for those with limited education. Table 8.3 contains information on the BNT–60 performance by age group and education level separately for the 167 community dwelling persons by age group. These individuals had completed a brief self-assessment of their medical history and those indicating a positive neurologic history or cognitive deficit had been excluded.

Ross, Lichtenberg, and Christensen (1995) examined BNT–60 performance in a group of 123 geriatric inpatients at an urban rehabilitation hospital. All persons observed or reported to have neurological, psychiatric, or alcohol abuse problems were excluded from the study. Sixty percent of the sample were African American and the mean education level was 11.05 years (*SD* = 3.38). As is apparent in Table 8.3, the means and standard deviations obtained for this sample were poorer than those seen in other studies. Ross et al. suggested these normative data are more appropriate for use in urban medical settings than those data obtained from optimally healthy samples.

A French language adaptation of the Boston Naming Test has also been developed (Colombo & Assal, 1992) with normative data collected for 420 persons living in the French part of Switzerland who were free of neurological or psychiatric disorders. All persons over age 70 were living independently in the community. Data are presented by gender, age (by decade from 20 to 89 years), and socioeconomic level (3 levels), with 10 persons per cell. They used the BNT–85 and removed 9 items judged to be inappropriate from a sociocultural perspective. Of the remaining 76 items, a single correct response was required for 64 items and two correct responses were allowable for 12 items. The test was divided into two shortened versions of 20 items. Corrections for socioeconomic level were determined and norms were developed on the distribution of the cumulated frequencies of the corrected scores for the short and long versions.

Nicholas, Brookshire, MacLennan, Schumacher, and Porrazzo (1989) noted a lack of interrater reliability data for the BNT–60 and that commercially available administration and scoring instructions lack clarity. They provided standard administration, response coding, and scoring procedures for the BNT–60. Prompts to be given following certain types of incorrect responses were also developed (Nicholas et al., 1989). They administered this revised BNT–60 (BNT–60–R) to 60 nonbrain-damaged persons age 40 to 78 and reported a high percentage of scoring agreements within the same rater (98%) and between raters (86%–95%). There was no correlation between the BNT–60–R and age and, as a group, the 60 persons in their study obtained a mean performance of 54.50 ($SD = 3.52$). Two response categories (i.e., Related Names and Don't Know) accounted for approximately 88% of all incorrect responses. Prompting following Related Name and Multiple Attempts responses frequently elicited the correct response, whereas prompts following other error responses did not. This information concerning the types of errors made by nonbrain-damaged persons may assist clinicians in evaluating the significance of these errors in clinical situations.

The *Controlled Oral Word Association Test* (CWAT; Benton & Hamsher, 1978), a commonly used measure of verbal fluency, requires that the respondent generate as many words as possible in response to a given stimulus letter over a 1-minute period. Three stimulus letters are presented successively. The total number of acceptable words constitutes the raw score, which is then corrected for educational level and sex. An age correction for the 60- 64-year level is also included. It has been suggested (Benton, Eslinger, & Damasio, 1981) that a corrected score of 22 or less denotes a defective performance (i.e., exceeded by 97% of normal persons).

A decline in verbal fluency performance has been found in elderly persons by some investigators (e.g., Benton et al., 1981). There are a number of possible explanations for these discrepancies in findings, including the difficulty level of the letters selected. It was noted by Bolla et al. (1990) that Benton's norms are for the letters *CFL* and *PRW*, even though many investigators use *FAS*. According to a study of the difficulty level for different letters by Borkowski, Benton, and Spreen (1967), *L* and *R* are of moderate difficulty and *FASCPW* are all classified as easy. Of note, it is not always specified which letters were used in the studies of the effects of age on verbal fluency production.

Although Benton and Hamsher's (1978) norms imply age, education and sex effects (in that corrections are provided for each of these three variables), Benton et al. (1981) noted that there is little evidence of decline in performance when the age correction specified for the 60 to 64 age group was applied to all persons from age 60 to 80. They reported that 11% of the 37 volunteers who considered themselves to be psychologically normal, in reasonably good health, with no history of neurologic or psychiatric disorders requiring hospitalization, and were age 80 or older performed below expectations (for the 60- 64-year-old group) on this measure. Later it was revealed that CWAT was one of the three measures contributing most to distinguishing between persons with dementia and normal persons matched on age, sex, and education (Eslinger, Damasio, Benton, & Van Allen, 1985). The mean performance for this control group was 37.9 (*SD* = 10.9).

K. M. Montgomery (1982) administered the FAS version of the CWAT to 85 volunteers over age 65 who were living independently in the community, had no history of psychiatric or neurologic disorders, and had adequate sight and hearing. Little effect of age was noted. The mean raw score performance for this group was 38.77 (*SD* = 12.87).

Farmer et al. (1987) administered the CWAT as part of the Framingham Heart Study (see chap. 2 for a description of this sample). They provided the means and standard deviations by gender and educational level for persons age 55 to 89 (see Table 8.4). No clear age effects are apparent but marked differences by educational level were noted.

TABLE 8.4
Means and Standard Deviations for Performance on the CWAT
from the Multilingual Aphasia Battery (Benton & Hamsher, 1978)

Age Group	Men			Women		
	8–11 Years Education	*12 Years Education*	*13+ Years Education*	*8–11 Years Education*	*12 Years Education*	*13+ Years Education*
65–69						
M	29.2	32.6	39.0	24.3	34.6	39.9
SD	14.0	8.4	12.8	8.6	11.6	12.3
n	27	42	29	38	52	70
70–74						
M	27.5	28.5	34.9	26.6	34.4	36.8
SD	8.3	8.2	12.0	9.2	7.8	11.1
n	29	20	37	36	35	50
75–79						
M	28.7	30.5	37.4	27.2	33.4	37.8
SD	10.0	11.0	11.9	11.6	15.1	10.0
n	15	8	16	29	35	22
80–84						
M	21.9	29.2	36.0	25.9	34.2	31.6
SD	10.8	9.1	9.3	10.3	11.6	10.9
n	14	5	9	16	15	19
85–89						
M			33.0	20.7	31.3	25.5
SD			11.8	5.2	10.4	9.3
n			3	6	3	4

M. S. Albert et al. (1988) examined the total raw score performance of 21 persons age 60 to 69 years and 23 persons between age 70 and 80 (see previous sample description) on the FAS version of the CWAT. They also requested that as many proper names as possible be generated in a 1-minute period. The older age group performed less well on each measure (FAS: $M = 39.65$, $SD = 10.44$; proper nouns: $M = 18.30$, $SD = 3.61$) than the younger group (FAS: $M = 45.33$, $SD = 11.56$; proper nouns, $M = 20.00$, $SD = 4.38$).

Bolla et al. (1990) examined the performance of 199 volunteers from the John's Hopkins Teaching Nursing Home Study of Normal Aging (see chap. 2 for a description of this sample). The score was the total number of words produced. Significant effects of verbal intelligence (as measured by the raw score from the Vocabulary subtest of the WAIS–R) and gender were found on FAS performance, but no age effect was evident. They noted that their sample was average or above average with respect to verbal intelligence and provided a caution when using this information to make judgments concerning individuals who do not exhibit similar levels of verbal intelligence.

Axelrod and Henry (1992) examined the performance of 20 persons in each decade from 50 through 80 (see chap. 2 for a description of this sample) on the FAS version of the CWAT and examined raw scores for each letter and the total number of words generated across all three letters. No age effect on CWAT performance was noted and there did not appear to be major differences in terms of the number of words generated for each letter (see Table 8.5).

Thus, although some minor deterioration with age has been reported, specifically over age 80, it seems that the CWAT appears to stay relatively stable with increasing age in the samples reported here. It is not always specified which version of the CWAT was used and this should be encouraged in the future.

TABLE 8.5
Means and Standard Deviations (in parentheses)
for Performance on the FAS Version of the CWAT by Age

Variable	60–69	70–79	80–89
F	14.2 (4.7)	11.8 (3.2)	13.1 (4.1)
A	11.2 (3.7)	10.8 (4.3)	11.5 (5.1)
S	14.2 (3.8)	13.4 (3.9)	13.2 (5.4)
FAS	39.6 (10.7)	36.0 (9.3)	37.8 (14.0)

Note. From "Age-related Performance on the Wisconsin Card Sorting, Similarities, and Controlled Oral Word Association Tests," by B. N. Axelrod and R. R. Henry, 1992, *Clinical Neuropsychologist, 6,* p. 22. Copyright © 1992 by Swets & Zeitlinger Publishers. Used with permission.

VISUOPERCEPTUAL AND MOTOR SKILLS

It is often noted that the most pronounced declines with increasing age are observed on measures requiring visuoperceptual and/or visuomotor skills (M. S. Albert, 1988; Lezak, 1995). These declines are particularly evident after age 70. Although Benton and Tranel (1993) used the terms *visuoperceptual, visuospatial,* and *visuoconstructive* when describing different types of disorders that may arise as a consequence of brain disease, this chapter discusses measures reflecting these constructs under the general rubric of visuoperceptual and motor skills. Of note, there is not extensive normative information available for older adults on many of the measures in these domains, except perhaps the performance scales from the WAIS–R (see chap. 4). Georgemiller and Hassan (1986) described assessment strategies for abilities such as route finding, route learning, and topographical memory in the context of the older adult.

The remainder of this chapter focuses on measures for which some normative information is available. The order of review proceeds from those that are primarily visual in nature to those that primarily involve tactile/motor functions.

Visuoperceptual Measures

The *Hooper Visual Organization Test* (HVOT; Hooper, 1958) is comprised of 30 pictures of jigsawlike cut-up common objects. The respondent must determine what the object would be if the pieces were put back together. This task requires the participant to mentally manipulate the visual stimuli to obtain the correct response. In some instances one-half credits can be awarded for partially correct responses.

All sources of information on HVOT performance across age concur that declines with advancing age are expected. K. M. Montgomery (1982) administered the HVOT to 85 volunteers over age 65 (see previous description of this sample). The HVOT correlated significantly with age ($r -.48$). An overall mean of 22.52 ($SD = 4.1$) was obtained for her sample. P. F. Farver and T. B. Farver (1982) administered the HVOT to 36 persons between age 60 and 89. These individuals were screened for significant neurological, psychiatric, and medical conditions that may affect cognition. However, 15 people were included who were taking hypertensive medication or had a head injury with no known neurological sequelae. All but 5 were living independently in the community. When scores were adjusted for educational level, the 60 to 69 and 70 to 79 age groups differed from the 80 to 89 group, suggesting that the most pronounced effect occurring after age 60 is for those over age 80. Tamkin and Jacobsen (1984) examined the HVOT performance in 211 male psychiatric inpatients and observed a continuous decline in HVOT scores as age increased. For persons age 70 and older, they indicated a score from 10–30 fell within 2 standard deviations of the mean, whereas scores of 6–9 indicated mild impairment, and scores of 2–5 indicated moderate impairment. Their sample performed differently from Montgomery's normal elderly sample, where scores above 14 were considered within the average range.

Benton, Sivan, Hamsher, Varney, and Spreen (1994) described a number of perceptual and motor measures for which they have obtained normative information for older adults. They are combined here for ease of description. Limited information concerning the characteristics of the normative samples is available from Benton et al. (1994).

The *Judgment of Line Orientation Task* requires the respondent to identify which lines, from a multiple choice array, match the lines on the stimulus card. The lines in the stimulus item are shorter than the lines in the response array and the respondent is asked to identify which lines are pointing in the same direction as those in the stimulus card. There are two forms of this measure. Each contains 5 practice items and 30 test items. A consistent decline in performance was noted with increasing age and a consistent difference of about 2 points was noted by gender favoring men. Corrections for these differences were developed and involved adding 3 points to the scores of persons between age 65 and 74 and 2 points for women in all age groups. Mean corrected scores of 25.7 and 25.8 were then obtained by men and women, respectively, between age 65 and 74.

The *Visual Form Discrimination* task requires the respondent to match the stimulus item to one in an array of four multiple-choice alternatives. There is no time limit for this task and there are 16 items. The maximum score per item is 2 and types of errors (e.g., peripheral error, major distortion) can be examined. In a sample of 85 normal persons, means of 29.3 and 30.3 were determined for the 15 men and 12 women, respectively, in the age 55 to 74 range. For persons below age 75, no age corrections were recommended (Benton et al., 1994), but Valdois, Poissant, and Joanette (1989) observed a considerable decline in the performance of persons between age 75 and 84 as compared to younger age groups.

The last of the Benton measures to be discussed here, the *Tactual Form Perception* task, requires the respondent to identify, on a multiple-choice display, each of 10 sandpaper figures by feeling them with the fingers of each hand. That is, 10 figures are identified using the right hand and 10 figures are identified using the left hand. A slight decline (i.e., 9/10 for each hand) was noted with advancing age for performance of the 61 to 70-year-old age group ($n = 32$).

The *Bender–Gestalt Test* (BGT) requires the respondent to copy increasingly difficult designs accurately. There are nine designs to be copied and various sets of instructions and scoring systems have been used when administering this task (see Lezak, 1995, for a thorough description).

Lacks and Storandt (1982) administered this measure to 334 persons age 60 and older who were of middle and lower-middle socioeconomic class with an average educational level of 8.8 years. All persons were assessed by their personal physicians to be sufficiently healthy to live independently. An adaptation of the Hutt–Briskin system (1960) was used to score the responses to the task. Two raters scored the protocols and an interrater agreement of .87 was obtained for a sample of 163 records. The frequencies of errors varied slightly across the five age groups (60–64, $n = 23$; 65–69, $n = 21$; 70–74, $n = 21$; 75–79, $n = 32$; 80+, $n = 26$) from a mean of 3.23 ($SD = 1.67$) for the youngest group to 3.45 ($SD = 1.99$) for the oldest group. Thus, the impairment criterion developed on younger adults (i.e., five or more errors) did not change substantially with advancing age.

The *Ruff Figural Fluency Test* (RFFT) was designed to assess the ability to perform fluently in a visuospatial mode and was meant to be analogous to verbal fluency tasks. It consists of five parts, each containing a different stimulus presentation (i.e., arrangement) of five dots. The participant is to connect two or more of the five dots using straight lines to make as many designs as possible. One minute is allowed for each of the five parts. The number of unique designs and the number of perseverative errors are recorded.

Ruff, Light, and Evans (1987) administered the RFFT to 85 volunteers who ranged from age 55 to 70 with approximately equal numbers in each of three education levels (i.e., lowest: < 12 years; middle: 13–15 years; highest: 16 or more years). All participants were screened to exclude those with a positive history of psychiatric hospitalization, chronic polydrug use, or neurological disorder. The total number of unique designs was related to level of education (highest: $M = 84.4$, $SD = 20.8$; middle: $M = 77.2$, $SD = 17.7$; lowest: $M = 67.5$, $SD = 19.9$). Error scores showed no differences by age, education, or gender, but the scores were very variable. The average number of perseverative errors was 9.2 with a standard deviation of 12.2. Little other information about the clinical utility of this measure is, as yet, available.

Tactual and Motor Tasks

The *Tactual Performance Test* (TPT) is a visuospatial performance task that was modified by Halstead (1947) to involve tactile memory. The respondent is blindfolded and required to place blocks of different shapes onto a board containing holes corresponding to the shapes of the blocks. The score is time to completion with the dominant and nondominant hands and when both hands are used together. After completing this portion of the task, the blindfold is removed and the respondent is asked to draw the board (i.e., indicate the shapes and their locations). This yields two additional scores: the number of shapes correctly recalled (i.e., Memory score) and the number of blocks placed in proper relation to the board and other blocks (i.e., Location score). Administration and scoring procedures may differ (see Lezak, 1995) by investigator and age contributes significantly to performance on this task.

Heaton et al. (1991) included a 10-item TPT as part of their expanded Halstead–Reitan Battery (see chap. 2 for a description of this sample). The TPT was administered to 378 persons (mean age = 41.8, SD = 16.7) from their base sample and 108 persons (mean age = 42.7, SD = 17.1) from their validation sample. A minutes-per-block score (i.e., number of minutes divided by the number of blocks correctly placed) for each of the three trials and the total time to complete all trials were the scores used in their normative system (see chap. 2 for a description of their approach). The number of shapes recalled (i.e., Memory) and the number of shapes placed in their correct locations (i.e., Locations) were also included as scores in their normative system.

The *Purdue Pegboard* (PP) is a commonly used measure of manual dexterity (Tiffin, 1968). The respondent is asked to place metal pins, one at a time, into a row of pegboard holes first with the dominant hand and then the nondominant hand. In a third trial, pins are placed in the pegboard holes with both hands simultaneously. In the last trial, a pin, washer, collar, and washer are assembled in an operation requiring the coordination of both hands.

Agnew, Bolla-Wilson, Kawas, and Bleecker (1988) administered the PP to 212 healthy volunteers from the Johns Hopkins Teaching Nursing Home Study of Normal Aging (see chap. 2 for a description of this sample). One hundred and twenty-five of these persons were age 60 and over. They administered three 30-second trials for each subtest except the assembly subtest for which three 60-second trials were administered. Scores were determined as the average performance across the three trials (i.e., number of pins or number of components properly placed). Gender and age effects were observed, but the rate of decline across age groups did not differ by gender (see Table 8.6). Women performed better than men and generalized slowing with increasing age was apparent.

For *Grooved Pegboard* (GP), the respondent must place pegs, which contain a ridge along one side, into holes on a small board containing a 5 × 5 matrix of slotted holes angled in different directions. The score is time to completion. The task may be performed with the preferred or nonpreferred hands.

Heaton et al. (1991) included the GP as part of their expanded Halstead-Reitan Battery (see chap. 2 for a description of this sample). The GP was administered to 368 persons (mean age = 41.4, SD = 16.7) from

TABLE 8.6
Means and Standard Deviations (in parentheses)
for Performance on the Purdue Pegboard

	Men			Women		
	60–69 Years	70–79 Years	80–89 Years	60–69 Years	70–79 Years	80–89 Years
Dominant Hand	13.6	13.0	10.8	14.6	13.8	12.9
	(1.74)	(1.90)	(1.33)	(2.03)	(1.27)	(1.80)
Nondominant Hand	13.1	12.4	10.6	13.9	12.9	11.2
	(1.56)	(1.48)	(1.84)	(1.78)	(1.52)	(2.05)
Both Hands	10.9	10.4	8.5	11.6	10.5	9.2
	(1.46)	(1.27)	(1.21)	(1.87)	(1.19)	(1.92)
Assembly	28.0	27.5	21.5	31.7	29.1	21.9
	(5.06)	(5.06)	(4.81)	(6.83)	(4.85)	(4.54)

Note. From "Purdue Pegboard Age and Sex Norms for People 40 Years Old and Older," by J. Agnew, K. Bolla-Wilson, C. H. Kawas, and M. L. Bleecker, 1988, *Developmental Neuropsychology, 4,* p. 32. Copyright © 1988 by Lawrence Erlbaum Associates, Inc. Adapted with permission.

their base sample and 107 persons (mean age = 42.5, *SD* = 17.1) from their validation sample. The total number of seconds required to place 25 pegs was the score used in their normative system (see chap. 2 for a description of their approach). Age appears to exert some effect, though not dramatic, in terms of *T*-score values (e.g., a raw score of 65 is equivalent to a scaled score of 10; for men with a grade 12 education, *T*-scores of 62, 67, and 70 are obtained by persons aged 60, 70, and 80, respectively).

Another common measure of manual dexterity is the *Finger Oscillation*, or *Finger Tapping Test* (FTT). For this task, the respondent is asked to tap a key attached to a device for recording the number of taps as quickly as possible over a 10-second interval. Typically, five trials are performed for each hand and the score is the average of the five trials. Some variations in administration and scoring have been noted (see Lezak, 1995, for a discussion of these). As with the PP, an age-related decline would be expected for the FTT.

R. R. Bornstein (1985) administered the FTT to 57 persons age 60 and older. Scores were based on the average of 5 trials within 5 points of each other to a maximum of 10 trials (see Table 8.7). Of note, the men perform better on this measure of manual dexterity than the women.

CONCLUSIONS

The two groups of tasks included in this chapter, those assessing language/communication and those assessing visuoperceptual/motor functions, each show changes with increasing age. The role of memory has

TABLE 8.7
Means and Standard Deviations on the Finger
Tapping Test for Persons Between Age 60 and 69

Hand	Male		Female	
	Less Than High School Education (n = 16)	High School Education or Better (n = 23)	Less Than High School Education (n = 22)	High School Education or Better (n = 34)
Preferred	39.1	43.0	29.7	32.2
Hand	(5.7)	(4.7)	(6.2)	(6.0)
Nonpreferred	35.2	39.3	29.8	32.0
Hand	(5.2)	(6.2)	(5.6)	(4.9)

Note. From "Normative Data on Selected Neuropsychological Measures From a Nonclinical Sample," by R. A. Bornstein, 1985, *Journal of Clinical Psychology, 41,* p. 656. Copyright © 1985 by John Wiley & Sons, Inc. Adapted by permission of John Wiley & Sons, Inc.

been noted with respect to the language measures and the role of motor speed has been noted as a possible confound in the performance of some visuoperceptual tasks. Gender and education effects are also observed for some of these measures. For these measures as for those discussed in the other chapters, the use of age-appropriate norms is imperative, particularly after age 75.

Chapter 9

Assessing Psychopathology

The geriatric neuropsychologist often wishes to assess for the presence of psychopathology, because such conditions can often mimic or exacerbate symptoms of dementia (Lezak, 1980). It is estimated that a minimum of 10% of people over age 65 have emotional and cognitive problems of clinical severity (Birren & Sloane, 1977). Although there is little research to support the assumption that mental disorders manifest themselves in similar ways in younger and older adults (La Rue, Dessonville, & Jarvik, 1985), the *DSM–IV* (American Psychiatric Association, 1994) criteria generally do not differentiate between these two groups. In addition, risk factors for psychiatric conditions may not be the same for young and old persons, as the latter may be more likely to suffer from sensory deficits, physical illness, bereavement, and social isolation (La Rue et al., 1985).

Traditionally, research work with elderly psychiatric patients has not been very popular, although in recent years there has been a tendency for such work to emerge (Gatz, 1995; La Rue et al., 1985). The relative lack of information in this area may complicate the assessment of psychopathology in elderly persons. For instance, somatic complaints are generally more common in later life but may also be evident in depression (Davison & Neale, 1994). Differentiating somatic symptoms of depression from symptoms due to physical decline may be difficult. Despite emerging interest in this field (e.g., Birren et al., 1992), attempts to develop psychometric instruments and tailor existing ones for use with elderly persons are relatively rare. Moreover, available information lacks detail and is relatively primitive in relation to work pursued with younger persons.

Rather than including an extended discussion of psychopathology in elderly persons, a brief overview of major psychopathology syndromes is presented and their assessment with reference to available psychometrically developed instruments is discussed. Also included is a selective review and norms pertaining to specific instruments that have been used with elders.

Generally, it is recommended that the geriatric neuropsychologist refer to the *DSM–IV* in attempting to diagnose mental disorders. Although the system is not specifically geared toward the elderly patient, it provides explicit definitions and behavioral criteria and is probably the diagnostic system that meets with the highest consensus in North America. The *DSM–IV* section most relevant to the geriatric neuropsychologist is "Delirium, Dementia and Other Cognitive Disorders." Psychological disorders often considered in neuropsychological assessment include depression, delusional (paranoid) disorders, schizophrenia and psychotic disorders, sleep disorders, hypochondriasis, and substance related disorders. A brief overview of these categories is provided.

A variety of instruments designed to assess adult psychopathology are available to the clinician. Great caution should be exercised when using such instruments, however, because most lack representative norms for elderly persons and this may limit their validity. Even where norms for elders exist, the best way to interpret findings is not always clear. Specifically, whether or not separate norms for elders must be used depends both on the magnitude and the meaning of age differences (Butcher et al., 1991). In some instances, it may be that scores obtained by elderly persons may not be statistically different from scores obtained by younger age groups. Such findings would argue against the need for separate norms for the elderly. Unfortunately, some of the studies reporting norms did not report statistical comparisons among different age groups. It is, therefore, difficult to evaluate the utility of the reported norms. In addition, as normative studies on psychopathology scales are typically cross sectional, age effects cannot be disentangled from cohort effects, and many of the differences may be due to historical effects and differences in physical health rather than personality and psychopathology per se (Butcher et al., 1991). Finally, norms derived from cognitively intact groups of subjects may be of limited usefulness in the assessment of people with cognitive impairments.

This chapter reviews instruments that have been developed for administration to the individual. First it discusses some multidimensional instruments (i.e., MMPI-2, Brief Symptom Inventory and projective tests). Such instruments may be useful for the assessment of a variety of conditions. Following the discussion of the multidimensional instruments, an examination of specific disorders and psychometric instruments that can be used to assess these is included. (Chapter 11 focuses on the role of collaborative informants in the assessment process and discusses proxy-administered measures that may assist in the assessment of psychopathology in elderly persons).

MULTIDIMENSIONAL PSYCHOPATHOLOGY
INSTRUMENTS

The *Minnesota Multiphasic Personality Inventory-2* (Butcher, Dahlstrom, Graham, Tellegen, & Kaemer, 1989) is a very widely used, empirically developed measure of psychopathology. Although it consists of 10 clinical scales, a configural interpretation of the instrument is recommended (Graham, 1993). Reliability varies from scale to scale but test–retest reliability for scales ranges from .58 to .92 (Butcher et al., 1989). The data also support the validity of the instrument (Graham, 1993). In a review of the literature, Graham (1993) concluded that elderly persons obtain somewhat higher MMPI scores on Scales 1 (hypochondriasis), 2 (depression), 3 (hysteria), and 0 (social introversion) and lower scores on Scales 4 (psychopathic deviate) and 9 (mania). Graham suggested that such elevations in the elderly should not be taken to reflect increased psychopathology but concern about health and decreases in activity levels. Graham also suggested that the decision as to whether age-specific norms should be used on the MMPI or the MMPI–2 depends on the context of the assessment. Does the assessor wish to determine whether the elderly person has somatic concerns relative to the population at large or relative to other persons the same age?

Although the normative sample of the MMPI–2 included older adults (Butcher et al., 1991), they were underrepresented. The committee did not include separate norms for elderly persons in the manual, but conducted appropriate analyses and concluded that age-specific norms are not needed (at least for older men). Specifically, Butcher et al. (1991) concluded that of the 567 MMPI–2 items, only 14 differed by more than 20% in endorsement and such differences probably reflected cohort effects. Based on current knowledge, Graham (1993) and Butcher et al. (1991) recommended that the use of age-specific norms for older adults does not seem appropriate at this time. Table 9.1 presents some norms for older men based on Butcher et al. (1991). Readers can refer to these for comparison purposes but it may be premature to use these norms at the present time as they are not the basis for the MMPI validation research. Butcher et al. (1991) presented additional statistical information pertinent to these norms.

Priest and Meunier (1993) studied a relatively small sample (valid $N = 26$) of well-educated elderly women and presented MMPI–2 norms based on their findings. Although some differences in the performance of this sample and younger adults were found, these were not large. Quite rightfully, they cautioned that their results are not large enough to warrant, in and of themselves, the disregarding of traditional normative information. Clearly, the question as to whether separate MMPI–2 norms are needed for elderly women, can be addressed using a larger and more diverse sample of adults.

Although cautions for the use of the previous version of the MMPI (L. W. Smith, Patterson, Grant, & Clopton, 1989) for the elderly have

TABLE 9.1
Age Differences in MMPI–2 Clinical Scales
for the Boston Normative Aging Sample

Scale	60–69 Years of Age (n = 591)		70–91 Years of Age (n = 241)	
	M	SD	M	SD
Lie (L)	4.94	2.36	5.10	2.58
Fake Bad (F)	3.67	2.62	3.69	2.69
Subtle Defensiveness (K)	17.21	4.65	16.74	4.50
Hypochondriasis (Hs)	5.24	4.10	5.83	4.06
Depression (D)	19.08	5.07	20.03	5.24
Hysteria (Hy)	21.50	4.93	21.20	4.99
Psychopathic Deviate (Pd)	14.78	4.19	13.77	3.75
Masculinity–Femininity (Mf)	22.69	4.25	23.35	4.15
Paranoia (Pa)	8.82	2.87	8.46	2.66
Psychasthenia (Pt)	8.38	6.61	8.91	6.43
Schizophrenia (Sc)	7.95	6.04	8.26	5.88
Hypomania (Ma)	14.52	3.71	14.17	3.88
Social Introversion (Si)	25.61	8.61	27.32	8.94

Note. MMPI–2 = revised Minnesota Multiphasic Personality Inventory. From "Personality and Aging: A Study of the MMPI–2 Among Older Men," by J. N. Butcher, C. M. Aldwin, M. R. Levenson, Y. S. Ben-Porath, A. Spiro III, and R. Bosse, 1991, *Psychology and Aging, 6,* p. 366. Copyright © 1991 by the American Psychological Association. Adapted with permission.

been raised in the literature, relevant norms on a short version of the original MMPI were presented by L. W. Smith et al. (1989). The clinician may wish to plot the MMPI profile based on norms for elderly persons (see, e.g., W. G. Dahlstrom, Welsh, & L. E. Dahlstrom, 1972, pp. 384–385) in addition to the profile based on the normative sample. However, R. L. Green (1980), in his interpretive guide for the MMPI–2, recommended that the actual interpretation should be based on the general normative sample profile as the interpretation and validation information is based on this sample. Thus, it is not clear what would be the validity of interpretations based on norms for the aged. Overall, more research is needed to determine the utility of the MMPI–2 with the elderly. However, the scale has clearly proven useful in the assessment of younger adults.

The *Brief Symptom Inventory* (BSI) is an abbreviated form of the Symptom Checklist–90 (SCL–90; Derogatis, 1977). It consists of 53 items and measures psychopathology on the dimensions listed in Table 9.2. These dimensions correspond and are highly correlated to the dimensions of the SCL–90 (Derogatis, 1977). Hale, Cochran, and Hedgepeth (1984) produced norms for persons over age 59 (see Table 9.2). They pointed out that the SCL–90 includes somatic items but these do not confound the depression scale as they appear in a separate somatization scale. Because the scores

TABLE 9.2
Normative Information on the Brief Symptom Inventory

	Female (n = 364)		Male (n = 201)	
	M	SD	M	SD
Age	73.54	7.04	73.92	7.06
Somatization	.50	.53	.45	.48
Obsessive-Compulsive	.83	.67	.73	.59
Interpersonal Sensitivity	.40	.56	.32	.47
Depression	.53	.59	.43	.50
Anxiety	.48	.54	.30	.39
Hostility	.29	.41	.34	.42
Phobic Anxiety	.25	.42	.17	.36
Paranoid Ideation	.37	.46	.44	.51
Psychoticism	.26	.37	.25	.36

Note. Ninety-five percent of the subjects were residing independently in the community. The remaining were living in nursing homes. From "Norms for the Elderly on the Brief Symptom Inventory," by W. D. Hale, C. D. Cochran, and B. E. Hedgepeth, 1984, *Journal of Consulting and Clinical Psychology, 52,* p. 321. Copyright © 1984 by the American Psychological Association. Adapted with permission.

for males and females differ along some scales, Hale et al. produced separate norms for each gender. In addition, their overall conclusion was that the use of special norms for the elderly would be appropriate as higher scores are obtained for older adults than young adults on many scales.

In terms of *projective approaches,* it is probably fair to say that they are not used commonly in geriatric neuropsychological assessments. They may prove useful, however, in some cases (e.g., in situations where an elderly person lacks testwise skills and is uncomfortable in answering direct questions). Although some normative work in the use of projective tests with the elderly has been done, the samples are generally small and validity evidence still remains to be accumulated (Hayslip & Lowman, 1986). Furthermore, the ability of such tests to assist in the diagnosis of psychopathology in the aged remains to be determined (Hayslip & Lowman, 1986).

UNIDIMENSIONAL PSYCHOPATHOLOGY INSTRUMENTS

Anxiety Scales

Estimates of prevalence for *anxiety disorders* in the elderly range from 3.5% to 10.2% (Flint, 1994) and tranquillizer medications are used by the elderly in disproportionately higher rates than by younger individuals (Hersen &

Van Hasselt, 1992). Nonetheless, Flint (1994) concluded that most studies show that anxiety disorders are somewhat less common in the elderly than they are in young adults. He also concluded that generalized anxiety and phobias account for most late-life anxiety. Agoraphobia (and possibly obsessive compulsive disorder for women) may occur for the first time late in life. Panic disorder, obsessive-compulsive disorder in males, and phobias can persist from younger years, or they may be attributable to another medical or psychiatric disorder. Finally, Flint (1994) concluded that comorbidity of anxiety with medical illness and alcoholism is lower in late life than it is in younger people.

Professionals must differentiate anxiety from physical disorders and conditions associated with anxietylike symptoms (e.g., hyperthyroidism, small stroke or ischemic attack, use of substances such as caffeine and alcohol).

Several psychometric instruments are available that may be used to measure anxiety and fear in older adults within the context of the clinical assessment. These include the BSI, the MMPI–2 (discussed earlier), the *State-Trait Anxiety Inventory* (Spielberger, Gorsuch, & Lushene, 1970; Spielberger, Gorsuch, Lushene, Vagg, & Jacobs, 1983), the *State Trait Anxiety Inventory for Children* (Spielberger, Gorsuch, Lushene, Montouri, & Platsek, 1973), and the *Self-Rating Anxiety Scale* (W. K. Zung, 1971). However, most developed assessment techniques assume that the elderly patient does not present with cognitive impairment and the norms that exist have been based primarily on community dwelling elders. Thus, they may not be appropriate for institutionalized persons. The progression of dementia can limit the opportunity for the direct assessment of the elderly person and much of the assessment information can be better derived from interviews with a proxy or by observation. Given the limited norms that are applicable to elders, objective behavioral assessment procedures such as behavioral avoidance tests, functional analysis, self-monitoring, and other related procedures (see Bellack & Hersen, 1988) may be particularly useful for this group. Finally, as depression is often comorbid with anxiety, the clinician may also wish to use a depression scale that has been normed for elders.

The *State–Trait Anxiety Inventory* (STAI; Spielberger et al., 1970) consists of two main scales: a State and a Trait scale. When filling out the State scale, individuals are asked to respond to the items in reference to how they feel at the moment the questionnaire is being filled out. In the Trait part of the instruments, the person is asked to indicate how they generally feel. The items in the two scales are not identical. Responses are provided along 4-point scales. The manual of this instrument reports data supporting its reliability and validity (Spielberger et al., 1970).

Limited norms for the STAI (Spielberger et al., 1970) are available and are listed in Table 9.3 (Knight, Waal-Manning, & Spears, 1983). However, the normative samples are rather small and the STAI New Zealand norms

TABLE 9.3
Normative Information for Older Adults
on the State Trait Anxiety Inventory

Age Group	Measure	
	STAI–State	STAI–Trait
Male		
60–69 ($n = 59$)	30.39 (7.18)	32.94 (7.26)
70–79 ($n = 29$)	32.44 (8.49)	32.15 (7.49)
Female		
60–69 ($n = 80$)	32.59 (9.49)	35.15 (8.40)[a]
70–79 ($n = 37$)	33.49 (9.05)[b]	34.47 (8.45)

Note. STAI–State = State Trait Anxiety Inventory–State; STAI–Trait = State Trait Anxiety Inventory–Trait. The data are based on a sample recruited from a small New Zealand community. From "Some Norms and Reliability Data for the State-Trait Anxiety Inventory and the Zung Self-Rating Depression Scale," by R. G. Knight, H. J. Waal-Manning, and G. F. Spears, *British Journal of Clinical Psychology, 22*, p. 247. Copyright © 1983 by the British Psychological Society. Adapted with permission.
[a]$n = 78$.
[b]$n = 36$.

of Knight (1984) may be of limited generalizability to North American samples. In addition, representative norms for elderly persons are needed using the more recent version of the STAI (Spielberger et al., 1983). The Knight (1984) normative information suggests, however, that (at least in their sample) there were no substantial differences in scores over the life span. Although research has supported the factorial validity of the STAI in a psychogeriatric sample (Nesselroade, Mitteness, & Thompson, 1984), it has been argued that the form may be too complicated for some elderly persons to complete (Patterson, O'Sullivan, & Spielberger, 1980; Rankin, Gfeller, & Gilner, 1993). The simplified three-choice format for the children's version of the STAI (STAIC; Spielberger et al., 1973) may be more appropriate for use with some elders. Patterson et al. (1980) presented evidence in support of the convergent and discriminant validity of the STAIC when used with elderly patients. Normative data (Rankin et al., 1993) for elders are presented in Table 9.4. The norms presented by Rankin et al. (1993) on the STAIC are based on a larger sample than Knight's (1984) STAI norms, but include only people recruited in seniors' centers. Rankin et al. concluded in their study of six age cohorts that anxiety scores on the STAIC do not increase with age.

The *Self-Rating Anxiety Scale* (W. K. Zung, 1971) has also been normed for elderly persons. It contains 20 items and was designed to assess anxiety symptoms. Respondents are asked to indicate how much each item applies

TABLE 9.4
Normative Information for Older Adults on the
State Trait Anxiety Inventory for Children–State

Age Group	M	SD
60–69 years (n = 21)	28.2	4.3
70–74 years (n = 32)	30.2	3.8
75–79 years (n = 31)	29.7	4.5
80–84 years (n =27)	29.4	5.1

Note. The data are based on a sample of 38 male and 89 female subjects recruited from senior's centers and similar organizations. The subjects were not receiving active treatment for anxiety or depression nor had they any significant clinical illnesses. Reprinted from the Journal of Psychiatric Research, 27, by E. J. Rankin, J. D. Gfeller, and F. H. Gilner, Measuring anxiety states in the elderly using the State-Trait Anxiety Inventory for Children, p. 113, 1993, with kind permission from Elsevier Science Ltd, The Boulevard, Langford Lane, Kidlington 0X5 1GB, UK.

to them (none or little of the time, some of the time, good part of the time, most or all of the time). Zung presented validity evidence for the scale. W. K. Zung and R. L. Green (1973) reported that persons age 65 and older (n = 47), judged to be normal on the basis of their ability to carry out age-appropriate activities, obtained a mean score of 40 (SD = 7.0).

Multidimensional psychopathology instruments such as the BSI have normative information based on larger and more representative samples than the unidimensional inventories reviewed. Overall, the lack of adequate normative information for the measurement of anxiety symptomatology in the elderly is striking. It appears that the scales reviewed here can be used with the elderly but clinicians should exercise great caution both in interpreting individual scores relative to the normative data presented here and in drawing diagnostic and prognostic conclusions from the instruments. Given the lack of adequate psychometric information, objective behavioral information such as behavioral avoidance tests, functional analysis, self-monitoring, and other related procedures (see Bellack & Hersen, 1988) may often prove to be more useful indicators of anxiety than psychometric scales. Future research examining the psychometric characteristics of such scales in elders may improve their clinical utility.

Depression Scales

According to the Epidemiologic Catchment Area Study, the prevalence of clinically diagnosable mood disorders in persons over age 65 ranges between .5% and 2.2% for men and 3.1% and 5% for women (Myers et al., 1984). With bipolar conditions being extremely rare in community dwelling elderly persons and believed to almost always have an onset before age 65 (e.g., Davison & Neale, 1994; Jamison, 1979), these estimates reflect largely unipolar conditions. If bipolar-like symptoms appear in late life, the possibility of organic impairment should be assessed. Nonetheless, prevalence figures for mood disorders vary from study to study with some investigators reporting higher rates than others (Blazer, Hughes, & George, 1987). Although prevalence estimates for affective disorders in elders are somewhat lower than those reported for younger people, it has been suggested that elderly persons may experience symptoms of depression (as opposed to clinical depression) more frequently (Norris, Gallagher, A. Wilson, & Winograd, 1987).

Although depression accounts for many acute psychiatric admissions of elders (Gurland & Cross, 1982), it seems to be less common in older than it is in younger adults (Regier et al., 1988). Furthermore, there may be differences in the way symptoms of depression manifest themselves in the young and the old (Davison & Neale, 1994). Blazer (1982) tabulated a comparison of symptoms based on age. The information was derived from the preexisting literature and suggested that elderly persons seem less likely to report suicidal ideation and guilt feelings and more likely to report somatic symptoms. Blazer (1982) based his conclusions on only 19 patients over age 60. Nonetheless, Musetti et al. (1989) studied a large sample and reported findings indicating less suicidal ideation, greater motor retardation, more weight loss, less hostility, and more general decline in elderly patients with depression. Despite such reports of reduced suicidal ideation in elders, the numbers of actual attempts and completed suicides are high in this population (Davison & Neale, 1994). This should be taken into account when assessing suicide risk.

Obtaining information from caregivers can be helpful in the assessment of patient symptomatology. Teri and Wagner (1992) concluded, however, that caregiver and patient reports of symptoms of depression do not always correspond and generally patients with Alzheimer's disease tend to report fewer symptoms than their caregivers. Thus, when depression in such patients is assessed, it is important to consider both patient and caregiver reports. In addition to obtaining information about depressive symptomatology, eliciting material on current and previous health status as well as medication use could assist in the interpretation of the interview responses (Gallagher, 1986).

It is important to note some problems associated with studies of depression in older adults. Specifically, Thompson, Heller, and Rody (1994) concluded that studies of depression in older adults often exclude 25% to 35% of potential participants. They suggested that depressed older adults may be especially likely to refuse participation. This could limit the generalizability of the conclusions drawn by many researchers. It also implies that normative studies of depression in older adults would also be affected and clinicians may wish to keep that in mind when comparing a patient's scores with the normative group. Regardless of this limitation, Teri and Wagner (1992) argued that almost no normative information on established depression measures is available for people with dementia and that difficulties with language abilities may interfere with the validity of these instruments.

In assessing for depression, the clinician may supplement interview information with a variety of psychometric instruments. As suicide rates among the elderly are quite high, the clinician must assess carefully for the presence of suicide risk. This can be done both through careful interviewing of the person and caregiver but may also be evaluated through the examination of critical item responses in psychometric instruments such as the Beck Depression Inventory (Beck, Ward, Mendelson, Mock, & Erbaugh, 1961) and the Minnesota Multiphasic Personality Inventory–2 (Butcher et al., 1989). When using any psychometric instrument, one must consider the type of population the patient represents. As an example, Harper, Kotik-Harper, and Kirby (1990) concluded that psychometric instruments may underestimate depression in specific subgroups of elders. Specifically, they found that psychometric instruments tended to underestimate depression in elders who were thought by physicians and relatives to show significant and unexplained deterioration in their functioning. Thus, special care should be taken to reduce false negative rates when working with such patients.

The *Schedule for Affective Disorders and Schizophrenia* (SADS; Spitzer & Endicott, 1978) is an instrument that has good reliability and validity. Gallagher (1986) made extensive use of the scale with reliable and valid findings in older adults. This schedule explores aspects of affective distress but is time consuming and requires considerable training on the part of the examiner. Gallagher (1986) suggested that clinicians working in settings in which time and financial considerations may preclude the use of the SADS, could construct a comprehensive but shorter interview based on SADS questions. SADS questions that would not be applicable to individual clients could be omitted.

With respect to self-report instruments, it is generally recommended to avoid those with high somatic content because this may be confounded with the increasing number of physical problems that often accompany old age (e.g., Yesavage, 1986). The *Geriatric Depression Scale* (GDS) is a brief self-report depression scale that has been specifically designed to assess depression in older people (Brink et al., 1982; Yesavage et al., 1983). It consists of 30 items, has a yes–no format, and assesses affective and behavioral symptoms of depression. Vegetative symptoms are not assessed. One of its advantages over other screening instruments is that it focuses on psychological aspects of depression by not emphasizing somatic items. The scale can also be read to the subject as its yes–no format makes it amenable to such administration when the patient has problems that could interfere with reading. The measure has established reliability and validity among independent community residents, those receiving medical or psychiatric treatments in outpatient and inpatient settings, as well as institutionalized elders (Koenig, Meador, Cohen, & Blazer, 1988; Norris et al., 1987; Parmallee, Lawton, & Katz, 1989; Rapp, Parisi, Walsh, & Wallace, 1988; Yesavage et al., 1983). In fact, Parmalee et al. (1989) concluded that there were no differences in the reliability and validity of the instrument for cognitively impaired and intact patient groups and the correlation of the GDS with the Blessed Dementia Rating Scale (Blessed et al., 1968; see chap. 3) was of negligible magnitude. Overall, the GDS appeared to be quite robust when used with mildly to moderately cognitively impaired as well as cognitively intact aged (Parmallee et al., 1989).

Yesavage (1983) reported sensitivity and specificity information corresponding to different cutoffs. The criterion for depression was based on Spitzer, Endicott, and Robins' (1978) Research Diagnostic Criteria. When a cutoff of 11 is used, the sensitivity and specificity values are 84% and 95%, respectively. A cutoff score of 13 results in 80% sensitivity and 100% specificity. Normative data for groups of elders appear on Table 9.5. Table 9.6 contains original and more extensive GDS normative data for persons with and without dementia who were referred to a dementia assessment clinic.

The *Beck Depression Inventory* (BDI; A. T. Beck et al., 1961) has also been used as a screening instrument for the identification of depression in the elderly (Gallagher, Breckenridge, Steinmetz, & Thompson, 1983). The instrument has satisfactory reliability and validity (see Spreen & Strauss, 1991) and it is brief and easy to administer. Allen-Burge, Storandt, Kinscherf, and Rubin (1994) studied a sample of 191 geriatric inpatients and concluded that both the GDS and the BDI were less effective in identifying depression in male than female geriatric patients. The BDI has been criticized because its somatic content may be inappropriate for older adults (Hyer & Blount, 1984; Rapp et al., 1988), but the effects of these items in the number of false positives is not entirely clear (e.g., Olin, Schneider, Eaton, Zemansky, & Pollock, 1992). Nonetheless, there is some evidence that the GDS is easier for older adults to complete (Olin et al., 1992) and for that reason may be preferred.

A. T. Beck and R. W. Beck (1972) introduced a short, 13-item version of the Beck Depression Inventory for use in screening medical patients for depressive features. The short form correlates with the full version at .96 (A. T. Beck & R. W. Beck, 1972) and has satisfactory reliability and validity (Reynolds & Gould, 1981). Knight (1984) presented norms collected in a New Zealand community on the Short Form of the Beck Depression Inventory arguing that the A. T. Beck and R. W. Beck (1972)

TABLE 9.5
Normative Information on Depression Scales for Elderly Subjects

Depression Scale	Source	Sample	M	(SD)
Geriatric Depression Scale	Yesavage et al. (1983)	Elderly persons recruited from seniors' centers ($n = 40$)	5.75	(4.34)
	Hadjistavropoulos et al. (1994)	Elderly persons referred for assessment to an outpatient dementia clinic ($n = 136$)	8.01	(5.61)
Hamilton Rating Scale for Depression	Yesavage et al. (1983)	Elderly persons recruited from seniors' centers ($n = 40$)	5.43	(4.98)
Centre for Epidemiological	Data derived from proxies	65–69 years ($n = 42$)	5.95	(8.37)
Studies Depression Scale	associated with case controls	70–74 years ($n = 63$)	6.27	(7.16)
	in the Canadian Study on	75–79 years ($n = 58$)	5.85	(6.22)
	Health and Aging	80–84 years ($n = 42$)	4.86	(5.87)
		85+ years ($n = 14$)	6.71	(6.80)
Zung Self-Rating Scale for	Yesavage et al. (1983)	Elderly persons recruited from seniors' centers ($n = 40$)	34.31	(6.66)
Depression	W. K. Zung & R. L. Green (1973)	Persons over age 65 ($n = 169$)	48	(10)
	Knight et al. (1983)	Males 60–69 ($n = 58$)	33.46	(6.49)
		Females 60–69 ($n = 78$)	37.18	(7.51)
		Males 70–79 ($n = 28$)	33.86	(6.93)
		Females 70–79 ($n = 34$)	34.83	(7.43)
Short Form of Beck Depression	Knight (1984)	Males 60–69 ($n = 52$)	2.29	(2.22)
Inventory		Females 60–69 ($n = 64$)	2.89	(2.90)
		Males 70–79 ($n = 27$)	3.00	(1.75)
		Females 70–79 ($n = 47$)	2.83	(2.20)
Beck Depression Inventory	Gallagher et al. (1983)	Elderly persons recruited from seniors' centers ($n = 82$)	5.54	(4.67)
Memorial University of		Elderly persons over age 66 ($n = 100$)	16.62	(6.59)
Newfoundland Scale of Happiness				

TABLE 9.6
Original Geriatric Depression Scale Norms Based on
Outpatients Referred to a Diagnostic Dementia Clinic

Age Group	M	SD
Individuals Diagnosed With Dementia		
65–69 (*n* = 75)	8.50	5.76
70–74 (*n* = 130)	8.10	5.61
75–79 (*n* = 108)	6.30	4.28
80–84 (*n* = 55)	7.60	5.07
85+ (*n* = 12)	6.00	4.00
Individuals Judged as "Not Having Dementia"		
65–69 (*n* = 37)	8.00	6.58
70–74 (*n* = 35)	9.10	6.13
75–79 (*n* = 30)	8.30	5.86
80–84 (*n* = 13)	8.00	4.76

Note. The GDS was administered as part of the assessment at the Clinic for Alzheimer Disease and Related Disorders, Vancouver Hospital and Health Sciences Centre, Vancouver, British Columbia, Canada. Diagnostic conclusions (e.g., demented vs. not demented) were drawn after the administration of the GDS.

sample was smaller and atypical in that it was collected at a hospital setting. Table 9.5 presents data for persons over age 60 derived from Knight (1984). Knight's data suggest that average scores of normal persons do not change substantially across the life span but information from clinical samples varying in age would be useful in determining whether a depression by age interaction plays a role in the scores. The generalizability of these New Zealand norms to North American samples may also be limited.

Norris et al. (1987) compared the sensitivity and specificity of the BDI and the GDS in a sample of elderly outpatients with medical problems. These estimates are different from sensitivity and specificity estimates reported using other samples (e.g., Brink et al., 1982). With a cutoff score of 10 for either scale and *DSM–III* diagnosis of depression as criterion, sensitivity and specificity were 89% and 82%, respectively, for the BDI and 89% and 73%, respectively, for the GDS. When using a cutoff of 17 for the BDI, sensitivity and specificity were 50% and 92%, respectively. A cutoff of 14 on the GDS leads to 78% sensitivity and 86% specificity. Thus, lower cutoff scores yield higher sensitivity and lower specificity estimates than high cutoff scores. Clinicians often prefer to achieve high sensitivity because of the potential costs of false positive misclassification from a screening instrument are potentially lower than that of false negative misclassification. Researchers, however, may often desire higher specificity and may select higher cutoff scores (Norris et al., 1987).

The *Hamilton Depression Rating Scale* (Hamilton, 1960) has been used in many studies involving elders, but some reservations about its use have been expressed (Gallagher, 1986) on the basis that validity information for samples of elders is lacking. The scale is used within the context of an interview with the patient. Based on the interview, the clinician makes ratings on 23 dimensions, such as depressed mood (ranging from 0 = absent to 4 = patient reports virtually only these feeling states in his spontaneous verbal and nonverbal communication) and work and activities (ranging from 0 = no difficulty to 4 = stopped working because of present illness). Yesavage et al. (1983) reported that with a cutoff score of 11, sensitivity and specificity on this instrument is 86% and 80%, respectively, when using the Research Diagnostic Criteria for depression (Spitzer & Endicott, 1978). Normative information is presented in Table 9.5. A related scale that has been evaluated with a sample of cognitively intact elderly medical patients (Rapp, Smith, & Britt, 1990) is the *Extracted Hamilton Depression Rating Scale* (XHDRS; Endicott, Cohen, Nee, Fleiss, & Sarantakos, 1981). This 17-item instrument matches items from the SADS interview to the original Hamilton Depression Scale by content. That is, the 7-point rating scale of the SADS was converted to the original 4-point rating scale of the Hamilton. Rapp et al. (1990) presented evidence of good reliability and validity. One hundred and nine geriatric/surgery patients who did not meet the Research Diagnostic Criteria (Spitzer et al., 1978) for a psychiatric diagnosis obtained a mean total score of 4.94 (pooled $SD = 6.01$). These norms, however, may not be applicable to cognitively impaired and community dwelling elderly persons. Rapp et al. (1990) concluded that the XHDRS had improved overall performance compared to the BDI and GDS for their sample of medical patients largely because of its better specificity. For example, when sensitivity equals 83%, the Beck and the GDS both had specificity of 65%, whereas the XHDRS had specificity of 92%. Other screening instruments include the *Carroll Rating Scale for Depression* (Carroll, Feinberg, Smouse, Rawson, & Greden, 1981), which is a transformation of the Hamilton Rating Scale for Depression (Hamilton, 1960) into a self-rating format. Like the Hamilton, the Carroll contains somatic items.

The *Center for Epidemiologic Studies–Depression Scale* (CES–D; Raddloff, 1977) requires estimation of symptom frequency that may make it cumbersome for some elders to complete. Nonetheless, respondents are given a card with four possible alternatives ranging from "Rarely or none of the time (less than once a day)" to "Most or all of the time (5–7 times per day)." The four response alternatives are applied to 20 statements (e.g., "During the past week I did not feel like eating; my appetite was poor"). The psychometric properties of this measure have not been investigated adequately with elderly persons.

The CES–D was administered to elderly proxies associated with the case controls of the Canadian Study of Health and Aging (Canadian Study of Health and Aging Work Group, 1994). Cognitively normal case controls were drawn at random from the CSHA community sample who screened 78 or above on the 3MS. Original norms on the proxies associated with these individuals are presented on Table 9.5.

Norms also exist for the *Zung Self-Rating Depression Scale* (W. K. Zung & R. L. Green, 1973). This 20-item scale has a 4-point format and has been reported to have satisfactory internal consistency and validity (Yesavage et al., 1983) when used with older adults. These investigators reported that using the Research Diagnostic Criteria (Spitzer & Endicott, 1978) for depression, a score of 46 achieves 80% sensitivity and 85% specificity in elderly samples. Some relevant norms on the Zung are presented on Table 9.5. From this table, it is apparent that the sample of W. K. Zung and R. L. Green (1973) obtained higher scores than the other samples reported. Unfortunately, W. K. Zung and R. L. Green's (1973) sample was not described explicitly. Hence, it is difficult to interpret the discrepancy in the scores between the samples.

The *Memorial University of Newfoundland Scale of Happiness* (MUNSH; Kozma & Stones, 1980) is a measure that can be used to assess level of well-being in elders. The measure has 24 items and is intended to assess affect within the range from happiness to subclinical depression. Responses are obtained using a yes–no–I don't know format. Several studies have shown the internal consistency of this measure to be high (Kozma, Stones, & McNeil, 1991). In addition, the scale correlates highly with psychopathology scales and particularly depression (Kozma, Stones & Kazarian, 1985) as well as with other life satisfaction and morale scales, and avowed happiness (Kozma & Stones, 1983, 1987, 1988). The effects of social desirability and acquiescence biases are minimal (Kozma & Stones, 1987, 1988; Kozma et al., 1991). Norms on this instrument are presented in Table 9.5. The norms are based on a volunteer sample of community residents of an eastern Canadian urban center (Kozma, di Fazio, Stones, & Hannah, 1992). Generally, scores on this instrument appear to stay quite stable across the life span.

The Geriatric Depression Scale is recommended for the psychometric assessment of depression in the elderly not only because of the availability of normative information but also because more extensive research has been conducted on this scale than any other for samples of elders. This scale could supplement interview questions directed toward both the patient and a proxy. When time allows, a measure of well-being, such as the MUNSH, may be used to supplement the information obtained from unidimensional depression scales.

Substance Use Measures

Illicit drug use among the elderly is very rare. The major substance-related disorders in the elderly typically involve the use of alcohol and prescription tranquillizers. As noted in chapter 11, various patterns of cognitive functioning may be associated with alcohol use. Recognition of alcohol use disorders in elderly persons is important both from a differential diagnostic viewpoint and for determining the validity of the assessment results (e.g., if the person is intoxicated during the assessment). To assess for the presence of alcoholism, Zimberg (1987) recommended asking specifically whether use of alcohol in the elderly has been associated with marked changes in behavior/personality, memory loss and confusion, social isolation, argumentativeness, neglect of hygiene and self-care, missing medical appointments, neglect of medical regimen, interference with income management, problems with the law, and problems with neighbors.

Problems with drug overdose involving prescription medications may be seen in elders who are estimated to comprise 2% to 6% of overdose problems seen in acute care medical settings (Heller & Wynne, 1975; La Rue et al., 1985; D. M. Petersen & Thomas, 1975). As cognitive impairment and other factors (e.g., sensory deficits) may interfere with compliance to the medical prescription, it is necessary for the geriatric neuropsychologist to obtain detailed information about any and all drugs that a patient may be using. Such drugs may have effects on cognitive function. In addition, misuse could potentially be prevented if it is discovered early that the patient is not following the physician's recommendations.

In addition to interview information that can be obtained by the clinician, a variety of assessment procedures for substance abuse are available. Sobell, Toneatto, and Sobell (1994) described structured interviews and self-report methods that have been used with success in adults. Nonetheless, the utility of such methods with samples of elders has not been sufficiently addressed (C. J. King, Van-Hasselt, Segal, & Hersen, 1994). In addition, organic impairment can interfere with the patient's ability to provide accurate self-report through interviews and questionnaires.

The utility of a small number of screening tools for alcoholism has been investigated with samples of elderly persons. The *CAGE* (Ewing, 1984) is a brief alcohol screening measure that consists of four questions (e.g., "Have you ever had a drink first thing in the morning to steady your nerves or get rid of a hangover?") and has been shown to have excellent sensitivity and specificity for young persons (M. King, 1986). Buchsbaum, Buchanan, Welsh, Centor, and Schnoll (1992) studied 323 general medical patients age 60 or older, 33% of whom were found to have problems with alcohol use as assessed using *DSM–III* criteria. With a cutoff score of 1, the CAGE had sensitivity and specificity of 86% and 78%. With a cutoff score of 2, specificity improved to 90% but sensitivity dropped to 70%. Thus, it appears that a cutoff score of 1 is appropriate when screening samples of elderly medical patients with a high incidence of alcohol problems, whereas a cutoff score of 2 may be preferable when screening community dwelling elders (King et al., 1994).

Data are also available on the *Michigan Alcoholism Screening Test* (MAST; Selzer, 1971). The 25 items of this true–false inventory can be differentially weighted to yield a highest possible score of 50. Ten- (B–MAST) and 13-item (S–MAST) short versions of the instrument have also been developed (B. J. Zung, 1979). The use of these scales in elders was studied by Willenbring, Christensen, Spring, and Rasmussen (1987). These investigators administered the long and short versions of the MAST to 52 elders (mean age 64 +/– 2.8 years) hospitalized for substance abuse treatment and a similarly aged control group of 33 elders who were hospitalized for problems unrelated to alcohol. Using a cutoff score of 6 or greater, the MAST had a sensitivity of 100% and a specificity of 90%. When weighted scoring was employed, the sensitivity and specificity were 96% and 86% when a cutoff score of 3 was used.

The briefer B-MAST yielded sensitivity and specificity of 91% and 83% when a cutoff score of 4 was employed. A cutoff of six positive responses resulted in sensitivity of 82% and specificity of 100%. A cutoff score of 2 in the S-MAST resulted in sensitivity of 98% and specificity of 72%. Given the overall better sensitivity of the full version of the MAST, it is recommended that it be preferred over the briefer versions (C. J. King et al., 1994).

In summary, it appears that the initial data on the use of screening tools for alcohol-related problems in samples of elders are very promising. Proxy report and biochemical procedures (breath alcohol tests, urine tests, saliva tests) can also be of value in detecting and monitoring substance consumption (Sobel et al., 1994), particularly in cases where there are doubts about the accuracy of self-reports.

ASSESSMENT FOR OTHER FORMS OF PSYCHOPATHOLOGY

Personality Disorders

Vaillant and Perry (1980) suggested that with aging, a true decrease in the incidence of personality disorders occurs. La Rue et al. (1985) suggested, however, that such estimates of age-related reduction in personality disorders may be due to patterns of service utilization rather than prevalence changes per se. Although early community surveys (reviewed by La Rue et al., 1985) estimate the prevalence of personality disorders in older adults to be 2.8% to 11% research using recent *DSM* criteria is needed.

Christinson and Blazer (1988) discussed the evolution of personality disorders in the elderly. They pointed out that interpersonally focused coping mechanisms that a person uses may evolve into personality disorders under the stress of physical or psychiatric problems. Persons with paranoid features may experience an exacerbation of characteristics, such as suspiciousness and hypersensitivity, because of problems developing with various sensory modalities. They also suggested that persons with histrionic features may find that the effectiveness of seductive and dramatic behaviors they previously relied on may be reduced. As the stresses of life may make it difficult for persons with narcissistic features to maintain their fragile self-esteem, such individuals may be expected to experience dysthymia. Individuals with obsessive-compulsive traits may become increasingly rigid and perfectionistic with difficulties associated in decision making. Finally, Christinson and Blazer concluded that illnesses associated with aging may become legitimate means of gratifying the dependency needs of people with depended personalities. Such views, however, are based largely on clinical experience and intuition. Longitudinal empirical investigations could shed more light on the evolution of personality disorders across the life span. Nonetheless, in their review of the literature, Christinson and Blazer also concluded that core personality traits show relative stability over a lifetime. There is research in support of this view (Costa & McCrae, 1980).

Assessment for personality disorders is approached much the same way in older adults as for younger persons (e.g., MMPI–2). The added caution is, once again, that the presence of cognitive impairment may limit the validity of some established assessment methods. The clinician must be cautious, however, as personality disorders may manifest themselves differently in the old than they do in the young. As research is lacking, it is difficult to determine what type of age differences in personality disorder manifestations exist.

Hypochondriasis and Health Anxiety

The frequency of *hypochondriasis* among the aged is sometimes considered high (e.g., Straker, 1982). Data suggest, however, that this condition is no more frequent among the aged than it is among the young (Siegler & Costa, 1985). Although actual health problems increase with age, there is no corresponding increase in health concern. Regier et al. (1988) found that only .1% of persons over age 65 can be diagnosed with somatization disorder, a rate comparable to rates reported with younger age groups. Costa and McCrae (1985) concluded that age influences the number of health complaints only insofar as it increases actual disease. Health concerns of the elderly are no more exaggerated than are health concerns of people in other age groups. Regardless of whether hypochondriasis is suspected, reports of physical symptoms and health-related concerns should be followed up with appropriate medical examinations. Only if a medical examination does not support the validity of the elderly person's health concerns, a diagnosis of hypochondriasis may be made.

Insomnia

It is well established that the prevalence of insomnia increases with age (Mellinger, Balter, & Uhlenhuth, 1985), with 45% of persons between age 65 and 79 having some difficulty with sleeping. Furthermore, use of sleeping medications among the elderly is common (Mellinger et al., 1985). Bootzin and Engle-Friedman (1987) concluded that frequent awakenings are very common among elders, as are other related problems. The medications that elderly persons take to combat difficulties with sleep typically result in quick tolerance (Mellinger et al., 1985). In addition, some tranquillizers (such as the benzodiazepines) often result in impairments in learning new information and thinking clearly the next day (Ghoneim & Mewaldt, 1990). It is important for the geriatric neuropsychologist to take note of any such medications elderly persons might be receiving and the effects these may have on cognitive function. Cognitive behavioral treatment programs have been shown to be effective alternatives in treating insomnia in older adults (Edinger, Hoelscher, Marsh, Ipper, & Ionescu-Pioggia, 1992), but may be less effective in persons with cognitive impairments. Behavioral assessment procedures for insomnia have been developed (e.g., sleep diaries, polysomnography, mechanical devices, and ancillary measures). Refer to Lacks and Morin (1992) for a review. Such assessments may be tailored for the elderly.

For the geriatric psychologist, it is important to remember that insomnia can have a variety of causes, including stress and situational factors, psychiatric disorders, substance withdrawal, sleep-induced respiratory impairment (i.e., apnea), myoclonus, and restless leg syndrome (Spielman, 1986). It is important to assess for the presence of sleep apnea and neurological conditions that could interfere with sleep. In many instances, polysomnography and a neurological referral will be indicated in order to comprehend the factors that cause and maintain the condition and to assist in a treatment regiment.

CONCLUSIONS

Clinical research on the psychometric assessment of psychopathology in elders with cognitive impairments is very limited. Limited age-appropriate norms exist for some standardized instruments, but the clinical utility of such norms has not been adequately established. Thus, clinicians should exercise great caution when they assess psychopathology in the elderly in general and when deciding on appropriate normative comparison groups in particular.

Chapter 10

Age-Associated Conditions Affecting Cognition

One of the primary purposes of conducting a neuropsychological evaluation in persons over age 65 is to assist in diagnostic decision making. In this context, it is necessary to determine if cognitive impairment (i.e., change in cognitive functioning greater than that expected as part of the normal aging process) is present. When cognitive impairment is identified, examination of the pattern of performance, within the context of historical information concerning the emergence of the difficulties and demographic characteristics of the individual, may suggest or support a particular diagnosis.

The *Diagnostic and Statistical Manual for Mental Disorders* (*DSM–IV*; American Psychiatric Association, 1994) criteria for specific forms of cognitive disorders are probably the most commonly applied, but other sets of criteria exist for specific disorders and, where appropriate, are highlighted in this chapter. *Dementia* refers to an overall decline in mental capacity (one or more cognitive domains) that renders the individual unfit to meet the diverse intellectual demands associated with the obligations of everyday life. Central to this diagnosis, as defined by the *DSM–IV*, is impairment of memory. At least one other area of functioning—including disturbances in language (aphasia), motor planning (apraxia), visual perception, and recognition (agnosia)—and/or executive functions—must also be impaired. It becomes evident that there are instances where memory impairment does not appear central to a neurodegenerative condition and where a single primary area of cognitive impairment may be apparent long before other areas of deficit emerge. The *DSM–IV* provides categories for such disorders (e.g., cognitive disorders not otherwise specified, amnestic disorders) and this chapter refers to these as *circumscribed (focal)*, or *mild, cognitive/behavioral deficits*.

Disorders that emerge in late life are the focus of this chapter. These have been organized as *circumscribed (focal), or mild, cognitive/behavioral deficits*, and *pervasive disturbances of cognition and behavior.* These syndromes of cognitive and behavioral functioning may or may not be linked to specific etiologies. Where possible, each syndrome is described briefly within the framework of elements of the neuropsychological assessment identified in chapter 1 (see Table 10.1). In this context, it is important to note that the cognitive and behavioral presentations may change or evolve across the course of the disorder. Moreover, what is known about the disorders affecting cognition in later life has grown tremendously and is likely to continue to evolve.

Although these disorders are presented in "pure form" as discrete entities, it must be noted that it is possible that one or more conditions may be present. For example, it has been noted that depression may accompany various neurological conditions (e.g., poststroke, Alzheimer's disease, Parkinson's disease). The identification of coexisting (comorbid) conditions is of importance, because treatment for remediable disorders may improve the quality of life of the individuals and/or those around them. In addition, the factors described in chapter 1 (e.g., vision, hearing, medications, isolation) may have an effect on how a specific disorder is manifested.

TABLE 10.1
Key Features for Differential Diagnosis

Testing		
Arousal level		
Attention		
Language	i)	Comprehension
	ii)	Expression (naming, repetition, fluency, phrase length, response speed, word finding, paraphasic errors [literal: sounds like; semantic: similar meaning])
Motor	i)	Movements (facial, gait, tremor)
Memory	i)	New learning
	ii)	Verbal, visual
	iii)	Personal information
	iv)	Remote memory or information learned in the past
Visuospatial reasoning		
Verbal reasoning		
Mood		
History	i)	Onset
	ii)	Duration
	iii)	Course
	iv)	Demographic information (education, occupation)
	v)	Living situation, hobbies, alcohol consumption
	vi)	Medical condition (meds, surgeries, anesthetics, psychiatric/neurological status)

MILD AND FOCAL COGNITIVE AND BEHAVIORAL DEFICITS

Mild Cognitive Decline

The significance of cognitive impairment that does not meet criteria for dementia in elderly persons is, as yet, unknown. It may be that within this group some persons are exhibiting the very early signs of a degenerative process (e.g., Derenzi, 1986; Heath, Kennedy, & Kapur, 1983), whereas others have stable or reversible conditions. Although a number of diagnostic terms incorporating the concept of mild impairment of cognition have emerged in the literature (Dawe, Procter, & Philpot, 1992), there is, as yet, no one accepted criteria (Berg, 1990; Morris & Rubin, 1991).

Little is known about features that might differentiate among reversible conditions, those with a benign course, and those that may show progressive deterioration over time. Minor cognitive deficits may result from many factors, including fatigue, depression, visual, or auditory impairment, or nonneurological physical disability—none of which imply dementia (Berg, 1990).

Zaudig (1992) described methods for diagnosing mild cognitive impairment based on the *DSM–III–R* and International Classification of Diseases–10th edition (ICD–10; World Health Organization, 1992) criteria for dementia. Memory impairment is central to both the *DSM–III–R* and *ICD–10* criteria and, hence, is reflected when using these criteria for diagnosing Mild Cognitive Impairment (MCI). The proposed criteria for MCI identify subtypes with memory impairment only, memory and intellectual impairment, or memory and intellectual impairment coexisting with deterioration of emotional control, social behavior, or motivation.

Although measures of memory functioning have proved most useful in differentiating between groups of individuals who deteriorate and meet criteria for dementia over the study time and those who did not (e.g., Katzman et al., 1989; Linn et al., 1995; Rubin, Morris, Grant, & Vendegna, 1989; Tuokko et al., 1991), memory impairment is not always the primary feature in disorders affecting cognitive functioning. Thus, Zaudig's criteria may only capture this specific subgroup of persons with mild cognitive decline. Moreover, with the introduction of changes to the *DSM–IV* criteria for dementias, the utility of Zaudig's criteria may be brought into question.

Refinement of the criteria employed to diagnose and subclassify MCI is clearly important with respect to the early identification of degenerative processes. In addition, it has been observed that this diagnostic group is slightly more common than dementia (Canadian Study of Health and Aging Work Group, 1994). One goal of CSHA–2, the longitudinal follow-up study to CSHA–1, is to examine the utility of a variety of methods for examining the relations between MCI and early dementia.

Age-associated Memory Impairment

Crook et al. (1986) proposed criteria to identify the loss of memory function that occurs as a consequence of normal aging. Age-Associated Memory Impairment (AAMI) describes otherwise healthy persons over age 50 whose memory is poorer than that of healthy young adults. It is expected that AAMI would affect most of the population over age 50 years (McEntree & Crook, 1990; G. Smith et al., 1991). Despite the age-consistent nature of this "disorder," in practice many clinicians inadvertently use the term *AAMI* to refer to circumscribed memory impairment. That is, memory functions impaired in relation to other persons of the same age. AAMI was not intended to identify that specific subset of individuals.

A case has been made for using this diagnostic category in the context of the development of pharmaceutical agents as treatments for normal aging-related memory decline that would "benefit millions of elderly people who are not demented or disabled, but feel at a disadvantage in the conduct of their lives" (McEntree & Crook, 1990, p. 528). Of note, the AAMI criteria are not useful as an indicator for the development of dementia over time. In an 8-year longitudinal study of a random sample of 146 persons over age 65, Snowdon and Lane (1994) found the mortality rate and development of dementia among those fulfilling criteria for AAMI to be similar to other nondemented groups.

Blackford and La Rue (1989) suggested revisions to the criteria for AAMI. In addition to restricting the age range and recommending the use of a standardized self-report memory questionnaire to determine the extent of subjective complaints, they proposed guidelines for identifying more select subgroups with age-consistent memory impairment (ACMI) and late-life forgetfulness (LLF). Whether or not these distinctions will be of benefit is yet to be determined.

Amnestic Disorders

Amnestic disorders, as defined by the *DSM–IV*, are conditions in which only memory functions are impaired. These disorders may appear in relation to general medical conditions, substance abuse, or exposure, or for unknown reasons. There is ample evidence to suggest that exposure to specific toxins (Hartman, 1995) may result in circumscribed memory problems and, for this reason, it is of the utmost importance to obtain accurate historical information concerning exposures (e.g., carbon monoxide poisoning, toluene exposure in house painters).

An often underestimated potential source of cognitive deficits, and specifically memory problems, in older adults is alcohol abuse. It has been estimated that alcohol abuse affects some 10% of older men and 2% of older women (Larkin & Seltzer, 1994). However, it has also been noted that there is insufficient information for defining and delineating the prevalence and patterns of alcohol use disorders in geriatric populations (Rains & Ditzler, 1993). Elderly persons with alcohol use disorders may present with falls, confusion, self-neglect, unusual behaviors, injuries, malnutrition, incontinence, and other manifestations characteristic of a dementia (Rains & Ditzler, 1993). Although there is potential for significant recovery of cognitive functioning with abstinence (Grant, 1987; Salmon, Butters, & Heindel, 1993; Willenbring, 1988), many older persons with alcohol use disorders also have multiple medical problems, polypharmacy, and other confounding events (e.g., a history of trauma and falls). Despite this, the role of alcohol in the presentation of cognitively impaired persons is an important diagnostic consideration that needs to be addressed even when regular consumption is as low as 1 drink per day (Rains & Ditzler, 1993).

Wernicke–Korsakoff (WK) syndrome is perhaps the most striking disorder associated with chronic alcohol consumption. The initial stage of the disorder (Wernicke's encephalopathy) is characterized by abnormal eye movements, gait ataxia, and a state of global confusion. Typically, the person emerges from the acute effects of the Wernicke's encephalopathy with Korsakoff's syndrome. This is characterized by a severe and permanent amnestic condition with marked apathy and passivity (Salmon et al., 1993; see Table 10.2). The cardinal features of the syndrome are severe inabilities to learn new information and to recall events occurring within a 20-year period prior to the onset of the disorder (retrograde amnesia). A tendency to confabulate is often present (though not necessary) during the acute phases of the disorder. However, general intellectual abilities remain relatively well preserved.

The profound amnesia seen in Korsakoff syndrome has been attributed to deficits in episodic memory (memory for specific events and episodes dependent on temporal or spatial cues for their retrieval). Semantic memory or knowledge of general principles, associations, and rules that are independent of the context in which they were learned (e.g., arithmetical procedures, vocabulary knowledge) typically remains intact.

Persons with Korsakoff's syndrome may also have difficulty performing other tasks dependent on new learning or requiring the types of conceptualization and problem solving often associated with integrity of the frontal lobes. For example, impairments have been demonstrated on visuospatial processing tasks such as digit symbol substitution (Glosser, Butters, & Kaplan, 1977; Kapur & Butters, 1977) and on tasks requiring the learning and shifting of problem-solving strategies (Salmon et al., 1993).

TABLE 10.2
Presentation of Wernicke–Korsakoff
Encephalopathy and Chronic Alcoholism

Domain	Wernicke–Korsakoff Syndrome	Chronic Alcoholism
Attention and Arousal	Low motivation, perseveration	
Language		
Motor		
Memory	Recent very impaired; remote memory discontinuous; islands of preservation	Relatively mild; may be limited to visual modality; little evidence of retrograde amnesia; not susceptible to proactive interference
Problem Solving	Impaired if requires new learning or visuoperceptual processing	Impaired if requires new learning or visuoperceptual processing
	Inability to plan, initiate, or consistently apply an optimal problem-solving strategy	Inability to plan, initiate, or consistently apply an optimal problem-solving strategy
Everyday and Social	Lack initiative	
Emotional, Personality, Thought Content	Unaware of or undisturbed by problems, placid, cooperative, apathy, sometimes confabulation	
History Features		
Onset	Sudden or gradual	Gradual
Course	Stable	?
Medical condition	Nutritional deficit; chronic alcoholism	?

Chronic alcohol consumption that does not result in Wernicke–Korsakoff syndrome may also manifest with memory impairment (see Table 10.2). However, memory impairment seen with chronic alcohol consumption is relatively mild, may be limited to the visual modality, and does not include retrograde amnesia. As with WK, these persons typically do not manifest semantic memory deficits. The other specific cognitive deficits (i.e., visuoperceptual and planning) noted for WK may also be seen with chronic alcoholism.

The nonmemory deficits seen in WK and chronic alcoholics have been ascribed to the direct toxic effects of alcohol to the association cortex (Salmon et al., 1993). The truly amnesic state seen in WK has been attributed to the development of small hemorrhagic lesions in the midline diencephalon region following thiamine deprivation (Victor, Adams, &

Collins, 1989). The specific structures most often affected are the dorsomedial nucleus of the thalamus and the mamilliary bodies of the hypothalamus. Damage to the basal forebrain has also been implicated in the profound memory deficits seen in WK and alcoholic dementia (e.g., Lishman, 1986, 1990). It has been suggested (Salmon et al., 1993) that persons particularly vulnerable to the toxic effects of alcohol may develop alcoholic dementia rather than WK due to more widespread cortical damage and perhaps greater involvement of the basal forebrain structures.

Disorders Primarily Affecting Language

Since Mesulam (1982) first brought the syndrome of *primary progressive aphasia* to clinical attention, there have been a number of reports of cases presenting with isolated progressive language dissolution (e.g., Chawluk et al., 1986; Heath et al., 1983; Kirshner, Tanridag, Thurman, & Whetsell, 1987; Mesulam, 1987; Sapin, Anderson, & Pulaski, 1989). The language disorder has been characterized in a variety of ways: as an anomic aphasia with reduced verbal output (Mesulam, 1982), as a Broca-type aphasia (Craenhals, Raison-Van Ruymbeke, Rectem, Seron, & Laterre, 1990), and as a hypokinetic dysarthria with anomia (Kempler et al., 1989). None of these fits neatly into the Benson–Geshwind classification scheme for aphasia (Mesulam, 1987). Thus, it appears that any specific disorder primarily affecting speech and/or language is captured by this syndrome designation.

The early isolated deficits seen with progressive aphasia may evolve into a more global dementia over time (J. Green, Morris, Sandson, McKeel, & Miller, 1990; Kirshner, Webb, Kelly, & Wells, 1984; Poeck & Luzzatti, 1988; Wechsler, 1977). Kempler et al. (1990), in summarizing findings about the syndrome, note that a uniform symptom complex is not apparent, evolution to a full-blown dementia complex is not necessarily seen, and the rate of progression varies greatly from case to case. It has been suggested that "quantifiable neuropsychological assessment" may reveal subtle disturbances in other areas of cognitive functioning and the lack of such evidence may be a source of discrepancy between studies (Foster & Chase, 1983).

EEG and PET scan findings have tended to reflect focal abnormalities in the perisylvian region of the left hemisphere (Chawluk et al., 1986; Craenhals et al., 1990; Mesulam, 1982, 1987). Biopsy or autopsy findings have confirmed the presence of Pick's disease (Craenhals et al., 1990; A. F. Wechsler, Verity, Rosenchein, Fried, & Scheibel, 1982), spongiform changes and astrocytosis of cortical layer 2 (Kirshner et al., 1987), Creutzfeldt-Jacob disease (Mandell, Alexander, & Carpenter, 1989), Alzheimer's disease (Kempler et al., 1990) with disproportionate involvement of the left inferior parietal cortex (J. Green et al., 1990), or nonspecific changes with an absence of specific histopathological markers (J. Green et al., 1990; Kirshner et al., 1987).

Disorders Primarily Affecting Behavior

Although primary disorders affecting frontotemporal functioning have been categorized as forms of dementia, the typical memory disturbances central to *DSM–IV* definitions of dementia are not present. Instead, *frontotemporal dementia* (FTD), is characterized by progressive personality change, and breakdown in social conduct. Investigators in Manchester, UK, and Lund, Sweden, have produced a set of criteria to aid in identifying this disorder (The Lund and Manchester Groups, 1994).

Often the earliest and most striking features of FTD (see Table 10.3) are marked changes in social behavior, which may include the emergence of disinhibited behaviors (e.g., violent behavior, unrestrained sexuality), misdemeanors (such as shoplifting), changes in oral behaviors (e.g., excessive eating or drinking), or lack of initiative (e.g., withdrawal from social activities, deterioration in hygiene and grooming). Behaviors may be stereotyped or perseverative (e.g., wandering, ritualistic preoccupations such as hoarding, toileting, dressing, and unrestrained exploration of objects in the environment). The person lacks concern about actions and may appear emotionally indifferent or withdrawn. Speech output is often reduced through lack of spontaneity.

Because apathy, inertia, excessive sentimentality, and suicidal or fixed ideation may also be present, the role of depression may be questioned early in the course. Clients with FTD may be misdiagnosed as eccentric or as suffering from psychotic disorders. Apathetic and withdrawn individuals may be described as having "Diogenes syndrome," a condition characterized by extreme self-neglect, social retreat, and hoarding of worthless objects. Disinhibited consumption of alcohol may be misidentified as alcoholism.

TABLE 10.3
Features Associated With Frontotemporal Dementia (FTD)

Domain	FTD
Attention and Arousal	Distractible
Language	Often first sign; anomia, circumlocution, paraphasias, repetitive use of stereotyped responses, echolalia, comprehension
Motor	
Memory	Relatively well preserved until late in the course
Problem Solving	Visuospatial relatively well preserved until late in the course
Everyday and Social	Everyday behavior affected; social behavior changed
Emotional, Personality, Thought Content	Marked personality change; blunting, apathy, irritability Cognitive deficits minimal (motivation to perform?)
Onset	Insidious
Course	Progressive
History	More common in females; onset age 40–60; prevalence after age 65 unknown

Clients with FTD are an enigma for care providers. Although they may be forgetful, they do not exhibit marked memory impairments or disorientation. The forgetfulness appears more a function of poor abilities to plan and initiate behavior rather than "true" impairments of new learning. Moreover, visuospatial functioning and praxis are fairly well preserved, although thinking may be concrete. This, in fact, is the opposite picture to that of classical Alzheimer's Disease (AD), which exhibits early memory impairment and little or no disturbance in social skills until late in the disease's course.

Care providers may feel that because the individual is capable of learning and remembering, requests for assistance and reminders are reflections of "bloody-mindedness" or "manipulative" behaviors. Similarly, the often marked apathy may be viewed as an unwillingness to engage or take part in activities rather than an inability to self-initiate behaviors. The lack of insight into everyday problems may result in uncooperative behavior, skepticism, or withdrawal from the "interference" of concerned parties.

Onset before age 65, a positive family history of a similar disorder in a first-degree relative, and evidence of motor neuron disease (e.g., bulbar palsy, muscular weakness and wasting, fasciculations) are supportive features for this diagnosis.

EEG studies are normal, despite clinically evident behavior disturbance, and brain imaging studies show predominant frontal and/or anterior temporal abnormality. According to the Lund and Manchester Groups (1994), two types of histological change underlie the frontotemporal cerebral atrophy seen in this disorder. The first and most common, designated as frontal lobe degeneration, is characterized by nerve cell loss and spongiform changes (microvasculation) with mild to moderately severe astrocytic gliosis in the outer cortical layers. The second is the typical Pick-like histology characterized by intense astrocytic gliosis with intraneuronal inclusion bodies or inflated neurons in all cortical layers. FTD results from bilateral pathology in the frontotemporal regions. Asymmetrical degeneration may result in primarily linguistic rather than behavioral symptoms if the language-dominant area is affected. Here then is the link to the clinical entity of *primary progressive aphasia* with both disorders forming part of the clinical spectrum of lobar atrophy and sharing the same spectrum of histology (Neary, Snowden, & Mann, 1993). The underlying pathology distinguishes the clinical syndrome of FTD from other disorders that may also affect frontotemporal structures (e.g., AD, Creutzfeldt–Jacob disease, subcortical vascular disease).

Disorders Primarily Affecting Movement

Movement disorder may be present in someone suspected of cognitive decline or impairment. When this is the case, it is important that disorders affecting subcortical structures be considered. Bradykinesia (i.e., slowed movements), rigidity, poor coordination, a variety of hyperkinesias (such as tremor, chorea, myoclonus, and tics), and dysarthria are characteristic manifestations of the involvement of subcortical brain structures (e.g., striatum, thalamus, substantia nigra, subthalamic nuclei, and deep white matter tracts).

The term *subcortical dementia* has been used to refer to the cognitive deficits seen in relation to these disorders and has attracted much discussion (e.g., M. L. Albert, 1978; Cummings & Benson, 1984; Whitehouse, 1986). The typical clinical features associated with the subcortical dementias (see Table 10.4) include impairment of recall, slowness of thought process (bradyphrenia), poor abstraction and strategy formation, apathy, and disturbances of mood (e.g., depression). Of note, deficits in language, praxis, and recognition (aphasia, apraxia, and agnosia) are rarely present (M. L. Albert, 1978).

A variety of specific disorders may affect subcortical regions of the brain including: (a) degenerative disorders such as Parkinson's disease, Huntington's disease, idiopathic calcification of the basal ganglia, progressive supranuclear palsy; (b) vascular disorders; (c) metabolic disorders such as Wilson's disease or hypoparathyroidism; or, (d) demyelinating disorders such as multiple sclerosis (see M. L. Albert & Knoefel, 1994; Cummings, 1990). Two disorders that carry with them particularly important specific treatment implications are briefly described here: *Lewy Body disease,* a relatively new diagnostic entity that often presents with the extrapyramidal features of Parkinson's disease and, *hydrocephaly.*

TABLE 10.4
Features Associated With Subcortical Dementias

Domain	Subcortical Dementia
Attention and Arousal	May be poor
Language	No aphasia but may be nonspecific word finding when condition is severe
Motor	Slowness of movement, stooped posture, small-stepped gait, difficulty initiating movement (bradykinesia), tremor, tics, dystonias present, speech may be dysarthric
Memory	Recall may be affected but recognition generally intact
Problem Solving	Calculation preserved until late; visuospatial impaired (with or without motor component)
Everyday and Social	
Emotional, Personality,	Apathy, depression
Thought Content	Typically mild deficits
History Features	
Onset	Insidious
Course	Slow and progressive

Note. Includes information from Cummings (1990).

A variety of terms (e.g., diffuse cortical Lewy Body disease, diffuse Lewy Body disease, senile dementia of the Lewy Body type) have been used to refer to this disorder, which is characterized by Lewy Body formation in the brain stem and cerebral cortex. It has been estimated that dementia associated with Lewy Bodies is the second most common cause of cognitive impairment in elderly persons (Hansen & Galsko, 1992) and exceeds the prevalence of vascular dementia. Given the frequency with which Lewy Bodies are implicated as contributing to cognitive impairment, operational criteria for senile dementia of the Lewy Body type (SDLT) have been proposed by McKeith, Perry, Fairbairn, Jabeen, and Perry (1992; see Table 10.5). In comparison to persons with AD, those with confirmed Lewy Bodies more often show fluctuating cognitive impairment, psychotic features (including visual and auditory hallucinations and paranoid delusions), depressive symptoms, frequent falling, and unexplained losses of consciousness. Moreover, persons with SDLT frequently show often irreversible adverse reactions indicative of neuroleptic sensitivity syndrome when administered neuroleptic medications. The survival time of persons treated with neuroleptic medication was reduced by 50%.

Hydrocephaly also carries specific treatment implications. It has been estimated that between 6% and 12% of all cases presenting with dementia may have a hydrocephalic etiology (Strub & Black, 1988). Hydrocephaly

TABLE 10.5
Proposed Operational Criteria for Senile
Dementia of Lewy Body Type (SDLT)

A. Fluctuating cognitive impairment affecting both memory and higher cortical actions (such as language, visuospatial ability, praxis, or reasoning skills). The fluctuation is marked by the occurrence of both episodic confusion and lucid intervals, as in delirium, and is evident either on repeated tests of cognitive function or by variable performance in daily living skills.

B. At least one of the following:
   (1) visual and/or auditory hallucinations, which are usually accompanied by secondary paranoid delusions;
   (2) mild spontaneous extrapyramidal features or neuroleptic sensitivity syndrome, i.e., exaggerated adverse responses to standard doses of neuroleptic medication;
   (3) repeated unexplained falls and/or transient clouding or loss of consciousness.

C. Despite the fluctuating pattern the clinical features persist over a long period of time (weeks or months) unlike delirium, which rarely persists as long.

D. Exclusion of any underlying physical illness adequate to account for the fluctuating cognitive state, by appropriate examination and investigation.

E. Exclusion of past history of confirmed stroke and/or evidence of cerebral ischaemic damage on structural brain imaging.

Note. From "Operational Criteria for Senile Dementia of Lewy Body Type (SDLT)," by I. G. McKeith, R. H. Perry, A. F. Fairbairn, S. Jabeen, and E. K. Perry, 1992, *Psychological Medicine, 22*, p. 920. Copyright © 1992 by Cambridge University Press. Reprinted with permission.

TABLE 10.6
Features Associated With Communicating
(Normal Pressure) Hydrocephalus

Domain	Normal Pressure Hydrocephalus
Attention and Arousal	Low motivation, perseveration; generally impaired early in illness
Language	Generally preserved
Motor	Slowness, gait disorder (spastic, apraxic), incontinence, shuffling, retropulsive psychomotor retardation
Memory	Deficits are mild to moderate in severity
Problem Solving	Visuospatial problem-solving deficits frequently but not consistently
Everyday and Social	
Emotional, Personality, Thought Content	Apathy, loss of initiative, and spontaneity the cardinal feature
History Features	
Onset	Sudden or gradual
Course	Progressive
History	Idiopathic or secondary to trauma (hemorrhage, tumor, infection, etc.)

refers to enlargement of the ventricles resulting from impaired absorption of the cerebral spinal fluid (CSF). Obstructive hydrocephaly results from a blockage of movement of the CSF, whereas nonobstructive (i.e., communicating or normal pressure hydrocephalus) results from an imbalance of the production and absorption of CSF. This latter condition is traditionally recognized clinically by a specific triad of disturbances: gait and balance disturbance, urinary incontinence, and relatively mild cognitive impairment characterized by "frontal" or subcortical deficits (including slowness in mentation, loss of initiative and spontaneity; see Table 10.6).

The primary method of treatment is surgical insertion of a shunt to divert the CSF, allowing it to be absorbed by the body more effectively. The results of surgical intervention show substantial variability (see Stambrook, Gill, Cardoso, & Moore, 1993). Stambrook et al. (1988) noted that despite postsurgical improvement in gait, balance, incontinence, and many mental functions, cognitive functioning did not necessarily return to normal. Although there are a number of factors that need to be taken into consideration regarding the treatment for this condition, accurate early identification is an important first step in the treatment process.

Disorders Primarily Affecting Attention

Disturbance of attention may be viewed as the hallmark of *acute confusional state* (*ACS*) or *delirium*. The person's ability to focus, sustain, and shift attention, selectively and voluntarily, is impaired (Lipowski, 1994). Thus, the person is distractible and awareness of self and environment is blurred. The condition tends to fluctuate over the course of the day. Closely associated with this disturbance of attention is disturbance of the sleep–wake continuum. The person with an ACS may be drowsy during the day and insomnic at night. Abnormal psychomotor activity is also an essential feature of ACS (Lipowski, 1994). Three clinical subtypes of ACS have been described that incorporate the domains of alertness (or readiness to respond to stimuli) and psychomotor activity level: hyperalert–hyperactive, hypoalert–hypoactive, and a mixed type (Lipowski, 1994). ACS related to withdrawal from alcohol or sedative-hypnotic drugs may be hyperactive, whereas hypoactivity (sluggishness) is the most common ACS reaction seen in older persons.

The onset is typically sudden (i.e., hours to days) and may be preceded by a period characterized by difficulty concentrating, irritability, restlessness, or fleeting illusions or hallucinations. ACS is a serious indicator of illness in an elderly person and is to be viewed as requiring immediate medical attention. In many cases, persons recover when the underlying disorder is treated appropriately. However, ACS in an older person may also signal the exacerbation of a chronic, perhaps life-threatening, disease. Moreover, survivors do not necessarily recover fully (Lipowski, 1994). Of particular note is that older persons may take far longer to recover from ACS than younger persons and monitoring of this improvement is important to ensure ample recovery time before far-reaching decisions are made on the person's behalf. For example, postoperative ACS occurs in 10% to 15% of older persons undergoing surgery and may last for weeks (Mesulam & Geschwind, 1976).

ACS may be superimposed on an underlying dementia and the signal of an emergent medical condition (e.g., urinary tract infection or pneumonia). Thus, it is of utmost importance that the symptoms of ACS be identified. It is an attentional disorder that affects global cognitive functioning, has an acute onset, fluctuates in severity over the course of the day, is most severe at night, often presents with hallucinations, and often includes restlessness or sluggishness. The most common precipitating events are physical illness (e.g., infections, metabolic disorders, cardiovascular disorders, cerebrovascular disorders), injury, surgery, anticholinergic, or recent change in medication use.

Disorders Primary Affecting Mood or Thought Processes

Many disorders affecting mood and thought processes common to younger adults may also be seen in the older adult and have been described in detail elsewhere (e.g., Birren et al., 1992). Discussion here is limited to two conditions that show little or no evidence of cognitive deficits but marked behavior disturbances: depression and paraphrenia.

Depressive syndromes are very commonly seen in later life even though the prevalence of depressions with marked symptomatology is much lower in older persons than in younger adults (Birren et al., 1992). The *DSM–IV* provides criteria for diagnosing a number of forms of mood disturbance (e.g., major depressive episode, dysthymic disorders, adjustment disorders, bereavement). The term *pseudodementia* has been used to describe reversible cognitive impairment associated with depression (Wells, 1979). However, longitudinal evaluations of persons with these apparently reversible conditions (Alexopoulos, 1989) and the acceptance of the simultaneous presentation of depression and dementia (Reifler, 1982) have helped to clarify the significance of cognitive deficits coexisting with depressive symptomatology.

Certain clinical features may help to distinguish between persons with depression and those with dementia of the Alzheimer's type (see Table 10.7). However, it must be noted that intermittent depressive symptoms have been reported in up to 50% of persons with dementia (P. Ernst, Badash, Beran, Kosovky, & Kleinhauz, 1977) and 20% to 30% of persons with AD (Reifler, Larson, Teri, & Poulsen, 1986). Whether depression

TABLE 10.7
Features Associated With Alzheimer's-type Dementia and Depression

Domain	Alzheimer's-type Dementia	Depression (pseudodementia)
Attention and Arousal	Distractible	Low motivation; decreased attention to detail
Language	Decreases over time	Limited spontaneous elaboration
Motor	Dressing apraxia; other apraxias over time	Psychomotor retardation
Memory	Recent and remote memory impairments	Secondary to attention
Problem Solving	Abstract reasoning; visuospatial over time	Mental processing slowed
Everyday and Social		
Emotional, Personality, Thought Content	Apathy; personality change may be paranoid or sexually inappropriate	Preoccupation with affective state
Other Features	Rarely self-referred; female > male; no identifiable cause	"Don't know" responses; transposition errors; cautious errors; typically higher functioning than complaints indicate
History Features		
Onset	Insidious	Relatively sudden preceded by dysphonic symptoms
Course	Progressive	Variable

presents with or without cognitive impairment, treatment is warranted as demented depressed persons may show a reversal of affective symptoms even though their cognitive functioning remains impaired (Reifler et al., 1989). Thus, the excess disability created by the depression can be alleviated and a better quality of life can be achieved.

Psychotic phenomena, including delusions and hallucinations, have been reported in late life in elderly persons with early-onset schizophrenia (e.g., Cohen, 1990); persons with a variety of dementia syndromes (e.g., Absher & Cummings, 1993); and elderly persons for whom there is a clear absence of an affective syndrome, progressive cognitive impairment, or other obvious organic cause (Pearlson & Petty, 1994). These latter syndromes have been referred to as *late-life schizophrenia,* or *late-onset paraphrenia.* There has been much debate concerning the use of separate criteria for late-onset paraphrenia as distinct from late-life schizophrenia (e.g., Almeida, Howard, Forstl, & Levy, 1992; Almeida, Howard, Levy, & David, 1995a; Munro, 1991). Both the *DSM–IV* and the *ICD–10* support the classification of persons presenting in this manner into the general diagnostic category of schizophrenia or a variety of other diagnostic categories dependent on the impact of the symptomatology and duration of the condition (e.g., Delusional Disorder, in which daily functioning is not markedly impaired; Schizophreniform, if symptoms present for less than 6 months; Brief Psychotic Episode, if symptoms present for less than 1 month in duration). No distinctions are made by age of onset.

Almeida et al. (1995a) argued that including late paraphrenia in the diagnosis of schizophrenia or delusional disorder has poor empirical and theoretical bases and late paraphrenia (see Table 10.8) may still be the best option for the classification of these late-onset psychotic states. Munro (1991) also argued that this group of persons, who differ from cases of delusional disorder and schizophrenia, are potentially being "lumped" into the indeterminate category of "Psychotic disorder, not otherwise specified." He proposed a similar set of criteria to that of Almeida et al. (1995a) for paraphrenia.

Although, by definition, this group of individuals does not exhibit cognitive deficits, it is important for neuropsychologists to be aware of the diagnostic issues surrounding this symptom presentation. It is not uncommon for persons presenting in this way to be referred for evaluation of their cognitive status. It is of interest that there appear to be more women than men presenting with this condition, whereas more men than women present with earlier onset schizophrenia. Moreover, sensory and social isolation are often present to a greater extent than seen in the general age-related population, as are neurological soft signs, which may suggest an organic basis for this condition (Almeida, Howard, Levy & David, 1995b).

TABLE 10.8
Inclusion and Exclusion Criteria for Diagnosis of Late Paraphrenia

Inclusion
(a) Onset of symptoms at or over age 55
(b) Symptoms must have been present for at least 6 months
(c) At least one of the following:
  • Delusions of any kind that are independent of affective symptoms (delusion must remain unchanged in absence of symptoms)
  • Thought echo, insertion, broadcasting, or withdrawal
  • Persistent hallucinations in any modality, when accompanied by either fleeting or half-formed delusions without clear affective content, or by persistent overvalued ideas, or when occurring every day for weeks or months on end

Exclusion
(a) Lack of adequate corroboration of history by medical notes
(b) Dementia and other diagnosable organic disorders (ICD–10)
  • Evidence of neurological, metabolic, or similar disorder that could cause psychotic symptoms
  • MMSE < 24
  • Presence of major brain lesions on MRI scan such as stroke or tumors
(c) Presence of past or current moderate/severe depressive episode (ICD–10)
(d) Harmful substance use or dependence (ICD–10)
(e) Past history as psychiatric in-patient or treatment with neuroleptics, antidepressants, or lithium at any time before age 55
(f) Illiteracy
(g) Severe visual impairment (unable to read 24-point print)
(h) No informed consent

Note. From "Psychotic States Arising in Late Life (Late Paraphrenia): Psychopathology and Nosology," by O. P. Almeida, R. J. Howard, R. Levy, and A. S. David, 1995a, *British Journal of Psychiatry, 166,* p. 206. Copyright © 1995 by Royal Society Medicine Press. Reprinted with permission.

PERVASIVE DISTURBANCES OF COGNITION AND BEHAVIOR

As noted earlier, the term *dementia,* as defined in the *DSM–IV,* refers to deficits in more than one area of cognitive functioning. As more areas of functioning become impaired, it becomes more difficult to differentiate among conditions on the basis of cognitive performance. The history and course characteristics are of primary importance in the diagnostic process. Although many conditions produce dementia, cognitive profiles typical of, or specific to, these disorders may not be readily apparent. In addition, the evolution of cognitive symptomatology over time may mask or obscure differentiating features among these conditions. Once deterioration in global cognitive functioning is evident, diagnostic issues tend to be of somewhat less concern and management issues typically become the focus for the affected individuals and their care provider(s). However, observation (through neuropsychological evaluation) of the emergence of new features may help clarify the diagnosis in persons initially presenting with more circumscribed or focal disorders (as described previously). Two conditions that typify how the patterns of characteristics (e.g., onset, course, history) can be useful in making etiological distinctions when pervasive disturbances of cognition and behavior are present are Alzheimer's disease (AD) and Vascular dementias.

Alzheimer's Disease

The most common source of generalized cognitive impairment (or dementia) of insidious onset and progressive course affecting persons over age 65 is Alzheimer's disease. Among the most commonly applied criteria for identifying AD are those described by the National Institute of Neurological and Communicative Disorders and Stroke–Alzheimer's Disease and Related Disorders Association (NINCDS–ADRDA; McKhann et al., 1984), which include the presence of the dementia syndrome as established by clinical examination and confirmed by neuropsychological testing, deficits in two or more areas of cognition, progressive worsening of memory and other cognitive functions, no disturbance of consciousness, onset between age 40 and 90 and most often after age 65, and absence of systemic disorders or other brain diseases that could account for the progressive deficits in memory and cognition. Of note, impairment in a domain of functioning is operationally defined as a score falling below the fifth percentile compared to appropriate normative data controlling for age, gender, and education.

The pathological hallmark of this neurodegenerative disorder is a proliferation of neuritic plaques and neurofibrillary tangles distributed through cortical and subcortical regions of the brain. Although variations in the pattern of distribution of these plaques and tangles may occur, typically the parietotemporal and limbic regions are predominantly affected (T. L. Kemper, 1994). However, it has been noted that multiple neurotransmitter and neuromodulator abnormalities exist in the AD brains. The primary pathological process is unknown.

Behaviorally, AD typically presents with impairment of new learning. Initially deficits may only affect the retrieval of new information. As the disease progresses, impairments in the acquisition and retention of new material also become apparent. In addition, the individual may also begin to have difficulty recalling information learned in the past and/or familiar persons and places. As a consequence of this memory impairment, individuals with AD may have difficulty concentrating or may loose track of what they are doing and appear distractible. It is not uncommon for marked disturbances in visuospatial processing also to be apparent relatively early in the course of the disorder. Thus, copying visual material may prove difficult (e.g., drawings or block designs) and the comprehension of spatial relations may be poor. Disturbances in language may also emerge characterized by empty speech, circumlocutions, and inappropriate word selection as the disease progresses. Eventually both expression and comprehension are affected. Motor functions, per se, remain intact well into the course of the disorder, but problems completing motor sequences (e.g., dressing apraxia) may be apparent in moderate to late stages. The most common change in character or personality associated with AD is apathy (Bozzola, Gorelick, & Freels, 1992). Persons loose interest in hobbies and activities and may sit unoccupied, or performing a repetitive task, for long periods of time.

The "stages" of AD have been captured in unidimensional (e.g., Reisberg, Ferris, De Leon, & Crook, 1982) and multidimensional scales (e.g., Clinical Rating Scale: Berg, 1988; Functional Rating Scale: Tuokko, 1993). The advantage of multidimensional scales over unidimensional scales is that individual differences in presentation and course can be reflected. For example, Martin (1987) noted that persons with AD may present with different patterns of performance. Persons presenting with relatively more impaired word-finding problems than visuospatial deficits showed significantly greater hypometabolism in the left temporal lobe than other cortical regions. Conversely, persons with greater constructional deficits than word-finding problems displayed significantly greater hypometabolism in the right temporal and parietal areas.

It has been noted that measures, useful for the early detection of AD, may not necessarily be those most sensitive to change across the course of the disease. Floor and ceiling effects for specific instruments will emerge at different stages of the dementia (e.g., Christensen, Hadzi-Pavlovic, & Jacomb, 1991). Various batteries of tests have been recommended for use when evaluating persons with dementia (see Zec, 1993, for a review). In addition, specific tools have been designed for assessing severe AD (e.g., M. Albert & Cohen, 1992; Volicer, Hurley, Lathi, & Kowall, 1994) or frail elderly persons (Coval et al., 1985), which are most useful for defining areas of cognitive strengths and weaknesses for care planning. Thus, the purpose of the assessment is of utmost importance when choosing measures to assess cognition in persons with suspected AD (e.g., early detection, monitoring behavior change, providing information for care plans of severely impaired persons). Different measures are most appropriate for different purposes.

Vascular Disorders

The relations between vascular disorders and cognitive functioning have undergone much scrutiny and continue to be a difficult area to define clearly. Fundamental to understanding this issue is the realization that there are a number of conditions affecting the circulatory system, which supplies the brain and spinal cord, that may be related to cognitive impairment (e.g., thrombo-embolic disorders, anoxic-ischemic disorders, hemorrhagic disorders). Moreover, the predominant location of the resulting brain damage is related to the type of cognitive impairment demonstrated. Cummings and Benson (1992) described two principal vascular dementia syndromes: disorders resulting from the occlusion of arteriole-size vessels irrigating the deep gray and white matter structures (e.g., lacunar states and Binswanger's disease), which primarily affect subcortical structures; and disorders involving extracranial (carotid) or intracranial vessels or the small vessels supplying cortical regions. Subcortical states may affect the basal ganglia, thalamus, internal capsule, or subcortical white matter and common features in the fully developed syndrome include rigidity, spasticity, pseudobulbar palsy, limb weakness, exaggerated muscle stretch reflexes, and extensor plantar responses. The characteristics of the cognitive impairment are variable and not well defined (Cummings & Benson, 1992), but many persons show features typical of other subcortical dementias, including apathy and loss of tact. Cortical insults may result in well-defined focal syndromes reflective of the location of damage. When a number of infarctions have occurred (i.e., multiple and often bilateral), the clinical picture may be that of a more generalized dementia syndrome.

The two methods most widely used in the past to define vascular disorders were the multi-infarct criteria in the *DSM–III–R* and Hachinski's ischemic score (Hachinski, Lassen, & Marshall, 1974). Each of these measures has been found to be lacking (e.g., Dening & Berrios, 1992; Metter & R. S. Wilson, 1993; Rosen, Terry, Fuld, Katzman, & Peck, 1980) and new sets of criteria have emerged that more accurately reflect the diversity of vascular conditions that may affect cognition. In Chui et al.'s (1992) system for probable ischemic vascular dementia, radiologic evidence of at least one supratentorial lesion and evidence of a stroke temporally linked to the dementia or two or more other strokes is required. The National Institute of Neurological Disorders and Stroke–Association Internationale pour Recherche et L'Enseignement en Neurosciences (NINDS–AIREN) system (Roman et al., 1993) for probable vascular dementia requires clinical (i.e., history, examination) or radiological (neuroimaging) evidence of cerebrovascular disease, and a plausible temporal relation between the cognitive dysfunction and cerebrovascular disease.

It would be expected, given the diversity of brain regions potentially affected by vascular disorders, that there may be many different types of clinical presentation associated with vascular disorders. Despite the inherent differences between the forms of vascular disorders that may affect cognition, there are characteristics seen commonly in vascular disorders in general that may aid in their identification (see Table 10.9) and differ-

TABLE 10.9
Features Associated With Alzheimer's-type
Dementia and Vascular Dementia

Domain	Alzheimer's-type Dementia	Vascular Dementia
Attention and Arousal	Distractible	
Language	Decreases over time	
Motor	Dressing apraxia; other apraxias over time	Often sensory-motor signs secondary to infarction in the basal ganglia, internal capsule, thalamus; dysarthria, dysphagia
Memory	Recent and remote memory impairments	Relatively well preserved
Problem Solving	Abstract reasoning; visuospatial over time	WAIS performance scores poorer than in AD
Everyday and Social		
Emotional, Personality, Thought Content	Apathy; personality change may be paranoid or sexually inappropriate	Pseudobulbar affect
Other Features		Subtle changes; hypertension; focal neurological signs (numbness, tingling, weakness, slurred speech)
History Features		
Onset	Insidious	Sudden or insidious
Course	Progressive	Stepwise or smooth progression
History	Rarely self-referred; female > male; no identifiable cause	Steep increase in occurrence after age 65; male > female; strokes; TIAs; MIs

entiation from AD. These include historical features such as abrupt onset, stepwise deterioration, fluctuating course, previous hypertension and a history of neurological symptoms of transient ischemic attacks (e.g., Erkinjuntti et al., 1988; Hachinski et al., 1975). However, as noted by Cummings and Benson (1992), a gradual deterioration, as seen in neurodegenerative disorders, and the absence of typical historical features does not preclude the diagnosis. Typical factors associated with vascular origins of cognitive decline include hypertension, heart disease, cigarette smoking, diabetes mellitus, alcohol consumption, and hyperlipidemia (Meyer, McClintic, Rogers, Sims, & Mortel, 1988).

For the most part, neuropsychological research has not differentiated among the vascular syndromes and, although some research exists on specific well-defined subtypes (Bernard et al., 1990, 1992), it is not possible to make specific comments about the neuropsychological differentiation of these conditions from others. The most common characteristic noted is a "patchy" distribution of intellectual deficits that may differ among individuals (American Psychiatric Association, 1987).

SUMMARY OF KEY FEATURES

Although the pattern of cognitive and behavioral functioning has been the focus of the previous discussion, key features may be of assistance when formulating diagnostic hypotheses. These include the type of onset (i.e., sudden or gradual), and course (i.e., rapid decline, insidious decline, stepwise decline, fluctuating), in addition to the pattern of strengths and weaknesses observed during the assessment process. For example, the presence of a relatively sudden onset of symptomatology would be most suggestive of acute confusional states, depression, trauma (e.g., minor blow to the head or fall), or signify a cerebrovascular accident (CVA). For most degenerative disorders, such as Alzheimer's disease, the onset is slow and insidious and informants may have great difficulty identifying when the first changes in functioning were noted.

Table 10.10 describes some of the conditions associated with various course characteristics. Acute confusional states (ACS or delirium) may be associated with a variety of underlying conditions and may present as a rapid deterioration in functioning or a person's level of functioning may fluctuate. In geriatric populations, acute confusional states are life threatening and require prompt and immediate medical intervention. Practitioners working in acute care or long-term care settings may come in contact with person's presenting with ACS more than practitioners in other settings.

TABLE 10.10
Course Characteristics Associated With Specific Conditions

Course	Disorder
Rapid decline	Acute Confusional State (ACS)
	Creutzfeld–Jacob
Stepwise deterioration	Vascular dementia
Stable (following sudden decline)	Wernicke–Korsakoff encephalopathy
	Anoxia
	Large vessel cerebrovascular accident
Progressive decline	Neurodegenerative disorders (e.g., Alzheimer's disease, Parkinson's disease)
Improvement with time or intervention	Vascular conditions
	ACS
	Depression
Fluctuating	ACS
	Frontal-type Dementia
	Lewy Body Dementia

A stepwise course is often heralded as a key identifying feature of vascular dementia (Hachinski et al., 1974). In some forms of this condition, the individual repeatedly suffers small CVAs, which may not present with the classic features of motor weakness seen in larger CVAs. Episodes of flu-like symptoms may be reported following which the individual no longer is able to perform at their previous level of functioning. This pattern of decline differs from that more typically associated with CVAs where there is a large vascular event with marked disturbance of functioning, followed by a period of "recovery" of some function and a relatively stable course thereafter.

Often depression and ACS will improve with intervention and so too will the functioning of the individual. Particularly in cases where depression coexists with another condition (e.g., poststroke or Alzheimer's disease), it is important to distinguish between improved functioning due to alleviation of depression or ACS symptomatology and improvement (or reversal) of the coexisting neurological condition. Misinterpretation of the nature and extent of improvement in functioning may place persons at risk (e.g., sent home from hospital without supports even though underlying deficits still exist).

Marked fluctuations in functioning may occur with ACS but may also be a feature of other degenerative disorders such as Lewy Body disease and frontotemporal dementias. As noted earlier, ACS requires immediate medical intervention and must be ruled out as the source of fluctuations in behavior. The fluctuations seen in LBD and FTD tend to occur across days (or testing sessions), whereas ACS fluctuations may be more moment-to-moment in nature.

Table 10.11 describes some of the diagnoses suspected when particular cognitive strengths and weaknesses are observed during the assessment process. As a general rule, movement (including speech) disorders suggest damage to subcortical structures of the brain though some movement disorders may be benign or idiopathic (e.g., tremor and facial dyskinesias). It should also be noted that movement disorders may arise for other reasons than disorders of the central nervous system (e.g., arthritis) and it is important to distinguish between these sources when making diagnostic decisions.

Marked fluctuations in attention and concentration during the course of the assessment may suggest the presence of an ACS, particularly if consciousness is clouded. Distractibility during the assessment and/or responding to irrelevant stimuli (e.g., distracted by noise outside testing room or objects within the room) may be seen with FTDs.

When language deficits are the primary presenting feature, the syndrome of Progressive Aphasia may be considered, although the underlying neurological disorder characterized by this behavior presentation may be

TABLE 10.11
Behavioral Presentations Associated With Specific Conditions

Observed Impairment	Raises the Question of:
Arousal and Attention	
Clouded consciousness or fluctuations in concentration	Acute confusional state (ACS)
High distractibility	Disorders affecting the frontal lobes; acute confusional state
Language	Primary progressive aphasia
Motor	
Gait	Communicating (Normal Pressure) hydrocephalus (NPH) subcortical disturbances including Parkinson's disease, progressive supranuclear palsy (PSP), multisystem degeneration
Tremor	Benign; Parkinson's disease; Lewy Body dementia
Tics, facial dyskinesias	Neuroleptic medications; idiopathic Basal Ganglia calcification
Slowness in response	Psychomotor retardation of depression
Initiation problems	Disorders affecting the subcortical and/or frontal regions
Speech	Disorders affecting subcortical structures such as amyotrophic lateral sclerosis or vascular disorders
Memory	
Subjective complaint exceeds objective deficits	Depression
New learning only	Amnestic disorder (e.g., Wernicke–Korsakoff encephalopathy, WK); early Alzheimer's disease (AD)
Relatively spared	Vascular disorders; disorders affecting the frontal lobes
Mood/Emotion/Thought Content	
Preoccupation with affective state	Depression
Unconcern or lack of awareness	WK; AD; disorders affecting the frontal lobes
Pseudobulbar affect	Vascular conditions
Marked personality alteration	Disorders affecting the frontal lobes
Delusional ideation	Paraphrenia; various dementia syndromes (e.g., AD, vascular); ACS
Depressive symptomatology	May be present in a variety of dementia syndromes as well as stand alone

unclear. Alzheimer's disease may present in this fashion but so may other nonspecific neurodegenerative disorders.

Typically, the cardinal feature of Alzheimer's disease (AD) is memory impairment. Early in the course this may be relatively restricted to deficits in new learning that evolve throughout the course to include most aspects of memory functioning. However, other disorders may also present with

circumscribed new learning deficits, including various subcortical dementias and Wernicke–Korsakoff syndrome. Within the *DSM–IV*, there is a
category of amnestic disorder that may be related to specific medical conditions or may be idiopathic (not otherwise specified). When memory
functioning is relatively spared in the context of other areas of cognitive
impairment, this may suggest the presence of a vascular origin to the
deficits, or FTD. Moreover, when subjective complaints of memory impairment (on the part of the person being assessed) exceed the objective
evidence of little if any memory deficits, then depression may be suspected.

Although typically assessed through observation rather than formal testing, disorders of emotion, thought content, and personality may also be
suggestive of specific disorders. For example, preoccupation with affective
status is seen most commonly in persons with a major depression. Persons
who show pseudobulbar affect (i.e., strong affect triggered by mild stimu-
lation) may have sustained damage to the bulbar region of the brain
through trauma or vascular events. Marked apathy and/or lack of concern
about their situation may be seen with AD, FTD, or Wernicke–Korsakoff
syndrome. Marked personality change early in the course of the disorder
is thought to be primarily associated with FTD and may bring the person
into contact with police for the first time late in life. Delusional ideation
may accompany a variety of organic conditions (e.g., AD, FTD) but may
also be present in ACS. In the context of intact cognition, delusions may
be present in late–onset schizophrenia, or paraphrenia.

Differentiation of these conditions is of importance for identifying all
remediable sources of cognitive change. Moreover, clarification of the
diagnosis may also assist in care planning through the establishment of
appropriate expectations concerning the present capacities of the individuals and their future needs.

The Role of the Caregiver in Neuropsychological Assessment

Caregivers and proxies of patients can play an important role in the assessment process. In the case of elderly persons with cognitive impairments, these individuals may serve as legal guardians and provide consent for assessment and/or treatment on behalf of the affected individual. In all cases, they can provide valuable background information about the person's condition and, if applicable, rate of cognitive decline. This chapter focuses on nonprofessional caregivers, typically family members (i.e., usually spouses or children).

Two main areas of caregiver assessment are covered here. The first area relates to the role of the caregiver as a provider of information about the cognitively impaired individuals and their functioning. The second area focuses on the assessment of caregiver stress that can interfere with effective provision of care.

THE CAREGIVER AS AN INFORMATION PROVIDER

Regardless of the degree of cognitive impairment, a caregiver has the potential of being a rich source of information about an individual's functioning. In some multidisciplinary settings, family and genetic histories are often collected by somebody other than the neuropsychologist. Even in such circumstances it is important for the neuropsychologist to interview the caregiver to obtain more specific information about the person's cognitive functioning. Questions concerning the onset and duration of symptoms noticed by the caregiver are important, as are those concerning

205

disruptions of specific behaviors (e.g., When were the first changes noticed? What types of changes have you noticed in language functions? What types of changes have you noticed in memory functions? What types of changes came first? Was the deterioration gradual or were there relatively sudden changes noticed? How is the person's everyday functioning? How did it change recently?). In addition to a personal interview, standardized, valid, and reliable instruments may be useful for collecting information from caregivers.

It is important to note that the correspondence between the responses of proxies and aged persons in the community varies depending on the nature of the information sought, characteristics of the person, characteristics of the proxies, and the proxies' ability to observe the care recipient (Zimmerman & Magaziner, 1994). Specifically, Zimmerman and Magaziner (1994) reviewed the literature on some of the factors that affect proxy responses and found the following: (a) The more objective and concrete the question, the higher the correspondence between care recipient and proxy reports; (b) proxy–person agreement on ratings of cognitive ability is relatively good (but not as good as it is for measures of physical abilities), whereas proxy–subject agreement on ratings of affective status varies across studies; (c) if subjects are in good health, then agreement is better on measures of satisfaction and instrumental activities of daily living (e.g., ability to use the telephone) than for physical activities of daily living (e.g., eating) and agreement is maximized when the subjects are impaired; and (d) although generally proxies indicate more impairment and disability than respondents do, there are some exceptions (Basset, Magaziner, & Hebe, 1990). Overall, the most concrete finding seems to be that the highest agreement between respondent and proxy reports is obtained for objective items that ask about specific and observable aspects of functioning and that proxies tend to report more disability than the care recipient (Zimmerman & Magaziner, 1994).

Normative information on some important instruments that are used to assist in diagnosis by obtaining information from a caregiver is presented here. The goal of using such instruments is typically to determine whether or not the functioning of the elderly person differs from that of normal elderly persons. Thus, normative data collected from informants responding about normal elders would constitute an appropriate comparison group. Some information reported by proxies of people with dementia were also included because they may prove useful in some cases.

Measures of Cognitive and General Functioning

The *Present Functioning Questionnaire* (PFQ; Crockett, Tuokko, Koch, & Parks, 1989) is an interview-administered measure that consists of 60 items developed to form five scales: personality (assesses for psychopathology symptoms), everyday functioning (e.g., "problems handling money" and "problems shopping"), language skills, memory, and self-care (e.g., "Must be bathed by someone else"). A copy of the questionnaire appears in Tuokko and Crockett (1991). Scores reflect the number of problems endorsed by the caregiver. The questionnaire was developed for administration to collaborative informants (typically caregivers of people with dementia) and represents the caregivers' impressions of the subjects' deficits. This measure has satisfactory reliability and validity (Crockett et al., 1989; Hadjistavropoulos, Taylor, Tuokko, & Beattie, 1994). Such an instrument could be administered in conjunction with a caregiver interview and contains very specific questions centered around symptomatology that could be followed up by the interviewer. Normative data for this instrument (based on a community sample) are presented on Table 11.1. Although the neuropsychologist can obtain information through the PFQ about the activities of daily living (ADL) and instrumental activities of daily living (IADL), several additional instruments exist for that purpose and are presented later.

The *Revised Memory and Behaviour Problems Checklist* (RMBPC; Teri et al., 1992) is another instrument designed for caregivers reporting on the symptoms exhibited by care recipients. Each behavior is rated on two scales: (a) *Frequency*, representing the rate of occurrence of specific behaviors (0 = never occurs; 1 = occurs infrequently and not in the last week; 2 = occurred 1–2 times in the last week; 3 = occurred 3–6 times in the last week; and 4 = occurs daily or more often); and (b) a *Reaction rating*, representing the degree to which individual behaviors bother or upset the caregiver (0 = not at all, 1 = a little; 2 = moderately; 3 = very much; 4 = extremely). Thus, this instrument also provides information on caregiver stress. Teri et al. derived three subscales based on factor analysis: Depression, Disruption (e.g., includes verbal aggression, destroying property, arguing, etc.), and Memory-Related

TABLE 11.1
Normative Information on the Present Functioning Questionnaire

Scales	M	SD
Personality Scale	1.40	1.91
Everyday Tasks Scale	.17	.59
Language Skills Scale	.16	.65
Memory Scale	.80	1.62
Self-care Scale	.09	.44
Total Score	2.60	3.68

Note. Collaborative informants who reported on 70 normal elderly volunteers from senior's activity groups. Data from Crockett, D., Tuokko, H., Koch, W., & Parks, R. (1989). Copyright © 1989 by The Haworth Press Inc., Binghamton, NY. Clinical Gerontologist, The assessment of everyday functioning using the Present Functioning Questionnaire and the Functional Rating Scale in elderly samples 8(3), p. 15. Adapted with permission.

Problems. They also presented means and standard deviations obtained by collaborative informants who reported on elderly persons, most of whom were diagnosed with dementia. The internal consistency was .75 and .87 for Frequency and Reaction, respectively, and validity evidence (in terms of relation to other scales) has been presented (Teri et al., 1992). This scale may be useful when it comes to assessing the course and severity of geriatric disorders. Its specificity and sensitivity in differentiating normal elders from those with dementia, however, requires further investigation. In that sense, the PFQ might prove to be a more useful instrument than the RMBPC as norms on normal elders are available. The RMBPC was published in its entirety in Teri et al. (1992, appendix).

Jorm and Jacomb (1989) presented general population norms as well as psychometric information on the *Informant Questionnaire on Cognitive Decline in the Elderly* (IQCODE). The instrument was specifically developed to assess decline from a premorbid level. The caregiver reports on degree of change over a 10-year period. The measure consists of 26 items. It contains questions pertinent to memory, language abilities, and everyday functioning. Responses are provided on 5-point format ranging from Much Better (1) to Much Worse (5). The questionnaire has high internal consistency and was found to discriminate between informants derived from the general population and informants reporting on persons with dementia. The mean correlation with the MMSE is .59 and correlations with education have been near zero (Jorm, 1996). The lack of correlation with education is a major strength of this instrument. Jorm and Jacomb (1989) included the questionnaire in its entirety in an appendix. General population norms were derived from a volunteer Australian sample (Jorm & Jacomb, 1989). The persons, whose names were taken from the electoral role for the Australian Capital Territory, were contacted and asked if they knew of an elderly person. Of the 815 persons who responded and indicated they knew an elderly person, 613 filled out the questionnaire. The norms are based on these individuals and are presented as percentages.

Another instrument commonly used with caregivers is the *Blessed Dementia Rating Scale* (BDS; Blessed et al., 1968). The second part of the BDS was developed for administration to the care recipient and was discussed in chapter 3. The first part of the instrument is administered to the caregiver and assesses changes in daily living, self-care, cognitive capacity, and personality domains (Blessed et al., 1968). Higher scores are indicative of more severe deficits. It consists of 22 items and is administered to a proxy using an interview format. Three domains are assessed: changes in performance of everyday activities (e.g., inability to find way about familiar streets); changes in habits (e.g., eating); and changes in personality, interests, drive (e.g., hobbies relinquished). Scores on the instrument relate to neuropsychological testing and can differentiate between different de-

grees of dementia (Erkinjuntti, Hokkanen, Sulkava, & Palo, 1988). Erkinjuntti, Hokkanen, et al. (1988) discussed a revised version of the BDS
(consisting of the sum of Items 1–11) that achieved higher sensitivity and
specificity than the unrevised version. Specifically, a cutoff score of 4 in
the unrevised version gave a sensitivity of 90% and specificity of 84%. In
the revised version (RDS), a cutoff score of 1.5 gave a sensitivity of 93%
and a specificity of 97%. The average BDS score for community dwelling
elderly persons ($n = 105$) was 2.23 (+/−.23). Recent research has shown
that the interrater reliability between two raters who, working independently, interviewed each of 47 caregivers of persons with dementia,
was low (Cole, 1990). It would be interesting for future research to determine whether similar interrater reliability problems are also found with
respect to other instruments administered to caregivers.

Williams (1991a) discussed the *Cognitive Behavior Rating Scales,* which
are measures that can be administered to relatives or other caregivers of
persons with dementia. This 117-item questionnaire covers the following
areas of functioning: Language Deficits, Apraxia, Disorientation, Agitation,
Need for Routine, Depression, Higher Cognitive Deficits, Memory Disorder, and Dementia. Satisfactory reliability and validity data on the instrument are available (Williams, 1991a). The manual of the scale discusses
small age effects that appear for the subscales focusing on Agitation, Depression, and Dementia. It also presents norms for persons up to age 89.
These persons were recruited through advertisments and were screened
for neurological and psychiatric disorders. Responses were provided by
family members who lived with the care recipient. Williams (1991a) pointed
out that the persons he studied for the development of the manual for
these scales did not include a sufficient number of mild cases. Relatives
may be less able to provide valid responses for subjects with mild impairment. This criticism may hold for many other proxy-administered instruments reviewed here and more research is needed to address this issue.

Chapter 3 of this volume indicated that the *Cambridge Mental Disorders
of the Elderly Examination* (CAMDEX; Roth et al., 1986) includes an informant interview that addresses the areas of orientation, memory, general
intellectual functioning, behavior, personality, mood, and activities of daily
living of the care recipient. Each item is coded on a 3-point scale with a
maximum score of 63. Some validity evidence for the scale exists (O'Connor, Pollitt, Brook, & Reiss, 1989). For instance, the informant memory
and orientation scores correlate with memory and orientation tests. O'Connor et al. (1989) presented means but not standard deviations of total
scores derived from informants reporting about persons with mild, moderate, and severe dementia. Spouse interviews resulted in mean scores of
11.92, 25.95, and 36.43 for mild ($n = 24$), moderate ($n = 19$), and severe
cases ($n = 7$), respectively. Interview scores derived from nurse and child

informants did not differ significantly from the scores obtained during interviews with spouses.

During the last several years, instruments have been developed to diagnose dementia based solely on informant data (see Jorm, 1996). These instruments may prove useful in unusual situations during which it is impossible to examine and assess the person (e.g., postmortem). As this area of instrument development is relatively new, however, more research is needed before the clinical utility of such instruments can be established. For example, the *Informant Based Questionnaire* (Barber, Snowdon, & Craufurd, 1995) was designed to differentiate Alzheimer's disease from frontotemporal dementia. It takes approximately 1 hour and 20 minutes to administer and includes a series of questions focusing on language, memory/orientation, personality, spatial skills, and other related domains. Barber et al. were able to devise a scoring system that separated perfectly 20 early-onset Alzheimer's disease cases and 18 confirmed cases of frontotemporal dementia. Clearly, however, cross validation and normative research is needed on this instrument.

Measures Assessing Activities of Daily Living

Although some of the caregiver strain scales reviewed later in this chapter as well as the PFQ allow for an assessment of activities of daily living (ADL), more specialized instruments exist. ADL assessment instruments are often administered to caregivers when patients are unable to complete them. An ADL measure could be self-report, proxy-administered, or based on observation. Generally, the validity of ADL scales can be compromised when they are administered to persons of diminished capacity.

One of the most widely used measures is the *Index of ADL* (Katz, Downs, Cash, & Grotz, 1970). Six ADL functions are rated in a dichotomous fashion: bathing, dressing, going to the toilet, transfering, continence, and feeding. One point is given for each item for which the person requires assistance. Satisfactory validity and reliability evidence for the scale can be found in the literature. For example, Katz et al. (1970) found that the scale relates in the predicted direction to indices of adaptive capacity and Sherwood, Morris, Morr, and Gutkin (1977) found that the measure has high reproducibility. The original intent of the scale was to be administered to knowledgeable informants who would report on the person's status.

Law and Letts (1989) wrote a review of ADL scales tapping basic activities such as eating, dressing, and grooming. Of the scales they reviewed, they concluded that the *Barthel Index* (Mahoney & Barthel, 1965), the Index of ADL (Katz, Ford, Moskowitz, Jackson, & Jaffee, 1963), the *Level of Rehabilitation Scale* (LORS–II; Carey & Posavac, 1982), and the *Physical Self-Maintenance Scale* (PSMS; Lawton & Brody, 1969) have satisfactory psychometric properties and are short. They also concluded that these scales would make good diagnostic measures. Law and Letts (1989) hypothesized that the best potential for responsibly measuring change in ADL function is reflected on the Barthel Index (Mahoney & Barthel, 1965), the *Kenny Self-Care Evaluation* (Schoening et al., 1965), and the *Klein–Bell ADL* scale (Klein & Bell, 1982). Nonetheless, they stressed that this potential remains to be evaluated. More reliability evidence is needed, for example, for both the Kenny Self-Care Evaluation and the Klein–Bell ADL scale. Other reviewers have argued that the Katz Index is adequate for most purposes and is used widely (A. R. Kane & L. R. Kane, 1981). For hospital-based clinicians, working with patients with chronic long care needs and multiple disabilities, more detailed scales such as the Barthel Index (Mahoney & Barthel, 1965) may be particularly useful (A. R. Kane & L. R. Kane, 1981).

Instrumental Activities of Daily Living (IADL) measures tap more complex activities associated with daily living. These were reviewed in detail by A. R. Kane and L. R. Kane (1981). Many were developed for administration to the person and some are proxy administered. However, it is common for clinicians to administer scales to caregivers that were originally developed as self-report measures.

The *Functional Health Status Test* (Rosow & Breslow, 1966) is a relatively pure IADL measure and contains 25 questions. It is a Guttman-type hierarchically organized scale. The items range from questions concerning ability to go to a church meeting and the movies to the ability to engage in strenuous physical work such as shoveling snow. More research is needed to establish the psychometric properties of the scale. The *Philadelphia Geriatric Centre Instrumental Activities of Daily Living* (Lawton, 1972) also has a Guttman format and taps ability to use the telephone, shopping, food preparation, housekeeping, laundry, public transportation, taking medications, and handling finances. Reproduceability was high but the investigators commented that it may be more suitable for women and it does not tap the full range of ADL.

The *Older Americans Resources Service (OARS): IADL scale* (Fillenbaum, 1988) was administered to caregivers who participated in the Canadian Study of Health and Aging. The items range from ability to eat and dress to ability to manage money. In other words, it includes both ADL and IADL items (see Tables 11.2 and 11.3). Reliability and limited validity evidence exist for this instrument (Duke University Centre for the Study of Aging and Human Development, 1978), although studies are needed to determine the extent to which reliability and validity of the instrument are affected depending on whether the instrument is administered to a patient or a caregiver. Items are rated "without help," "with help," or "unable to perform." The scale results in a global score of ADL and IADL. An overall 1 to 6 rating can also be made by a rater (1 = excellent and 6

TABLE 11.2
Canadian Study on Health and Aging Norms on the OARS
ADL/IADL Scale Based on Caregivers of Persons Who
Scored Greater Than 77 on the 3MS ($n = 484$)

Items	Number of Persons Able to Perform With No Help (%)	Number of Persons Able to Perform With Some Help (%)	Number of Persons Unable to Do This (%)
Can subject eat?	477 (98.6)	6 (1.2)	1 (.2)
Can subject dress and undress?	471 (97.3)	12 (2.5)	1 (.2)
Can subject take care of appearance?	472 (97.5)	10 (2.1)	2 (.4)
Can subject walk?	455 (94.0)	29 (6.0)	—
Can subject get in and out of bed?	477 (98.6)	7 (1.4)	—
Can subject take a bath or shower?	426 (88.0)	48 (9.9)	9 (1.9)
Can subject use the bathroom or toilet?	481 (99.4)	2 (.4)	—
Can subject use the telephone?	451 (93.2)	29 (6.0)	4 (.8)
Can subject get to distant places?	395 (81.6)	76 (15.7)	9 (1.9)
Can subject go shopping?	362 (74.8)	85 (17.6)	33 (6.8)
Can subject prepare own meals?	405 (83.7)	52 (10.7)	25 (5.2)
Can subject do housework?	284 (58.7)	149 (30.8)	48 (9.9)
Can subject take own medicine?	454 (93.8)	26 (5.4)	3 (.6)
Can subject manage own money?	443 (91.5)	33 (6.8)	8 (1.7)

Note. The items from the OARS come from *Multidimensional Functional Assessment of Older Adults* (pp. 143–145) by G. G. Fillenbaum, 1988, Hillsdale, NJ: Lawrence Erlbaum Associates. Copyright © 1975 by the Duke University Center for the Study of Aging and Development. Adapted with permission.

= totally impaired) based on the subject's responses to the various items. Frequencies of the responses on individual items of caregivers reporting on people who obtained scores of 78 or greater on the 3MS (Teng & Chui, 1987) appear on Table 11.2. Information on the responses of caregivers of persons with dementia appear on Table 11.3. Frequencies of overall ADL ratings obtained in the CSHA study appear on Table 11.4.

Earlier in this chapter, findings concerning patient–proxy agreement in symptom reporting were discussed. Some research of this kind focused specifically on ADL/IADL. Rubenstein, Schairer, Wieland, and Kane (1984) found that scores on ADL and IADL scales may vary depending on who provides the information about the person's functioning. These investigators administered (to a group of hospitalized patients over age 65) the Index of ADL (Katz et al., 1970), the PSMS (Lawton & Brody, 1969), and the IADL scale developed at the Philadelphia Geriatric Centre (see Rubenstein et al., 1984). The investigators concluded that information sources about functioning cannot be used interchangeably. This is consistent with the findings of Zimmerman and Magaziner (1994). Although proxies' and self reports of functioning can often be similar, the similarities may not be strong enough

TABLE 11.3
Canadian Study on Health and Aging Norms
on the OARS ADL/IADL Scale Based on
Caregivers of Persons With Dementia (n = 353)

Items	Number of Persons Able to Perform With No Help (%)	Number of Persons Able to Perform With Some Help (%)	Number of Persons Unable to Do This (%)
Can subject eat?	308 (87.3)	37 (10.5)	8 (2.3)
Can subject dress and undress?	243 (68.8)	73 (20.7)	36 (10.2)
Can subject take care of appearance?	265 (75.1)	53 (15.0)	35 (9.9)
Can subject walk?	274 (77.6)	55 (15.6)	24 (6.8)
Can subject get in and out of bed?	312 (88.4)	20 (5.7)	21 (5.9)
Can subject take a bath or shower?	160 (45.3)	120 (34.0)	72 (20.4)
Can subject use the bathroom or toilet?	294 (83.3)	31 (8.8)	27 (7.6)
Can subject use the telephone?	180 (51.0)	39 (26.3)	74 (21.0)
Can subject get to distant places?	84 (23.8)	167 (47.3)	95 (26.9)
Can subject go shopping?	73 (20.7)	110 (31.2)	164 (46.5)
Can subject prepare own meals?	90 (25.5)	105 (29.7)	151 (42.8)
Can subject do housework?	58 (16.4)	116 (32.6)	170 (48.2)
Can subject take own medicine?	129 (36.5)	115 (32.6)	97 (27.5)
Can subject manage own money?	82 (23.2)	89 (25.2)	176 (49.9)

Note. The items from the OARS come from *Multidimensional Functional Assessment of Older Adults* (pp. 143–145) by G. G. Fillenbaum, 1988, Hillsdale, NJ: Lawrence Erlbaum Associates. Copyright © 1975 by the Duke University Center for the Study of Aging and Development. Adapted with permission.

TABLE 11.4
Frequencies of Overall ADL Ratings Based on the
Responses of Caregivers of Persons With Dementia and
Caregivers of Persons Who Obtained Greater than 77
on the 3MS (Canadian Study on Health and Aging)

Level of Impairment	Caregivers of Persons With Dementia (%)	Caregivers of Persons With score >77 on 3MS (%)
No impairment (2)	5.6	32.5
Mild Impairment (3)	13.0	20.8
Moderate Impairment (4)	26.9	20.7
Severe Impairment (5)	21.5	11.0
Total Impairment (6)	32.9	14.9

to consider the two types of reports equivalent. Generally, self-reported scores tended to be indicative of higher functioning than scores derived from proxies. Zimmerman and Magaziner speculated on the reasons for this discrepancy. Specifically, it may be due to denial on the part of the individual or to the burdened caregiver's tendency to underestimate the activities that the individuals are capable of performing on their own. In the case of hospitalized patients, the hospitalized status could function as a stereotype that could lead caregivers to underestimate the patients' capabilities.

Weinberger et al. (1992) compared self and proxy perceptions using a modified version of Index of ADL and Instrumental Activities of Daily Living in a sample of medical patients seen in a geriatric evaluation and treatment clinic. They concluded that patient and proxy ratings were concordant when it came to ability to perform ADL tasks. With respect to IADL, concordance was high for patients whose MMSE score was 24 or higher and relatively poor for patients with MMSE scores lower than 24. When disagreement occurred, proxies rated the patients as more impaired than the patients rated themselves. These findings seem to suggest that, in many instances, patients may overrate their ability to carry out instrumental activities of daily living.

Of the instruments reviewed here, the PFQ (Crockett et al., 1989) has the advantage of covering several areas of patient functioning (i.e., cognitive, psychological, ADL, and IADL) and norms for normal individuals are available. In addition, satisfactory reliability and validity evidence exists on this instrument. The IQCODE could also prove to be a very useful index of cognitive decline, as is suggested by the extensive available validity and reliability evidence (Jorm, 1996). The interested reader is referred to Jorm (1996) for a more detailed discussion of informant instruments that could be used for the assessment of cognitive decline. When more elaborate information on ADL and IADL is needed, other more focused scales (e.g., the OARS; Fillenbaum, 1988) may prove useful. Nonetheless, there is a need for additional normative and/or validity information for ADL and IADL measures.

ASSESSING THE PSYCHOLOGICAL CONSEQUENCES OF CAREGIVING

Caring for a person with dementia is a very demanding task with potentially serious psychological consequences for the caregiver. In a 2-year longitudinal study of Alzheimer's caregivers, Schultz and Williamson (1991) found that levels of depression among continuous caregivers were more serious than they were for noncaregivers. Furthermore, female caregivers were significantly more distressed than male caregivers. Nonetheless, male caregivers showed significant increases in depression symptoms over time. In another study of psychological distress among caregivers of dementia patients, Anthony-Bergstone, S. H. Zarit, and Gatz (1988) administered the Brief Symptom Inventory. Compared to age-matched norms, caregivers were elevated on the hostility subscale. Both younger and older women scored higher than the norms on the anxiety subscale, and older women were also elevated significantly on three other subscales. Means derived from this study are presented in Table 11.5. The standard deviations were not reported.

S. H. Zarit (1990) wrote that caregiver outcomes such as decreased well-being are determined by an interplay of factors, including patient deficits, appraisals of strain, social support, other stressors in the caregivers' lives, appraisals of coping by caregivers, and contextual factors such as the relationship of the caregiver with a patient. Some support for Zarit's assertions exists. Cantor (1983) found, for instance, that caregiver burden varies depending on the nature of the relationship of the caregiver with the person with dementia (e.g., child vs. parent vs. friend). Hadjistavropoulos et al. (1994) found that caregiver burden was affected substantially by the caregiver's perception of the care recipient's symptoms and only indirectly by actual symptoms. In addition, caregiver perceptions of the degree to which the care recipient's mood was dysphoric was more likely to contribute to caregiver burden than perceptions concerning other areas of functioning (e.g., memory and language skills). Such findings suggest that when well-

TABLE 11.5
Brief Symptom Inventory Subscale Scores of Caregivers

Subscale	Older Women[a]	Older Men[b]	Younger Women[c]	Younger Men[d]
Somatization	.70	.44	.43	.21
Obsessive-Compulsive	1.20	.87	.88	.75
Interpersonal Sensitivity	.61	.40	.42	.50
Depression	.92	.44	.61	.53
Anxiety	1.02	.53	.78	.74
Hostility	.90	.62	.72	.85
Phobic Anxiety	.30	.19	.19	.13
Paranoid Ideation	.53	.29	.44	.72
Psychoticism	.51	.24	.31	.32

Note. From "Symptoms of Psychological Distress Among Caregivers of Dementia Patients," by C. R. Anthony-Bergstone, S. H. Zarit, and M. Gatz, 1988, *Psychology and Aging, 3*, pp. 246–247. Copyright © 1988 by the American Psychological Association. Adapted with permission.
[a]$n = 77$; age 60 or older.
[b]$n = 47$; age 60 or older.
[c]$n = 47$; age 59 or younger.
[d]$n = 13$; age 59 or younger.

being of caregivers is assessed, it is important for the clinician to obtain information on as many of the dimensions discussed by Zarit as possible (i.e., social supports, nature of the caregiver–patient relationship, etc.).

Caregiver burden has been conceptualized within a stress and coping framework (S. H. Zarit, 1990). Two processes (coping and cognitive appraisal) have been identified as important mediators between a stressful situation such as caregiving and the psychological consequences for the individual (Lazarus & Folkman, 1984). Through *appraisal*, individuals evaluate whether they have anything at stake in any particular encounter and whether anything can be done to prevent or overcome harm or improve the chances for benefit. Coping refers to cognitive or behavioral efforts to manage demands that are appraised as taxing or as exceeding the person's resources (Lazarus & Folkman, 1984). *Secondary appraisal* refers to how well people evaluate the adequacy of their resources for coping with threats posed by stressors (Lazarus & Folkman, 1984). The relevant *primary stressors* are the stressors or demands that result from the elder's illness and disability. S. H. Zarit (1990) pointed out that these may have both objective (i.e., specific and necessary care tasks) and subjective components (i.e., the degree to which a caregiver feels distress as a result of the disability). *Secondary stressors* refer to the consequences of providing care in other areas of the caregiver's life. Primary and secondary stressors are believed to make contributions to caregiving outcomes such as decreased well-being. Furthermore, their effects are believed to be moderated by mediators such as coping, social support, and appraisals (S. H. Zarit, 1990). Such dimensions could also be evaluated during the interview with the caregiver.

For the assessment of the psychological consequences of caregiving, a brief interview with focused screening questions (e.g., How do you cope with having to care for your relative? Do you manage okay?) is recommended. Establishing adequate rapport with the caregiver is important in order to get sincere answers to such questions. Caregiver functioning can be assessed more systematically through the administration of general measures of psychological functioning (e.g., the *Brief Symptom Inventory*). Caregiver norms on some psychopathology scales are presented in Tables 11.5 and 11.6. Specifically, Table 11.5 presents norms on the Brief Symptom Inventory based on samples of caregivers of persons with dementia. All were living in the community. The data are broken down by caregiver sex and age. Table 11.6 presents data on the *Center for Epidemiologic Studies Depression* scale. These data were collected through the Canadian Study on Health and Aging. These instruments are discussed in more detail in chapter 9. In some instances, the clinician may be interested in comparing the caregiver's functioning with that of persons in the general population. General population norms would have to be used for that purpose. In

TABLE 11.6
Center of Epidemiologic Studies Depression Scale Scores
Obtained by Caregivers of People With Dementia
(Canadian Study on Health and Aging)

Age	Gender	n	M	SD
65–69	M	30	6.00	9.13
	F	77	8.61	9.01
70–74	M	19	7.32	8.31
	F	67	8.18	9.32
75–79	M	14	11.29	12.66
	F	51	10.67	9.59
80–84	M	16	12.75	8.18
	F	30	10.53	8.51
85+	M	9	6.33	5.59
	F	6	15.50	8.12

chapter 9, population norms for elderly persons are presented for several instruments developed to assess psychological symptoms.

In addition to interview and general measures of functioning, specialized instruments that assess caregiver burden exist. Because the goal of such instruments is to determine the degree to which a caregiver is burdened relative to other caregivers of dementia victims, it seems that appropriate normative groups would be caregivers of dementia victims or caregivers of people with suspected dementia.

Vitaliano, Young, and Russo (1991) published a major review of a variety of instruments developed specifically for the assessment of caregiver burden (e.g., Greene, R. Smith, Gardiner, & Timbury, 1982; Kinney & Parris-Stephens, 1989; Lawton, Kleban, Moss, Rovine, & Glicksman, 1989; R. J. V. Montgomery, Gonyea, & Hooyman, 1985; Novak & Guest, 1989; Pearlin & Schooler, 1978; Poulshock & Deimling, 1984; Rabins, Mace, & Lucas, 1982; Vitaliano, Russo, Young, Becker, & Maiuro, 1991; S. H. Zarit, Reever, & Bach-Petersen, 1980). Some instruments separately assess objective caregiver experiences as well as the caregiver's own response to such experiences. Other instruments confound subjective with objective dimensions. Although this section focuses on obtaining information about caregiver functioning, some of the instruments developed for that purpose (e.g., Poulshock & Deimling, 1984) also include questions that relate to the care recipient's functioning in areas such as activities of daily living (ADL) and thus, overlap with some of the ADL instruments reviewed in the previous section.

The *Burden Interview* (BI; S. H. Zarit & J. M. Zarit, 1982; Whitlatch, S. H. Zarit, & von Eye, 1991) is probably the most widely used instrument in this area. This 22-item scale (S. H. Zarit, Orr, & J. M. Zarit, 1985) assesses the extent to which caregivers view their responsibilities as having an adverse impact on their social life, health, emotional well-being, and finances. The caregivers respond to the items (e.g., Do you feel stressed between caring for your relative and trying to meet other responsibilities for your family or work?) along 5-point scales anchored by the polar opposites "Never" and "Nearly always." The scale has satisfactory reliability and validity (Whitlatch et al., 1991). The BI (S. H. Zarit & J. M. Zarit, 1990) was administered to caregivers in the Canadian Study on Health and Aging. Relevant norms are presented on Table 11.7. In terms of stress and coping conceptualizations, the scale taps appraisal of secondary stressors and secondary appraisal (S. H. Zarit, 1990).

Lawton et al. (1989) proposed five dimensions of burden based on a factor analysis of items they drew from a variety of scales. They proposed that caregiver appraisals of the caregiving process are multifaceted and include caregiver burden. The following dimensions were derived: impact of caregiving burden (analogous to secondary appraisal), impact of caregiving (analogous to secondary stressors), caregiving mastery, caregiving satisfaction, and cognitive reappraisal (a coping strategy) (S. H. Zarit, 1990). Although Lawton et al. derived some support for these dimensions, the appraisal dimensions were not conclusively confirmed. Additional research on this instrument is needed to determine its clinical utility. However, the main contribution of Lawton and colleagues was the expansion of the measurement of the caregiving experience to include several dimensions of appraisal.

Poulshock and Deimling's (1984) approach involves indices of burden that correspond to dependency and mental impairment. *Dependency* refers to activities of daily living. Specifically, for each ADL (bathing, dressing, toileting, mobility, incontinence, and eating), caregivers indicate along a

TABLE 11.7
Burden Interview (22-item version; S. H. Zarit & J. M. Zarit, 1990)
Scores of Caregivers of Patients With Dementia
(Canadian Study of Health and Aging)

Age	Gender	n	M	SD
65–69	M	28	13.29	10.08
	F	78	18.45	15.42
70–74	M	19	14.16	12.78
	F	65	17.17	17.89
75–79	M	14	16.36	16.29
	F	52	17.59	15.17
80–84	M	17	18.35	14.64
	F	29	15.14	11.37
85+	M	9	16.11	12.87
	F	4	35.25	19.45

0 to 3 scale whether they find the assistance tiring, difficult, or upsetting. For mental impairment, they indicate along a 0 to 3 scale how upset they feel as a result of the patient's level sociability (8 items), disruptive behavior (7 items), and cognitive incapacity (8 items). To measure caregiving impact, items similar to Zarit's Burden Interview are used. Impact is operationalized in terms of both negative changes in the elder/caregiver family relationships (11 items) and in terms of restrictions in the caregiver's activities (8 items). Reliability and construct validity evidence is also presented. A strength of this approach is that the caregiving experience can be measured in relation to specific symptoms.

Another interesting approach was discussed by Novak and Guest (1989). They developed the *Caregiver Burden Inventory* (CBI) that involves five factor analytically derived scales (Time-Dependence Burden, Developmental Burden, Physical Burden, Social Burden, and Emotional Burden). The CBI consists of 24 items. Adjusted raw scores derived from these scales can be used to plot caregiver burden profiles that graphically represent the degree to which each of the five areas measured is problematic relative to the rest. More evidence on the construct validity of this measure is needed.

Greene et al. (1982) described the development of two scales: a *Behavior and Memory Disturbance Scale* (BMDS) and a *Relative's Stress Scale* (RSS). The first scale contains 34 items tapping behavioral problems that the care recipients may be displaying (e.g., talk aloud to themselves) and the latter consists of 15 items and relates to negative feelings that caregiving may lead the caregiver to experience (e.g., Do you ever get cross and angry with . . . ?). The responses are given along 5-point scales corresponding to each item. The scales were factor analyzed using a very small sample ($N = 39$) and, thus, the factor analytically derived subscales (within each of the two main scales) may reflect an unstable solution. Although both objective and subjective aspects of burden are tapped by the scales, there is no direct correspondence between the items of the BMDS scale tapping objective burden and the RSS tapping subjective burden. Some validity evidence was presented but more research is needed to determine the utility of this scale.

Kinney and Parris-Stephens (1989) developed a *Caregiver Hassles Scale*. This 42-item instrument differs from others reviewed here in that it focuses on the day-to-day experience of caregiving rather than caregiving events or responsibilities occurring over longer periods of time. The five scales of the instrument are Basic Activities of Daily Living, Instrumental Activities of Daily Living, Cognitive Status, Patient Behavior, and the Caregiver's Social Network. The caregiver indicates whether or not each event occurred over the past week and then every occurrence is rated with respect to whether or not it represented a hassle along a 4-point scale. Construct validity and some reliability evidence was also presented.

R. J. V. Montgomery et al. (1985) developed two measures; the first consists of nine items designed to assess *objective burden*. The questions assess consequences of caregiving on the caregiver's life (e.g., amount of privacy at home, amount of time you have to yourself) and are scored along 5-point scales anchored by the polar opposites "a lot more" and "a lot less." The second scale consists of 13 items and aims to assess *subjective burden* (e.g., "I feel it is painful to watch my [relative] age"; "I feel useful in my relationship with my relative"). Some reliability and validity evidence was presented. A criticism of this approach is that the items in the two scales do not show a conceptual correspondence.

Only one of the instruments (*Screen for Caregiver Burden*; Vitaliano et al., 1991) reviewed by Vitaliano, Young, and Rousso (1991) met all three of the following criteria: examined prevalence of caregiver demands (Objective Burden), examined caregiver response to these specific demands (Subjective Burden), and has been studied with respect to criterion validation as well as sensitivity to change. This measure combines features of primary appraisal and subjective evaluation of secondary stressors. All items in the scale are included in Vitaliano, Russo, et al. (1991). Some normative information on the subjective burden portion of the scale was given by Vitaliano et al. (1991). The sample from which these norms were developed consisted of 79 spouse caregivers who were living with a person with possible/probable Primary Degenerative Dementia. The normative information is presented in quartiles. Caregivers of less than 65 years of age with a score higher than 42.2 would be at the top 25%, whereas they would fall at the bottom 25% if their score were less than 31. The means and standard deviations reported by Vitaliano and colleagues were 9.01 ($SD = 4.30$) for objective burden and 35.54 ($SD = 8.02$) for subjective burden (average caregiver age = 67.4 years). Vitaliano et al. presented data collected at two different points in time. The data for people over age 65 collected at Time 2 appeared somewhat elevated compared to those at Time 1. The information presented here is based on Time 1 data.

At this point there does not seem to be a consensus as to what is the best way to measure caregiver burden. More research is needed to determine the relative utility of global versus specific measures. Based on the previous review and keeping in mind the limitations discussed, clinicians may select the measure that taps best the area they are interested in assessing. The BI is probably the scale on which the greatest amount of information is available. Other scales, however, tap information not assessed by the BI. Furthermore, in comparing the data to norms, it is important to note the composition of the caregiver normative groups because caregiver's response to burden could be affected by factors such as demographic characteristics.

CONCLUSIONS

In most circumstances, a knowledgeable proxy should be interviewed in order to provide information about the care recipient's symptomatology. Standardized measures developed for such a purpose could supplement the clinical interview. The interview could also include some screening questions regarding the degree to which the caregiver/proxy is burdened by the patient's condition. Knowledge about caregiver burden is important not only because it may lead the caregiver to experience symptoms of psychological distress but also because caregiver burden could potentially interfere with effective patient care. Many clinicians may wish to pursue with the caregiver the possibility of an assessment of burden and caregiver functions through the use of standardized assessment tools and more elaborate interviewing. The purpose of the assessment should determine the measure of choice.

Chapter 12

Ethics in the Assessment of Elderly Persons

Most ethical issues pertaining to the assessment of elderly persons are common to the assessment of all populations. For the purposes of this discussion, several references are made to psychologists and codes of ethics developed by psychologists. However, the principles articulated here are relevant to the practices of many types of health professionals who work with elders. It is recommended that all practitioners using psychological and cognitive tests become familiar with the Standards for Educational and Psychological Testing (American Psychological Association, 1985), the General Guidelines for Providers of Psychological Services (American Psychological Association, 1987) and/or the Practice Guidelines for Providers of Psychological Services (Canadian Psychological Association, 1989), Specialty Guidelines for the Delivery of Services by Clinical Psychologists (American Psychological Association, 1981), as well as with the Ethical Principles and Code of Conduct (American Psychological Association, 1992) and the Canadian Code of Ethics for Psychologists (Canadian Psychological Association, 1991). Additional ethical guidelines and standards of practice are available for physicians (e.g., Council on Ethical and Judicial Affairs, 1994), social workers (e.g., National Association of Social Workers, 1993), and other health professionals.

Several important general issues need to be considered when conducting any psychological assessment (e.g., Keith-Spiegel & Koocher, 1985). First, to be competent, practitioners must have received specialized training in the type of population with whom they work. In the case of geriatric neuropsychologists, extensive supervision and training in both general and geriatric neuropsychology is required. Second, practitioners should be familiar with measurement theory and issues of test reliability and validity. This allows for an evaluation of the adequacy of the psychometric instruments they employ. They should also be familiar with the factors that could bias the results of psychological testing. Such factors were discussed in chapters 1 and 2 and include cultural and language issues. In addition, the content of psychological tests must be kept secure because test validity could be compromised if test security is violated and members of the public become familiar with the content of psychological tests. Test validity is affected when individuals become exposed to the items of a test before they are administered that test.

Another important concern is the use of computerized scoring and interpretation services as discussed by Matarazzo (1986). Any reports derived from computerized scoring systems should be viewed as means of generating hypotheses about the person's deficits. They should not be accepted at face value because they may be of limited validity. The computer program may fail to present more than one hypotheses for the clinician's consideration and to integrate interpretations with background history (Matarazzo, 1986). Computerized test interpretations are often simulations of clinicians' decision-making rules and are subject to error (Matarazzo, 1986). Thus, they should be checked against other sources of data (e.g., other psychological tests, background information). It is imperative that computerized packages provide sufficient evidence for the validity of their interpretations and the reports they generate. Such reports should never be used by individuals who do not have good knowledge of psychological assessment procedures and the limitations of such procedures.

Keith-Spiegel and Koocher (1985) stressed the importance of informed consent and the client's right to know the purpose of the assessment and the potential use of assessment results. These issues are of particular importance in geriatric assessment because the capacity to provide informed consent may be compromised by dementing illness and, in some institutional and/or family contexts, the voluntariness of informed consent may also be compromised. The issue of informed consent is especially salient when it comes to the assessment of elderly persons and is addressed in more detail later.

It is recommended that test scores be retained in a client's file only as long as they serve a valid and useful purpose (Keith-Spiegel & Koocher, 1985). In the cognitive assessment of elderly persons, test results are of special importance with respect to potential future use because they provide a baseline for determining the presence or absence of cognitive deterioration.

Questions about third-party access to psychological test data and its effects can often arise. In the case of elderly persons with dementia, there may be the complicating factor of family members wishing access to such data. When a client is cognitively impaired, a legal guardian may be entitled to legal access (Keith-Spiegel & Koocher, 1985). Keith-Spiegel and Koocher recommended that from the beginning of the working relationship, parties should be informed of the limits of confidentiality and an early discussion of the types of information to be shared should take place. Other questions pertaining to third-party access apply to most assessment situations and are discussed in detail elsewhere (see Keith-Spiegel & Koocher, 1985; Ogloff, 1995).

Geriatric neuropsychologists, by virtue of their role, will be dealing with a disproportionate number of elderly persons who suffer cognitive impairments and are, therefore, vulnerable. Thus, it is imperative that they be aware of the ethical issues involved in the assessment of such elders. Although the number of ethical issues that may arise is potentially high, two are discussed in more detail because they are of special importance in geriatric assessments. Specifically, issues pertaining to informed consent and assessment feedback are examined.

INFORMED CONSENT

Obtaining Consent

A substantial portion of elders are victims of dementia (Canadian Study of Health and Aging Work Group, 1994), so consent concerning health care decisions involving dementia victims is often obtained from proxy decision makers (e.g., family members). Rozovsky (1990) wrote that three elements must be present for consent to be legally and ethically valid: *voluntariness, mental capacity,* and *adequate information.* In the case of cognitively intact elderly persons, addressing the issue of competence is not terribly complicated. When, on the other hand, there is evidence that mental capacity is significantly compromised, consent for the assessment must be sought from an appropriate proxy (e.g., legal guardian).

Recent research evidence suggests that practitioners may have to be more conservative in their determinations of competence to provide consent. Abramovitch, Finstad, and Silberfeld (1993) conducted a study to investigate the issue of informed consent for mental capacity assessments. They concluded that it was the assessor's impression that everyone who participated in the capacity assessment provided informed consent at least to some degree. However, at the end of the assessment, it was found that eight clients (47% of the total group) were found to have only a general sense of being tested or showed no understanding at all for the reason of the assessment. Four of these clients showed no understanding of why they had come to the clinic. Abramovitch et al. recommended that more attention be paid when it comes to the determination of capacity to give consent and suggested an informal assessment of that capacity with some interview questions. Clients could be asked with appropriate probes about why they came to the clinic and about their expectations.

Tymchuk and Ouslander (1990) recommended an initial basic assessment of the person's ability to hear and see (i.e., can the person see, discriminate, and label words?) followed by a brief assessment of mental capacity to determine whether there is a need for proxy consent. They also supported assessment of reading capacity, presentation of consent material developed in a format and at difficulty level to match the person's ability, assessment of comprehension of consent material, and a follow-up to determine whether comprehension of the information remains at criterion level. These suggestions imply that a brief screening tool such as the Mini-Mental State exam (M. L. Folstein et al., 1975) combined with a test such as the Wide Range Achievement Test–Revised (Jastak & Wilkinson, 1984) could be used as quick assessment tools for capacity to consent in the case of some individuals (chapter 3 includes additional discussion of competency assessments). Although a problem with this suggestion is that persons would be given psychological tests in order to assess their capacity to agree to be given more psychological tests, the procedure is probably justified on ethical grounds because consent could be potentially obtained for a variety of other purposes (e.g., implementation of assessment recommendations, release of records). Perhaps, in the future, a videotaped format could be developed with information that could facilitate the consent process—especially in individuals of relatively lower educational attainment (Tymchuk & Ouslander, 1990).

Although proxy consent is often obtained when working with the elderly person, assent should be sought in all instances. Under no circumstances may a person be forced to participate in neuropsychological testing or research. It has been suggested that a professional activity may proceed without assent only if the service is of direct benefit to the person of diminished capacity (Canadian Psychological Association, 1991). Lack of assent and cooperation in neuropsychological assessment would typically jeopardize the validity of psychological test results and testing without assent is unlikely to be significantly beneficial to the person. In some instances, it may benefit the person to derive assessment information from a caregiver even if the individual refuses to participate in neuropsychological testing. In most cases, obtaining assent is not difficult. In a supportive environment, most people are cooperative with the assessment process.

Although at first glance the process of proxy consent may appear straightforward, Kapp (1991) discussed several caveats pertaining to proxy consent. First, elderly persons must be protected against family coercion masquerading in the guise of shared decision making. Furthermore, potential conflicts of interest between the person and the family may occur and service providers should be alert to these issues. For example, the family that refuses consent for routine beneficial care and/or assessment in order to save money and conserve future estate is not acting in the person's best interest. In extreme cases, it may be necessary to seek formal legal protection for the person.

Limits of Confidentiality

In general, practitioners must inform their clients of the limits to confidentiality before any assessment is undertaken and informed consent is obtained (American Psychological Association, 1992). Where the individual's mental abilities are compromised, it would be appropriate to inform their legal guardian of these limits. These limits may vary from jurisdiction to jurisdiction but generally involve situations such as suspicion of child abuse, danger to a person (and, in some cases, risk of substantial damage to property), and court order (see Ogloff, 1995). Some jurisdictions have adopted legislation that makes the reporting of elder abuse mandatory (Ogloff, 1995). Psychologists must be well aware of the relevant laws of their jurisdiction and be prepared to act accordingly. In all instances, appropriate support should be offered to the person and/or the family.

A common situation in the assessment of elders involves suspicion that the individual is unable to drive. Many jurisdictions require health professionals to inform the authorities if a person continues to drive despite impaired capacity. The act of driving is very important for many elders and removing their privilege to drive may be tantamount to removing their independence. Thus, it is very important for the geriatric neuropsychologist to be sensitive to these types of issues and support individuals in their attempt to adapt to a new lifestyle through consultation and/or appropriate referral.

GIVING FEEDBACK

The role of the neuropsychologist has been redefined to encompass, in addition to assessment, a more active involvement with the client and treatment team of health professionals (Gass & Brown, 1992). As part of such involvement, neuropsychologists provide assessment feedback to the family, the client, and other professionals. From an ethical point of view, it is important to recognize the person's right to self-determination and, as such, feedback to the person must be a concern to the neuropsychologist. Clinically, feedback can be a vehicle for providing persons with decision-making guidelines. For example, provincial and state laws outline specific rules with respect to competence to drive. Feedback pertaining to competence in this and other areas could be discussed with the patient. Involvement of family members is necessary when the person's ability to participate in the feedback process is compromised. During the process of feedback, the neuropsychologist can provide the person and family with support as the realization of the impact of neurological conditions often has negative emotional consequences. In addition, during the provision of feedback, recommendations can be made that could benefit the person and the family.

Gass and Brown (1992) provided some guidelines for the provision of assessment feedback to persons with brain dysfunction. Specifically, they recognized that no single approach to feedback can be used with all individuals and suggested the following steps: review the purpose of testing (this is especially important when it comes to persons with memory problems), define the tests as behavior samples assessing behavioral skills related to the functional integrity of the brain, explain test results and behavior in a manner the person can understand, describe strengths and weaknesses, address diagnostic and prognostic issues (it is often prudent to defer the diagnosis to a physician who can assess the psychologist's report in relation to medical diagnostic data), and make recommendations. Pope (1992) discussed the importance of ensuring that the client understands the limitations of psychological assessment procedures. Gass and Brown (1992) also stressed that the way the feedback is provided is important. Specifically, potentially stigmatizing terminology (e.g., demented, retarded) should be avoided and every effort should be made for feedback to be given in a way that is understandable to the clients. The emotional needs of the person may affect the timing of the feedback and the way this is given. Gass and Brown (1992) suggested, for instance, that some persons may require a supportive approach in which their relative strengths are stressed. Although denial on the part of the person and the family is a common initial response, and some degree of denial may be psychologically adaptive, the occurrence of prolonged denial may cause major problems (Gass & Brown, 1992). Such denial could prevent the person and the family from preparing for the future and for implementing treatment recommendations. Given such potential difficulties, the role of the geriatric neuropsychologist in the feedback process is delicate and professionals must consider carefully, and with a high degree of sensitivity, the issus pertaining to neuropsychological assessment feedback of each individual person.

NEUROPSYCHOLOGICAL RESEARCH
WITH GERIATRIC POPULATIONS

The ethical concerns relating to informed consent and vulnerability become especially potent when engaging in testing for research as opposed to clinical purposes. Although testing for clinical purposes is intended to directly benefit the person, this is not necessarily the case when it comes to research. Typically, in research studies, written consent must be obtained. Although consent forms are meant to be written in lay language, they may be technical and difficult to understand without a high level of education and/or technical background. In addition, many elderly persons have visual, auditory, and/or other impairments that could interfere with their ability to read consent forms. Adaptations for elderly persons may involve the use of large print and easy-to-understand language (Sachs, Rhymes, & Cassel, 1994).

Where the person is unable to provide consent, it would be appropriate to obtain proxy consent. But, testing for the purposes of research should not be attempted without assent of the participant. If the subject—no matter how impaired—objects to being in the study either verbally or behaviorally, then participation should be discontinued (Sachs et al., 1994). It has been suggested that persons with diminished capabilities should not be sought as research participants unless the research questions cannot be answered with another group of individuals who are more able to consent (Canadian Psychological Association, 1991). Sachs et al. (1994) endorsed the concept of advance directives for research with elders. Specifically, they suggested that institutionalized elderly persons or those without dementia may be given the opportunity to instruct others on their wishes regarding participation in research if they ever lose their decision-making capability.

ETHICS CODES AND THE RESOLUTION
OF ETHICAL DILEMMAS

The codes of ethics of the American Psychological Association (APA; American Psychological Association, 1992) and Canadian Psychological Association (CPA; Canadian Psychological Association, 1991) recognize the special care that should be taken in the assessment of vulnerable persons. The ethical principles of psychologists published by the APA are listed in Table 12.1.

Principles A to E apply directly to the types of dilemmas encountered by the geriatric neuropsychologist and Principle F (*Social Responsibility*) applies indirectly. First, the practitioner must consider issues pertaining to *Competence*. Are practitioners qualified to draw the conclusions they have reached both with respect to the person's cognitive function and psychological state? Have they assessed the person adequately? The Principle of *Integrity* is also important in so far as health professionals must consider the need to provide services with honesty and respect toward their clients. The principle of *Professional and Scientific Responsibility* must be considered

TABLE 12.1
Ethical Principles

American Psychological Association (1992)
Principle A: Competence
Principle B: Integrity
Principle C: Professional and Scientific Responsibility
Principle D: Respect for People's Rights and Dignity
Principle E: Concern for Other's Welfare
Principle F: Social Responsibility
Canadian Psychological Association (1991)
Principle I: Respect for the Dignity of Persons
Principle II: Responsible Caring
Principle III: Integrity in Relationships
Principle IV: Responsibility to Society

as well. Specifically, a decision should be made concerning collaboration with other professionals (e.g., referrals and consulations). Moreover, practitioners should be prepared to accept responsibility for any professional decision they make. Appropriate respect for the person's dignity, as specified in *Respect for People's Rights and Dignity*, must also be shown. Clinicians must consider the welfare of the client and the consequences that any action they might take could have for the client (*Concern for Others' Welfare*). Finally, clinicians should work for the benefit of their community and show respect for the law (*Social Responsibility*).

In addition to its ethical principles, APA's code outlines a variety of standards that must be maintained by psychologists. The section of standards referring specifically to assessment includes a discussion of the importance of a professional context, competence, and test security. The appropriate construction, use, and interpretation of tests is also discussed. The code specifically stresses in the section "Use of Assessment with Special Populations" that psychologists must identify situations in which particular interventions or assessment techniques or norms may not be applicable because of factors such as the individual's ethnicity, language, and other demographic characteristics. In addition, the importance of providing feedback that is reasonably understandable to the person and/or guardian is also stressed.

The Canadian code comprises four ethical principles that are hierarchically listed in order of importance (see Table 12.1). These principles apply in a manner similar to those of the APA code. Specifically, the three most relevant CPA principles are: *Respect for the Dignity of Persons, Responsible Caring,* and *Integrity in Relationships.* Like the APA's corresponding principle, the fourth principle of the CPA code (*Responsibility to Society*) applies indirectly. Regardless of whether psychologists consult the APA code, the CPA code, or both, they should also review more specific standards outlined in the codes that may be pertinent to each dilemma with which they are dealing. Both the APA and CPA codes outline standards referring broadly to issues such as informed consent, confidentiality, and competence.

The geriatric neuropsychologist will often encounter ethical dilemmas. These must be considered carefully and any decision taken must be able to withstand scrutiny. The decision-making approach recommended by the CPA's ethics code is particularly useful in the resolution of ethical dilemmas. Specifically, the Canadian Code of Ethics for Psychologists outlines seven steps for resolving ethical dilemmas. Psychologists must first identify the ethically relevant issues and practices. In other words, they should consider how each ethical principle of the codes applies to their situation. Second, they should consider alternative courses of action. Third, they should analyze all likely risks and benefits for each course of action. Fourth, practitioners must select an appropriate course of action after conscientious application of existing principles, standards, and moral values. Fifth, they should take appropriate action with a commitment to assume responsibility for the consequences of the selected course of action. Sixth, they must evaluate carefully the consequences of the course of action. Finally, practitioners must assume responsibility for consequences of their action. This could involve the correction of any negative consequences or the reengaging of the decision-making process if the ethical problem is not resolved.

Sometimes as practitioners consider alternative courses of action, they may realize that there will be times when ethical principles are in conflict. There may be a situation, for instance, where the need to give maximal protection to clients' welfare has to be balanced with the need to show concern for their dignity. The need to protect clients' dignity is maximized when they are given full and complete information about assessment conclusions. On the other hand, the disclosure of such information could sometimes have devastating emotional consequences for clients and, in rare occasions, it could lead them to cease their cooperation with the health service provider. In such a case, the ethical principles concerned with protection of dignity are in conflict with ethical principles concerned with protection of welfare. A health care provider could, therefore, become tempted to proceed with appropriate referral while being somewhat evasive about the assessment conclusions. The CPA code deals with such situations by having its principles organized in a hierarchical fashion. Principle I (*Respect for the Dignity of Persons*) is considered to be the most important. Thus, in situations where principles are in conflict, the hierarchical organization of the code could lead to resolution. In contrast, the principles of the APA code are not organized hierarchically, making the code less helpful for guiding actions. It is important to point out, however, that the intent of the hierarchical organization of the CPA code is not to undermine the importance of showing responsible caring and protecting client welfare. In the scenario discussed, a psychologist should take all reasonable steps to protect client welfare and minimize and correct any negative consequences that a selected course of action could have. The psychologist should ensure, for instance, that appropriate follow-up and/or referral is arranged if the assessment results have negative emotional consequences for a client.

Ethical dilemmas usually do not have perfect solutions and the CPA code points out that there are exceptions to the hierarchical organization of its principles. It states, for instance, that *Respect for the Dignity of Persons* should be given the highest weight except in situations where there is clear and imminent danger to the physical safety of any individual. Naturally, psychologists and other practitioners should also be familiar with laws and precedence-setting cases affecting their jurisdiction and take these into account in their chosen course of action. As stated in the APA code of ethics, "whether or not a psychologist has violated the ethics code does not by itself determine whether he or she is legally liable in any court action" (American Psychological Association, 1992, p. 1598). It is important to consult with colleagues when in doubt about any situation involving the resolution of ethical dilemmas in practice or research.

References

Abikoff, H., Alvir, J., Hong, G., Sukoff, R., Orazio, J., Solomon, S., & Saravay, S. (1987). Logical memory subtest of the Wechsler Memory Scale: Age and education norms and alternate-form reliability of two scoring systems. *Journal of Clinical and Experimental Neuropsychology, 9*, 435–448.

Abraham, I. L., Manning, C., Boyd, M. R., Neese, J. B., Newman, M. C., Plowfield, L. A., & Reel, S. (1993). Cognitive screening of nursing home residents: Factor structure of the Modified Mini Mental State Examination. *International Journal of Geriatric Psychiatry, 8*, 133–138.

Abramovitch, R., Finstad, M., & Silberfeld, M. (1993). Preliminary report on mental capacity assessments. *Canadian Journal on Aging, 12*, 373–381.

Absher, R., & Cummings, J. L. (1993). Noncognitive behavioural alterations in dementia syndromes. In F. Boller & J. Grafman (Eds.), *Handbook of neuropsychology* (Vol. 8, pp. 315–338). Amsterdam: Elsevier Science.

Adams, R. L., Boake, C., & Crain, C. (1982). Bias in a neuropsychological test classification related to education, age, and ethnicity. *Journal of Consulting and Clinical Psychology, 50*, 143–145.

Adams, R. L., Smigielski, J., & Jenkins, R. L. (1984). Development of a Satz–Mogel short form of the WAIS–R. *Journal of Consulting and Clinical Psychology, 52*, 908.

Agnew, J., Bolla-Wilson, K., Kawas, C. H., & Bleecker, M. L. (1988). Purdue Pegboard age and sex norms for people 40 years old and older. *Developmental Neuropsychology, 4*, 29–35.

Albert, M., & Cohen, C. (1992). The test for severe impairment: An instrument for the assessment of patients with severe cognitive dysfunction. *Journal of the American Geriatrics Society, 40*, 449–453.

Albert, M. L. (1978). Subcortical dementia. In R. Katzman, R. D. Terry, & K. L. Bick (Eds.), *Alzheimer's disease: Senile dementia and related disorders* (pp. 173–180). New York: Raven.

Albert, M. L., & Knoefel, J. E. (Eds.). (1994). *Clinical neurology of aging* (2nd ed.). New York: Oxford University Press.

Albert, M. S. (1981). Geriatric neuropsychology. *Journal of Consulting and Clinical Psychology, 49*, 835–850.

Albert, M. S. (1988). Cognitive function. In M. S. Albert & M. B. Moss (Eds.), *Geriatric neuropsychology* (pp. 33–56). New York: Guilford.

Albert, M. S., Heller, H. S., & Milberg, W. (1988). Changes in naming ability with age. *Psychology and Aging, 3,* 173–178.

Albert, M. S., & Moss, M. B. (1988). *Geriatric neuropsychology.* New York: Guilford.

Alekoumbides, A., Charter, R. A., Adkins, T. G., & Seacat, G. F. (1987). The diagnosis of brain damage by the WAIS, WMS, and Reitan Battery utilizing standardized scores corrected for age and education. *International Journal of Clinical Neuropsychology, 9,* 11–28.

Alexopoulos, G. S. (1989). Late-life depression and neurological brain disease. *International Journal of Geriatric Psychiatry, 4,* 187–190.

Allen-Burge, R., Storandt, M., Kinscherf, D. A., & Rubin, E. H. (1994). Sex differences in the sensitivity of two self-report depression scales in older depressed inpatients. *Psychology and Aging, 9,* 443–445.

Almeida, O. P., Howard, R. J., Forstl, H., & Levy, R. (1992). Late paraphrenia: A review. *International Journal of Geriatric Psychiatry, 7,* 543–548.

Almeida, O. P., Howard, R. J., Levy, R., & David, A. S. (1995a). Psychotic states arising in late life (late paraphrenia): Psychopathology and nosology. *British Journal of Psychiatry, 166,* 205–214.

Almeida, O. P., Howard, R. J., Levy, R., & David, A. S. (1995b). Psychotic states arising in late life (late paraphrenia): The role of risk factors. *British Journal of Psychiatry, 166,* 215–228.

American Psychiatric Association. (1987). *Diagnostic and statistical manual of mental disorders* (3rd, rev. ed.). Washington, DC: Author.

American Psychiatric Association. (1994). *Diagnostic and statistical manual of mental disorders* (4th ed.). Washington, DC: Author.

American Psychological Association. (1981). Specialty guidelines for the delivery of services by clinical psychologists. *American Psychologist, 36,* 640–651.

American Psychological Association. (1985). *Standards for educational and psychological testing.* Washington, DC: Author.

American Psychological Association. (1987). General guidelines for providers of psychological services. *American Psychologist, 42,* 712–723.

American Psychological Association. (1992). Ethical principles of psychologists and code of conduct. *American Psychologist, 47,* 1597–1611.

Ammons, R. B., & Ammons, C. H. (1962). The Quick Test (QT): Provisional manual. *Psychological Reports, 11,* 111–161.

Anastasi, A. (1988). *Psychological testing* (6th ed.). Upper Saddle River, NJ: Prentice-Hall.

Angoff, W. H. (1971). Scales, norms and equivalent scores. In R. L. Thorndike (Ed.), *Educational measurement* (2nd ed., pp. 508–600). Washington, DC: American Council on Education.

Angoff, W. H., & Robertson, G. R. (1987). A procedure for standardizing individually administered tests, normed by age or grade level. *Applied Psychological Measurement, 11,* 33–46.

Anthony, J. C., Le Resche, L., Niaz, L., Von Korff, M. R., & Folstein, M. F. (1982). Limits of the Mini-mental state as a screening test for dementia and delirium among hospital patients. *Psychological Medicine, 12,* 397–408.

Anthony-Bergstone, C. R., Zarit, S. H., & Gatz, G. (1988). Symptoms of psychological distress among caregivers of dementia patients. *Psychology and Aging, 3,* 245–248.

Aronson, H. (1985). *Manual of administration and scoring: Aronson Shopping List, Form I and II.* Unpublished manuscript.

Axelrod, B. N., & Henry, R. R. (1992). Age-related performance on the Wisconsin Card Sorting, Similarities, and Controlled Oral Word Association Tests. *Clinical Neuropsychologist, 6,* 16–26.

Axelrod, B. N., Jiron, C. C., & Henry, R. R. (1993). Performance of adults ages 20 to 90 on the Abbreviated Wisconsin Card Sorting Test. *Clinical Neuropsychologist, 7,* 205–209.

Bak, J. S., & Greene, R. L. (1980). Changes in neuropsychological functioning in an aging population. *Journal of Consulting and Clinical Psychology, 48,* 395–399.

Banks, P. G., Dickson, A. L., & Plasay, M. T. (1987). The Verbal Selective Reminding Test: Preliminary data for healthy elderly. *Experimental Aging Research, 13,* 203–207.

Barber, R., Snowdon, J. S., & Craufurd, D. (1995). Frontotemporal dementia and Alzheimer's disease: Retrospective differentiation using information from informants. *Journal of Neurology, Neurosurgery and Psychiatry, 59,* 61–79.

Barer, M. L., Evans, R. G., & Hertzman, C. (1995). Avalanche or glacier? Health care and the demographic rhetoric. *Canadian Journal on Aging, 14,* 193–224.

Barona, A., & Chastain, R. (1986). An inproved estimate of premorbid IQ for blacks and whites on the WAIS–R. *International Journal of Clinical Neuropsychology, 8,* 169–173.

Barona, A., Reynolds, C. R., & Chastain, R. (1984). A demographically based index of premorbid intelligence for the WAIS–R. *Journal of Consulting and Clinical Psychology, 52,* 885–887.

Basset, S. S., Magaziner, J., & Hebe, J. R. (1990). Reliability of proxy response on mental health indices for aged, community-dwelling women. *Psychology and Aging, 5,* 127–132.

Bayles, K. A., Boone, D. R., Tomoeda, C. K., Slauson, T. J., & Kaszniak, A. W. (1989). Differentiating Alzheimer's patients from the normal elderly and stroke patients with aphasia. *Journal of Speech and Hearing Disorders, 54,* 74–87.

Bayles, K. A., & Kaszniak, A. W. (1987). *Communication and cognition in normal aging and dementia.* Boston: Little, Brown.

Bayles, K. A., & Tomoeda, C. (1991). *Arizona Battery for Communication Disorders of Dementia.* Gaylord, MI: National Rehabilitation Services.

Beck, A. T., & Beck, R. W. (1972). Screening depressed patients in family practice: A rapid technique. *Postgraduate Medicine, 52,* 81–85.

Beck, A. T., Ward, C. H., Mendelson, M., Mock, J., & Erbaugh, J. (1961). An inventory for measuring depression. *Archives of General Psychiatry, 4,* 561–571.

Beland, R., & Lecours, A. R. (1990). The MT–86β Aphasia Battery: A subset of normative data in relation to age and level of school education. *Aphasiology, 4,* 439–462.

Beland, R., Lecours, A. R., Giroux, F., & Bois, M. (1993). The MT–86β Aphasia Battery: A subset of normative data in relation to age and level of school education: II. *Aphasiology, 7,* 359–382.

Bellack, A. S., & Hersen, M. (1988). *Behavioral assessment: A practical handbook* (3rd ed.). New York: Pergamon.

Bender, M. (1975). The incidence and type of perceptual deficiencies in the aged. In W. S. Fields (Ed.), *Neurological and sensory disorders in the elderly* (pp. 15–30). Miami, FL: Symposia Specialists.

Bender, M. (1979). Defects in reversal of serial order of symbols. *Neuropsychologia, 17,* 125–138.

Benson, D. F. (1993). Aphasia. In K. M. Heilman & E. Valenstein (Eds.), *Clinical neuropsychology* (3rd ed., pp. 17–36). New York: Oxford University Press.

Benton, A. L. (1974). *Revised Visual Retention Test* (4th ed.). San Antonio, TX: Psychological Corporation.

Benton, A. L., Eslinger, P. J., & Damasio, A. R. (1981). Normative observations on neuropsychological test performances in old age. *Journal of Clinical Neuropsychology, 3,* 33–42.

Benton, A. L., & Hamsher, K. (1978). *Multilingual Aphasia Examination manual.* Iowa City: University of Iowa Press.

Benton, A. L., Sivan, A. B., Hamsher, K. deS., Varney, N. R., & Spreen, O. (1994). *Contributions to neuropsychological assessment* (2nd ed.). New York: Oxford University Press.

Benton, A. L., & Tranel, D. (1993). Visuoperceptual, visuospatial and visuoconstructive disorders. In K. M. Heilman & E. Valenstein (Eds.), *Clinical neuropsychology* (3rd ed., pp. 165–214). New York: Oxford University Press.

Berg, L. (1988). Clinical Dementia Rating (CDR). *Psychopharmacology Bulletin, 24,* 637–639.

Berg, L. (1990). Minor cognitive deficits and the detection of mild dementia. *Psychiatric Journal of the University of Ottawa, 15,* 230–231.

Berkowitz, B., & Green, R. F. (1963). Changes in intellect with age: I. Longitudinal study of Wechsler–Bellevue scores. *Journal of Genetic Psychology, 103,* 3–21.

Bernard, B. A., Wilson, R. S., Gilley, D. W., Bennett, D. A., Waters, W. F., & Fox, J. H. (1992). Memory failure in Binswanger's disease and Alzheimer's disease. *Clinical Neuropsychologist, 6,* 230–240.

Bernard, B. A., Wilson, R. S., Gilley, D. W., Gross, D. A., Bennett, D. A., Whalen, M. E., & Fox, J. H. (1990). Performance of patients with BD and AD on the Mattis Dementia Rating Scale. *Journal of Clinical and Experimental Neuropsychology, 12,* 22.

Berry, D. T., Allen, R. S., & Schmitt, F. A. (1991). Rey–Osterrieth Complex Figure: Psychometric characteristics in a geriatric sample. *Clinical Neuropsychologist, 5,* 143–153.

Berry, D. T., & Carpenter, G. S. (1992). Effect of four different delay periods on recall of the Rey–Osterrieth Complex Figure by older persons. *Clinical Neuropsychologist, 6,* 80–84.

Binet, A., & Simon, T. (1908). Le developpement de l'intelligence chez les enfants [The development of intelligence in children]. *L'Anee Psychologique, 14,* 1–94.

Bird, H. R., Canino, G., Stipec, M. R., & Shrout, P. (1987). Use of the Mini-Mental State Examination in a probability sample of Hispanic population. *Journal of Nervous and Mental Disease, 175,* 731–737.

Birren, J. E., & Sloane, R. B. (1977). *Manpower and training needs in mental health and illness of the aging.* Los Angeles: Ethel Percy Andrus Gerontology Center, University of Southern California.

Birren, J. E., Sloane, R. B., & Cohen, G. D. (1992). *Handbook of mental health and aging* (2nd ed.). San Diego: Academic Press.

Blackford, R. C., & La Rue, A. (1989). Criteria for diagnosing age-associated memory impairment: Proposed improvements from the field. *Developmental Neuropsychology, 5,* 295–306.

Blair, J. R., & Spreen, P. (1989). Predicting premorbid IQ: A revision of the National Adult Reading Test. *Clinical Neuropsychologist, 3,* 129–136.

Blazer, D., Hughes, D., & George, L. K. (1987). Stressful life events and the onset of a generalized anxiety syndrome. *American Journal of Psychiatry, 144,* 1178–1183.

Blazer, D. G. (1982). *Depression in late life.* St. Louis: Mosby.

Blessed, G., Black, S. E., Butler, T., & Kay, W. K. (1991). The diagnosis of dementia in the elderly: A comparison of CAMCOG (the cognitive section of CAMDEX), the AGECAT program, *DSM–III,* the Mini-Mental State Examination and some short rating scales. *British Journal of Psychiatry, 159,* 193–198.

Blessed, G., Tomlinson, G. E., & Roth, M. (1968). The association between quantitative measures of dementia and of senile change in the cerebral grey matter of elderly subjects. *British Journal of Psychiatry, 114,* 797–811.

Bolla, K. I., Lindgren, K. N., Bonaccorsy, C., & Bleecker, M. L. (1990). Predictors of verbal fluency (FAS) in the healthy elderly. *Journal of Clinical Psychology, 46,* 623–628.

Bolla-Wilson, K., & Bleecker, M. L. (1986). Influence of verbal intelligence, sex, age, and education on the Rey Auditory Verbal Learning Test. *Developmental Neuropsychology, 2,* 203–211.

Bondi, M. W., Monsch, A. U., Butters, N., Salmon, D. P., & Paulsen, J. S. (1993). Utility of a modified version of the Wisconsin Card Sorting Test in the detection of dementia of the Alzheimer type. *Clinical Neuropsychologist, 7,* 161–170.

Boone, K. B., Lesser, I. M., Hill-Gutierrez, E., Berman, N. B., & D'Elia, L. F. (1993). Rey–Osterrieth Complex Figure performance in healthy, older adults: Relationship to age, education, sex and IQ. *Clinical Neuropsychologist, 7,* 22–28.

Boone, K. B., Miller, B. L., & Lesser, I. M. (1993). Frontal lobe cognitive functions in aging: Methodologic considerations. *Dementia, 4,* 232–236.

Bootzin, R. R., & Engle-Friedman, M. (1987). Sleep disturbances. In L. L. Carstersen & B. A. Edelstein (Eds.), *Handbook of clinical gerontology* (pp. 238–251). New York: Pergamon.

Borkowski, J., Benton, A. L., & Spreen, O. (1967). Word fluency and brain damage. *Neuropsychologia, 5,* 135–140.

Bornstein, R. A., & Matarazzo, J. D. (1982). Wechsler VIQ versus PIQ differences in cerebral dysfunction: A literature review with emphasis on sex differences. *Journal of Clinical Neuropsychology, 4,* 319–334.

Bornstein, R. R. (1985). Normative data on selected neuropsychological measures from a nonclinical sample. *Journal of Clinical Psychology, 41,* 651–660.

Borod, J. C., Goodglass, H., & Kaplan, E. (1980). Normative data on the Boston Diagnostic Aphasia Examination, parietal lobe battery, and the Boston Naming Test. *Journal of Clinical Neuropsychology, 2,* 209–215.

Botwinick, J. (1977). Intellectual abilities. In J. E. Birren & K. W. Schaie (Eds.), *Handbook of the psychology of aging* (pp. 580–605). New York: Van Nostrand Reinhold.

Botwinick, J., & Storandt, M. (1974). *Memory, related functions and age.* Springfield, IL: Thomas.

Bozzola, F. G., Gorelick, P. B., & Freels, S. (1992). Personality changes in Alzheimer's disease. *Archives of Neurology, 49,* 297–300.

Brandt, J. (1991). The Hopkins Verbal Learning Test: Development of a new memory test with six equivalent forms. *Clinical Neuropsychologist, 5,* 125–142.

Brink, T. L., Capri, D., DeNeeve, V., Janakes, C., & Oliveira, C. (1978). Senile confusion: Limitations of assessment by the Face–Hand Test, Mental Status Questionnaire, and staff ratings. *Journal of the American Geriatrics Society, 26,* 380–382.

Brink, T. L., Yesavage, J. A., Lum, O., Heirsema, P., Adey, M., & Rose, T. L. (1982). Screening tests for geriatric depression. *Clinical Gerontologist, 1,* 37–43.

Brinkman, S. D., & Braun, P. (1984). Classification of dementia patients by a WAIS profile related to central cholinergic deficiencies. *Journal of Clinical Neuropsychology, 6,* 393–400.

Brittain, J. L., La Marche, J., Reeder, K. P., Roth, D. L., & Boll, T. J. (1991). Effects of age and IQ on Paced Auditory Serial Addition Task (PASAT) performance. *Clinical Neuropsychologist, 5,* 163–175.

Bromley, D. (1957). Effects of age on intellectual output. *Journal of Gerontology, 12,* 318–323.

Brooker, B. H., & Cyr, J. J. (1986). Tables for clinicians to use to convert WAIS–R short forms. *Journal of Clinical Psychology, 42,* 982–986.

Buchsbaum, D. G., Buchanan, R. G., Welsh, J., Centor, R. M., & Schnoll, S. H. (1992). Screening for drinking disorders in the elderly using the CAGE questionnaire. *Journal of the American Geriatrics Society, 40,* 662–665.

Burke, H. R. (1985). Raven's Progressive Matrices (1938). More on norms, reliability and validity. *Journal of Clinical Psychology, 41,* 231–235.

Buschke, H. (1973). Selective reminding for analysis of memory and learning. *Journal of Verbal Learning and Verbal Behavior, 12,* 543–546.

Buschke, H. (1984). Cued recall and amnesia. *Journal of Clinical Neuropsychology, 6,* 433–440.

Butcher, J. N., Aldwin, C. M., Levenson, M. R., Ben-Porath, Y. S., Sprio, A., & Bosse, R. (1991). Personality and aging: A study of the MMPI-2 among older men. *Psychology and Aging, 6,* 361–370.

Butcher, J. N., Dahlstrom, W. G., Graham, J. R., Tellegen, A., & Kaemer, B. (1989). *Minnesota Multiphasic Personality Inventory–2 (MMPI–2): Manual for administration and scoring.* Minneapolis, MN: University of Minnesota.

Cahan, S. (1989). A critical examination of the "reliability" and "abnormality" approaches to the evaluation of subtest score differences. *Educational and Psychological Measurement, 49,* 807–814.

Canadian Psychological Association. (1989). *Practice guidelines for providers of psychological services.* Ottawa, Canada: Author.

Canadian Psychological Association. (1991). *Canadian code of ethics for psychologists.* Ottawa, Canada: Author.

Canadian Study of Health and Aging Work Group. (1994). Canadian Study of Health and Aging: Study methods and prevalence of dementia. *Canadian Medical Association Journal, 150,* 899–913.

Cantor, M. H. (1983). Strain among caregivers: A study of experience in the United States. *The Gerontologist, 23,* 597–604.

Carey, R. G., & Posavac, E. J. (1982). Rehabilitation program evaluation using a revised Level of Rehabilitation Scale (LORS–II). *Archives of Physical Medicine and Rehabilitation, 63,* 367–370.

Carroll, B. J., Feinberg, M., Smouse, P. E., Rawson, S. G., & Greden, J. F. (1981). The Carroll Rating Scale for Depression: I. Reliability and validation. *British Journal of Psychiatry, 138,* 194–200.

Cauthen, N. R. (1977). Extension of the Wechsler memory scale norms to older age groups. *Journal of Clinical Psychology, 33,* 208–211.

Chawluk, J. B., Mesulam, M. M., Hurtig, H., Kushner, M., Weintraub, S., Saykin, A., Rubin, N., Alavi, A., & Reivich, M. (1986). Slowly progressive aphasia without generalized dementia: Studies with positron emission tomography. *Annals of Neurology, 19,* 68–74.

Christensen, H., Hadzi-Pavlovic, D., & Jacomb, P. (1991). The psychometric differentiation of dementia from normal aging: A meta-analysis. *Psychological Assessment, 3,* 147–155.

Christinson, C., & Blazer, D. (1988). Clinical assessment of psychatric symptoms. In M. S. Albert & M. B. Moss (Eds.), *Geriatric neuropsychology* (pp. 82–99). New York: Guilford.

Chui, H. C., Victoroff, J. I., Margolin, D., Jagust, W., Shankle, R., & Katzman, R. (1992). Criteria for the diagnosis of ischemic vascular dementia proposed by the state of California Alzheimer's disease diagnostic and treatment centers. *Neurology, 42,* 473–480.

Coblentz, J. M., Mattis, S., Zingesser, L. H., Kassoff, S. S., Wisniewshi, H. M., & Katzman, R. (1973). Presenile dementia. *Archives of Neurology, 29,* 299–308.

Cohen, C. I. (1990). Outcome of schizophrenia into later life: An overview. *The Gerontologist, 30,* 790–797.

Cole, M. G. (1990). Interrater reliability of the Blessed Dementia Scale. *Canadian Journal of Psychiatry, 35,* 328–330.

Colombo, F. T., & Assal, G. (1992). Francais du test de denomination de Boston Versions abregees [An abbreviated, French version of the Boston Naming Test]. *Revue europeenne de Psychologie Appliqué, 42,* 67–71.

Costa, P. T., & McCrae, R. R. (1980). Still stable after all these years: Personality as a key to some issues in adulthood and old age. *Life-Span Development and Behavior, 3,* 65–102.

Costa, P. T., & McCrae, R. R. (1985). Hypochondriasis, neuroticism, and aging: When are somatic complaints unfounded? *American Psychologist, 40,* 19–28.

Council on Ethical and Judicial Affairs. (1994). *Code of medical ethics: Current opinions with annotations.* Chicago: American Medical Association.

Coval, M., Crockett, D., Holliday, S., & Koch, W. (1985). A multi-focus assessment scale for use with frail elderly populations. *Canadian Journal on Aging, 4,* 101–109.

Craenhals, A., Raison-Van Ruymbeke, A., Rectem, D., Seron, X., & Laterre, E. C. (1990). Is slowly progressive aphasia actually a new clinical entity? *Aphasiology, 4,* 485–509.

Craik, F.I.M. (1977). Age differences in human memory. In J. E. Birren & K. W. Schaie (Eds.), *Handbook of the psychology of aging* (pp. 384–420). New York: Van Nostrand Reinhold.

Craik, F.I.M. (1990). A functional account of age differences in memory. In F. Klix & H. Hagendorf (Eds.), *Human memory and cognitive capabilities: Mechanisms and performances. Symposium in memoriam Hermann Ebbinghaus 1885, Berlin Humboldt University 1985* (pp. 409–422). Amsterdam: Elsevier/North-Holland.

Crawford, J. R. (1989). Estimation of premorbid intelligence: A review of recent developments. In J. R. Crawford & D. M. Parker (Eds.), *Developments in clinical and experimental neuropsychology* (pp. 55–74). New York: Plenum.

Crawford, J. R. (1990). Assessing the validity of NART-estimated premorbid IQs in the individual case. *British Journal of Clinical Psychology, 29*, 435–436.

Crawford, J. R., Cochrane, R.H.B., Besson, J.A.O., Parker, D. M., & Stewart, L. E. (1990). Premorbid IQ estimates obtained by combining the NART and demographic variables: construct validity. *Personality and Individual Differences, 11*, 209–210.

Critchley, M. (1953). *The parietal lobes.* New York: Hafner.

Crockett, D., Tuokko, H., Koch, W., & Parks, R. (1989). The assessment of everyday functioning using the Present Functioning Questionnaire and the Functional Rating Scale in elderly samples. *Clinical Gerontology, 8*, 3–25.

Crockett, D. J., Coval, M., Tuokko, H., Buree, B., & Koch, W. (1991). *Multifocus Assessment Scale for the frail elderly–Revised form (MAS–R): Procedure manual.* Vancouver Hospital and Health Sciences Centre–UBC Site. Unpublished manuscript.

Cronbach, L. J. (1990). *Essentials of psychological testing* (5th ed.). New York: Harper & Row.

Crook, T., Bartus, R. T., Ferris, S. H., Whiterhouse, P., Cohen, G. D., & Gershon, S. (1986). Age-associated memory impairment: Proposed diagnostic criteria and measures of clinical change–Report of a National Institute of Mental Health Work Group. *Developmental Neuropsychology, 2*, 261–276.

Crook, T., Gilbert, J. G., & Ferris, S. (1980). Operationalizing memory impairment for elderly persons: The Guild Memory Test. *Psychological Reports, 47*, 1315–1318.

Crook, T. H., & Larrabee, G. J. (1992). Normative data on a self-rating scale for evaluating memory in everyday life. *Archives of Clinical Neuropsychology, 7*, 41–51.

Crum, R. M., Anthony, J. C., Bassett, S. S., & Folstein, M. F. (1993). Population-based norms for the Mini-Mental State Examination by age and education level. *Journal of the American Medical Association, 269*, 2386–2391.

Cullum, C. M., Butters, N., Troster, A. I., & Salmon, D. P. (1990). Normal aging and forgetting rates on the Wechsler Memory Scale–Revised. *Archives of Clinical Neuropsychology, 5*, 23–30.

Cummings, J. L. (1990). Introduction. In J. L. Cummings (Ed.), *Subcortical dementia* (pp. 1–16). New York: Oxford University Press.

Cummings, J. L., & Benson, D. F. (1984). Subcortical dementia: Review of an emerging concept. *Archives of Neurology, 41*, 874–879.

Cummings, J. L., & Benson, D. F. (1992). *Dementia: A clinical approach* (2nd ed.). Boston: Butterworth Heinemann.

Cyr, J. J., & Brooker, B. H. (1984). Use of appropriate formulas for selecting WAIS–R short forms. *Journal of Clinical and Consulting Psychology, 52*, 903–905.

Dahlstrom, W. G., Welsh, G. S., & Dahlstrom, L. E. (1972). *An MMPI handbook: Vol. 1. A clinical interpretation* (rev. ed.). Minneapolis, MN: University of Minnesota Press.

Daignault, S., Braun, M. J., & Whitaker, H. (1992). Early effects of normal aging in perseverative and non-perseverative prefrontal measures. *Developmental Neuropsychology, 8*, 99–114.

Dalton, J. E., Peterson, S. L., Blon, B. E., & Holmes, N. R. (1987). Diagnostic errors using the Short Portable Mental Status Questionnaire with a mixed clinical population. *Journal of Gerontology, 42*, 512–514.

D'Arcy, C. (1994). Socio-economic status as a risk factor for dementia: Results from the CSHA. *Chronic Diseases in Canada, 15*, S14–S15.

Darley, F., Aronson, A., & Brown, J. (1975). *Motor speech disorders.* Philadelphia: Saunders.

Dastoor, D. P., Schwartz, G., & Kurtzman, D. (1991). Clock-drawing: An assessment technique in dementia. *Journal of Clinical and Experimental Gerontology, 13*, 69–85.

Davies, A.D.M. (1968). The influence of age on Trail Making Test performance. *Journal of Clinical Psychology, 24*, 96–98.

Davison, G. C., & Neale, J. M. (1994). *Abnormal psychology* (6th ed.). New York: Wiley.

Dawe, B., Procter, A., & Philpot, M. (1992). Concepts of mild memory impairment in the elderly and their relationship to dementia—a review. *International Journal of Psychogeriatrics, 7,* 473–479.

DeFilippis, N. A., McCampbell, E., & Rogers, P. (1979). Development of a booklet form of the Category Test: Normative and validity data. *Journal of Clinical Neuropsychology, 1,* 339–342.

D'Elia, L., Satz, P., & Schretlen, D. (1989). Wechsler Memory Scale: A critical appraisal of the normative studies. *Journal of Clinical and Experimental Neuropsychology, 11,* 551–568.

Delis, D. C., Kramer, J. H., Kaplan, E., & Ober, B. A. (1987). *California Verbal Learning Test.* San Antonio, TX: Psychological Corporation.

Dening, T. R., & Berrios, G. E. (1992). The Hachinski Ischaemic Score: A reevaluation. *International Journal of Geriatric Psychiatry, 7,* 585–589.

Denton, F. T., & Spencer, B. G. (1995). Demographic change and the cost of publicly funded health care. *Canadian Journal on Aging, 14,* 174–192.

Deptula, D., Singh, R., Goldsmith, S., Block, R., Bagne, C. A., & Pomara, N. (1990). Equivalence of five forms of the Selective Reminding Test in young and elderly subjects. *Psychological Reports, 67,* 1287–1295.

Derenzi, E. (1986). Slowly progressive visual agnosia or apraxia without dementia. *Cortex, 22,* 171–180.

Derogatis, L. R. (1977). *The SCI–90 Manual I: Scoring, administration and procedures for the SCI–90.* Baltimore, MD: Johns Hopkins University School of Medicine, Clinical Psychometrics Unit.

desRosiers, G., & Ivison, D. (1986). Paired associate learning: Normative data for differences between high and low associate word pairs. *Journal of Clinical and Experimental Neuropsychology, 8,* 637–642.

Diesfeldt, H., & Vink, M. (1989). Recognition memory for words and faces in the very old. *British Journal of Clinical Psychology, 28,* 247–253.

Dixon, R. A., & Hultsch, D. F. (1984). The Metamemory in Adulthood (MIA) instrument. *Psychological Documents, 14,* 3.

Doppelt, J. E. (1956). Estimating the full scale score on the Wechsler Adult Intelligence Scale from scores on four subtests. *Journal of Consulting Psychology, 20,* 63–66.

Doppelt, J. E., & Wallace, W. L. (1955). Standardization of the Wechsler Adult Intelligence Scale for older persons. *Journal of Abnormal and Social Psychology, 51,* 312–330.

Doyon, J., Bouchard, R., Morin, G., Bourgeois, C., & Cote, D. (1991). Nouveau système du cotation quantitative de test de l'horlage: Sensibilite et specificite dans la demence de type Alzheimer [New system of quantitative scoring of clock drawing: Sensitivity and specificity in dementia of the Alzheimer type]. *L'Union Medicale du Canada (Mars/Avril), 119* (abstract).

Duckett, S. (Ed.). (1991). *The pathology of the aging human nervous system.* Philadelphia: Lea & Febiger.

Duke University Centre for the Study of Aging and Human Development. (1978). *Multidimensional functional assessment: The OARS Methodology.* Durham, NC: Duke University Press.

Edelstein, H., Nygren, M., Northrop, L., Staats, N., & Pool, D. (1993, August). *Assessment of capacity to make financial and medical decisions.* Paper presented at the 101st annual meeting of the American Psychological Association, Toronto, Ontario, Canada.

Edinger, J. D., Hoelscher, T. H., Marsh, G. R., Ipper, S., & Ionescu-Pioggia, M. (1992). A cognitive behavioral therapy for sleep maintenance insomnia in older adults. *Psychology and Aging, 7,* 282–289.

Eisdorfer, C. R., & Cohen, D. (1980). Diagnostic criteria for primary neuronal degeneration of the Alzheimer's type. *Journal of Family Practice, 11,* 553–557.

Endicott, J., Cohen, J., Nee, J., Fleiss, J., & Sarantakos, S. (1981). Hamilton Depression Rating Scale: Extracted from regular and change versions of the schedule for affective disorders and schizophrenia. *Archives of General Psychiatry, 35,* 836–844.

Eppinger, M. G., Craig, P. L., Adams, R. L., & Parsons, O. A. (1987). The WAIS–R index for estimating premorbid intelligence: Cross validation and clinical utility. *Journal of Consulting and Clinical Psychology, 55,* 86–90.

Erber, J. T. (1974). Age differences in recognition memory. *Journal of Gerontology, 29,* 177–181.

Erkinjuntti, T., Haltia, M., Palo, J., Sulkava, R., & Paetau, A. (1988). Accuracy of the clinical diagnosis of vascular dementia: A prospective clinical and post-mortem neuropathological study. *Journal of Neurology, Neurosurgery and Psychiatry, 51,* 1037–1044.

Erkinjuntti, T., Hokkanen, L., Sulkava, S., & Palo, J. (1988). The Blessed Dementia Scale as a screening test for dementia. *International Journal of Geriatric Psychiatry, 3,* 267–273.

Erkinjuntti, T., Sulkava, R., Wikstrom, J., & Autio, L. (1987). Short-Portable Mental Status Questionnaire as a screening test for dementia and delirium among the elderly. *Journal of the American Geriatrics Society, 35,* 412–416.

Ernst, J. (1987). Neuropsychological problem-solving skills in the elderly. *Psychology and Aging, 2,* 363–365.

Ernst, P., Badash, D., Beran, B., Kosovky, R., & Kleinhauz, M. (1977). Incidence of mental illness in the aged: Unmasking the effects of chronic brain syndrome. *Journal of the American Geriatrics Society, 8,* 371–375.

Eslinger, P. J., Damasio, A. R., Benton, A. L., & Van Allen, M. (1985). Neuropsychologic detection of abnormal mental decline in older adults. *Journal of the American Medical Association, 253,* 670–674.

Eson, M. E., Yen, J. K., & Bourke, R. S. (1978). Assessment of recovery from serious head injury. *Journal of Neurology, Neurosurgery and Psychiatry, 41,* 1036–1042.

Essex-Sorlie, D. (1995). *Medical biostatistics and epidemiology.* Norwalk, CT: Appleton & Lange.

Ewing, J. A. (1984). Detecting alcoholism: The CAGE questionnaire. *Journal of the American Medical Association, 252,* 1905–1907.

Faibish, G. M., Auerbach, V. S., & Thornby, J. I. (1986). Modifications of the Halstead–Reitan in geriatrics. *British Journal of Psychiatry, 149,* 698–709.

Farmer, M. E., White, L. R., Kittner, S. J., Kaplan, E., Moes, E., McNamara, P., Wolz, M. M., Wolf, P. A., & Feinleib, M. (1987). Neuropsychological test performance in Framingham: A descriptive study. *Psychological Reports, 60,* 1023–1040.

Farver, P. F., & Farver, T. B. (1982). Performance of normal older adults on tests designed to measure parietal lobe functions. *American Journal of Occupational Therapy, 36,* 444–449.

Feher, E. P., Mahurin, R. K., Inbody, S. B., Crook, T., & Pirozzolo, F. J. (1991). Anosagnosia in Alzheimer's disease. *Neuropsychiatry, Neuropsychology and Behavioral Neurology, 4,* 136–146.

Ferguson, G. A. (1981). *Statistical analyses in psychology and education* (5th ed.). Toronto, Canada: McGraw-Hill.

Feurst, D. R. (1993). A review of the Halstead–Reitan Neuropsychological Battery norms program. *Clinical Neuropsychologist, 7,* 96–103.

Fillenbaum, G. G. (1980). Comparison of two brief tests of organic brain impairment: The MSQ and the Short Portable MSQ. *Journal of the American Geriatrics Society, 28,* 381–384.

Fillenbaum, G. G. (1988). *Multidimensional functional assessment of older adults.* Hillsdale, NJ: Lawrence Erlbaum Associates.

Fillenbaum, G. G., George, L. K., & Blazer, D. G. (1988). Scoring nonresponse on the Mini-Mental State Examination. *Psychological Medicine, 18,* 719–726.

Flint, A. (1994). Epidemiology and comorbidity of anxiety disorders in the elderly. *American Journal of Psychiatry, 151,* 640–649.

Folstein, M. L., Folstein, S. E., & McHugh, P. R. (1975). Mini-mental state: A practical method for grading the cognitive status of patients for the clinician. *Journal of Psychiatric Research, 12,* 189–198.

Foster, N. L., & Chase, T. N. (1983). Diffuse involvement in progressive aphasia. *Annals of Neurology, 13,* 224–225.

Fozard, J. L. (1990). Vision and hearing in aging. In J. E. Birren & K. W. Schaie (Eds.), *Handbook of the psychology of aging* (3rd ed., pp. 150–170). New York: Academic Press.

Freedman, M., Leach, L., Kaplan, E., Winocur, G., Shulman, I., & Delis, D. C. (1994). *Clock drawing: A neuropsychological analysis.* New York: Oxford University Press.

Fuld, P. (1984). Test profile of cholingeric dysfunction and of Alzheimer-type dementia. *Journal of Clinical Neuropsychology, 6,* 380–392.

Galasko, D., Klauber, M. R., Hofstetter, R., Salmon, D. P., Lasker, B., & Thal, L. J. (1990). The Mini-Mental State Examination in the early diagnosis of Alzheimer's disease. *Archives of Neurology, 47,* 49–52.

Gallagher, D. (1986). Assessment of depression by interview methods and by psychiatric rating scales. In L. W. Poon (Ed.), *Handbook for clinical memory assessment of older adults* (pp. 202–212). Washington, DC: American Psychological Association.

Gallagher, D., Breckenridge, J., Steinmetz, J., & Thompson, L. (1983). The Beck Depression Inventory and research diagnostic criteria: Congruence in an older population. *Journal of Consulting and Clinical Psychology, 51,* 945–946.

Ganguli, M., Ratcliffe, G., Huff, J., Belle, S., Kancel, M. J., Fischer, L., & Kuller, L. H. (1990). Serial sevens versus world backwards: A comparison of the two measures of attention from the MMSE. *Journal of Clinical and Experimental Neuropsychology, 17,* 203–207.

Gass, C. S., & Brown, M. C. (1992). Neuropsychological test feedback to patients with brain dysfunction. *Psychological Assessment, 4,* 272–278.

Gatz, M. (Ed.). (1995). *Emerging issues in mental health and aging.* Washington, DC: American Psychological Association.

Geffen, G., Moar, K. J., O'Hanlon, A. P., Clark, C. R., & Geffen, L. B. (1990). Performance measures of 16- to 86- year-old males and females on the Auditory Verbal Learning Test. *Clinical Neuropsychologist, 4,* 45–63.

Georgemiller, R., & Hassan, F. (1986). Spatial competence: Assessment of route-finding, route-learning, and topographical memory in normal aging. *Clinical Gerontologist, 5,* 19–37.

Ghoneim, M. M., & Mewaldt, S. P. (1990). Benzodiazepines and human memory: A review. *Anesthesiology, 72,* 926–938.

Gilbert, J. G., & Levee, R. F. (1971). Patterns of declining memory. *Journal of Gerontology, 26,* 70–75.

Gilbert, J. G., Levee, R. F., & Catalano, F. L. (1968). A preliminary report on a new memory scale. *Perceptual and Motor Skills, 27,* 277–278.

Gilewski, M. J., & Zelinski, E. M. (1986). Questionnaire assessment of memory complaints. In L. W. Poon, T. Crook, K. L. Davis, C. Eisdorfer, B. J. Gurland, A. W. Kaszniak, & L. W. Thompson (Eds.), *Handbook for clinical memory assessment of older adults* (pp. 93–107). Washington, DC: American Psychological Association.

Gilewski, M. J., Zelinski, E. M., Schaie, K. W., & Thompson, L. W. (1983, August). *Abbreviating the Metamemory Questionnaire: Factor structure and norms for adults.* Paper presented at the meeting of the American Psychological Association, Anaheim, CA.

Glosser, G., Butters, N., & Kaplan, E. (1977). Visuoperceptual processes in brain-damaged patients on the digit symbol substitution tests. *International Journal of Neuroscience, 7,* 59–66.

Golden, C. J., Moses, J. A., Jr., Graber, B., & Berg, R. A. (1981). Objective clinical rules for interpreting the Luria-Nebraska Neuropsychological Battery: Derivation, effectiveness, and validation. *Journal of Consulting and Clinical Psychology, 49,* 616–618.

Goodglass, H. (1980). Naming disorders in aphasia and aging. In L. K. Obler & M. L. Albert (Eds.), *Language and communication in the elderly: Clinical, therapeutic and experimental issues* (pp. 37–46). Lexington, MA: Heath.

Goodglass, H., & Kaplan, E. (1972). *The assessment of aphasia and related disorders.* Philadelphia: Lea & Febiger.

Goranson, T., Tuokko, H., Rosenblood, L., & Frerichs, R. (1997, October). *Serial sevens: Myths and realities*. Poster session presented at the meeting of the Canadian Association on Gerontology, Calgary, Alberta, Canada.

Graf, P., Uttl, B., & Tuokko, H. (1995). Color- and picture-word Stroop tests: Performance changes in old age. *Journal of Clinical and Experimental Neuropsychology, 17*, 390–415.

Graham, J. R. (1993). *MMPI–2 assessing personality and psychopathology* (2nd ed.). New York: Oxford University Press.

Granick, S., & Friedman, A. L. (1967). The effect of education on the decline of psychomotor test performance with age. *Journal of Gerontology, 22*, 191–195.

Grant, I. (1987). Alcohol and the brain: Neuropsychological correlates. *Journal of Consulting and Clinical Psychology, 55*, 310–324.

Green, J., Morris, J. C., Sandson, J., McKeel, D. W., Jr., & Miller, J. W. (1990). Progressive aphasia: A precursor of global dementia? *Neurology, 40*, 423–429.

Green, R. L. (1980). *The MMPI: An interpretive guide* (2nd ed.). New York: Grune & Stratton.

Greene, J. G., Smith, R., Gardiner, M., & Timbury, G. C. (1982). Measuring behavioral disturbance of elderly demented patients in the community and its effect on relatives: A factor analytic study. *Age and Ageing, 11*, 121–126.

Greifenhagen, A., Kurz, A., Wiseman, M., Haupt, M., & Zimmer, R. (1994). Cognitive assessment in Alzheimer's disease: What does the CAMCOG assess? *International Journal of Geriatric Psychiatry, 9*, 743–750.

Grigsby, J., Kaye, K., & Robbins, L. J. (1992). Reliabilities, norms and factor structure of the Behavioral Dyscontrol Scale. *Perceptual and Motor Skills, 74*, 883–892.

Grisso, T. (1994). The clinical assessment of competence of older adults. In M. Storandt & G. R. VandenBos (Eds.), *Neuropsychological assessment of dementia and depression in older adults: A clinician's guide* (pp. 119–139). Washington, DC: American Psychological Association.

Grober, E., & Buschke, H. (1987). Genuine memory deficits in dementia. *Developmental Neuropsychology, 3*, 13–36.

Grober, E., Buschke, H., Crystal, H., Bang, S., & Dresner, R. (1988). Screening for dementia by memory testing. *Neurology, 38*, 900–903.

Grober, E., & Sliwinski, M. (1991). Development and validation of a model for estimating premorbid verbal intelligence in the elderly. *Journal of Clinical and Experimental Neuropsychology, 13*, 933–949.

Gronlund, N. E. (1973). *Preparing criterion-referenced tests for classroom instruction*. New York: Macmillan.

Gulliksen, H. (1950). *Theory of mental tests*. New York: Wiley.

Gurland, B., & Cross, P. S. (1982). Epidemiology of psychopathology in old age. *Psychiatric Clinics of North America, 5*, 11–26.

Haaland, K. Y., Linn, R. T., Hunt, W. C., & Goodwin, J. S. (1983). A normative study of Russell's variant of the Wechsler Memory Scale in a healthy elderly population. *Journal of Consulting and Clinical Psychology, 51*, 878–881.

Haaland, K. Y., Vranes, L. F., Goodwin, J. S., & Garry, P. J. (1987). Wisconsin card sorting test performance in a healthy elderly population. *Journal of Gerontology, 42*, 345–346.

Hachinski, B. C., Iliff, L. D., Zilhka, E., DuBoulay, G. H., McAllister, V. L., Marshall, J., Russell, R.W.R., & Symon, L. (1975). Cerebral blood flow in dementia. *Archives of Neurology, 32*, 632–637.

Hachinski, B. C., Lassen, N. A., & Marshall, J. (1974). Multi-infarct dementia: A cause of mental deterioration in the elderly. *Lancet, 2*, 207–210.

Hadjistavropoulos, T., Taylor, S., Tuokko, H., & Beattie, B. L. (1994). Neuropsychological deficits, caregivers' perception of deficits and caregiver burden. *Journal of the American Geriatrics Society, 42*, 308–314.

Haglund, R.M.J., & Schickit, M. A. (1976). A clinical comparison of tests of organicity in elderly patients. *Journal of Gerontology, 31*, 654–659.

Hale, W. D., Cochran, C. D., & Hedgepeth, B. E. (1984). Norms for the Brief Symptom Inventory. *Journal of Consulting and Clinical Psychology, 52,* 321–322.

Hallenbeck, C. E., Fink, S. L., & Grossman, J. S. (1965). Measurement of intellectual inefficiency. *Psychological Reports, 17,* 339–349.

Halstead, W. C. (1947). *Brain and intelligence: A quantitative study of the frontal lobes.* Chicago: University of Chicago Press.

Hamilton, M. (1960). A rating scale for depression. *Journal of Neurology, Neurosurgery, and Psychiatry, 23,* 56–61.

Hansen, L. W., & Galsko, D. (1992). Lewy body disease. *Current Opinion in Neurology and Neurosurgery, 5,* 889–894.

Harper, R. G., Kotik-Harper, D., & Kirby, H. (1990). Psychometric assessment of depression in an elderly general population. *Journal of Nervous and Mental Disease, 178,* 113–119.

Hartman, D. E. (1995). *Neuropsychological toxocology: Identification and assessment of human neurotoxic syndromes* (2nd ed.). New York: Plenum.

Harwood, E., & Naylor, G.F.K. (1969). Recall and recognition in elderly and young subjects. *Australian Journal of Psychology, 21,* 251–257.

Hasher, L., & Zacks, R. T. (1979). Automatic and effortful processes in memory. *Journal of Experimental Psychology, 108,* 358–388.

Hayman, M. (1942). Two minute test measurement of intellectual impairment in psychiatric disorders. *Archives of Neurology and Psychiatry, 47,* 454–464.

Hayslip, B., & Lowman, R. L. (1986). The clinical use of projective techniques with the aged: A critical review and synthesis. *Clinical Gerontologist, 5,* 63–94.

Heath, P. D., Kennedy, P., & Kapur, N. (1983). Slowly progressive aphasia without generalized dementia. *Annals of Neurology, 13,* 687–688.

Heaton, R. K. (1981). *Wisconsin Card Sorting Test manual.* Odessa, FL: Psychological Assessment Resources.

Heaton, R. K. (1992). *Comprehensive norms for an expanded Halstead–Reitan Battery: A supplement for the Wechsler Adult Intelligence Scale–Revised.* Odessa, FL: Psychological Assessment Resources.

Heaton, R. K., Chelune, G. J., Talley, J. L., Kay, G. G., & Curtiss, G. (1993). *Wisconsin Card Sorting Test manual: Revised and expanded.* Odessa, FL: Psychological Assessment Resources.

Heaton, R. K., Grant, I., & Matthews, C. G. (1986). Differences in neuropsychological test performance associated with age, education and sex. In I. Grant & K. M. Adams (Eds.), *Neuropsychological assessment of neuropsychiatric disorders* (pp. 100–120). New York: Oxford University Press.

Heaton, R. K., Grant, I., & Matthews, C. G. (1991). *Comprehensive norms for an expanded Halstead–Reitan Battery: Demographic corrections, research findings and clinical applications.* Odessa, FL: Psychological Assessment Resources.

Heller, F. J., & Wynne, R. (1975). Drug misuse in the elderly: Indications and treatment suggestions. In E. Senvay, V. Shorty, & H. Alkasne (Eds.), *Developments in the field of drug abuse* (pp. 945–955). Cambridge, MA: Schenkman.

Hersen, M., & Van Hasselt, V. B. (1992). Behavioral assessment and the treatment of anxiety in the elderly. *Clinical Psychology Review, 12,* 619–640.

Hoffman, R. G., & Nelson, K. S. (1988). Cross-validation of six short forms of the WAIS–R in a healthy geriatric sample. *Journal of Clinical Psychology, 44,* 952–957.

Hooper, H. E. (1958). *The Hooper Visual Organization Test: Manual.* Beverly Hills, CA: Western Psychological Services.

Horn, J. L. (1968). Organizational abilities and the development of intelligence. *Psychological Review, 79,* 242–259.

Horn, J. L., & Cattell, R. B. (1967). Age differences in fluid and crystallized intelligence. *Acta Psychobiologica, 26,* 107–129.

Howell, S. C. (1972). Familiarity and complexity in perceptual recognition. *Journal of Gerontology, 27*, 364–371.

Howieson, D. B., Holm, L. A., Kaye, J. A., Oken, B. S., & Howieson, J. (1993). Neurologic function in the optimally healthy oldest old: Neuropsychological evaluation. *Neurology, 43*, 1882–1886.

Huff, F. J. (1990). Language in normal aging and age-related neurological diseases. In R. D. Nebes & S. Corkin (Eds.), *Handbook of neuropsychology* (Intelligence ed., Vol. 4, pp. 251–264). Amsterdam: Elsevier.

Huff, F. J., Collins, C., Corkin, S., & Rosen, T. J. (1986). Equivalent forms of the Boston Naming Test. *Journal of Clinical and Experimental Neuropsychology, 8*, 556–562.

Hulicka, I. M. (1966). Age differences in Wechsler Memory Scale scores. *Journal of Genetic Psychology, 109*, 135–145.

Hutt, M., & Briskin, G. (1960). *The clinical use of the revised Bender Gestalt Test.* New York: Grune & Stratton.

Hyer, L., & Blount, J. (1984). Concurrent and discriminant validities of the Geriatric Depression Scale with older psychiatric inpatients. *Psychological Reports, 54*, 622–626.

Ivnik, R. J., Malec, J. F., Smith, G. E., Tangalos, E. G., Petersen, R. C., Kokmen, E., & Kurland, L. T. (1992a). Mayo's Older Americans Normative Studies: WAIS–R norms for ages 56–97. *Clinical Neuropsychologist, 6*(Suppl.), 1–30.

Ivnik, R. J., Malec, J. F., Smith, G. E., Tangalos, E. G., Petersen, R. C., Kokmen, E., & Kurland, L. T. (1992b). Mayo's Older Americans Normative Studies: WMS–R norms for ages 56 to 94. *Clinical Neuropsychologist, 6*(Suppl.), 49–82.

Ivnik, R. J., Malec, J. F., Tangalos, E. G., Petersen, R. C., Kokmen, E., & Kurland, L. T. (1990). The Auditory-Verbal Learning Test (AVLT): Norms for ages 55 years and older. *Psychological Assessment, 2*, 304–312.

Ivnik, R. J., Malec, J. F., Tangalos, E. G., Petersen, R. C., Kokmen, E., & Kurland, L. T. (1992c). Mayo's Older Americans Normative Studies: Updated AVLT norms for ages 56 to 97. *Clinical Neuropsychologist, 6*(Suppl.), 83–104.

Ivnik, R. J., Smith, G. E., Tangalos, E. G., Petersen, R. C., Kokmen, E., & Kurland, L. T. (1991). Wechsler Memory Scale: IQ-dependent norms for persons ages 65 to 97 years. *Psychological Assessment, 3*, 156–161.

Jamison, K. R. (1979). Manic depressive illness in the elderly. In O. J. Kaplan (Ed.), *Psychopathology of aging* (pp. 79–95). New York: Academic Press.

Jarvik, L. F. (1988). Aging of the brain: How can we prevent it? *The Gerontologist, 28*, 739–747.

Jastak, S., & Wilkinson, G. (1984). *The Wide-Range Achievement Test Revised.* Wilmington, DE: Jastak Associates.

Jenkyn, L. R., Reeves, A. G., Warren, T., Whiting, R. K., Clayton, R. J., Moore, W. W., Rizzo, A., Tuzun, I. M., Bonnett, J. C., & Culpepper, B. W. (1985). Neurologic signs in senescence. *Archives of Neurology, 42*, 1154–1157.

Jensen, A. R., & Rohwer, W. D. (1966). The Stroop Color-Word Test: A review. *Acta Psychologica, 25*, 36–93.

Jorm, A. F. (1996). Assessment of cognitive impairment and dementia using informant reports. *Clinical Psychology Review, 16*, 51–73.

Jorm, A. F., & Jacomb, P. A. (1989). The Informant Questionnaire on Cognitive Decline in the Elderly (IQCODE): Socio-demographic correlates, reliability, validity and some norms. *Psychological Medicine, 19*, 1015–1022.

Joynt, R. J., & Shoulson, I. (1979). Dementia. In K. M. Heilman & E. Valenstein (Eds.), *Clinical neuropsychology* (pp. 475–498). New York: Oxford University Press.

Kahn, R. L., Goldfarb, A. I., Pollack, M., & Peck, A. (1960). Brief objective measures for the determination of mental status in the aged. *American Journal of Psychiatry, 117*, 326–328.

Kane, A. R., & Kane, L. R. (1981). *Assessing the elderly: A practical guide to measurement.* Lexington, MA: Heath.

Kaplan, E., Goodglass, H., & Weintraub, S. (1978). *The Boston Naming Test.* Philadelphia: Lea & Febiger.

Kaplan, E., Goodglass, H., & Weintraub, S. (1983). *The Boston Naming Test* (2nd ed.). Philadelphia: Lea & Febiger.

Kapp, M. B. (1991). Health care decision making by the elderly: I get by with a little help from my family. *The Gerontologist, 31,* 619–623.

Kapur, N., & Butters, N. (1977). Visuoperceptive deficits in long-term alcoholics with Korsakoff's psychosis. *Journal of Studies on Alcohol, 38,* 2025–2035.

Kareken, D., & Williams, M. (1994). Human judgment and estimation of premorbid intellectual function. *Psychological Assessment, 6,* 83–91.

Kaszniak, A. (1990). Psychological assessment of the aging individual. In J. E. Birren & K. W. Schaie (Eds.), *Handbook of the psychology of aging* (3rd ed., pp. 427–445). San Diego: Academic Press.

Katz, S., Downs, T. D., Cash, H. R., & Grotz, R. C. (1970). Progress in development of the index of ADL. *The Gerontologist, 10,* 20–30.

Katz, S., Ford, A. B., Moskowitz, R. W., Jackson, B. A., & Jaffee, M. W. (1963). Studies of illness in the aged. The index of ADL: A standardized measure of biological and psychosocial function. *Journal of the American Medical Association, 12,* 914–919.

Katzman, R., Aronson, M., Fuld, P., Kawas, C., Brown, T., Morgenstern, H., Frishman, W., Gidez, L., Eder, H., & Ooi, W. L. (1989). Development of dementing illnesses in an 80 year old volunteer cohort. *Annals of Neurology, 25,* 317–324.

Kaufman, A. S. (1975). Factor analysis of the WAIS–R at 11 age levels between 6½ and 16½ years. *Journal of Clinical and Consulting Psychology, 43,* 135–147.

Kaufman, A. S. (1976). A four-test short form of the WISC–R. *Contemporary Educational Psychology, 1,* 180–196.

Kaufman, A. S. (1977). Should short-form validity coefficients be corrected? *Journal of Consulting and Clinical Psychology, 45,* 1159–1161.

Kaufman, A. S. (1990). *Assessing adolescent and adult intelligence.* Boston: Allyn & Bacon.

Kaufman, A. S., & Kaufman, N. L. (1990). *Kaufman Brief Intelligence Test (K–BIT). Manual.* Circles Pines, MN: American Guidance Service.

Kaufman, A. S., & Kaufman, N. L. (1993). *Kaufman Adolescent and Adult Intelligence Test (KAIT). Manual.* Circles Pines, MN: American Guidance Service.

Kaufman, A. S., & Kaufman, N. L. (1994). *Kaufman Short Neuropsychological Assessment Procedure (K–SNAP). Manual.* Circles Pines, MN: American Guidance Service.

Kausler, D. H., & Lair, C. V. (1966). Associative strength and paired-associate learning in elderly subjects. *Journal of Gerontology, 21,* 278–280.

Keith-Spiegel, P., & Koocher, G. P. (1985). *Ethics in psychology: Professional standards and cases.* New York: Random House.

Kemper, S., Kynette, D., Rash, S., O'Brien, K., & Sprott, R. (1989). Life-span changes to adults' language: Effects of memory and genre. *Applied Psycholinguistics, 10,* 49–66.

Kemper, T. L. (1994). Neuroanatomical and neuropathological changes during aging and dementia. In M. L. Albert & J. E. Knoefel (Eds.), *Clinical neurology of aging* (2nd ed., pp. 68–78). New York: Oxford University Press.

Kempler, D., Jackson, C. A., Metter, E. J., Benson, D. F., Hanson, W. R., & Riege, W. H. (1989). Slowly progressive aphasia. *Clinical Aphasiology, 18,* 257–270.

Kempler, D., Metter, E. J., Riege, W. H., Jackson, C. A., Benson, D. F., & Hanson, W. R. (1990). Slowly progressive aphasia: Three cases with language, memory, CT and PET data. *Journal of Neurology, Neurosurgery and Psychiatry, 53,* 987–993.

Kendrick, D. C. (1982a). Psychometrics and neurological models: A reply to Dr. Rabbitt. *British Journal of Clinical Psychology, 21,* 61–62.

Kendrick, D. C. (1982b). Why assess the aged? A clinical psychologist's view. *British Journal of Clinical Psychology, 21,* 47–54.

Kennedy, K. J. (1981). Age effects on Trail Making Test performance. *Perceptual and Motor Skills, 52,* 671–675.

Kiernan, R. J., Mueller, J., Langston, W., & Van Dyke, C. (1987). The Neurobehavioral Cognitive Status Examination: A brief but differentiated approach to cognitive assessment. *Annals of Internal Medicine, 107,* 481–485.

King, C. J., Van-Hasselt, V. B., Segal, D. L., & Hersen, M. (1994). Diagnosis and assessment of substance abuse in older adults: Current strategies and issues. *Addictive Behaviors, 19,* 41–55.

King, M. (1986). At risk drinking among general practice attendees: Validation of the CAGE questionnaire. *Psychological Medicine, 16,* 213–217.

Kinney, J. M., & Parris-Stephens, M. A. (1989). Caregiving hassles scale: Assessing the daily hassles of caring for a family member with dementia. *The Gerontologist, 29,* 328–332.

Kirshner, H. S., Tanridag, O., Thurman, l., & Whetsell, W. P. (1987). Progressive aphasia without dementia: Two cases with focal spongiform degeneration. *Annals of Neurology, 22,* 527–532.

Kirshner, H. S., Webb, W. G., Kelly, M. P., & Wells, C. E. (1984). Language disturbance: An initial symptom of cortical degeneration and dementia. *Archives of Neurology, 41,* 491–496.

Klein, R. M., & Bell, B. (1982). Self care skills: Behavioural measurement with the Klein–Bell ADL Scale. *Archives of Physical Medicine and Rehabilitation, 63,* 335–338.

Klonoff, H., & Kennedy, M. (1965). Memory and perceptual functioning in octogenarians and nonagenarians in the community. *Journal of Gerontology, 20,* 328–333.

Klonoff, H., & Kennedy, M. (1966). A comparative study of cognitive functioning in old age. *Journal of Gerontology, 21,* 239–243.

Knight, R. G. (1984). Some general population norms for the short form Beck Depression Inventory. *Journal of Clinical Psychology, 40,* 751–753.

Knight, R. G., Waal-Manning, H. A., & Spears, G. F. (1983). Some norms and reliability data for the State-Trait Anxiety Inventory and the Zung Self Rating Depression Scale. *British Journal of Clinical Psychology, 22,* 245–249.

Koenig, G., Meador, K. G., Cohen, H. G., & Blazer, D. G. (1988). Self-rated depression scales and screening for major depression in the older hospitalized patient with medical illness. *Journal of the American Geriatrics Society, 36,* 699–706.

Koss, E., Haxby, J. V., & Decarli, C. (1991). Pattern of performance preservation and loss in healthy elderly. *Developmental Neuropsychology, 7,* 99–113.

Kozma, A., di Fazio, R., Stones, M. J., & Hannah, T. E. (1992). Long- and short-term affective states in happiness: Age and sex comparisons. *Social Indicators Research, 4,* 293–310.

Kozma, A., & Stones, M. J. (1980). The measurement of happiness: Development of the Memorial University of Newfoundland Scale of Happiness (MUNSH). *Journal of Gerontology, 35,* 906–912.

Kozma, A., & Stones, M. J. (1983). Revalidation of the Memorial University of Newfoundland Scale of Happiness. *Canadian Journal on Aging, 2,* 27–29.

Kozma, A., & Stones, M. J. (1987). Social desirability in measures of subjective well being: A systematic evaluation. *Journal of Gerontology, 42,* 56–59.

Kozma, A., & Stones, M. J. (1988). Social desirability in measures of subjective well being: Age comparisons. *Social Indicators Research, 20,* 1–14.

Kozma, A., Stones, M. J., & Kazarian, S. (1985). The usefulness of the MUNSH as an index of overall well-being and psychopathology. *Social Indicators Research, 17,* 49–55.

Kozma, A., Stones, M. J., & McNeil, K. (1991). *Subjective well being in later life.* Toronto, Canada: Butterworths.

La Rue, A. (1992). *Aging and neuropsychological assessment.* New York: Plenum.

La Rue, A., Dessonville, E., & Jarvik, L. F. (1985). Aging and mental disorders. In J. E. Birren & K. W. Schaie (Eds.), *Handbook of the psychology of aging* (2nd ed., pp. 664-702). New York: Van Nostrand Reinhold.

LaBarge, E., Edwards, D., & Knesevich, J. W. (1986). Performance of normal elderly on the Boston Naming Test. *Brain and Language, 27,* 380–384.

Lacks, P., & Morin, C. (1992). Recent advances in the assessment and treatment of insomnia. *Journal of Consulting and Clinical Psychology, 60,* 586–594.

Lacks, P., & Storandt, M. (1982). Bender Gestalt performance of normal older adult. *Journal of Clinical Psychology, 38,* 624–627.

Larkin, J. P., & Seltzer, B. (1994). Alcohol abuse and Alzheimer's disease. *Hospital and Community Psychiatry, 45,* 1040–1041.

Larrabee, G. J., Trahan, D. E., Curtiss, G., & Levin, H. S. (1988). Normative data for the Verbal Selective Reminding Test. *Neuropsychology, 2,* 173–182.

Law, M., & Letts, L. (1989). A critical review of scales of activities of daily living. *American Journal of Occupational Therapy, 43,* 522–528.

Lawton, M. P. (1971). The functional assessment of elderly people. *Journal of the American Geriatrics Society, 19,* 465–481.

Lawton, M. P. (1972). Assessing the competence of older people. In D. Kent, R. Kastenbaum, & S. Sherwood (Eds.), *Research planning and action for the elderly* (pp. 122–143). New York: Behavioural Publications.

Lawton, M. P., & Brody, E. M. (1969). Assessment of older people: Self maintaining and instrumental activities of daily living. *The Gerontologist, 9,* 179–186.

Lawton, M. P., Kleban, M. H., Moss, M., Rovine, M., & Glicksman, A. (1989). Measuring caregiver appraisal. *Journal of Gerontology, 44,* 61–67.

Lazarus, R. S., & Folkman, S. (1984). *Stress, appraisal and coping.* New York: Springer.

Leckliter, I. N., Matarazzo, J. D., & Silverstein, A. B. (1986). A literature review of factor analytic studies of the WAIS–R. *Journal of Clinical Psychology, 42,* 332–342.

Levin, H. S., Benton, A. L., & Grossman, R. G. (1982). *Neurobehavioral consequences of closed head injury.* New York: Oxford University Press.

Levine, H. R. (1971). Validation of the Quick Test for intelligence screening of the elderly. *Psychological Reports, 29,* 167–172.

Lezak, M. (1980). *Neuropsychological assessment.* New York: Oxford University Press.

Lezak, M. (1983). *Neuropsychological assessment* (2nd ed.). New York: Oxford University Press.

Lezak, M. D. (1995). *Neuropsychological assessment* (3rd ed.). New York: Oxford University Press.

Lichtenberg, P. A., & Christensen, B. (1992). Extended normative data for the Logical Memory Subtests of the Wechsler Memory Scale–Revised: Responses from a sample of cognitively intact elderly medical patients. *Psychological Reports, 71,* 745–746.

Lindeboom, J., Ter-Horst, R., Hooyer, C., Dinkgreve, M., & Jonker, C. (1993). Some psychometric properties of the CAMCOG. *Psychological Medicine, 23,* 213–219.

Linn, R. T., Wolf, P. A., Bachman, D. L., Knoefel, J. E., Cobb, J. L., Belanger, A. J., Kaplan, E. F., & D'Agostino, R. B. (1995). The "preclinical phase" of probable Alzheimer's disease. *Archives of Neurology, 52,* 485–490.

Lipowski, Z. J. (1994). Acute confusional states (delirium) in the elderly. In M. L. Albert & J. E. Knoefel (Eds.), *Clinical neurology of aging* (2nd ed., pp. 347–362). New York: Oxford University Press.

Lishman, W. A. (1986). Alcoholic dementia: A hypothesis. *Lancet, 1,* 1184–1185.

Lishman, W. A. (1990). Alcohol and the brain. *Journal of Psychiatry, 156,* 635–644.

The Lund and Manchester Groups. (1994). Clinical and neuropathological criteria for frontotemporal dementia. *Journal of Neurology, Neurosurgery and Psychiatry, 57,* 416–418.

Luria, A. R. (1966). *Higher cortical functions in man.* New York: Basic Books.

Lynch, G., McGaugh, J. L., & Weinberger, N. M. (1984). *Neurobiology of learning and memory.* New York: Guilford.

MacInnes, W. D., Gillen, R. W., Golden, C. J., & Graber, B. (1983). Aging and performance on the Luria–Nebraska Neuropsychological Battery. *International Journal of Neuroscience, 19,* 179–190.

Mack, J. L., & Carlson, J. (1978). Conceptual deficits and aging: The Category Test. *Perceptual and Motor Skills, 46,* 123–128.

Mack, W. J., Freed, M., Williams, W., & Henderson, V. W. (1992). Boston Naming Test: Shortened versions for use in Alzheimer's disease. *Journal of Gerontology: Psychological Sciences, 47,* P154–P158.

MacLeod, C. M. (1991). Half a century of research on the Stroop effect: An integrative review. *Psychological Bulletin, 109,* 163–203.

Mahoney, F. I., & Barthel, D. W. (1965). Functional evaluation: The Barthel Index. *Maryland State Medical Journal, 14,* 61–65.

Malec, J. F., Ivnik, R. J., & Hinkeldey, N. S. (1991). Visual Spatial Learning Test. *Psychological Assessment, 3,* 82–88.

Malec, J. F., Ivnik, R. J., Smith, G. E., Tangalos, E. G., Petersen, R. C., Kokmen, E., & Kurland, L. T. (1992). Visual Spatial Learning Test: Normative data and further validation. *Psychological Assessment, 4,* 433–441.

Mandell, A. M., Alexander, M. P., & Carpenter, S. (1989). Creutzfeldt–Jacob disease presenting as isolated aphasia. *Neurology, 39,* 55–58.

Margolis, R. B., Taylor, J. M., & Greenlief, C. L. (1986). A cross validation of two short forms of the WAIS–R in a geriatric sample suspected of dementia. *Journal of Clinical Psychology, 42,* 145–146.

Martin, A. (1987). Representation of semantic and spatial knowledge in Alzheimer's patients: Implications for models of preserved learning in amnesia. *Journal of Clinical and Experimental Neuropsychology, 9,* 191–224.

Masur, D. M., Fuld, P. A., Blau, A. D., Thal, L. J., Levin, H. S., & Aronson, M. K. (1989). Distinguishing normal and demented elderly with the selective reminding test. *Journal of Clinical and Experimental Neuropsychology, 11,* 615–630.

Matarazzo, J. D. (1972). *Wechsler's measurement and appraisal of adult intelligence* (5th ed.). Baltimore: Williams & Wilkins.

Matarazzo, J. D. (1986). Computerized clinical test interpretations. *American Psychologist, 41,* 14–24.

Matarazzo, J. D., Bornstein, R. A., McDermott, P. A., & Noonan, V. (1986). Verbal IQ versus performance IQ difference scores in males and females from the WAIS–R standardization sample. *Journal of Clinical Psychology, 42,* 965–974.

Matarazzo, J. D., & Herman, D. O. (1984). Base rate differences for the WAIS–R: Test–retest stability and VIQ–PIQ differences. *Journal of Clinical Neuropsychology, 6,* 351–366.

Matarazzo, J. D., & Herman, D. P. (1985). Clinical uses of the WAIS–R: Base rates of differences between VIQ and PIQ in the WAIS–R standardization sample. In B. B. Wolman (Ed.), *Handbook of intelligence: Theories, measurements and applications* (pp. 899–932). New York: Wiley.

Mattis, S. (1976). Mental status examination for organic mental syndrome in the elderly patient. In L. Bellak & T. B. Karasu (Eds.), *Geriatric psychiatry* (pp. 77–121). New York: Grune & Stratton.

Mattis, S. (1988). *Dementia Rating Scale (DRS): Professional manual.* Odessa, FL: Psychological Assessment Resources.

McCue, M., Goldstein, G., & Shelly, C. (1989). The application of a short form as the Luria–Nebraska Neuropsychological Battery to discriminate between dementia and depression in the elderly. *International Journal of Clinical Neuropsychology, 11,* 21–29.

McCue, M., Shelly, C., & Goldstein, G. (1985). A proposed short form of the Luria–Nebraska Neuropsychological Battery oriented toward assessment of the elderly. *International Journal of Clinical Neuropsychology, 7,* 96–101.

McDowell, I., & Newell, C. (1996). *Measuring health: A guide to rating scales and questionnaires* (2nd ed.). New York: Oxford University Press.

McEntree, W. J., & Crook, T. H. (1990). Age-associated memory impairment: A role for catecholamines. *Neurology, 40,* 526–530.

McFie, J. (1975). *Assessment of organic intellectual impairment.* New York: Academic Press.

McGlynn, S. M., & Kaszniak, A. W. (1991). Unawareness of deficits in dementia and schizophrenia. In G. P. Prigatano & D. L. Schacter (Eds.), *Awareness of deficit after brain injury* (pp. 84–110). New York: Oxford University Press.

McKeith, I. G., Perry, R. H., Fairbairn, A. F., Jabeen, S., & Perry, E. K. (1992). Operational criteria for senile dementia of the Lewy body type (SDLT). *Psychological Medicine, 22,* 911–922.

McKhann, G., Drachman, D. A., Folstein, M. F., Katzman, R., Price, D., & Stadlan, E. M. (1984). Clinical diagnosis of Alzheimer's disease: Report of the NINCDS–ADRDA work group under the auspices of the Department of Health and Human Services task force on Alzheimer's disease. *Neurology, 34,* 939–944.

McLean, J. E., Kaufman, A. S., & Reynolds, C. R. (1989). Base rates of WAIS–R subtest scatter as a guide for clinical and neuropsychological assessment. *Journal of Clinical Psychology, 45,* 919–926.

Measso, G., Zappala, G., Cavarzeran, F., Crook, T. H., Romani, L., Pirozzolo, F. J., Grigoletto, F., Amaducci, L. A., Massari, D., & Lebowitz, B. D. (1993). Raven's colored progressive matrices: A normative study of a random sample of healthy adults. *Acta Neurologica Scandinavica, 88,* 70–74.

Meehl, P. E., & Rosen, A. (1955). Antecedent probabilities and the efficiency of psychometric signs, patterns, on cutting scores. *Psychological Bulletin, 52,* 194–216.

Mellinger, G. D., Balter, M. B., & Uhlenhuth, E. H. (1985). Insomnia and its treatment. *Archives of General Psychiatry, 42,* 225–232.

Meneilly, G. S., & Tuokko, H. (1994). Normal aging of the nervous system. In D. B. Calne (Ed.), *Neurodegenerative diseases* (pp. 383–398). Philadelphia: Saunders.

Mesulam, M. M. (1982). Slowly progressive aphasia without generalized dementia. *Annals of Neurology, 11,* 592–598.

Mesulam, M. M. (1987). Primary progressive aphasia—differentiation from Alzheimer's disease. *Annals of Neurology, 22,* 533–534.

Mesulam, M. M., & Geschwind, N. (1976). Disordered mental status in the postoperative period. *Urologic Clinics of North America, 3,* 199–215.

Metter, E. J., & Wilson, R. S. (1993). Vascular dementias. In R. W. Parks, R. F. Zec, & R. S. Wilson (Eds.), *Neuropsychology of Alzheimer's disease and other dementias* (pp. 416–437). New York: Oxford University Press.

Meyer, J. S., McClintic, K. L., Rogers, R. L., Sims, P., & Mortel, K. F. (1988). Aetiological considerations and risk factors for multi-infarct dementia. *Journal of Neurology, Neurosurgery and Psychiatry, 51,* 1489–1497.

Meyerink, L. H. (1982). Intellectual functioning: The nature and pattern of change with aging. *Dissertation Abstracts International, 43*(3-B), 855.

Mitrushina, M., & Satz, P. (1989). Differential decline of specific memory components in normal aging. *Brain Dysfunction, 2,* 330–335.

Mitrushina, M., & Satz, P. (1991). Effect of repeated administration of a neuropsychological battery in the elderly. *Journal of Clinical Psychology, 47,* 790–801.

Mittenberg, W., Hammeke, T. A., & Rao, S. M. (1989). Intrasubtest scatter on the WAIS–R as a pathognomic sign of brain injury. *Psychological Assessment, 1,* 273–276.

Mittenberg, W., Thompson, G. B., Schwartz, J. A., Ryan, J. J., & Levitt, R. (1991). Intellectual loss in Alzheimer's dementia and WAIS–R intrasubtest scatter. *Journal of Clinical Psychology, 47,* 544–547.

Montgomery, K. M. (1982). *A normative study of neuropsychological test performance of a normal elderly sample.* Unpublished master's thesis, University of Victoria, Victoria, British Columbia, Canada.

Montgomery, R.J.V., Gonyea, J. G., & Hooyman, N. R. (1985). Caregiving and the experience of subjective and objective burden. *Family Relations, 34,* 19–26.

Morgan, S. F., & Hatsukami, D. K. (1986). Use of the Shipley Institute of Living Scale for neuropsychological screening of the elderly: Is it an appropriate measure for this population? *Journal of Clinical Psychology, 42,* 796–798.

Morris, J. C., & Rubin, E. H. (1991). Clinical diagnosis and course of Alzheimer disease. *Psychiatric Clinics of North America, 14,* 223–236.

Mortimer, J. A. (1995). The epidemiology of Alzheimer's disease: Beyond risk factors. In K. Iqbal, J. A. Mortimer, B. Winblad, & H. M. Wisniewski (Eds.), *Research advances in Alzheimer's disease and related disorders* (pp. 3–14). New York: Wiley.

Moses, J. A., Schefft, B. K., Wong, J. L., & Berg, R. A. (1992). Revised norms and decision rules for the Luria–Nebraska Neuropsychological Battery, Form II. *Archives of Clinical Neuropsychology, 7,* 251–269.

Mountain, M. A., & Snow, W. G. (1993). Wisconsin Card Sorting Test as a measure of frontal pathology: A review. *Clinical Neuropsychologist, 7,* 108–118.

Munro, A. (1991). A plea for parphrenia. *Canadian Journal of Psychiatry, 36,* 667–672.

Murden, R. A., McRae, T. D., Kaner, S., & Buchman, M. E. (1991). Mini-Mental State Exam scores vary with education in blacks and whites. *Journal of the American Geriatrics Society, 39,* 149–155.

Musetti, L., Perugi, G., Soriani, A., Rossi, V. M., Casano, G. B., & Akiskal, H. S. (1989). Depression before and after age 65: A re-examination. *British Journal of Psychiatry, 155,* 330–336.

Myers, J. K., Weissman, M. M., Tischler, G. L., Holzer, C. E., Leaf, P. J., Orvaschel, H., Anthony, J. C., Boyd, J. H., Burke, J. D., Kramer, M., & Stolzman, R. (1984). Six month prevalence of psychiatric disorders in three communities: 1980 to 1982. *Archives of General Psychiatry, 41,* 959–967.

National Association of Social Workers. (1993). *Code of ethics of the National Association of Social Workers.* Washington, DC: Author.

Naugle, R. I., Cullum, C. M., & Bigler, E. D. (1990). Evaluation of intellectual and memory function among dementia patients who were intellectually superior. *Clinical Neuropsychologist, 4,* 355–374.

Neary, D., Snowden, J. S., & Mann, D. M. A. (1993). The clinical pathological correlates of lobar atrophy. A review. *Dementia, 4,* 154–159.

Neils, J., Baris, J. M., Carter, C., Dell'aira, A. L., Nordlock, S. J., Weiler, E., & Weisiger, B. (1995). Effects of age, education, and living environment on Boston Naming Test performance. *Journal of Speech and Hearing Research, 38,* 1143–1149.

Nelson, H. E. (1976). A modified card sorting test sensitive to frontal lobe defects. *Cortex, 12,* 313–324.

Nelson, H. E. (1982). *The National Adult Reading Test (NART): Test manual.* Windsor, England: NFER-Nelson.

Nelson, H. E., & McKenna, P. (1975). The use of current reading ability in the assessment of dementia. *British Journal of Social and Clinical Psychology, 14,* 259–267.

Nelson, H. E., & O'Connel, A. (1978). Dementia: The estimation of premorbid intelligence levels using the National Adult Reading Test. *Cortex, 12,* 313–324.

Nesselroade, J. R., Mitteness, L. S., & Thompson, L. K. (1984). Older adulthood: Short term changes in anxiety, fatigue, and other psychological states. *Research on Aging, 6,* 3–28.

Nicholas, E., Brookshire, R. H., MacLennan, D. L., Schumacher, J. G., & Porrazzo, S. A. (1989). Revised administration and scoring procedures for the Boston Naming Test and norms for non-brain-damaged adults. *Aphasiology, 3,* 569–580.

Nickols, J. E. (1963). Structural efficiency of the WAIS subtests. *Journal of Clinical Psychology, 19,* 420–423.

Norris, J. T., Gallagher, D., Wilson, A., & Winograd, C. H. (1987). Assessment of depression in geriatric medical outpatients: The validity of two screening measures. *Journal of the American Geriatrics Society, 35,* 989–995.

Novak, M., & Guest, C. (1989). Application of a multidimensional caregiver burden inventory. *The Gerontologist, 29,* 798–803.

Nunnally, J. (1970). *Introduction to psychological measurement.* New York: McGraw-Hill.

Obler, L. K., & Albert, M. L. (1981). Language and aging: A neurobehavioral analysis. In D. S. Beasley & G. A. Davis (Eds.), *Aging: Communication processes and disorders* (pp. 107–122). New York: Grune & Stratton.

Obler, L. K., Woodward, S., & Albert, M. L. (1984). Changes in cerebral lateralization in aging? *Neuropsychologia, 22,* 235–240.

O'Carroll, R. (1992). Predicting premorbid intellectual ability in dementia. *Clinical Neuropsychologist, 6,* 113–115.

O'Connor, D. W., Pollitt, P. A., Brook, P. B., & Reiss, B. B. (1989). The validity of informant histories in a community study of dementia. *International Journal of Geriatric Psychiatry, 4,* 203–208.

Ogloff, J. (1995). Navigating the quagmire: Legal and ethical guidelines for mental health intervention. In D. Martin & A. Moore (Eds.), *First steps in the art of intervention* (pp. 347–376). Pacific Grove, CA: Brooks/Cole.

O'Leary, U. M., Rusch, K. M., & Guastello, S. J. (1991). Estimating age-stratified WAIS–R IQs from scores on the Raven's Standard Progressive Matrices. *Journal of Clinical Psychology, 47,* 277–284.

Olin, J. T., Schneider, L. S., Eaton, E. M., Zemansky, M. F., & Pollock, V. (1992). The Geriatric Depression Scale and the Beck Depression Inventory as screening instruments in an older adult outpatient population. *Psychological Assessment, 4,* 190–192.

Orme, J. E. (1966). Hypothetically true norms for the Progressive Matrices Tests. *Human Development, 9,* 222–230.

Paolo, A. M., & Ryan, J. J. (1992a). Generalizability of two methods of estimating premorbid intelligence in the elderly. *Archives of Clinical Neuropsychology, 7,* 135–143.

Paolo, A. M., & Ryan, J. J. (1992b). Unusual combinations of verbal and performance IQs in normal and neurologically impaired elderly. *Journal of Clinical Psychology, 48,* 230–233.

Paolo, A. M., & Ryan, J. J. (1993a). Is the WAIS–R an acceptable test for the elderly? Opinions of examinees 75 years and older. *Journal of Clinical Psychology, 49,* 720–723.

Paolo, A. M., & Ryan, J. J. (1993b). Test–retest stability of the Satz–Mogel WAIS–R Short Form in a sample of normal persons 75 to 87 years of age. *Archives of Clinical Neuropsychology, 8,* 397–404.

Paolo, A. M., & Ryan, J. J. (1993c). WAIS–R abbreviated forms in the elderly: A comparison of the Satz–Mogel with a seven-subtest short form. *Psychological Assessment, 5,* 425–429.

Paolo, M., Ryan, J. J., & Troster, A. I. (in press). Estimating premorbid WAIS–R intelligence in the elderly: An extension and cross validation of new regression equations. *Journal of Clinical Psychology.*

Parasuraman, R., & Davies, R. (1984). *Varieties of attention.* New York: Academic Press.

Parmallee, P. A., Lawton, M. P., & Katz, I. R. (1989). Psychometric properties of the Geriatric Depression Scale among the institutionalized aged. *Psychological Assessment, 1,* 331–338.

Patterson, R. L., O'Sullivan, M. J., & Spielberger, C. D. (1980). Measurement of state and trait anxiety in elderly mental health clients. *Journal of Behavioral Assessment, 2,* 89–97.

Pauker, J. D. (1988). Constructing overlapping cell tables to maximize the clinical usefulness of normative test data: Rationale and an example from neuropsychology. *Journal of Clinical Psychology, 44,* 930–933.

Payne, R. W., & Jones, H. G. (1959). Statistics for the investigation in individual cases. *Journal of Clinical Psychology, 13,* 115–121.

Pearlin, L. J., & Schooler, C. (1978). The structure of coping. *Journal of Health and Social Behavior, 19*, 2–21.

Pearlson, G. D., & Petty, R. G. (1994). Late-life-onset psychoses. In C. E. Coffey & J. L. Cummings (Eds.), *The American Psychiatric Press textbook of geriatric psychiatry* (pp. 261–277). Washington, DC: American Psychiatric Press.

Peck, D. F. (1970). The conversion of Progressive Matrices and Mill Hill Vocabulary raw scores into deviation IQs. *Journal of Clinical Psychology, 26*, 67–70.

Petersen, D. M., & Thomas, C. W. (1975). Acute drug reactions among the elderly. *Journal of Gerontology, 30*, 552–556.

Petersen, R. C., Smith, G., Kokmen, E., Ivnik, R. J., & Tangalos, E. G. (1992). Memory function in normal aging. *Neurology, 42*, 396–401.

Pfeiffer, E. (1975). A Short Portable Mental Status Questionnaire for the assessment of organic brain deficit in elderly patients. *Journal of the American Geriatrics Society, 23*, 433–441.

Plude, D. J., Milberg, W. P., & Cerella, J. (1986). Age differences in depicting and perceiving tridimensionality in simple line drawings. *Experimental Aging Research, 12*, 221–225.

Poeck, K., & Luzzatti, C. (1988). Slowly progressive aphasia in three patients: The problem of accompanying neuropsychological deficit. *Brain, 111*, 151–168.

Pontius, A. A., & Yudowitz, B. S. (1980). Frontal lobe system dysfunction in some criminal actions as shown in the narratives test. *Journal of Nervous and Mental Disease, 168*, 111–117.

Pope, K. (1992). Responsibilities in providing test feedback to clients. *Psychological Assessment, 4*, 268–271.

Poulshock, S. W., & Deimling, G. T. (1984). Families caring for elders in residence: Issues in the measurement of burden. *Journal of Gerontology, 39*, 230–239.

Price, L. J., Fein, G., & Feinberg, I. (1980). Neuropsychological assessment of cognitive function in the elderly. In L. W. Poon (Ed.), *Aging in the 1980's* (pp. 78–85). Washington, DC: American Psychological Association.

Priest, W., & Meunier, G. F. (1993). MMPI-2 performance of elderly women. *Clinical Gerontologist, 14*, 3–11.

Query, W. T., & Megran, J. (1983). Age-related norms for AVLT in a male patient population. *Journal of Clinical Psychology, 39*, 136–138.

Rabins, D., Mace, N., & Lucas, M. (1982). The impact of dementia on the family. *Journal of the American Medical Association, 248*, 333–335.

Raddloff, L. S. (1977). The CES-D Scale: A self-report depression scale for research in the general population. *Applied Psychological Measurement, 1*, 385–401.

Rae, S. (1995). *A comparison of clock scoring approaches for dementia screening in an elderly population.* Unpublished master's thesis, Simon Fraser University, Burnaby, British Columbia, Canada.

Rains, B. S., & Ditzler, T. F. (1993). Alcohol use disorders in cognitively impaired patients referred for geriatric assessment. *Journal of Addictive Diseases, 12*, 55–64.

Rankin, E., Gfeller, J. D., & Gilner, F. H. (1993). Measuring anxiety states in the elderly using the State-Trait Anxiety Inventory for Children. *Journal of Psychiatric Research, 27*, 111–117.

Rapp, S. R., Parisi, S. A., Walsh, D. A., & Wallace, C. E. (1988). Detecting depression in elderly medical inpatients. *Journal of Consulting and Clinical Psychology, 56*, 509–513.

Rapp, S. R., Smith, S. S., & Britt, M. (1990). Identifying comorbid depression in elderly medical patients: Use of the Extracted Hamilton Depression Rating Scale. *Psychological Assessment, 2*, 243–247.

Raven, J. C. (1965). *Guide to using the Coloured Progressive Matrices.* London: H. K. Lewis.

Raven, J. C., Court, J. H., & Raven, J. (1976). *Manual for Raven's Progressive Matrices.* London: H. K. Lewis.

Raven, J. C., Court, J. H., & Raven, J. (1990). *Manual for Raven's Progressive Matrices and Vocabulary Scales.* Oxford, England: Oxford Psychologist's Press.

Reeves, D., & Wedding, D. (1994). *The clinical assessment of memory: A practical guide.* New York: Springer.

Regier, D. A., Boyd, J. H., Burke, J. D. J., Rae, D. S., Myers, J. K., Kramer, M., Robins, L. N., George, L. K., Karno, M., & Locke, B. Z. (1988). One month prevalence of mental disorders in the United States: Based on five epidemiologic catchment area sites. *Archives of General Psychiatry, 45*, 977–986.

Reifler, B. V. (1982). Arguments for abandoning the term pseudo-dementia. *Journal of the American Geriatrics Society, 30*, 665–668.

Reifler, B. V., Larson, E., Teri, L., & Poulsen, M. (1986). Dementia of the Alzheimer's type and depression. *Journal of the American Geriatrics Society, 34*, 855–859.

Reifler, B. V., Teri, L., Raskind, M., Veith, R., Barnes, R., White, E., & McLean, P. (1989). Double-blind trial of imipramine in Alzheimer's disease patients with and without depression. *American Journal of Psychiatry, 146*, 45–49.

Reisberg, B., Ferris, S. G., De Leon, M. J., & Crook, T. (1982). The Global Deterioration Scale for assessment of primary degenerative dementia. *American Journal of Psychiatry, 139*, 1136–1139.

Reitan, R. M., & Davidson, L. A. (1974). *Clinical neuropsychology: Current status and applications.* New York: Winston/Wiley.

Reitan, R. M., & Wolfson, D. (1986). The Halstead–Reitan Neuropsychological Battery and aging. *Clinical Gerontologist, 5*, 39–61.

Reitan, R. M., & Wolfson, D. (1993). *The Halstead–Reitan Neuropsychological Test Battery: Theory and clinical interpretation.* Tucson, AZ: Neuropsychology Press.

Resnick, R. J., & Entin, A. D. (1971). Is an abbreviated form of the WISC valid for Afro-Americans? *Journal of Consulting and Clinical Psychology, 36*, 97–99.

Retzlaff, P. D., & Gibertini, M. (1994). Neurometric issues and problems. In R. D. Vanderploeg (Ed.), *Clinician's guide to neuropsychological assessment* (pp. 185–209). Hillsdale, NJ: Lawrence Erlbaum Associates.

Rey, A. (1964). *L'examen clinique en psychologie* [Clinical examination in psychology]. Paris: Presses Universitaires de France.

Reynolds, W. M., & Gould, J. W. (1981). A psychometric investigation of the standard and short form Beck Depression Inventory. *Journal of Consulting and Clinical Psychology, 49*, 306–307.

Rinn, W. E. (1988). Mental decline in normal aging: A review. *Journal of Geriatric Psychiatry and Neurology, 1*, 144–158.

Robertson-Tehabo, E. A., & Arenberg, D. (1989). Assessment of memory in older adults. In T. Hunt & C. Lindley (Eds.), *Testing older adults* (pp. 200–231). Austin, TX: Pro-Ed.

Roccaforte, W. H., Burke, W. J., Bayer, B. L., & Wengel, S. P. (1992). Validation of a telephone version of the Mini-Mental State Examination. *Journal of the American Geriatrics Society, 40*, 697–702.

Rodenburg, M., Hopkins, R. W., Hamilton, P. F., Ginsburg, L., Nashed, Y., & Minde, N. (1991). The Kingston standardized cognitive assessment. *International Journal of Geriatric Psychiatry, 6*, 867–873.

Roman, D. D., Edwall, G. E., Buchanan, R. J., & Patton, J. H. (1991). Extended norms for the Paced Auditory Serial Addition Task. *Clinical Neuropsychologist, 5*, 33–40.

Roman, G. C., Tatemichi, T. K., Erkinjuntti, T., Cummings, J. L., Masdeu, J. C., Garcia, J. H., Armaducci, L., Orgogozo, M., Brun, A., Gofman, A., Chui, H. C., Moody, D. M., O'Brien, M. D., Amaguchi, T., Grafman, J., Drayer, B. P., Bennett, D. A., Fisher, M., Ogata, J., Kokmen, E., Bermejo, F., Wolf, P. A., Gorelick, P. B., Bick, K. L., Pajeau, A., Bell, M. A., DeCarli, C., Culebras, A., Korczyn, A. D., Bogousslavsky, J., Hartmann, A., & Scheinberg, P. (1993). Vascular dementia: Diagnostic criteria for research studies. Report of the NINDS–AIREN International Work Group. *Neurology, 43*, 250–260.

Rosen, W. G., Terry, R. D., Fuld, P. A., Katzman, P., & Peck, A. (1980). Pathological verification of ischemic score in differentiation of dementias. *Annals of Neurology, 7*, 486–488.

Rosenbek, J. C., & LaPointe, L. L. (1981). Motor speech disorders and the aging process. In D. S. Beasley & G. A. Davis (Eds.), *Aging: Communication processes and disorders* (pp. 159–174). New York: Grune & Stratton.

Rosow, I., & Breslow, N. (1966). A Guttman scale for the aged. *Journal of Gerontology, 21,* 556–559.

Ross, T. P., Lichtenberg, P. A., & Christensen, B. K. (1995). Normative data on the Boston Naming Test for elderly adults in a demographically diverse medical sample. *Clinical Neuropsychologist, 9,* 321–325.

Roth, M., Tym, E., Mountjoy, C. Q., Huppert, F. A., Hendrie, H., Verma, S., & Goddard, R. (1986). A standardized instrument for the diagnosis of mental disorder in the elderly with special reference to the early detection of dementia. *British Journal of Psychiatry, 149,* 698–709.

Royall, D. R., Mahurin, R. K., & Gray, K. F. (1992). Bedside assessment of executive cognitive impairment: The executive interview. *Journal of the American Geriatrics Society, 40,* 1221–1226.

Royall, D. R., Mahurin, R. K., True, J. E., Anderson, B., Brock, I. P., Freeburger, L., & Miller, A. (1993). Executive impairment among the functionally dependent: Comparisons between schizophrenic and elderly subjects. *American Journal of Psychiatry, 150,* 1813–1819.

Rozovsky, F. A. (1990). *Consent to treatment: A practical guide* (2nd ed.). Boston: Little-Brown.

Rubenstein, L. Z., Schairer, C., Wieland, G. D., & Kane, R. (1984). Systematic biases in functional status assessment of elderly adults: Effects of different data sources. *Journal of Gerontology, 39,* 686–691.

Rubin, E. H., Morris, J. C., Grant, E. A., & Vendegna, T. (1989). Very mild senile dementia of the Alzheimer type: I. Clinical assessment. *Archives of Neurology, 46,* 379–382.

Ruff, R. M., Light, R. H., & Evans, R. W. (1987). The Ruff Figural Fluency Test: A normative study with adults. *Developmental Neuropsychology, 3,* 37–51.

Ruff, R. M., Light, R. H., & Quayhagen, M. (1989). Selective Reminding Tests: A normative study of verbal learning in adults. *Journal of Clinical and Experimental Neuropsychology, 11,* 539–550.

Russell, E. (1972). WAIS factor analysis with brain damaged subjects using criterion measures. *Journal of Consulting and Clinical Psychology, 39,* 133–139.

Rutman, D., & Silberfeld, M. (1992). A preliminary report on the discrepancy between clinical and test evaluations of competence. *Canadian Journal of Psychiatry, 37,* 634–639.

Ryan, C. M. (1988). Neurobehavioral disturbances associated with disorders of the pancreas. In R. E. Tarter, D. H. Van Thief, & K. L. Edwards (Eds.), *Medical neuropsychology* (pp. 121–158). New York: Plenum.

Ryan, F. F., & Sattler, J. M. (1988). Wechsler Adult Intelligence Scale–Revised (WAIS–R), *Assessment of Children* (3rd ed., pp. 219–244). San Diego: J. M. Sattler.

Ryan, J. J. (1983). Clinical utility of the WAIS–R short form. *Journal of Clinical Psychology, 39,* 261–262.

Ryan, J. J., Georgemiller, R. J., & McKinney, B. E. (1984). Application of the four-subtest WAIS–R short form with an older clinical sample. *Journal of Clinical Psychology, 40,* 1033–1036.

Ryan, J. J., Paolo, A. M., & Brungardt, T. M. (1990). Standardization of the Wechsler Adult Intelligence Scale–Revised for persons 75 years and older. *Psychological Assessment, 2,* 404–411.

Ryan, J. J., & Paolo, A. M. (1992a). Base rates of intersubtest scatter in the old age standardization sample of the WAIS–R. *Archives of Clinical Neuropsychology, 7,* 515–522.

Ryan, J. J., & Paolo, A. M. (1992b). A screening procedure for estimating premorbid intelligence in the elderly. *Clinical Neuropsychologist, 6,* 53–62.

Ryan, J. J., & Paolo, A. M. (1992c). Verbal performance IQ discrepancies on the WAIS–R: An examination of the old-age standardization sample. *Neuropsychology, 6,* 293–298.

Ryan, J. J., Paolo, A. M., & Brungardt, T. M. (1990). Factor analysis of the Wechsler Adult Intelligence Scale–Revised for persons 75 years and older. *Professional Psychology Research and Practice, 21,* 177–181.

Ryan, J. J., Paolo, A. M., & Brungardt, T. M. (1992). WAIS–R test–retest stability in normal persons 75 years and older. *Clinical Neuropsychologist, 6,* 3–8.

Ryan, J. J., Paolo, A. M., Pehlert, M. E., & Coker, M. C. (1991). Relationship of sex, race, age, education and level of intelligence to the frequency of occurrence of a WAIS–R marker for dementia of the Alzheimer's type. *Developmental Neuropsychology, 7,* 451–458.

Sachs, G. A., Rhymes, J., & Cassel, C. K. (1994). Biomedical and behavioral research in nursing homes: Guidelines for ethical investigators. *Journal of the American Geriatrics Society, 41,* 771–777.

Salmon, D. P., Butters, N., & Heindel, W. C. (1993). Alcoholic dementia and related disorders. In R. W. Parks, R. F. Zec, & R. S. Wilson (Eds.), *Neuropsychology of Alzheimer's disease and other dementias* (pp. 186–209). New York: Oxford University Press.

Sapin, L. R., Anderson, F. H., & Pulaski, P. D. (1989). Progressive aphasia without dementia: Further documentation. *Annals of Neurology, 25,* 411–413.

Sattler, J. M. (1982). *Student's manual to accompany the assessment of children's intelligence and special abilities* (2nd ed.). Boston: Allyn & Bacon.

Satz, P., & Mogel, S. (1962). An abbreviation of the WAIS for clinical use. *Journal of Clinical Psychology, 18,* 77–79.

Satz, P., & Van Gorp, W. G. (1987). WAIS–R marker for dementia of the Alzheimer type? An empirical and statistical induction test. *Journal of Clinical and Experimental Neuropsychology, 9,* 767–774.

Schaie, K. W. (1980). Cognitive development and aging. In L. K. Obler & M. L. Albert (Eds.), *Language and communication in the elderly* (pp. 7–26). Lexington, MA: Heath.

Scherr, P. A., Albert, M. S., Funkenstein, H. H., Cook, N. R., Hennekens, C. H., Branch, L. G., White, L. R., Taylor, J. O., & Evans, D. A. (1988). Correlates of cognitive function in an elderly community population. *American Journal of Epidemiology, 128,* 1084–1101.

Schmidt, J. P., Tombaugh, T. N., & Faulkner, P. (1992). Free-recall, cued-recall and recognition procedures with three verbal memory tests: Normative data from age 20 to 79. *Clinical Neuropsychologist, 6,* 185–200.

Schmidt, R., Freid, W., Fazekas, F., Reinhart, B., Grieshefer, P., Koch, M., Eber, B., Schumaker, M., Palmin, K., & Lechner, H. (1994). The Mattis Dementia Rating Scale: Normative data from 1001 healthy volunteers. *Neurology, 44,* 964–966.

Schoening, H. A., Anderegg, L., Bergstrom, D., Fonda, M., Steinke, N., & Ulrich, P. (1965). Numerical scoring of self-care status of patients. *Archives of Physical Medicine and Rehabilitation, 46,* 689–697.

Schultz, R., & Williamson, G. (1991). A 2-year longitudinal study of depression among Alzheimer's caregivers. *Psychology and Aging, 6,* 569–578.

Schwamm, L. H., Van Dyke, C., Kiernan, R. J., Merrin, E. L., & Mueller, J. (1987). The Neurobehavioral Cognitive Status Examination: Comparison with the Cognitive Capacity Screening Examination in a neurosurgical population. *Annals of Internal Medicine, 107,* 486–491.

Selzer, M. L. (1971). The Michigan Alcoholism Screening Test: The quest for a new diagnostic instrument. *American Journal of Psychiatry, 127,* 1653–1658.

Shallice, T., & Burgess, P. (1991). Deficits in strategy application following frontal lobe damage in man. *Brain, 114,* 727–741.

Sharpe, K., & O'Carroll, R. (1991). Estimating premorbid intellectual level in dementia using the National Adult Reading Test: A Canadian study. *British Journal of Clinical Psychology, 30,* 381–384.

Sherwood, S., Morris, J., Mor, V., & Gutkin, C. (1977). *Compendium of measures for describing and assessing long term care populations.* Boston: Hebrew Rehabilitation Centre for the Aged.

Shipley, W. C. (1940). A self-administering scale for measuring intellectual impairment and deterioration. *Journal of Psychology, 9*, 371–377.

Shipley, W. C., & Burlingame, C. C. (1941). A convenient self-administered scale for measuring intellectual impairment in psychotics. *American Journal of Psychiatry, 97*, 1313–1325.

Shulman, K., Sheldetsky, R., & Silver, I. (1986). The challenge of time: Clock-drawing and cognitive function in the elderly. *International Journal of Geriatric Psychiatry, 1*, 135–140.

Shulman, K. I., Pushkar Gold, D., Cohen, C. A., & Zucchero, C. A. (1993). Clock drawing and dementia in the community: A longitudinal study. *International Journal of Geriatric Psychiatry, 8*, 487–496.

Siegler, I. C., & Costa, P. T. (1985). Health behavior relationships. In J. E. Birren & K. W. Schaie (Eds.), *Handbook of the psychology of aging* (2nd ed., pp. 144–166). New York: Van Nostrand Reinhold.

Silverstein, A. B. (1981). Reliability and abnormality of test score differences. *Journal of Clinical Psychology, 37*, 392–394.

Silverstein, A. B. (1982a). Two and four-subtest short forms of the Wechsler Adult Intelligence Scale–Revised. *Journal of Consulting and Clinical Psychology, 50*, 415–418.

Silverstein, A. B. (1982b). Validity of a Satz–Mogel–Yudin-type short forms. *Journal of Consulting and Clinical Psychology, 50*, 20–21.

Silverstein, A. B. (1985). An appraisal of three criteria for evaluating the usefulness of WAIS–R short forms. *Journal of Clinical Psychology, 11*, 677–680.

Silverstein, A. B. (1987). Unusual combinations of Verbal and Performance IQs on Wechsler's intelligence scales. *Journal of Clinical Psychology, 43*, 720–722.

Silverstein, A. B. (1990). Notes on the reliability of Wechsler short forms. *Journal of Clinical Psychology, 46*, 194–196.

Sinnett, E. R., Holen, M. C., & Davie, M. J. (1988). Quick Test scores among persons over sixty. *Psychological Reports, 62*, 397–398.

Smith, A. (1967). The serial sevens subtraction test. *Archives of Neurology, 17*, 78–80.

Smith, G., Ivnik, R. J., Petersen, R. C., Malec, J. F., Kokmen, E., & Tangalos, E. (1991). Age-associated memory impairment diagnoses: Problems of reliability and concerns for terminology. *Psychology and Aging, 6*, 551–558.

Smith, G. E., Ivnik, R. J., Malec, J. F., Kokmen, E., Tangalos, E. G., & Kurland, L. T. (1992). Mayo's Older Americans Normative Studies (MOANS): Factor structure of a core battery. *Psychological Assessment, 4*, 382–390.

Smith, L. W., Patterson, T. L., Grant, I., & Clopton, C. (1989). A shortened MMPI useful for psychiatric screening of the non-institutionalized elderly. *Journal of Clinical Psychology, 45*, 359–365.

Snow, W. G., Freedman, L., & Ford, L. (1986). Lateralized brain damage, sex differences and the Wechsler Intelligence Scales: A re-examination of the literature. *Journal of Clinical and Experimental Neuropsychology, 8*, 179–189.

Snow, W. G., Tierney, M. C., Zorzitto, M. L., Fisher, R. H., & Reid, D. W. (1989). WAIS–R test–retest reliability in a normal elderly sample. *Journal of Clinical and Experimental Neuropsychology, 11*, 423–428.

Snowdon, J., & Lane, F. (1994). A longitudinal study of age-associated memory impairment. *International Journal of Geriatric Psychiatry, 9*, 779–787.

Sobel, L. C., Toneatto, T., & Sobell, M. B. (1994). Behavioral assessment and treatment planning for alcohol, tobacco, and other drug problems: Current status with an emphasis on clinical applications. *Behavior Therapy, 25*, 533–580.

Speirs, P. A. (1981). Have they come to praise Luria or to bury him? The Luria–Nebraska Battery controversy. *Journal of Consulting and Clinical Psychology, 49*, 331–341.

Spielberger, C. D., Gorsuch, R. L., & Lushene, R. E. (1970). *Manual for the State-Trait Anxiety Inventory.* Palo Alto, CA: Consulting Psychologists Press.

Spielberger, C. D., Gorsuch, R. L., Lushene, R. E., Montouri, J., & Platsek, D. (1973). *STAIC: Preliminary manual for the State-Trait Anxiety for Children.* Palo Alto, CA: Consulting Psychologists Press.

Spielberger, C. D., Gorsuch, R. L., Lushene, R. E., Vagg, P. R., & Jacobs, G. A. (1983). *Manual for the State-Trait Anxiety Inventory (form Y).* Palo Alto, CA: Consulting Psychologists Press.

Spielman, A. (1986). Assessment of insomnia. *Clinical Psychology Review, 6,* 11–25.

Spitzer, R. L., & Endicott, J. (1978). *NIMH clinical research collaborative program on the psychobiology of depression: Schedule for affective disorders and schizophrenia (SADS).* New York: New York State Psychiatric Institute, Biometrics Research Division.

Spitzer, R. L., Endicott, J., & Robins, E. (1978). Research diagnostic criteria: Rationale and reliability. *Archives of General Psychiatry, 35,* 773–782.

Spitzform, M. (1982). Normative data in the elderly on the Luria–Nebraska Neuropsychological Battery. *Clinical Neuropsychology, 4,* 103–105.

Spreen, O., & Benton, A. L. (1969). *Neurosensory Centre Comprehensive Examination for Aphasia.* Victoria, Canada: University of Victoria.

Spreen, O., & Strauss, E. (1991). *A compendium of neuropsychological tests: Administration, norms and commentary.* New York: Oxford University Press.

Squire, L. R. (1987). *Memory and brain.* New York: Oxford University Press.

Stambrook, M., Cardoso, E. R., Hawryluk, G. A., Erikson, P., Piated, D., & Sicz, G. (1988). Neuropsychological changes following the surgical treatment of normal pressure hydrocephalus. *Archives of Clinical Neuropsychology, 3,* 323–330.

Stambrook, M., Gill, D. D., Cardoso, E. R., & Moore, A. D. (1993). Communicating (normal-pressure) hydrocephalus. In R. W. Parks, R. F. Zecs, & R. S. Wilson (Eds.), *Neuropsychology of Alzheimer's disease and other dementias* (pp. 283–307). New York: Oxford University Press.

Stanton, B. A., Jenkins, C. D., Savageau, J. A., Zyzanski, S. J., & Aucoin, R. (1984). Age and educational differences on the Trail Making Test and Wechsler Memory Scales. *Perceptual and Motor Skills, 58,* 311–318.

Stebbins, G. T., Gilley, D. W., Wilson, R. S., Bernard, B. A., & Fox, J. H. (1990). Effects of language disturbances on premorbid estimates of IQ in mild dementia. *Clinical Neuropsychologist, 4,* 64–68.

Stebbins, G. T., Wilson, R. S., Gilley, D. W., Bernard, B. A., & Fox, J. H. (1990). Use of the National Adult Reading Test to estimate premorbid IQ in dementia. *Clinical Neuropsychologist, 4,* 18–24.

Straker, M. (1982). Adjustment and personality disorders in the aged. *Psychiatric Clinics of North America, 5,* 121–129.

Streiner, D. L., & Norman, G. R. (1995). *Health measurement scales: A practical guide to their development and use* (2nd ed.). New York: Oxford University Press.

Stroop, J. R. (1935). Studies of interference in serial verbal reactions. *Journal of Experimental Psychology, 18,* 643–662.

Strub, R. C., & Black, F. W. (1988). *Neurobehavioral disorders: A clinical approach.* Philadelphia: Davis.

Sunderland, T., Hill, J. L., Mellow, A. M., Lawlor, B. A., Gundersheimer, J., Newhouse, P. A., & Grafman, J. H. (1989). Clock drawing in Alzheimer's disease: A novel measure of dementia severity. *Journal of the American Geriatrics Society, 3,* 725–729.

Sweet, J. J., Mober, P. J., & Tovian, S. M. (1990). Evaluation of Wechsler Adult Intelligence Scale–Revised premorbid IQ formulas in clinical populations. *Psychological Assessment, 2,* 41–44.

Talland, G. A. (1965). Three estimates of word span and their stability over the adult years. *Quarterly Journal of Experimental Psychology, 17,* 301–307.

Tamkin, A. S., & Jacobsen, R. (1984). Age-related norms for the Hooper Visual Organization Test. *Journal of Clinical Psychology, 40,* 1459–1463.

Teng, E. L., & Chui, H. C. (1987). The modified Mini-Mental State (3MS) Examination. *Journal of Clinical Psychiatry, 48,* 314–318.

Teri, L., Truax, P., Logsdon, R., Vomsto, J., Zarit, S., & Vitaliano, P. (1992). Assessment of behavioral problems in dementia: The revised memory and behavior problems checklist. *Psychology and Aging, 7,* 622–629.

Teri, L., & Wagner, A. (1992). Alzheimer's disease and depression. *Journal of Consulting and Clinical Psychology, 60,* 379–391.

Thompson, M. G., Heller, K., & Rody, C. (1994). Recruitment challenges in studying late-life depression: Do community samples adequately represent depressed older adults? *Psychology and Aging, 9,* 121–125.

Thorp, T. R., & Mahrer, A. R. (1959). Predicting potential intelligence. *Journal of Clinical Psychology, 15,* 286–288.

Tiffin, J. (1968). *Purdue Pegboard Examiner manual.* Chicago: Science Research Associates.

Tombaugh, T. (1989). *An itemized scoring system for the Taylor Complex Figure.* Unpublished research, Carleton University.

Tombaugh, T. N., McDowell, I., Kristjansson, B., & Hubley, A. M. (1996). Mini-Mental State Examination (MMSE) and the Modified MMSE (3MS): A psychometric comparison and normative data. *Psychological Assessment, 8,* 48–59.

Tombaugh, T. N., & McIntyre, N. J. (1992). The Mini-Mental State Examination: A comprehensive review. *Journal of the American Geriatrics Society, 40,* 922–935.

Tombaugh, T. N., & Schmidt, J. P. (1992). The learning and memory battery (LAMB): Development and standardization. *Psychological Assessment, 4,* 193–206.

Tombaugh, T. N., Schmidt, J. P., & Faulkner, P. (1992). A new procedure for administering the Taylor Complex Figure: Normative data over a 60-year age span. *Clinical Neuropsychologist, 6,* 63–79.

Trahan, D. E., Goethe, K. E., & Larrabee, G. J. (1989). An examination of verbal supraspan in normal adults and patients with head trauma or unilateral cerebrovascular accident. *Neuropsychology, 3,* 81–90.

Trahan, D. E., & Larrabee, G. J. (1993). Clinical and methodological issues in measuring rate of forgetting with the Verbal Selective Reminding Test. *Psychological Assessment, 5,* 67–71.

Tsang, M. H., Aronson, H., & Hayslip, B. (1991). Standardization of a learning and retention task with community reading older adults. *Clinical Neuropsychologist, 5,* 67–77.

Tuokko, H. (1993). Psychosocial evaluation and management of the Alzheimer's patient. In R. W. Parks, R. F. Zec, & R. S. Wilson (Eds.), *Neuropsychology of Alzheimer's disease and other dementias* (pp. 565–588). New York: Oxford University Press.

Tuokko, H., & Crockett, D. (1987). Central cholinergic deficiency WAIS profiles in a non-demented aged sample. *Journal of Clinical and Experimental Neuropsychology, 9,* 225–227.

Tuokko, H., & Crockett, D. (1989). Cued recall and memory disorders in dementia. *Journal of Clinical and Experimental Neuropsychology, 11,* 278–294.

Tuokko, H., Crockett, D., Holliday, S., & Coval, M. (1987). The relationship between performance on the Multi-focus Assessment Scale and functional status. *Canadian Journal on Aging, 6,* 33–45.

Tuokko, H., & Crockett, D. J. (1991). Assessment of everyday functioning in normal and malignant memory disordered elderly. In D. E. Tupper & K. D. Cicerone (Eds.), *The neuropsychology of everyday life: Issues in development and rehabilitation* (pp. 135–181). Boston: Kluwer.

Tuokko, H., & Hadjistavropoulos, T. (1994). *A comparison of the clinical utility of alternative approaches to the scoring of clock drawing.* Unpublished manuscript.

Tuokko, H., Hadjistavropoulos, T., Miller, J. A., & Beattie, B. L. (1992). The Clock Test: A sensitive measure to differentiate normal elderly from those with Alzheimer's disease. *Journal of the American Geriatrics Society, 40,* 579–584.

Tuokko, H., Hadjistavropoulos, T., Miller, J. A., Horton, A., & Beattie, B. L. (1995). *The Clock Test: Administration and scoring manual.* Toronto: Multi-Health Systems.

Tuokko, H., Hadjistavropoulos, T., Rae, S., & O'Rourke, N. P. *A comparison of the clinical utility of alternative approaches to the scoring of clock drawing.* Manuscript submitted for publication.

Tuokko, H., Kristjansson, E., & Miller, J. (1995). The neuropsychological detection of dementia: An overview of the neuropsychological component of the Canadian Study of Health and Aging. *Journal of Clinical and Experimental Neuropsychology, 17*, 352–373.

Tuokko, H., & Purves, B. (1993). *Understanding dementia: A problem approach for caregivers* [Videotape]. Available from the Alzheimer Society of BC, 20-601 West Cordova Street, Vancouver, British Columbia, Canada V6T 1G1.

Tuokko, H., Vernon-Wilkinson, R., Weir, J., & Beattie, B. L. (1991). Cued recall and early identification of dementia. *Journal of Clinical and Experimental Neuropsychology, 13*, 871–879.

Tuokko, H., & Woodward, T. (1996). Development and validation of a demographic correction system for the neuropsychological measures used in the Canadian Study of Health and Aging. *Journal of Clinical and Experimental Neuropsychology, 18*, 479–616.

Tymchuk, A., & Ouslander, J. G. (1990). Optimizing the informed consent process with elderly people. *Educational Gerontology, 16*, 245–257.

U.S. Bureau of the Census. (1950). *U.S. census of population: 1950* (Current population reports, series P-23, No. 128). Washington, DC: U.S. Government Printing Office.

U.S. Bureau of the Census. (1983). *America in transition: An aging society* (Current population reports, series P-23, No. 128). Washington, DC: U.S. Government Printing Office.

Uhlmann, R. F., Teri, L., Rees, T. S., Mozlowski, K. J., & Larson, E. B. (1989). Impact of mild to moderate hearing loss on mental status testing: Comparability of standard and written Mini-Mental State Examinations. *Journal of the American Geriatrics Society, 37*, 223–228.

Ulatowska, H. K., Hayashi, M. M., Cannito, P., & Fleming, S. G. (1986). Disruption of reference in aging. *Brain and Language, 28*, 24–41.

Vaillant, G. E., & Perry, J. C. (1980). Personality disorders. In H. Kaplan, A. Freedman, & B. Sadock (Eds.), *Comprehensive text of psychiatry* (3rd ed., pp. 1562–1590). Baltimore: Williams & Wilkins.

Valdois, S., Poissant, A., & Joanette, Y. (1989). Visual form discrimination in normal aging and dementia of the Alzheimer type. *Journal of Clinical and Experimental Neuropsychology, 11*, 91.

Vallardita, C. (1985). Raven's Colored Progressive Matrices and intellectual impairment in patients with focal brain damage. *Cortex, 21*, 627–634.

Van Gorp, W. G., & Mahler, M. (1990). Subcortical features of normal aging. In J. Cummings (Ed.), *Subcortical dementia* (intelligence ed., pp. 231–250). New York: Oxford University Press.

Van Gorp, W. G., Mitrushina, M., & Cummings, J. L. (1989). Normal aging the encephalopathy of AIDS: A neuropsychological comparison. *Neuropsychiatry, Neuropsychology and Behavioral Neurology, 2*, 5–20.

Van Gorp, W. G., Satz, P., Kiersch, M. E., & Henry, R. (1986). Normative data on the Boston Naming Test for a group of normal older adults. *Journal of Clinical and Experimental Neuropsychology, 8*, 702–705.

Van Gorp, W. G., Satz, P., & Mitrushina, M. (1990). Neuropsychological processes associated with normal aging. *Developmental Neuropsychology, 6*, 279–290.

Vanderploeg, R. D., & Schinka, J. A. (1995). Predicting WAIS–R IQ premorbid ability: Combining subtest performance and demographic variable predictors. *Archives of Clinical Neuropsychology, 10*, 225–239.

Victor, M., Adams, R. D., & Collins, G. H. (1989). *The Wernicke–Korsakoff syndrome.* Philadelphia: Davis.

Vitaliano, P. P., Russo, J., Young, H., Becker, J., & Maiuro, R. D. (1991). The screen for caregiver burden. *The Gerontologist, 31*, 76–83.

Vitaliano, P. P., Young, H. M., & Russo, J. (1991). Burden: A review of measures used among caregivers of individuals with dementia. *The Gerontologist, 31,* 67–75.

Volicer, L., Hurley, A. C., Lathi, D. C., & Kowall, N. W. (1994). Measurement of severity in advanced Alzheimer's disease. *Journal of Gerontology: Medical Sciences, 49,* M223-M226.

Wallin, A., & Gottfries, C. G. (1990). Biochemical substrates in normal aging and Alzheimer's disease. *Pharmacopsychiatry, 23,* 37–43.

Wang, P. L., & Ennis, K. E. (1996). Competency assessment in clinical populations: An introduction to the Cognitive Competency Test. In B. P. Uzzell & Y. Gross (Eds.), *Clinical neuropsychology of intervention* (pp. 119–133). Boston: Martinus Nijhoff.

Ward, L. C. (1990). Prediction of verbal, performance and full scale IQ's from seven subtests of the WAIS–R. *Journal of Clinical Psychology, 46,* 436–440.

Warrington, E. K. (1984). *Recognition Memory Test.* Windsor, England: NFER-Nelson.

Watkins, C. E., Mckay, B. L., Parra, R. A., & Polk, N. E. (1987). Using WAIS–R short forms with clinical outpatients: A cautionary note. *Professional Psychology: Research and Practice, 18,* 397–398.

Watson, C. G. (1965). Intrasubtest scatter in hospitalized brain damaged and schizophrenic patients. *Journal of Consulting Psychology, 29,* 596.

Watson, Y. I., Arfken, C. L., & Birge, S. J. (1993). Clock completion: An objective screening test for dementia. *Journal of the American Geriatrics Society, 41,* 1235–1240.

Wechsler, A. (1977). Presenile dementia presenting as aphasia. *Journal of Neurology, Neurosurgery and Psychiatry, 40,* 303–305.

Wechsler, A. F., Verity, M. A., Rosenchein, S., Fried, I., & Scheibel, A. B. (1982). Pick's disease: A clinical computed tomographic, and histologic study with olgi impregnation observations. *Archives of Neurology, 39,* 287–290.

Wechsler, D. (1945). A standardized memory scale for clinical use. *Journal of Psychology, 19,* 87–95.

Wechsler, D. (1981). *WAIS–R manual.* New York: Psychological Corporation.

Wechsler, D. (1987). *Wechsler Memory Scale–Revised manual.* San Antonio, TX: Psychological Corporation.

Wedding, D., & Faust, D. (1989). Clinical judgment and decision making in neuropsychology. *Archives of Clinical Neuropsychology, 4,* 233–265.

Weinberger, M., Samsa, G. P., Schmader, K., Greenberg, S. M., Carr, D. B., & Wildman, D. S. (1992). Comparing proxy and patients' perceptions of patients' functional status: Results from an outpatient geriatric clinic. *Journal of the American Geriatric Society, 40,* 585–588.

Wells, C. E. (1979). Pseudodementia. *American Journal of Psychiatry, 136,* 896–900.

Wentworth-Rohr, I., Mackintosh, R. M., & Flalkoff, B. S. (1974). Relationship of Hooper VOT score to sex, education, intelligence and age. *Journal of Clinical Psychology, 30,* 73–75.

Wetzel, L., & Boll, T. (1987). *Short Category Test, booklet format.* Los Angeles: Western Psychological Services.

Whitehouse, P. J. (1986). The concept of subcortical and cortical dementia: Another look. *Annals of Neurology, 19,* 1–6.

Whitlatch, C. J., Zarit, S. H., & von Eye, A. (1991). Efficacy of interventions with caregivers: A reanalysis. *The Gerontologist, 31,* 9–14.

Willenbring, M. L. (1988). Organic mental disorders associated with heavy drinking and alcohol dependence. *Clinics in Geriatric Medicine, 4,* 869–887.

Willenbring, M. L., Christensen, K. J., Spring, W. D., & Rasmussen, R. (1987). Alcoholism screening in the elderly. *Journal of the American Geriatrics Society, 35,* 864–869.

Williams, J. M. (1991a). *Cognitive Behavior Rating Scale.* Odessa, FL: Psychological Assessment Resources.

Williams, J. M. (1991b). *Memory assessment scales.* Odessa, FL: Psychological Assessment Resources.

Willshire, D., Kinsella, G., & Prior, M. (1991). Estimating WAIS–R IQ from the National Adult Reading Test: A cross validation. *Journal of Clinical and Experimental Neuropsychology, 13,* 204–216.

Wilson, B. A., Alderman, N., Burgess, P. W., Emslie, H., & Evans, J. J. (1996). *Behavioural Assessment of the Dysexecutive Syndrome.* Bury St. Edmunds: Thames Valley Test Company.

Wilson, R. S., Rosenbaum, G., & Brown, G. (1979). The problem of premorbid intelligence in neuropsychological assessment. *Journal of Clinical Neuropsychology, 1,* 49–54.

Winograd, C. H. (1984). Mental status tests and the capacity for self-care. *Journal of the American Geriatrics Society, 32,* 49–55.

Wolf-Klein, G. P., Silverstone, F. A., Levy, A. P., Brod, M. S., & Breuer, J. (1989). Screening for Alzheimer's disease by clock drawing. *Journal of the American Geriatrics Society, 37,* 730–734.

Wong, J. L., Schefft, B. K., & Moses, J. A. (1990). A normative study of the Luria–Nebraska Neuropsychological Battery, Form II. *International Journal of Clinical Neuropsychology, 12,* 175–179.

World Health Organization. (1992). *International statistical classification of diseases and related health problems* (10th ed.). Geneva: Author.

Yates, A. (1956). The use of vocabulary in the measurement of intelligence deterioration: A review. *Journal of Mental Science, 102,* 409–440.

Yesavage, J. A. (1986). The use of self-rating depression scales in the elderly. In L. W. Poon, T. Crook, K. L. Davis, C. Eisdorfer, B. J. Gurland, A. W. Kasniak, & L. W. Thompson (Eds.), *Handbook for clinical memory assessment of older adults* (pp. 213–217). Washington, DC: American Psychological Association.

Yesavage, J. A., Brink, T. L., Rose, T. L., Lum, O., Huang, V., Adey, M., & Leirer, V. O. (1983). Development and validation of a geriatric depression screening scale: A preliminary report. *Journal of Psychiatric Research, 17,* 37–49.

Youngjohn, J. R., Larrabee, G. J., & Crook, T. H. (1993). New adult age- and education-correction norms for the Benton Visual Retention Test. *Clinical Neuropsychologist, 7,* 155–160.

Zacharewicz, M., Pliskin, N., Neumann, C., Berent, S., & Buchtel, H. (1994, February). *The utility of premorbid IQ estimation across mild and moderate dementia populations.* Paper presented at the 22nd Annual Meeting of the International Neuropsychological Society, Cincinnati, OH.

Zachary, R. A. (1986). *Shipley Institute of Living Scale. Revised manual.* Los Angeles: Western Psychological Services.

Zachary, R. A., & Gorsuch, R. L. (1985). Continuous norming: Implications for the WAIS–R. *Journal of Clinical Psychology, 41,* 86–94.

Zarit, S. H. (1990, June). *Concepts and measures in family caregiving research.* Paper presented at the Conference on Conceptual and Methodological Issues in Family Caregiving Research, University of Toronto, Toronto, ON, Canada.

Zarit, S. H., Reever, K. E., & Bach-Petersen, J. (1980). Relatives of the impaired elderly: Correlates of feelings of burden. *The Gerontologist, 20,* 649–655.

Zarit, S. H., Orr, N. K., & Zarit, J. M. (1985). *The hidden victims of Alzheimer's disease: Families under stress.* New York: New York University Press.

Zarit, S. H., & Zarit, J. M. (1982). Families under stress: Interventions for caregivers of senile dementia patients. *Psychotherapy: Theory, Research and Practice, 19,* 461–471.

Zarit, S. H., & Zarit, J. M. (1983). Cognitive impairment. In P. M. Lewinsohn & L. Teri (Eds.), *Clinical geropsychology: New directions in assessment and treatment* (pp. 38–80). New York: Pergamon.

Zarit, S. H., & Zarit, J. M. (1990). *The memory and behavior problems checklist and the burden interview.* Unpublished manuscript.

Zaudig, M. (1992). A new systematic method of measurement and diagnosis of "mild cognitive impairment" and dementia according to ICD–10 and DSM–III–R criteria. *International Psychogeriatrics, 4,* 203–219.

Zec, R. (1993). Neuropsychological functioning in Alzheimer's disease. In R. W. Parks, R. F. Zec, & R. S. Wilson (Eds.), *Neuropsychology of Alzheimer's disease and other dementias* (pp. 3–80). New York: Oxford University Press.

Zimberg, S. (1987). Alcohol abuse among the elderly. In L. L. Carstersen & B. A. Edelstein (Eds.), *Handbook of clinical gerontology* (pp. 57–65). New York: Pergamon.

Zimmerman, S. I., & Magaziner, J. (1994). Methodological issues in measuring the functional status of cognitively impaired nursing home residents: The use of proxies and performance-based measures. *Alzheimer Disease and Associated Disorders, 8,* S281–S290.

Zung, B. J. (1979). Psychometric properties of the MAST and two briefer versions. *Journal of Studies on Alcohol, 40,* 845–859.

Zung, W. K. (1971). A rating instrument for anxiety disorders. *Psychosomatics, 12,* 371–379.

Zung, W. K., & Green, R. L. (1973). Detection of affective disorders in the aged. In C. Eisdorfer & W. E. Fann (Eds.), *Psychopharmacology and aging* (pp. 213–223). New York: Plenum.

Zweig, M. H., & Campbell, G. (1993). Receiver-operating characteristic (ROC) plots: A fundamental evaluation tool in clinical medicine. *Clinical Chemistry, 39,* 561–577.

Author Index

263

Subject Index